A Web-Based Introduction
to Programming

A Web-Based Introduction to Programming

Essential Algorithms, Syntax, and Control Structures Using PHP, HTML, and MySQL

Third Edition

Mike O'Kane

CAROLINA ACADEMIC PRESS

Durham, North Carolina

Library of Congress Cataloging-in-Publication Data

O'Kane, Mike, 1953-
  A web-based introduction to programming : essential algorithms, syntax, and control structures using PHP and XHTML / Mike O'Kane. -- Third edition.
    pages cm
  Includes bibliographical references and index.
  ISBN 978-1-61163-470-9 (alk. paper)
  1. Computer software--Development. 2. Internet programming. 3. Computer programming--Web-based instruction. 4. PHP (Computer program language) 5.
XHTML (Document markup language) I. Title.

  QA76.76.D47O43 2013
  006.7'6--dc23

                    2013016501

Carolina Academic Press
700 Kent Street
Durham, North Carolina 27701
Telephone (919) 489-7486
Fax (919) 493-5668

www.cap-press.com

Printed in the United States of America.

To my dear mother and father,
thank you for the love and light that you bestowed on us.

Contents

Preface

The problem I have tried to solve with this textbook is, quite simply, how to effectively introduce general programming concepts to students who have never programmed before. Perhaps like me, you have found yourself frustrated by textbooks that try to cover too much too fast, make inappropriate assumptions about what a student already knows, or take sudden leaps in complexity when providing examples and exercises.

I believe that the purpose of an introductory programming course is to help students gain confidence and develop their understanding of basic logic, syntax, and problem-solving. They do not need to learn all aspects of a language or even learn best practices—these are topics for the next course level. The question is: how to provide the kind of hands-on experience that supports active learning without overwhelming the beginning student with too much syntactical and programmatic detail?

I have tried many approaches over the years before settling on a Web-based approach, using minimal PHP and HTML code to develop small, interactive Web applications. This approach has proved very successful. Many students report how much they enjoy the course, how much they have learned, and how well the material has served them in subsequent courses and in their professional life. I also hear from many students who tell me that the course positively changed their opinion of programming as a career or subject of interest, which is most gratifying.

Some instructors may have concerns that my coverage of the PHP and HTML is insufficient. The book uses a minimal set of HTML tags and PHP functions and makes use of some arbitrary conventions to keep the focus on basic concepts that are common to most languages. To give a couple of examples: PHP **print** statements are used rather than **echo** statements, and these statements **always** include parentheses and double quotes so that the syntax is consistent with that of most other languages. And the code examples mostly use a pairing of **.html** and **.php** files of the same name (for example wages1.html and wages1.php) to produce simple interactive applications (the .html file provides a form that is processed by the .php file). The last chapter ("Where to Go From Here") explains which practices are standard and which are particular to the textbook, and also suggests best practices and areas for further study.

The third edition of the book includes a new chapter 14 that introduces MySQL. A brief (and optional) introduction to Object Oriented Programming is included in Chapter 13, but objects are not covered in any detail.

I hope that you will find the book useful for your purposes, and that, if you use the book, you will provide your own feedback and suggestions for the next edition.

Intended Audience

The book is designed to serve:

- Instructors teaching introductory programming, programming logic and design, or Web programming courses, who want a textbook that engages students and provides a solid preparation for subsequent courses, but avoids overwhelming beginners with too much syntactical detail or program complexity.
- Traditional and online students taking a first course in programming, programming logic and design, or Web programming.
- Web designers, graphic artists, technical communicators, and others who find that their work increasingly requires some degree of programming expertise, and need an effective, hands-on introduction.
- Others who wish to learn the basics of programming, either for personal interest, or to explore the possibility of a career in this field.

Approach

The book takes a fairly novel approach, allowing students to learn program logic and design by developing a large number of small Web-based applications. Students love working with the Web, and this approach has other important benefits:

- Important concepts such as client/server design, server-side processing, and interface-driven code modules can be introduced in the form of working applications, and then applied in hands-on exercises.
- Students not only learn the essential control structures and syntax of a programming language, but also learn to use a markup language (and style sheets). This makes sense in today's programming environment where markup and programming are integrated components of a networked application.
- The material is relevant to students across a range of disciplines: Computer Science, Information Systems, Technical Communications, Network Systems, Digital Media, Web Technologies, Mobile Applications, Database Programming, and other technology-related fields.
- The focus on hands-on problem-solving and fundamental structures prepare students for next-level, language-specific courses such as PHP, Java or

C++, without replicating a great deal of material, while the syntax covered here is generally consistent with these and other languages.

The book makes use of a programming language (PHP), a scripting language (HTML), and a database query language (MySQL), but does not attempt to provide a complete overview of these languages. Instead, students learn sufficient syntax to convert requirements into working applications using basic programming structures, arithmetic and logical expressions, user interfaces, functions, data files, and SQL queries. The focus remains on basic concepts, logic and design, algorithm development, and common programming procedures. The book provides context throughout, explaining why each topic is important, and referring students to related career paths.

Although the book focuses on Web-based applications, there is NO requirement for a network-based programming environment. The book uses a standalone Apache Web server (the open source xampp distribution provided by the Apache Friends group) that students can install on a USB drive or home computer simply by unzipping a file. Students can begin programming in HTML, PHP and MySQL in literally minutes.

Features

Each chapter begins with clearly stated learning outcomes. Each topic is introduced using examples of simple program requirements that are first developed as algorithms and interfaces and then realized in working code. Code statements and control structures are explained step by step.

Different programming topics are treated in separate chapters. Even topics that are commonly combined, such as counting loops and event-controlled loops, have their own chapters so that students have the chance to develop and apply their understanding of each separately.

Each chapter includes quizzes that have been carefully developed to test the student's understanding of the chapter's learning outcomes. The questions have been tested extensively in the classroom.

Three different types of coding exercise are provided at the end of each chapter:

- **Fixit** exercises provide small programs that include a single error of some kind. These exercises help students improve their problem-solving ability, test their understanding of key concepts, and develop tracing and debugging skills.
- **Modify** exercises provide working programs that must be modified to perform a somewhat different or additional function. These exercises help students determine how and where to add new code, and test their ability to read and understand existing code.
- **Code completion** exercises allow students to apply concepts and tools covered in the chapter by developing new applications. These exercises test the student's ability to: understand requirements, develop algorithms, and pro-

duce working code. The code completion exercises follow consistent themes that are developed throughout the book, so that students can more readily appreciate the value of new functionalities that they learn in each chapter.

Templates for each exercise contain partially completed code so students don't waste time typing (and debugging) code that is not relevant to the problem at hand. The templates also help instructors to streamline the grading process.

The textbook comes with a standalone Web server that can be installed on a fixed or portable drive simply by unzipping a file (so students can bring the software with them to work on computers at any location).

The server installation includes textbook folders that contain all code samples and exercise templates. Students can complete the exercises simply by opening, editing, and saving the appropriate files. Assignments can be turned in simply by zipping and submitting the appropriate chapter folder.

The textbook appendices provide additional learning resources designed to: (a) help individual students with particular needs or interests (for example file/folder management, additional references, and help debugging code); and (b) deliver useful topics not included in the chapters (for example data representation, additional control structures, and multi-dimensional arrays).

Textbook Web site

The textbook Web site ensures that both students and instructors have access to the most current resources associated with this textbook. The Web site includes everything required to install and use the Web server, and also provides hints and help for students, as well as additional exercises, test banks, slide presentations, quiz solutions, code solutions, and other instructional resources. The Web site can be found at:

http://www.mikeokane.com/textbooks/WebTech/

Changes to the Third Edition

As an instructor I know how frustrating it can be to adapt to changes in textbook editions, so I have tried not make any more significant structural changes than necessary for this new edition. I have made minor edits throughout, based on feedback and my own experiences in the classroom. These include small changes to quizzes and exercises. The previously lengthy Chapter 11 (arrays) has been broken down into two chapters so that numerically indexed arrays can be treated separately (in Chapter 11) from associative arrays (now in Chapter 12). This has also allowed additional coverage of both topics. For example Chapter 11 now includes more coverage of reading data from files into arrays. And Chapter 12 includes a worked example showing how, by testing $_POST array input, a single PHP file can combine the code to display an HMTL form with the code to process the form.. Chapter 13 (previously Chapter 12) now includes a section on the use of die() and exit() functions, and Appendix F has been expanded to include a longer list of useful PHP functions. The new Chapter 14 provides an introduction to the syntax and use of MySQL queries. And Chapter 15 (previously Chapter 13) has been updated to include some important new terms and technologies. The references to XHTML have been removed from the book in light of the growing significance of HTML 5. Reference to XHTML DOCTYPES have been removed for the same reason. The HTML in the book is syntactically consistent with both XHTML and HTML 5.

Chapter Overview

Chapter 1: Introducing Computer Programming. Students learn the relationship between machine language and high-level languages, and review common tasks that computer programs typically perform. The work of a programmer is described, and the software development cycle is explained. The chapter highlights and briefly summarizes design approaches such as algorithm development, interface design, client/server design and object oriented programming. Different programming languages are identified, and the distinction is made between interpreted and compiled languages, and between markup and programming languages. Standalone and network applications are also contrasted.

Chapter 2: Client/Server Applications — Getting Started. This chapter prepares students for the hands-on work they will perform in subsequent chapters. File types and local and Internet addressing schemes are explained. Instructions are provided to install, run, and test the required software. Students are shown how to create, store, and run a number of sample applications in order to become familiar with the process of using a text editor, saving files, running the Web server, and viewing the results in a Web browser.

Chapter 3: Program Design — from Requirements to Algorithms. The general characteristics and requirements of effective instructions are explored, using human and program examples. Students walk through the process of reviewing simple requirements, creating input, processing, and output (IPO) charts, designing the interface, and developing solution algorithms. The chapter introduces sequence, selection and control structures, variables and assignment operations, and arithmetic and logical expressions.

Chapter 4: Basics of Markup — Creating a User Interface with HTML. This chapter explains the significance of data rendering, and provides a brief overview and history of Hypertext Markup Language (HTML). Commonly used HTML tags are explained, and the student is shown how to apply these to create and organize simple Web pages. Cascading style sheets are introduced. Students are shown how to create HTML forms to obtain user input as a first step in developing interactive Web applications. HTML Tables are used to perform simple form layout.

Chapter 5: Creating a Working Program—Basics of PHP. This chapter teaches sufficient PHP language syntax to process user input received from HTML forms, perform simple arithmetic, and produce formatted output. In the process, students learn to code arithmetic expressions, use standard operators and functions, create and work with variables, and identify and fix both syntax and logical errors.

Chapter 6: Persistence—Saving and Retrieving Data. This chapter explains the difference between persistent and transient data, and introduces text file processing as well as basic database concepts. Students learn to: open, read, write, and close text files; work with multiple files; parse lines of data that contain multiple values separated by some kind of delimiter.

Chapter 7: Programs that Choose—Introducing Selection Structures. This chapter introduces selection control structures and demonstrates the use of algorithms to solve problems requiring simple selection. Students learn to use IF and IF..ELSE structures, Boolean expressions, relational operators, truth tables, simple string comparisons, and testing procedures.

Chapter 8: Multiple Selection, Nesting, ANDs and ORs. This chapter develops examples from Chapter 7 to handle problems associated with input validation and more complex requirements. Students explore the use of compound Boolean expressions, nested selection structures, chained IF..ELSEIF..ELSE selection structures, and multiple but independent selection structures.

Chapter 9: Programs that Count—Harnessing the Power of Repetition. This chapter introduces loop structures with a focus on count-controlled FOR loops. Students learn how to refer to the counting variable within the loop, and how to use loops to generate tables, crunch numbers, accumulate totals, find highest and lowest values in a series, select values from a file of records, and display bar charts.

Chapter 10: "While NOT End-Of-File"—Introducing Event-Controlled Loops. This chapter introduces WHILE loops and demonstrates the use of the priming read and the standard algorithm to process files of unknown length. The student is shown how WHILE loops can be used to perform various operations on a list of data values, and how a file of records can be processed and searched for specific records or field values.

Chapter 11: Structured Data—Working with Arrays. This chapter introduces numerically-indexed arrays, and shows how arrays can be used to store, access, and update multiple-related values. The use of the FOR loop to process arrays is explained, and various array-processing algorithms are demonstrated.

Chapter 12: Associative Arrays. This chapter introduces associative arrays. Students learn how to use associative arrays as lookups, and gain a better understanding of the $_POST array and the way that data is received from HTML forms. Web sessions are introduced, and students learn how to use the $_SESSION array to maintain session data between applications.

Chapter 13: Program Modularity—Working with Functions and Objects. This chapter demonstrates the importance of program modularity and introduces functions, include files and objects. Students learn to write their own functions, to build libraries of related functions, and to call functions from different applications as needed. Key concepts and examples of object oriented programming are also introduced in this chapter as an optional topic.

Chapter 14: Connecting to a Database—Working with MySQL. This chapter introduces databases queries as an important application tool. The relationship between relational databases and SQL is explained, along with the purpose and syntax of common queries (SELECT, INSERT, UPDATE and DELETE). Students learn to write code to open and close database connections, submit queries, handle errors, perform simple joins, and process results.

Chapter 15: Where to Go From Here. This last chapter provides a short overview of key concepts and technologies that the students may want to explore after completing this textbook.

The textbook also includes a number of useful appendices as follows:

Appendix A introduces data representation, and shows how binary values can store data for a wide range of purposes.

Appendix B provides an introduction to overview of file and folder management, file addressing schemes (including relative and absolute addresses), and the use of the command line with a list of common DOS and Unix command equivalents.

Appendix C provides help for students wishing to use different Web server installations.

Appendix D provides debugging help for students having trouble identifying and resolving PHP code errors.

Appendix E provides additional material and references for students wishing to learn more about HTML and style sheets.

Appendix F provides additional information regarding PHP data types, and provides a list of common PHP functions not covered in the book.

Appendix G provides additional coverage of common PHP operators and structures that were omitted from the chapters to avoid overwhelming the beginning student (for example, shortcut operators, the SWITCH statement, DO..WHILE loops, and multi-dimensional arrays).

Acknowledgments

This textbook could not have been created without the generous help and support of many others. In particular I want to thank my dear wife Constance Humphries for her invaluable technical advice, proof-reading, development of video tutorials, and daily encouragement and patience! My sincere thanks to Scott Sipe, Beth Hall, and all at Carolina Academic Press for their supportive style, professionalism and experience. Thanks to my fellow instructors at Asheville-Buncombe Technical Community College, especially to Charlie Wallin and Fred Smartt who field-tested the book, made invaluable suggestions and submitted any number of corrections. And thanks to all of those students who have learned with me and sometimes in spite of me as this book evolved in the classroom.

And a huge thank you to Kai 'Oswald' Seidler, Kay Vogelgesang, and all those who have contributed to the Apache Friends Project, and who continue to deliver and support the XAMPP distribution. So many of us owe you our great appreciation for your generosity of spirit!

About the Author

Mike O'Kane holds a master's degree in Systems Science (specializing in Advanced Technology) from Binghamton University. He has fifteen years experience teaching computer science courses, most recently at Asheville-Buncombe Technical Community College in North Carolina. He also has extensive practical experience in the use of technology for learning, having worked at IBM as a short-course developer, NC State University as an Instructional Coordinator, and the University of North Carolina system as the first Executive Director of the UNC Teaching and Learning with Technology Collaborative. He has a passion for developing effective instructional content, and learning environments that promote rather than hinder student learning.

A Web-Based Introduction to Programming

Chapter 1

Introducing Computer Programming

Intended Learning Outcomes

After completing this chapter, you should be able to:

- Explain the difference between computers and other machines.
- Describe the purpose of the microprocessor's instruction set.
- Explain the relationship between the instruction set and machine language.
- List some common tasks that computer programs perform.
- Describe what programmers do.
- Summarize the stages of the software development cycle.
- Explain the importance of writing and communications for programmers.
- Explain the relationship between high-level programming languages and machine language.
- Distinguish between the purpose of a compiler and an interpreter.
- Explain the difference between standalone and network applications.
- Explain the difference between programming languages and markup languages.

Introduction

Welcome! If you have never programmed before, this book is for you. By the time you complete the chapters and exercises, you will have a good grasp of the basic logic and design of computer programs. The book is designed to teach common programming syntax and control structures in a manner that will prepare for you for further study in this field. It will also provide you with sufficient expertise to develop small, interactive Web applications, using a combination of the HTML markup language and PHP programming language.

To get started, in this first chapter we will explore the general process of programming and define some important term and practices. For a book that is supposed to be hands-on this chapter is mostly descriptive! Don't be too concerned if some of the topics don't make complete sense yet. Your understanding will deepen as you work through the chapters and develop your own applications.

What Is a Computer Program?

A computer is a **programmable machine**. Most machines, such as vacuum cleaners or ceiling fans, are **hard-wired**, designed to perform one task only. But a computer is different. Computers can perform any number of tasks by reading and executing **computer programs**, or **software**. Each computer program contains instructions to direct the computer's operating system and hardware for a specific purpose. The ability to read and execute programs is achievable because each computer contains a **microprocessor** which includes the computer's **instruction set**. The instruction set defines all of the basic commands that the computer can execute. These basic commands are very low-level activities such as adding numbers, moving a piece of data from one location to another, or comparing values. The commands that make up the instruction set constitute the computer's machine language. Your programs work with the computer's operating system to issue commands to the microprocessor, so a computer program is essentially a set of instructions that tell the microprocessor to execute machine language commands in a particular sequence in order to provide a game, a Web browser, a business application, an email program, or some other useful service. If you've ever wondered why some programs run on one computer but not another, it is because different computers have different microprocessors and different operating systems.

Although different computer programs serve quite different purposes, all programs share some important characteristics. Here are some common tasks that any computer program might typically perform:

> **Provide interactive environments for users:** programs may use text-based input/output or Graphical User Interfaces (GUI's) to interact with users. Interfaces may include graphics, animations, audio, video, and other multimedia features.
>
> **Read and write data:** programs may access, create, modify or delete data that is stored in files and databases.
>
> **Perform numerical calculations:** programs can add, subtract, multiply, divide, and compare numbers, and can combine these operations to perform much more complex calculations.

Perform text-processing operations: programs can validate, convert, search, sort, compare, and replace text, and can construct reports, messages or documents such as this textbook.

Communicate with other programs and devices: programs may exchange data with other programs, cameras, scanners, Web browsers, satellites, cell phones, ATM machines, etc.

Control hardware: programs can control robots, satellites, aircraft, automobiles, printers, and other computers.

A single computer program may perform any combination of these operations. For example a computer game may look up player and game information in a file or database, provide an interactive multimedia environment for the player to play the game, perform numerical calculations, and communicate with programs running on other computers to allow multi-user play over the Internet. Similarly a payroll program may perform text-processing operations (such as validation and conversion), query and modify a database, perform numerical calculations, and send checks to a printer. What this means is that, as a programmer, you will want to know how to write programs that might include any or all of these operations.

What Do Programmers Do?

Programmers write program code, right? Well, actually programmers do a lot more than write code, and many programmers actually write very little code. One of the things that makes programming an attractive career for many men and women is that this work requires an appealing combination of **right-brain** (creative, problem-solving, brain-storming) and **left-brain** (logical, linear, sequential) activities. Another appeal is that there are a variety of career paths within the field, so if you have a general aptitude you have a good chance of finding work suited to your personal interests. For example if you like to work with people you may find yourself drawn to software design, interface development, usability, or training. If you prefer to work with data, you may prefer server-side application development, object design, or database administration.

Let's walk through the major stages in software development. This will clearly demonstrate the range of skills that programmers need in order to be successful in their work. Here we will simply summarize these steps so don't be concerned if this appears a little abstract right now. We will learn how to apply these steps to develop a working application in Chapter 3.

1. Evaluation of Requirements

In order to develop an effective software application we first need to determine the program's requirements. This usually requires careful reading and listening, asking questions, and careful documentation. Understanding and documenting requirements takes time and skill. A common mistake that beginning (and not just beginning) programmers make is to rush this important step in order to begin coding. Rushing the requirements phase can actually be very costly in terms of time, money and even professional relationships. So learn to go slowly and carefully when you are presented with a requirements document or when you first meet with a client. The more time you spend analyzing your program requirements (and asking questions if you are unsure about anything), the more easily the solution will appear. To repeat: the most important skills a programmer needs at this phase are to listen, read, ask questions, document carefully, and communicate effectively with clients, managers, and other programmers.

2. Software Design

Once you have a good idea of the software requirements, it's time to develop the design of your application. This may a one-person job in the case of a small application or may involve a design team. Software design can actually become a career path and some (often the most experienced) programmers spend most of their time evaluating requirements and designing applications that other programmers will then code.

Unless your requirements are quite simple, your application design will most likely consist of multiple code segments or **modules**, each of which can be developed separately. There are many advantages to a modular approach to software. Each module can be developed and tested **separately**, often by different programmers or programming teams. The modules can be developed **concurrently** which speeds up development time. This approach also allows each module to be developed by programmers with the most **suitable skills**. And a modular approach promotes **reusability**: some of the more useful modules can be shared by many different applications. Module design includes the development of testing procedures to test that a module will perform as expected when it is coded.

Client/server design is an essential feature of Web-based application development. A client application, such as a Web browser, provides an interface to the user and waits for the user to request a service, for example by clicking on a link, submitting a URL, or typing a URL. The client application then calls a server application to process the request and send back a response. When the client application receives the response this is presented to the user and the process repeats. You participate in a client/server interaction every time you use your browser.

For example, Figure 1-1 shows the screens for a very simple client/server application to calculate an employee's pay based on their hours worked and hourly wage. This example provides the user with two Web pages. When you type the URL to request the first page, the Web browser sends a request to the appropriate Web server, which sends back the data to display the page. The first page contains a form. When the user clicks the "Get Your Wage Report Now" button, the Web browser sends a second request to the Web server that includes the data that the user has entered into the form. The server executes a program that has been developed especially to process this data. This program generates the content for the second page, which the server sends back to the browser for display to the user.

Figure 1-1: A simple client/server interaction

In this book you will develop many small client/server applications similar to the example described above.

Object Oriented Programming (OOP) provides another modular design approach that is extremely important for modern application development. OOP allows programmers to share and reuse code very effectively and to design applications in a very structured and logical fashion, reducing costs and simplifying long term maintenance. This book does not cover OOP in any kind of detail, but Chapter 13 includes an optional section to introduce this important topic.

Whether your programs are simple or complex, it helps greatly to stay away from a computer in the early phases of application design! Explore your design ideas using a pen and paper, sticky notes, a white board, even the backs of napkins! If you go to work as a programmer, you will find that this is how software design teams usually work. The reason is simple: using disposable materials prevents you from becoming too invested in any particular approach too quickly and encourages brainstorming and creativity. You will find that sketching out ideas on paper before you start coding will help you think things through and save you time in the long run. Once you have a clear idea of what to do you will be ready to develop your algorithms and application structure.

Important skills for software designers are creative thinking, organization, familiarity with data structures, a background in object oriented programming, writing documentation, and experience with client-server programming and interface design.

3. Algorithm Development

Once you have a general design for your application, it is time to develop **algorithms** for each code module that the application will need. An algorithm is simply a set of clearly written, unambiguous instructions that have been developed to perform a task of any kind . Algorithms are a critical component of software design, often written in **pseudocode**, a mix of English and programming language syntax that programmers can easily understand. You will learn to develop algorithms using pseudocode in Chapter 3. The actual work of coding an application is ideally a fairly straightforward process of converting a carefully developed algorithm into a specific programming language.

The skills required for these activities include careful attention to detail, logical thinking, documentation (writing), and general programming experience.

4. Application Coding

This is the activity that is usually associated with programming! The algorithm for each program module is coded into a programming language. Each module is then carefully tested before the modules are assembled to produce the complete application. The most important skill required for coding is knowledge of the appropriate programming language, but programmers are expected to also have the experience to develop code efficiently, test thoroughly, find and fix errors (debugging) and document the code so that other programmers can refer to the documentation as needed.

Coding, testing, debugging and documenting require patience, thoroughness, and careful attention to detail.

5. Application Testing

Once the application has been assembled, it is time for thorough testing. While the development team may perform many tests for **correctness**, it is also important to test for **usability**. A development team may produce a terrific application that has been thoroughly tested and debugged but turns out to be a disaster when provided to end users. Why? Because the end users find the interface confusing and cannot easily perform the tasks that are most important for their purposes. Usability testing brings the users into the development process and ensures that the needs and concerns of the user are taken into account before the product is distributed. In the case of larger applications, usability testing is often undertaken by usability experts who may observe users working with the product to determine where improvements can be made. In smaller applications, the programmer may simply work with the client to find problems and get feedback.

Testing takes a great deal of patience, attention to detail, and thoroughness. Usability testing requires good listening skills, careful observation, and (if you are the programmer) humility! It's very easy for any programmer to be so focused on his or her own design that the needs of the user become secondary. If you notice yourself getting impatient with a user who cannot figure out how to use your product, or who wants the software to perform differently, then it's probably time to step back, pay attention to the user's concerns, and reconsider your own design assumptions.

6. User Support, Training, Software Maintenance

So now you have a complete and well-tested application. The development process does not end there! You will also need to develop online or printed manuals and other documentation for use by your end users. You may also need to deliver some form of training. And the software must be maintained. Users will find problems that must be corrected, and suggest additions and improvements that will need continued programming support. User support and training is a career path for those who like to work with non-technical people and who can also communicate effectively with programmers and software designers.

Important skills are the ability to communicate with both technical and non-technical people, the ability to listen and to explain (verbally and in writing) procedures clearly and carefully, patience, and often a sense of humor!

The Software Development Life Cycle

Taken together these activities constitute the software development life cycle:

- Evaluation of requirements
- Application design
- Algorithm development
- Application coding
- Application testing
- User support, training, software maintenance

This is not a precise list—in reality these various stages may not be so neat and sequential, and you will see somewhat different versions of this process in every programming textbook and in every workplace. Development teams may implement these various stages differently. But no matter how these stages are defined, no part of the development cycle should be treated carelessly. As you gain experience as a programmer you will more fully appreciate the special characteristics and importance of every step. And perhaps you can already see how the field of software design attracts people who are both creative and logical, who enjoy using both the left and right sides of their brain equally.

The Importance of Writing and Communicating

Documentation and writing are frequently mentioned as important skills for programmers. Documentation is critical to software development and wherever your own career path takes you in the field of software design and development, you will need to be able to write carefully and communicate effectively. Clients, designers and managers must refer to well-written documents that clearly define requirements, design and code specifications. Everyone involved in the development process must listen carefully and communicate effectively. Programmers must document their working code so that other programmers can easily read and modify it (often the programmer who develops a piece of code will **not** be the programmer who is asked to make changes for the next version). Programmers must often give presentations to clients or to their team. The testing phase also requires extensive documentation that indicates what tests were applied, the results of these tests, and how problems were resolved. Software users will need course manuals and training materials. Lastly all maintenance procedures must be documented so that a complete record is always available regarding the current state and history of the software.

What Are Programming Languages?

We have explored what a computer program **is**, and what programmers **do**, but what about programming **languages**? What is a programming language and why are there so many different languages?

As we have seen, a computer program is basically a sequence of instructions that direct the computer's microprocessor to perform various commands contained with the computer's instruction set. These commands are issued in machine language. Machine language commands are very **low-level** (for example adding two numbers, or copying a value from one memory location to another). It would be extremely time-consuming to write instructions in the 0s and 1s of machine language, and this code would be very error-prone and difficult to debug, maintain, or modify.

Instead of using machine language directly, we develop programs using **high-level programming** languages . Examples of current high-level languages are C++, C#, Java, PHP, Python, and Ruby. Examples of older high-level languages are C, Ada, BASIC, COBOL. Fortran, Pascal, and perl (older does not necessarily mean no longer used — many applications written in older languages are still in widespread use, and programmers are still needed to maintain and even update these programs).

A high-level programming language consists of a set of special words, symbols and operators that a programmer uses to write program instructions. These instructions are often referred to as the program's source code and the process of writing source code is often simply called coding . High-level languages are quite easy for programmers to learn, and applications written in these languages can be developed very quickly and efficiently. However the computer can only understand machine language, so once a program has been written in a high-level language, the code must then be translated into machine language instructions. There are actually two approaches to translating high-level code to machine language, either by compiling the code or by interpreting the code. The approach depends on the programming language that you are using.

Compilers and Interpreters

Some programming languages are **compiling** languages. This means that the entire source code for a program is converted (or compiled) into an executable file (.exe file) by special software known as a compiler. The .exe file that is produced by the compiler contains the necessary machine language instructions to perform the required task. Once a program has been compiled into an executable file, the source code is no longer required to run the program. End users of the program simply receive the .exe file. The programmers keep the source code in order to perform updates and produce new versions. Usually when you purchase standalone software from a store you are buying an executable program that has been compiled. Two advantages of compiled programs are:

- Compiled programs tend to run faster.
- The end user does not have access to the source code (and so cannot change the program).

Since a compiler generates an .exe file containing the machine language instructions for a specific microprocessor and operating system, the source code must be compiled separately for different platforms (Windows, Macintosh, Linux, etc). Also, each time the source code is modified, the new version must be compiled again to produce a new .exe file. The new .exe file must then be distributed to the end users.

Other programming languages are **interpreted** languages. Execution of programs written in interpreted languages is dependent on a special program known as an **interpreter**. An interpreter translates the source code into machine language one instruction at a time. Both the interpreter and the source code are needed **every time that the program is executed** since no executable file is created. One advantage of this approach is that the same source code can be used on any computer. For example computers running Windows, Macintosh or Linux operating systems can each use their own language interpreter to translate the source code into the appropriate machine language for that platform.

A disadvantage of using an interpreter is that in most cases we do not want to deliver the actual source code to the end user of the software. But this approach works very well for network-based programs, such as Web applications, since these programs are not distributed to end users. In these cases, the source code is located on a server computer and executed each time a request is submitted by a client application, such as a Web browser. The source code can be modified quickly and easily with no need to recompile and redistribute the software every time a change is made. PHP is an example of an interpreted programming language that is widely used to develop server-based Web applications.

Some languages provide both compiling **and** interpreting options, and some languages actually **combine** compiling with interpreting stages to achieve greater efficiency and platform independence. A notable example is the **Java** language. Java applications are compiled "up to a point" to produce an "almost executable" version in the form of

byte code that incorporates many of the efficiencies of the compilation process, and then Java interpreters are provided for different platforms so that the same byte code can be distributed for execution on any machine (Windows, Macintosh, Linux, etc.) in order to achieve platform independence.

So Many Languages!

As computer technology evolves, new programming languages are continually developed to take advantage of the latest hardware and software design strategies. For example new languages were developed to implement the functionality of object oriented programming, and to allow client/server application development. There are literally thousands of different programming languages and often a computer programmer is expert in only a few of these. While each programming language has its own special syntax and characteristics, most languages are very similar in their overall characteristics and functionality, and use the same basic logical structures to write instructions. We will learn about these common characteristics as we work through this book. A programmer who is familiar with the general logic of programming, and who has experience coding in one or two languages can usually learn new languages quite quickly.

Standalone and Network Applications

Computer programs can be designed for use on individual machines (as standalone applications), or across networks (as network applications).

A **standalone application** is designed to provide a complete service on the local computer, usually the computer sitting on the user's desk. Standalone applications do not require any network connectivity, interacting only with the computer's operating system and other **utility software** on the local machine. If a new version of the application becomes available, or if updates are required, these must be also installed on every user's computer. Examples of standalone software are traditional word-processing and spreadsheet applications, image-processing software, many games, etc. At this time, most of the programs that you install on your local computer are standalone applications.

Network applications are programs that run partly or entirely on remote computers, linked to the user across a network of some kind. The more traditional network application was simply installed on a single host computer and then accessed by many users remotely. Each user that signs on to the host computer is provided a user interface to work with the application. An increasingly important type of network application is a **client/server** application which consists of any number of component programs that work together across a network. Some components of a client/server application can be installed on a local computer, and perform as client programs. Other components of a network application are installed on network servers and perform as server programs. The server-based components respond to requests from client components of the application as needed. At the minimum the client component usually provides the user interface that allows the user to submit information and view the results, while the server component does most of the processing.

You are using a client/server application whenever you use your Web browser. The Web browser performs as a local client component, providing your user interface and allowing you to send requests to server programs all over the world. So you are using a client/server application whenever you use your Web browser to obtain information, shop online, or play an online game. Other common examples of client/server applications are ATM's and e-mail programs.

Client/server applications are becoming more and more common because they allow us to obtain services and perform tasks without need for special software on our local computer. We can expect to make increasing use of Web-based client/server applications as bandwidth increases since these require only a local Web browser and an Internet connection, rather than software that must be installed locally and continually updated. For example we are now seeing networked versions of word-processing and spreadsheet applications.

Markup Languages

So far we have discussed the purpose of programming languages. As you now know, the purpose of a programming language is to allow a programmer to write instructions that **process** data. In other words, programming languages are used to perform operations that read or modify existing data or generate new data for some purpose (for example to calculate wages, convert temperatures, or keep track of a game player's score).

Another type of language is a **markup language**. Markup languages are often used in conjunction with programming languages, but have a very distinct purpose. The purpose of a **markup language** is to provide markup instructions (usually in the form of tags) that simply **describe** data or indicate how data is to be **formatted**, or **rendered** (for example to define how data should be displayed on a Web page, or printed in a document). Markup languages are defined for wide range of purposes. For example, your word-processing program uses a markup language to save formatting instructions with your document as you type a report or letter.

The markup language that is used to render data for display in Web browsers is Hypertext Markup Language (HTML). We will learn the basics of HTML in order to format our Web-based applications.

Combining Markup and Programming Languages

In this course, you will learn the basics of programming by developing small, Web-based client/server applications using a programming language known as PHP, one of the most widely used programming languages for this type of application. Since you will use a Web browser to display your program output, you will also learn the basics of the HTML markup language to format your application input and output for display in your browser window.

Summary

A computer is a programmable machine. The computer's microprocessor includes the computer's **instruction set** which defines all of the basic commands that the computer can execute.

Commands to the microprocessor must be issued using the computer's **machine language**. A computer program is a set of machine language instructions that execute a sequence of commands to perform a useful task.

Different programs combine common components to achieve their purpose: interactive environments; read/write operations; numerical operations; text-processing, communication with other programs; control of hardware.

A software designer/developer requires a range of skills that combine creative problem-solving and logical processing. Documentation is an important part of the software process so writing and communication are important skills that are often not associated with this field.

Software development includes a number of stages: evaluation of requirements; application design; algorithm development; application coding; application testing; user support, training, software maintenance

Programs are written in programming languages which may be compiled or interpreted. The code containing the program instructions written in a specific language is known as source code. If the language is a compiler-based language the source code must be converted into an executable version which is then distributed for use. If the language is an interpreted language, the source code itself is distributed and this is then executed one line at a time by a language interpreter.

Some programs are designed to function as standalone applications, which means that they are installed locally and do not need access to other networks. A copy of a standalone application is required for every user. Network applications run over networks. A single network application can be installed on one computer and accessed across a network by many users.

An increasingly important type of network application is a client/server application, where client programs on local computers send requests to server programs on remote computers. These requests are processed and results returned to the client. A common example is a Web-based client/server application where a user's Web browser performs as a client to request services from server applications throughout the world.

Markup languages are not the same as programming languages. Programming languages provide instructions to **process** data. Markup languages provide tags to **describe** or format (**render**) data.

In this course you will learn to develop simple Web applications using the PHP programming language and HTML markup language.

Chapter 1 Review Questions

1. A web application is an example of:
   a. Object Oriented Programming
   b. Client/server design
   c. A microprocessor
   d. A standalone application

2. A program that requires the source code each time that it executes is using which method to convert the source code to machine language?
   a. A compiler
   b. An interpreter

3. Which approach is better when evaluating software requirements?
   a. Determine the requirements as quickly as possible in order to move on to the design and coding phases.
   b. Take time to analyze and clarify the application requirements.

4. What kind of thinking activities are most associated with the work of a programmer?
   a. Left brain activities
   b. Right brain activities
   c. Both left AND right brain activities
   d. Neither left NOR right brain activities

5. What language is often used to write algorithms?
   a. Markup language
   b. Pseudocode
   c. High-level programming language
   d. Machine language

6. Which language does the computer actually understand when it executes instructions for a program?
   a. Markup language
   b. High-level programming language
   c. Pseudocode
   d. Machine language

7. What is the computer's instruction set?
   a. The set of all programming languages that a computer can understand
   b. The set of all software that is currently available on the computer
   c. The basic set of commands that a computer can execute
   d. The rules for using a high-level programming language

8. What is source code?
    a. Programming instructions written in a programming language
    b. Program instructions that have been compiled into machine language
    c. The code used to identify text characters from languages all over the world
    d. The code used to identify memory addresses

9. What does an executable file contain?
    a. Programming instructions written in a programming language
    b. Program instructions that have been compiled into machine language.
    c. Formatted text
    d. An audio image

10. Which term applies to an application model where one program calls another program in order to have some task performed?
    a. Client/server
    b. Standalone program
    c. Instruction set
    d. An algorithm

11. What does an interpreter do?
    a. Reads and executes source code, one line at a time
    b. Converts source code into an executable file.
    c. Sends data from one program to another
    d. Converts and displays text that has been marked up

12. What does a compiler do?
    a. Reads and executes source code, one line at a time
    b. Converts source code into an executable file
    c. Sends data from one program to another
    d. Converts and displays text that has been marked up

13. When you use your Web browser to access information you are working with
    a. A client/server application
    b. A standalone application

14. What is an algorithm?
    a. A set of instructions to meet a requirement of some kind
    b. An executable file
    c. Program instructions that have been compiled into machine language
    d. Programming instructions written in a programming language

15. Which of the following is **not** a feature of modular application design?
    a. Concurrent development of each module
    b. Reusable code
    c. Separate testing of each module
    d. Less time needed to evaluate requirements

16. What category of language is used to describe or format data?
    a. Markup language
    b. High-level programming language
    c. pseudocode
    d. Machine language

17. What languages will you learn in this course?
    a. C++ and HTML
    b. XML and Java
    c. PHP and FORTRAN
    d. PHP and HTML

18. Which is the correct order for these stages in the software development life cycle?
    a. application coding, application design, algorithm development
    b. application design, algorithm development, application coding
    c. algorithm development, application design, application coding
    d. algorithm development, application coding, application design

19. Is a Web browser a client application or a server application?
    a. Client
    b. Server

20. What type of application runs entirely on your own computer?
    a. Client/server
    b. Networked
    c. Web-based
    d. Standalone

Chapter 2

Client/Server Applications — Getting Started

Intended Learning Outcomes

After completing this chapter, you should be able to:

- Explain how Web programs function as client/server applications.
- Identify the content of a file by referring to the file extension.
- Locate files using the Windows addressing scheme.
- Locate files using the Internet (IP) addressing scheme.
- Use the localhost domain to access a standalone Web server.
- Identify the languages we will use in this course.
- Identify the software you will need to complete the hands-on work.
- Install the required software.
- Create, save and open an HTML document that is stored on a local Web server.
- Create, save and run a PHP file that is stored on a local Web server.
- Create, save and run an interactive Web application consisting of an HTML document that includes a form, and a PHP application that processes the form.

Introduction

This chapter will prepare you for the hands-on activities that you will perform as you work through the subsequent chapters of this book. First we will review **client/server** design with a focus on Web-based applications. Next we will look at how files and folders are organized and located, using **local** addresses based on **disk drives**, and **Internet** addresses based on **domain names**. This is important since you will need to be careful to save files to the correct locations on your disk drive, and then open these files in your Web browser using the correct Internet address.

You will also install the server software that you need to work through the textbook and complete the exercises. This is a very straightforward procedure and you will be able to test that your server is running correctly by running some sample programs.

Once the server has been installed you will have the option to install a text editor, then you will be asked to type in a few small programs, save them, and run them using your Web browser. The code for these programs is provided. The idea is not to learn to develop programs (that comes later), but to simply learn the general process of using an editor to create code, saving your files to the correct location under your Web server, running the server, and then testing that your programs work correctly.

Client/Server Design in Web Applications

In a client/server design, client programs send requests to server programs to perform a task of some kind, just as you might ask someone else to do something for you. The server receives the request from the client and responds appropriately. The server program resides on a networked computer and can respond to hundreds, thousands or millions of client requests coming from any number of computers throughout an organization or from all over the world. Consider an online store that receives requests from many different customers all over the world every minute. An important advantage of client/server design is that new software installations and updates to existing software are performed on servers without requiring changes to the client computers.

Client/server applications are used world-wide across the **Internet**, and are also used to deliver services to members of an organization or company across **intranets** (an intranet is a private network).

A Web application is a familiar example of an Internet-based client/server design. In the case of Web applications, the client program is a Web browser. The Web browser runs on a user's personal or office computer. Each time the user enters a URL, or clicks on a link on a Web page, or clicks a Submit button after entering data into a Web form, the browser sends the user's request. The request is transmitted across the Internet to the appropriate Web server. The Web server receives and processes the request, then sends back a response for the browser to display in the form of a new Web page. Web server s may be located anywhere on the Internet and can accept requests from any client that has Internet access (Figure 2-1). In order to process each request, the server program may communicate with other programs or access databases or files.

This is a very efficient design since it allows the user to obtain all kinds of useful services without installing special software on their local computer (just the Web browser). Instead the user executes programs on remote servers, using an interface de-

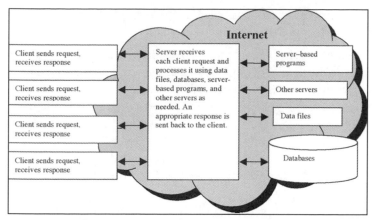

Figure 2-1: Example of client/server design

livered to his or her Web browser window. The server programs can be modified, and new programs added with no need for special installations on the user's computer.

In order to develop Web-based applications we must create files that contain the necessary instructions for our Web pages and programs, and store these files on a Web server. The server can then process the files as needed in response to requests.

In this course we will run a Web server on our **local** computer so that we can develop applications without any need for Internet access. In other words, our Web server will be located on the same computer as our Web browser. We will need to be careful to save our files to the correct locations so that our Web server can find them, and we will also need to provide the correct Web addresses (URL's) for these files when we wish to view them in our Web browser. Let's review how files and folders are organized on disks, and then learn how files can be located using the Windows and Internet addressing schemes.

Working with Files and Folders

Files are used to store data, all kinds of data. A file may contain text, images, videos, word-processing documents, programs, etc., but each file may only contain one type of data. The **file extension** usually indicates the format of the data that is stored in the file. This is very useful since the format indicates what type of program is needed to process the file. For example, a file with a **.jpg** extension contains image data stored using the **jpeg** image format, and can be opened by any image-viewing or image-processing program that can read this format. A file with an **.mp3** extension contains an MP3 audio file that can be handled by any MP3 player. A file with a **.zip** extension contains data that has been compressed using the ZIP compression scheme. To create zip files, or extract data from these files, you will need zip utility software.

Text files contain plain text (characters that can be typed on your keyboard). Text files can be viewed and edited using any text editing software. Files that contain plain text are often saved with a .txt extension. Often however, text files are given special extensions to indicate the specific purpose of the text that is stored in the file. In this course you will use a number of different extensions for your text files:

- **Plain text** files, using a **.txt** or **.dat** extension, will be used to store simple data for use by your programs. For example you might create a file named **scores.txt** that contains a list of student scores.
- HTML files, using an **.html** extension, will be used to store the markup instructions for Web pages. Our Web pages will include forms to allow the user to enter information that will be submitted for processing by our programs. For example you might create a file named wages.html that contains a Web page with a form for the user to submit their hours worked and hourly wage.
- **PHP** files, using a **.php** extension, will be used to store the source code for PHP programs. Our PHP programs will usually receive information from the user or look up data in files in order to perform useful processing operations and generate output. For example you might create a file named **wages.php** that contains the source code to receive wage information from a Web page, then calculate and display the pay.

Since these are all text files we can **create** and **modify** the content of using any text editor. However since these files contain text to serve different purposes, the file extension indicates what software is required to **process** the content of each file. A file with an **.html** extension is usually opened by a **Web browser**, since Web browsers are designed to interpret .html files and display the contents as Web pages. A file with a **.php** extension can only be executed as a set of PHP instructions if it is opened by a **PHP code processor**. A PHP code processor is included with the Web server that you will install as you work through this chapter.

Files are usually organized into **folders** for ease of management, and files and folders are stored on **portable** or **fixed** disks that are accessed through **disk drives** connected to computers. You can access files on disks located in **local** drives that are attached to your personal computer. You can also access files on disks in **remote** disk drives, attached to computers that are connected to your computer through a network such as the Internet. No matter where the drive is located, in order to locate a specific file on a disk, you need to be able to refer to some kind of **file addressing scheme**.

Locating Files and Folders on Computers Running a Windows Operating System

Most often when we want to locate a file or folder using a Windows operating system, we open **My Computer** (or **Windows Explorer**) and point and click our way to the file that we wish to work with. As a programmer, it is important to know that we can also reference a file by providing its unique **file path** or **address**. Every file and folder on a computer has a unique address that is based on its folder location and disk drive specification. Take a look at Figure 2-2, which displays a screen containing a list of four **folders**.

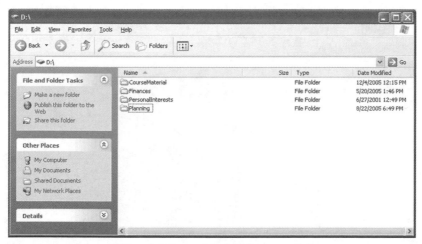

Figure 2-2: Examples of folders on a disk

Note that the address box shows the root address of these folders. They are located on the **D:** drive of the local computer. The address of the folder named **CourseMaterial** is therefore **D:\CourseMaterial**.

Folders can contain any combination of other folders and data files. Let's look inside **CourseMaterial** by double-clicking this folder (Figure 2-3).

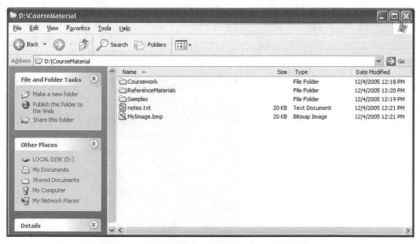

Figure 2-3: Inside the CourseMaterial folder

Notice the address in the address box is now **D:\CourseMaterial**, indicating that we have shifted our location to the CourseMaterial folder. This folder contains three folders (**CourseWork, ReferenceMaterials** and **Samples**) and two data files (**notes.txt** and **myImage.bmp**). The file extensions indicate the type of data stored in these two files: **notes.txt** contains plain text, while **myImage.bmp** contains a bitmap image. The complete address of the file named **notes.txt** is **D:\CourseMaterial\notes.txt** and the address of the folder named Coursework is **D:\CourseMaterial\Coursework**.

Now let's open the Coursework folder (Figure 2-4).

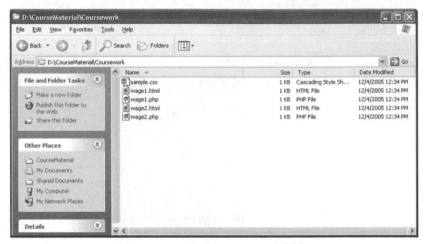

Figure 2-4: Inside the Coursework folder

Note that the address window now displays **D:\CourseMaterial\Coursework**. The Coursework folder contains five files named **sample.css**, **wage1.html**, **wage1.php**, **wage2.html**, and **wage2.php.** You can access any file directly using the file address. For example, instead of navigating to the Coursework folder by clicking through folders as we have done, we can open a file by simply typing the complete file address in the address window. For example, to access the **wage1.html** file we could just type: **D:\Course-Material\Coursework\wage1.html**.

Locating Files and Folders on the Internet

The Windows operating system assigns **drive letters** to identify each disk drive attached to your computer. The drive letter forms part of the address of any file stored on one of these disks. However this addressing scheme will not work when we need to locate files on the Internet, which consists of hundreds of thousands of disk drives attached to computers all over the world! An address that begins with **D:** would refer to a different drive on every computer in the network!

Instead all Internet addresses are based on the IP (Internet Protocol) addressing scheme. Each IP address references a specific **folder location** on a specific **disk** attached to a specific **computer** that is performing as a Web server somewhere in the world. Every IP address is unique so it is impossible for a single IP address to refer to two different locations. An example of an IP address is **69.147.83.197** which at the time of writing points to the PHP Group's Web site (this site supports the development and use of the PHP language). Try entering **http://69.147.83.197** in your Web browser's address window.

Imagine typing an IP address every time you needed to connect to a Web server! And how will anyone find our site if we move it to a different IP address? For ease of use and portability, we use **Internet domain names** to represent IP addresses. For example the domain name of the **69.147.83.197** address is **php.net**, so this domain name can be used in place of the IP address. Try typing **http://www.php.net**.

The Internet address of a specific file or folder usually combines a domain name with a file and folder path. For example, **http://www.php.net/license/index.php** is the Web address of a file named **index.php** which is located in the license folder. The exact folder and disk location of the license folder is referenced by the domain name **www.php.net**, which maps to an IP address that references a folder on a disk drive attached to a Web server, somewhere in the world. If these files are moved to a different Web server, the domain name is simply reassigned to point to the new IP address, so the URL does not need to be changed.

A Web address such as **http://www.php.net/license/index.php** is known as a **URL** (**Uniform Resource Locator**). Note that the separator used in URL's is the forward slash **/**, whereas the separator in our Windows addresses used the back slash ****. That's because the naming convention for Windows file paths derives from the **DOS** operating system which uses the back slash, whereas the naming convention for Internet addresses derives from the **Unix** operating system which uses the forward slash. Fortunately Windows now also allows you to use the Unix forward slash when typing Windows file paths.

Often we write URL's without specifying a file name at the end. For example, if we were to type **http://www.php.net/license/** into our Web browser's address box, we would actually receive a file even though we did not include a file name. That's because Web servers are configured to add default file names to URL's if none is provided. For example if a Web server is configured to open a file named index.php by default, then the URL **http://www.php.net/license/** would actually access a file in the **license** folder named **index.php** using the address **http://www.php.net/license/index.php**.

For more information about file and folder navigation and addresses, refer to Appendix B.

Working with a Local Web Server

You are going to learn the fundamentals of program logic and design by developing Web applications using our own Web server. In order to work simply and securely you will use special software that allows you to run a Web server on your local computer with no need for Internet access. Although the Web server will be installed locally, in all other respects it will perform exactly as an Internet-based server. The Web server will receive requests from our Web browser, process these requests and respond appropriately (we hope!). Your programs and files will be stored and accessed locally, however, if you were to copy these to a Web server located on the Internet, your applications would perform in exactly the same way across the Web. The required software is easily installed and easy to use.

The IP address of your standalone Web server will be **127.0.0.1** and the domain name will be **localhost**. This is a special non-unique IP address and domain name that allows you to reference your own computer instead of connecting to the **Internet**. So for example, in order to run a program named **myWeb1.php** which is in a folder named **samples**, in a folder named **WebTech** on your local Web server, you would type the URL:

http://localhost/Webtech/samples/myWeb1.php

Actually, if you type that URL into your Web browser right now you will get a message that the page cannot be displayed! That's because you are trying to connect to a Web server that is not actually running, which means that the localhost domain is not available. Once you install and run the Web server (later in this chapter) this URL will work.

What Languages Will I Use?

You will write your Web programs using a combination of two languages:

HTML (Hypertext Markup Language) provides the **markup instructions** that you will use to create and format the Web pages that display the user interface for your Web applications. You will use HTML to display headings, paragraphs, forms, tables, buttons, and images. Since this is a course in logic and design you will not learn everything there is to know about the HTML language. Nevertheless you will learn sufficient HTML to easily extend your skills in subsequent courses or personal research. Everything you learn will be based on current HTML standards.

PHP (**PHP Hypertext Preprocessor**) is a **programming language** that you will use to write server-based programs that process user requests by performing calculations, validating input, making decisions, reading data from files or databases, writing output to files or databases, returning results to the user, etc. This course covers sufficient PHP to teach basic programming logic and design as well as many important aspects of software development. This will prepare you for subsequent programming courses in PHP or other current programming languages.

Figure 2-5 shows the same example of a simple client/server application that you reviewed in Chapter 1.

Figure 2-5: Client/Server Example using HTML and PHP

Let's examine this a application more carefully. These are two Web pages. The first Web page is generated from HTML code located in an **.html** file on a Web server. The HTML code in this file has been designed to display a Web page that contains a heading, a form with two prompts and two input boxes, and two buttons.

When the user enters the information and presses the "Get Your Wage Report Now" button, the browser sends the user input (10.75 and 25 in this case) back to the server with a request to process a file containing PHP code. The code in the PHP file provides instructions to: (1) receive the data submitted from the first Web page; (2) calculate a wage based on this input; (3) generate a new HTML page to display the results. The second Web page is created by this PHP code and the server returns this to the Web browser for display to the user.

HTML and **PHP** are free technologies. You can find extensive information about HTML at **http://www.w3.org/MarkUp/** (the World Wide Web Consortium's HTML home page). You can learn more about PHP at **http://www.php.net/** (the PHP home page).

What Software Will I Need?

To complete your hands-on activities, you will need the following software:

- A **text editor** to create HTML and PHP files.
- A **Web browser** to submit requests to the Web server and display the Web pages that are returned for display.
- A **Web server** that can process requests sent to the localhost domain.

Read the following sections carefully and follow the instructions to install the necessary software for your computer. Once you have the software installed you will be ready to create and test some sample applications.

Installing a Text Editor

You will need a text editor to create and modify your HTML and PHP. You can use any text editor and there are many free editors available for both Windows and Macintosh computers. Some text editors are specifically designed for languages such as HTML and PHP, and contain special features that you will find useful as a programmer, for example code indentation, line numbering, and search and replace functions. Additionally a text editor that recognizes HTML and PHP will automatically apply different colors to special words, tags, and other syntactical elements of your code, which makes it easier to identify typing errors.

Three excellent freeware text editors for Windows are: **Crimson Editor** (an oldie but goody available from **http://www.crimsoneditor.com/**); Notepad++ (**http://notepad-plus-plus.org/**); and conTEXT (**http://www.contexteditor.org/**).

Macintosh users might consider **Textwrangler**, a highly regarded text editor that be found at: **http://www.textwrangler.com**

In all cases installation is simple and for most users the default installation settings will be fine. Take some time to get used to the basic operations to use your editor – you will have a chance to do this later in the chapter when you create some simple applications. Don't try and learn everything—you can explore the full functionality of your editor as you gain experience.

IMPORTANT NOTE: do not use a word-processor (such as MS Word) to create and edit your code. You need to save your code as plain text files.

Installing One or More Web Browsers

You need a Web browser to view the examples and your own programs. Any major browser should be fine and you will already have at least one browser already installed on your computer. Professional developers like to use two or three browsers so that they can test their Web sites more thoroughly. You are encouraged to work with multiple browsers for this reason but this is **not** required for the material in this textbook.

If you want to install additional browsers, **Mozilla Firefox** is an excellent and freely available browser that is available for Windows, Mac or Linux (**http://www.mozilla.com/firefox**). **Apple Safari** is another great browser available for Macintosh and Windows (**http://www.apple.com/safari**). And you might also consider **Google Chrome** (**http://www.google.com/chrome**) for Windows, Mac or Linux. In all cases, installation is simple and for most users the default installation settings will be fine.

Installing Your Web Server

You must also install a standalone Web server that will process your PHP code and deliver Web pages to your browser. The textbook CD contains the **Windows** version of the **XAMPPLite** standalone server along with a document that contains complete installation instructions (installation is simple but be sure to follow the instructions carefully). If you are running Windows be sure to install the Web server from the textbook CD and not from any Web site since the CD version includes the coursework and samples files that are used with the textbook. If you do not have the CD you can download the same version (and the installation instructions) from the textbook Web site at:

http://www.mikeokane.com/textbooks/WebTech/support.php

The CD also contains a document with instructions for **Macintosh** users to download and install the MAMP standalone server. These instructions also tell you how to add the **Webtech** folder (also provided on the CD). This folder contains the coursework and samples files that you will use as you work through the textbook. If you do not have the CD. these instructions are also available on the textbook site.

The installation documents also explain how to **run** and **stop** your Web server, and how to test your Web server to be sure that it is working correctly. The material that follows assumes that you have successfully installed and tested your Web server, that you have at least one Web browser, and that you have a text editor to create and edit your program code.

Using Your Web Server

Now let's learn how to use the server to run and test our Web applications! First start the Web server if you have not already done so. Now open any Web browser and type the following URL in the address window:

http://localhost/Webtech

Your installation is configured so that this URL will open a Web page (Figure 2-6) that will help you to use this textbook. If this page displays then your Web server is running successfully. As you will see, the page provides links that make it easy for you to view and work with the samples and coursework files that are discussed in each chapter. Note that your Web server must be running in order for you to view this page (or to view any page with a URL that begins **http://localhost**). If you were to stop your Web server, this URL would no longer work and your browser would report a connection error.

Let's run a simple program from the samples folder. Click the "Run files in the samples folder" link, and then click welcome.html from the list of files that appear.

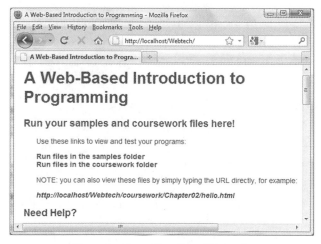

Figure 2-6: http://localhost/Webtech

This should bring up a welcome page with an interactive form for you to complete (Figure 2-7).

Figure 2-7: http://localhost/Webtech/samples/welcome.html

Try completing the form and the press the "Submit the Form" button. If a second welcome screen appears with a response to your submission, then everything is installed correctly and working fine.

Using URL's with Your Web Server

Every file on the Web has a unique URL, or Web address. The **URL** consists of a domain name, followed by the folders and a file name that indicate the location of the particular file on the server. Our local Web server has the domain name **localhost** and this domain name points to the **htdocs** folder which is in the folder that contains your installation).

Earlier you opened the file **welcome.html** from your **samples** folder. Open the file again and this time notice the URL in your browser's address window:

http://localhost/Webtech/samples/welcome.html

All of the URLs of files located on your Web server will begin **http://localhost** because **localhost** is the domain name of your local server. But how does the Web server know where to find the **welcome.html** file in order to send the contents of the file to your Web browser?

The answer is that, by default, the Web server looks in the **htdocs** folder of your Web server installation in response to any URL that begins **http://localhost**. In other words the URL **http://localhost** is associated with the **htdocs** file folder on your drive, and in case you're wondering, the name **htdocs** is a shortened version of "hypertext documents". Use **My Computer** (in Windows) or **Finder** (on a Macintosh) to locate the **htdocs** folder in your Web server installation.

So if the URL is **http://localhost/Webtech/samples/welcome.html** then the Web server will process the file named welcome.html that is located in the folder **htdocs/Webtech/samples**. Use **My Computer** or **Finder** to find this file on your disk — can you find it?

Be sure that you understand this. Each URL that begins **http://localhost/Webtech** refers to a file on your Web server that is located under the **htdocs/Webtech** folder and if you were to change the contents of any file inside this folder and the save your changes, the new version of the file would be displayed if you were to type the URL of the file in your Web browser.

As another example let's look at a file in your **coursework** folder. Type the URL **http://localhost/Webtech** and choose the **coursework** folder. Now click **Chapter02** and choose **hello.html**. This page displays a short introductory message about the kind of work you will do for each chapter (Figure 2-8).

Note that the URL for this file is:

http://localhost/Webtech/coursework/Chapter02/hello.html

Can you use **My Computer** (in Windows) or **Finder** (on a Mac) to locate this file on your disk?

We will keep all our work files in **two** folders under the **htdocs\Webtech** folder. The **samples** folder will contain all of the sample files referenced in the textbook. Try opening some of these programs in your browser now. You will notice that many files are listed in pairs with the same name but two different extensions (**.html** and **.php**). In these cases, click the **.html** files rather than the **.php** files to see what they do (the **.html** files display Web pages with forms that are used to "drive" the PHP programs). The **coursework** folder contains sub-folders for each chapter, and each chapter folder contains the files for your code exercises. If you were to try opening these files you will find

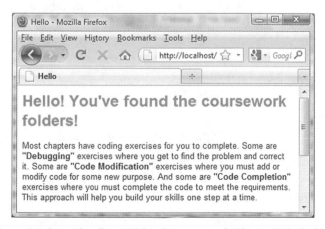

Figure 2-8: http://localhost/Webtech/coursework/Chapter02/hello.html

that many of them do not work correctly or generate errors—that's because they contain code that you will complete yourself as you work through the chapters.

To summarize, always remember to first **start** your Web server **before** you attempt to run your programs, and always **stop** the Web server and then **exit the Control Panel** once you have completed your work. The URL to your programs will always begin with **http://localhost/** and this should be followed by the names of any subfolders, followed by the name of the file that you wish to open. To avoid typing the complete URL's, you can just type **http://localhost/WebTech** (Figure 2-6) and then click through the links to open the file you want to view.

Always Use URL's to Run Your Web Applications!

As you probably know, in **Windows** you can often use **My Computer** to not only find a file but also to open the file (on a Macintosh you can use **Finder**). That's because your operating system associates the file type of a file with a default application that can handle that file type. For example, files with **.doc** and **.docx** files are usually associated the **MS Word** application, which is which why MS Word runs and opens the file when you click a file with one of these file types. Your computer usually associates **.htm** and **.html** files with your Web browser, so if you have a file with one of these extensions stored on your computer, and click this files in **My Computer** or **Finder**, the file will be displayed in your Web browser window. The page will display whether or not your Web server is running because you have opened it directly from your file system.

It's important to understand this because in this case you are not using a URL to request the file from your Web server, and that means that your Web server is not processing the file for use by the browser. Your .html pages will still display because these file do not require any special processing. But if you try to submit a form or if you click a .php file you will find a problem because .php files **must** be processed on the Web server before they can be viewed correctly by the browser. Since we are working with a combination of .html and .php files, you **must always** run the Web server and you **must always** use a URL that begins with the **localhost** domain to view your files in your Web browser.

To understand this better, let's try running a Web application without using a URL, just to see what happens.

Use **My Computer** (or **Finder** on a Macintosh) to navigate to the **samples** folder on your drive. Double-click the file named **addTwoNumbers.html**. A Web browser will probably start up, open the file and displays the Web page (Figure 2-9). This page looks fine, but notice the file path that is displayed in the browser's address window, which in Windows will be something like:

file://F:/xampplite/htdocs/Webtech/samples/addTwoNumbers.html

Because we opened the file in Windows, we see the Windows file path in the address window that begins **file://** rather than a URL that begins **http://localhost**. That tells you

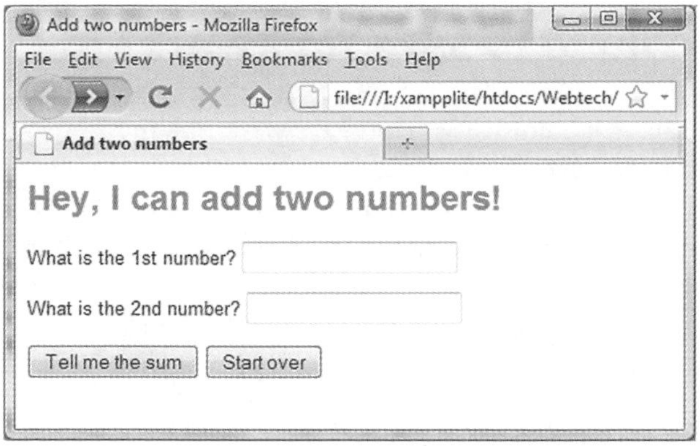

Figure 2-9: Opening addTwoNumbers.html using a Windows file path instead of a URL

that you are not connecting to the file through your Web server, which means you cannot process the form. If you type in two numbers and click the "Tell me the Sum" button, you will see something unexpected (Figure 2-10).

This doesn't make much sense! What is happening is that when the "Tell me the Sum" button was clicked, the Web browser opened a file named **twoNumbers.php** which contains the PHP instructions to process the form. However the browser was simply opening the file and displaying the contents. The browser was not submitting a request to your Web server to open and process the file. Your Web server includes the PHP processor which is necessary to execute the PHP instructions in this file. To access the Web server from your Web browser you **must** use URL's that begin with the domain name **localhost.**

So the correct way to view your .html and .php files is to always first run the Web server (if it is not already running), and then provide the URL to open the appropriate file. For example to correctly run the addTwoNumbers application, use the URL:

http://localhost/WebTech/samples/addTwoNumbers.html

Go ahead and do this to see that the application now works as expected.

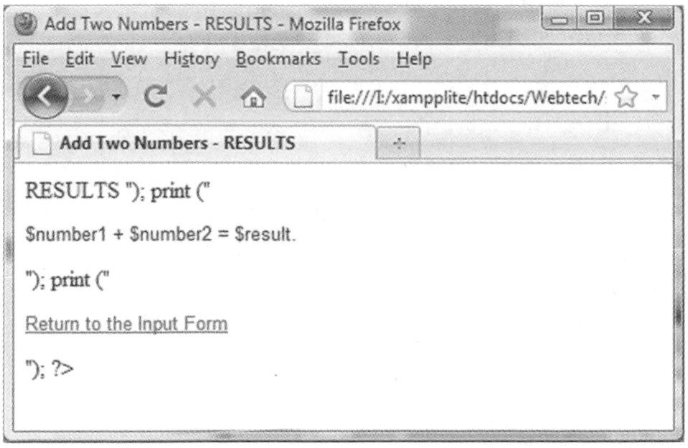

Figure 2-10: Result when opening addTwoNumbers.html without a URL

Where to Save Your Work Files

You will create and edit your HTML and PHP work files in the chapter folders under the **xampplite\htdocs\WebTech\coursework** folder. These files will produce small Web applications. You will use a text editor to develop the code for these files and then save them. It is important that you save these files in the correct location so that the Web server can find them when you type in the URL. Once you are ready to test your applications, be sure that the Web server is running and then use your Web browser to run your programs. The URL for your files will be:

   http://localhost/WebTech/coursework/ChapterXX/yyy

where ChapterXX is a chapter number (for example **Chapter02**) and yyy is the name of a specific file, for example **myFirst.html**. To avoid typing the entire URL, you can open just type **http://localhost/WebTech** and then click the links on that page to obtain the appropriate folder and file.

The Importance of Frequent Backups

Always keep a recent backup of your **Webtech** folder on a separate disk (for example on your hard drive at home if you are using a portable disk as your primary workplace, or on a portable disk if your hard drive is your primary workplace. It is good practice to back up your work every time you make major changes, or at least once a week. If your drive crashes, you can reinstall the Web server on a new drive and then copy the backup of your **Webtech** folder into the **htdocs** folder of your new installation. Take your backups seriously—there is nothing worse than losing hours, days, or weeks of hard work.

Creating an HTML Document

In order to get started, you will first create a simple HTML document, store it on your server and then send a request to open the document from your client Web browser. Don't be concerned about understanding this document right now—you will learn about HTML in Chapter 4.

Open **Crimson Editor** or any text editor that you wish to use. Type in the text for **myFirst.html**, but write your name instead of "YOUR NAME", write today's date instead of "TODAY'S DATE", and write something about yourself to replace the words "WRITE ABOUT YOURSELF HERE":

```
<!-- Author:   YOUR NAME
  Date:       TODAY'S DATE
  File:       myFirst.html
  Purpose:    HTML Practice
-->
<html>
<head>
  <title>HTML Example</title>
</head>
<body>

  <h1>My Web Page</h1>

  <p>Hi! My name is <strong>YOUR NAME</strong>. Let me tell you a
  little bit about myself ... </p>

  <p>WRITE ABOUT YOURSELF HERE</p>

</body>
</html>
```

Code Example: myFirst.html

Figure 2-11 shows how your file might look if you are using Crimson Editor as your text editor .

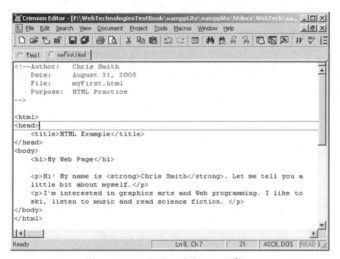

Figure 2-11: Using Crimson Editor

Choose **Save As** from the **File** menu and save the file as follows (your **Save in** address will reflect the actual location of your **xampplite** folder):

Save in: **xampplite\htdocs\WebTech\coursework\Chapter02**
File name: **myFirst.html**
Save as Type: **HTML**

The file has now been stored on the Web server. You can now submit a request to view this file from your Web browser. Be sure your server is running. Now type the following URL in your browser's address box:

http://localhost/WebTech/coursework/Chapter02/myFirst.html

When the browser submits this request, the Web server receives the URL and locates the file (myFirst.html). Since the file has an .html extension, the server simply sends the file contents back to the Web browser for display. Web browsers are designed to read HTML documents and treat any HTML tags as formatting instructions. We will learn more about this in the next chapter. Your HTML page should look similar to the screenshot in Figure 2-12.

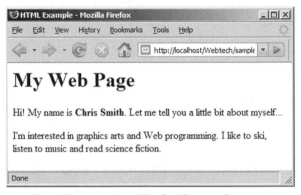

Figure 2-12: myFirst.html screenshot

If the link to **myFirst.html** does not work either your file name is different or the file is not in the correct location, or the Web server is not running.

If you wish to make changes to your document, simply edit your code in your text editor. Be sure to save your changes before viewing the file again and be sure to **refresh** the page in your Web browser otherwise your browser may continue to display the previous version.

Congratulations! You have just created a simple Web page, stored it on your local server, then accessed the page from a client (your Web browser)!

Creating a PHP program

Now let's create a simple PHP program. Don't be concerned about understanding this document right now—you will learn about PHP in Chapter 5. Type the code listing for **myFirst.php** in **Crimson Editor** (or your preferred text editor) exactly as written except type your name instead of "YOUR NAME" and today's date instead of "TODAY'S DATE". Note that you can copy and paste code from **myFirst.html** to save some time:

```
<!-- Author: YOUR NAME
   Date:      TODAY'S DATE
   File:      myFirst.php
   Purpose:   PHP Practice
-->
<html>
<head>
   <title>First PHP Example</title>
</head>
<body>

   <h1>Circle Calculation</h1>

   <?php
     $radius = 15.75;
     $area = pi() * pow ($radius, 2);
     $circumference = 2 * pi() * $radius;

     print("<p>A circle with a radius of $radius has an area of
         $area and a circumference of $circumference.</p>");

     print("<p>That's all that I have been designed to tell
         you!</p>");

   ?>
</body>
</html>
```

Code Example: myFirst.php

Choose **Save As** from the **File** menu and save the file as follows:

> Save in: **xampplite\htdocs\WebTech\coursework\Chapter02**
> File name: **myFirst.php**
> Save as Type: **PHP**

Now view this in your browser by typing the following URL:

> **http://localhost/WebTech/coursework/Chapter02/myFirst.php**

When the browser submits this request, the Web server receives the URL and locates the file (myFirst.php). Since the file has a .php extension, the server runs a PHP processor to execute any PHP code in the file and assemble a new HTML document. Once the PHP has been completely processed, the newly created HTML document is sent back to the Web browser for display. Your page should look something like the screenshot in Figure 2-13. We will learn more about this process in later chapters.

The text may wrap differently depending on the size of your browser window. If the link to **myFirst.php** does not work as expected, you may have used the wrong file name,

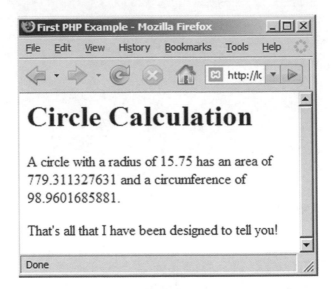

Figure 2-13: myFirst.php screenshot

or saved the files in the wrong location. Or you may have forgotten to start your Web server. You may receive an error message like this:

```
Parse error: parse error, unexpected T_VARIABLE in
F:\xampplite\htdocs\WebTech\coursework\myFirst.php on line 15
```

That means you have a syntax error in your PHP code. Programming languages such as PHP require a very precise syntax. There is a good chance that you may mistype something and your page may display differently (for example one or more numbers may not display as expected). Compare your code carefully with the example and see if you can find the errors. Once again remember to save your changes and remember to refresh the browser window to view your revised program.

Congratulations! You have just created a simple PHP program, stored it on your local Web server, and accessed it from a client (your Web browser)!

Creating an Interactive HTML and PHP Program

That last example displays information concerning a circle with a radius of **15.75**. We could improve the utility of this application by allowing the user to enter **any** radius. Next we will create a new version of this application that consists of two documents. The first (named **circle.html**) will be an HTML document that contains a form so that the user can submit a radius and submit this for processing. The second document (named **circle.php**) will contain a PHP program that receives the radius and calculates and displays the circumference and area of the circle. Here is the code for **circle.html**:

```
<!-- Author:  YOUR NAME
   Date:       TODAY'S DATE
   File:       circle.html
   Purpose:  PHP Practice
-->
<html>
<head>
  <title>Circle Calculation</title>
</head>
<body>

  <h1>Circle Calculation</h1>

  <form action="circle.php" method="post">
    <p>What is the radius of the circle?
    <input type="text" size="20" name="radius" /></p>
    <p><input type="submit" value="Tell me the area and
       circumference" /></p>
  </form>
</body>
</html>
```

Code Example: circle.html

Choose Save As from the File menu and save the file as follows (your Save in address will reflect the actual location of your xampplite folder):

Save in: **xampplite\htdocs\WebTech\coursework\Chapter02**
File name: **circle.html**
Save as Type: **HTML**

The file has now been stored on the Web server. You can now submit a request to view this file from your Web browser. Just type the following URL in your browser's address box:

http://localhost/WebTech/coursework/Chapter02/circle.html

If you do this you the document will display. Assuming that you typed everything correctly, you will see that it contains will see a Web page with a form (Figure 2-14).

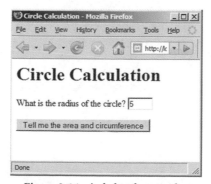

Figure 2-14: circle.html screenshot

If you enter a radius in to the text box and click the "Tell me the area and circumference" button, you will get an error message, similar to that shown in Figure 2-15.

Figure 2-15: Connecting to a page that does not exist

That's because the form on this Web page is designed to send the radius to a program named **circle.php** in order for it to be processed. The problem is that we haven't created the **circle.php** program yet! So let's do that right now!

Here is the code for **circle.php**:

```
<!-- Author:  YOUR NAME
   Date:      TODAY'S DATE
   File:      circle.php
   Purpose:   PHP Practice
-->
<html>
<head>
  <title> Circle Calculation</title>
</head>
<body>

  <h1>Circle Calculation</h1>

  <?php
    $radius = $_POST['radius'];
    $area = pi() * pow ($radius, 2);
    $circumference = 2 * pi() * $radius;

    print("<p>A circle with a radius of $radius has an area of
       $area and a circumference of $circumference.</p>");
  ?>
  <p><a href="circle.html">Calculate another circle?</a></p>

</body>
</html>
```

Code Example: circle.php

Choose **Save As** from the **File** menu and save the file as follows:

> Save in: **xampplite\htdocs\WebTech\coursework\Chapter02**
> File name: **circle.php**
> Save as Type: **PHP**

Now you should be able to use your form correctly. Open your Web document again:

> **http://localhost/WebTech/coursework/Chapter02/circle.html**

Type a radius into the text box and click the "Tell me the area and circumference" button. This time you should see a new page that displays the area and circumference of a circle with the radius that you submitted (Figure 2-16).

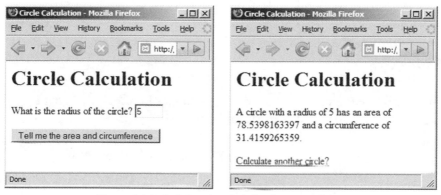

Figure 2-16: circle.html and circle.php screenshots

Note that you can click the "Calculate another circle?" link to return to the first page.

Congratulations! You have now created a simple Web application that: provides an input form, processes the input, and displays the result.

Do not be concerned about how these documents actually work at this point. The purpose of the current exercise is to give you practice using a text editor to type HTML and PHP code, saving your documents to the correct location on your disk, making corrections as needed, and viewing your applications in a Web browser using the correct URL. In the following chapters you will learn how to design and create Web applications that include HTML pages with forms and PHP programs that process these forms.

Summary

Client/Server applications are designed so that client-based software such as Web browsers can submit requests to server-based programs such as Web servers for processing. This makes it easy for large numbers of client programs to make use of common services. Another advantage is that new software installations and updates to existing software are performed on the server without requiring changes to the client computers. Client/server applications are used world-wide across the **Internet,** and are also used to deliver services on private **intranets.**

Web-based applications are developed by creating the required code and storing this on a Web server. Clients can submit requests to the server to process these files and return the results. When a server receives a request for an **.html** file, it simply locates and opens the file and returns the document for display by the Web browser. When a server receives a request for a **.php** file, it first processes the PHP instructions in the file and then returns the new HTML document that is generated. The Web server must be running in order for a client to submit requests.

Files usually include file extensions to indicate the data format that is stored in the file. Files can only be processed by programs designed to work with the file format. Text files can be opened by any text editing program, and sometimes contain text that requires specialized processing. In this course we will work with text files using three file extensions. Files with a **.txt** extension will be used to store data such as student scores or wage information. Files with an **.html** extension will contain HTML markup code for display in a Web browser. Files with a **.php** extension will contain PHP code that is processed by a PHP processor running on a Web server.

Under the Windows addressing scheme, file/folder locations are based on a drive letter to represent a specific disk drive, for example:

C:\xampplite\htdocs\WebTech\coursework\Chapter02\circle.html

Under the Internet addressing scheme, file/folder locations are based on an Internet domain name, for example:

http://localhost/WebTech/coursework/Chapter02/circle.html

The domain name is mapped to an IP address. In this case the IP address for the **localhost** domain is **127.0.0.1**

In this chapter you learned the basic steps to install, start and stop a local Web server. You also learned to create and modify HTML and PHP code using a text editor, and then view the results in a Web browser.

When you use the Web server, the URL's of your documents will always begin:

http://localhost/

This URL points to the **xampplite/htdocs** folder which is located wherever you installed the Web server on your disk. Be sure that the Web server is running before using this URL. Always be sure to use the Internet address when you attempt to view your .html and .php files. Do not use the Windows address, otherwise your .php programs will not be processed.

Don't be concerned about the actual content of the HTML and PHP code yet. The purpose of these exercises is to learn the procedures. You are now ready to learn how to design and code your own Web-based, client/server programs using HTML and PHP.

Chapter 2 Review Questions

1. Consider the following address: **D:\CourseMaterial\Coursework\wage1.html**
    Which statement is true?
    a. The file is stored in a folder named wage1.html
    b. The file is stored in a folder named Coursework
    c. The file is stored in a folder named CourseMaterial
    d. The file is stored in a folder named D:
    e. This address does not specify a file

2. Consider the following address: **D:\CourseMaterial\Coursework\wage1.html**
    What is the name of the file?
    a. wage1.html
    b. Coursework
    c. CourseMaterial
    d. D:
    e. This address does not specify a file

3. Consider the following address: **D:\CourseMaterial\Coursework\wage1.html**
    Where is the CourseMaterial folder located?
    a. Inside wage1.html
    b. Inside the Coursework folder
    c. On the D: drive
    d. It is not possible to tell from this address
    e. The address is incorrect

4. What type of address is this? D:\CourseMaterial\Coursework\wage1.html
    a. Internet address
    b. Microsoft Windows address

5. What is wrong with the following URL?
    http:\\www.w3.org\Markup\Guide\Style.html
    a. Internet addresses must use the forward slash / as a separator
    b. The file name is in the wrong location
    c. The domain name is the wrong location
    d. The file name is missing
    e. The drive letter is missing

6. What is wrong with the following URL?
     http://www.w3.org/Style.html/Markup/Guide/
     a. Internet addresses must use the back slash \ as a separator
     b. The file name is in the wrong location
     c. The domain name is the wrong location
     d. The file name is missing
     e. The drive letter is missing

7. Which component of a client/server application processes a PHP file?
     a. Client
     b. Server

8. What does HTML stand for?
     a. Highly Technical Markup Language
     b. Host Translated Markup Language
     c. Hypertext Markup Language
     d. Hands-on Technical Markup Language
     e. Hyper Transitional Markup Language

9. What is HTML?
     a. A markup language used to provide formatting instructions for text
     b. A programming language used to process input, perform calculations
        and other operations, and generate output
     c. An addressing scheme for URL's
     d. A name for a button on a user interface
     e. A form used to validate user input

10. What is PHP?
     a. A markup language used to provide formatting instructions for text
     b. A programming language used to process input, perform calculations
        and other operations, and generate output
     c. An addressing scheme for URL's
     d. A name for a button on a user interface
     e. A form used to validate user input

11. What is the domain name of the Internet address that you will use to access Web
     pages delivered by your standalone server?
     a. localhost
     b. www.w3.org
     c. WebTech
     d. samples
     e. welcome.html

12. Where should you save the html and php files that you create for this course?
    a. Anywhere on your disk is fine
    b. In the correct Chapter folder under
       xampplite\htdocs\WebTech\coursework\
    c. In the correct Chapter folder under
       xampplite\WebTech\htdocs\coursework\
    d. In the correct Chapter folder under xampplite\WebTech\coursework\
    e. In the correct Chapter folder under xampplite\coursework\

13. Which folder is divided into chapters?
    a. samples folder
    b. coursework folder

14. Which one of the following files can be found in your samples folder?
    a. gettingStarted.html
    b. gettingStarted.php
    c. courseWebSite.html
    d. quoteGenerator.html
    e. quoteGenerator.php

15. In your samples folder there is a file named tempConverter1.php. What should you
    do to run this program and find out what it does?
    a. Open the file using Windows Explorer
    b. Run your local Web server and then type the url
       http://localhost/WebTech/samples/tempConverter1.php
       in your browser window.
    c. Run your local Web server and type http://localhost/WebTech/ in your
       browser window, then click on samples and then click on
       tempConverter1.php.
    d. Either of the last two procedures will work but not the first one

16. In your samples folder, what happens if you run quoteGenerator.php in your
    browser window?
    a. The browser displays the same quote every time you run it.
    b. The browser displays a different quote each time you run it.
    c. The browser displays a different presidential quote each time you run
       it.
    d. The browser asks you to input a quote.

17. Which of the following file types does NOT appear in the samples folder?
    a. .bmp
    b. .html
    c. .jpg
    d. .php
    e. .txt

18. What is the correct URL for your myFirst.php document?
    a. http://localhost/WebTech/coursework/Chapter02/myFirst.php
    b. http://WebTech/coursework/Chapter02/myFirst.php
    c. http://localhost/coursework/Chapter02/myFirst.php
    d. http://WebTech/Chapter02/myFirst.php
    e. http://localhost/myFirst.php

19. In the samples folder, if you open welcome.html and submit the information but leave the first name and last name boxes blank, what does the resulting Web page display (among other things)?
    a. ERROR—INPUT IS MISSING!
    b. ERROR—YOU MUST ENTER YOUR FIRST NAME AND LAST NAME!
    c. Welcome!
    d. Welcome Whoever You Are!
    e. Welcome! You must enter your first name and last name!

20. In the samples folder, what is the difference between wage1.html and wage2.html?
    a. wage1.html allows you to input your hours worked and hourly wage but wage2.html does not
    b. wage2.html allows you to input your hours worked and hourly wage but wage1.html does not
    c. wage1.html allows you to input your name but wage2.html does not wage2.html allows you to input your name but wage1.html does not
    d. There is no difference between wage1.html and wage2.html

Chapter 2 Code Exercises

The exercises for this chapter are simply intended to ensure that (a) you have your software installed and working correctly, and (b) you are comfortable with the process of creating, editing and running your Web applications.

1. First be sure that you have installed your Web server. Now run the XAMPP Control Panel and start your server. If you have any problems when you do this, first review the steps to install and run your Web server before you assume there is a problem with your installation. Refer to the **Installation Problems** guide on the textbook Web site at:

    http://www.mikeokane.com/textbooks/WebTech/support.php

2. With your Web server started, open a Web browser and type the URL:

    http://localhost/Webtech/samples/artGallery.html

    You should see a Web page that displays a "Welcome to the Art Gallery" heading and allows you to choose an artist from a drop down list. If you do not see this and receive an error message instead, first be sure that you typed the URL correctly. If you still receive an error, then (a) your Webtech folder was not included in your installation (use **My Computer** to ensure that this folder is located in your **xampplite/htdocs** folder), or (b) your server is not running (the server may not be running if you also get an error message when you type the URL **http://localhost** in your browser address window), or (c) your server was not installed correctly (this may be the case if you received an error message when you started the server in the XAMPP Control Panel). Make a careful note of all error messages and anything else that might be useful, then refer to the **Installation Problems** guide on the textbook Web site for help.

3. Assuming that the artGallery page is displayed, select an artist and then click the "Show me an Artwork" button. An artwork should now be displayed along with some additional information. If you do not see this, check the URL in your Web browser's address window. If the URL begins with **file://** then you are not using the right URL and you are not connecting to the Web server. Go back and use the correct URL. Remember that, to connect to your Web server, your URLs must **always** begin **http://** and in this case the URL should be:

    http://localhost/Webtech/samples/artGallery.html

4. If the artGallery application performed successfully then you are ready to work. To become familiar with the procedure that we will follow throughout this textbook, use your text editor as directed in this chapter to create **myFirst.html**, **myFirst.php**, **circle.html**, and **circle.php** and save these files in the **Chapter02** folder of your coursework folder if you have not already done this. Test each of these by running your Web server, opening a Web browser, and typing the appropriate URLs. You may need to fix some of your code but eventually each program should run as described in the chapter. **Do not bypass this exercise.** You need to be comfortable creating and running your applications and using your Web server in order to work through this book.

Chapter 3

Program Design —
From Requirements to Algorithms

Intended Learning Outcomes

After completing this chapter, you should be able to:

- Describe important characteristics of successful instructions.
- Identify sequence, selection and repetition structures.
- Identify key elements of a simple requirements document.
- Develop an Input, Processing, Output (IPO) chart based on a simple requirements document.
- Develop a user interface design based on a simple requirements document.
- Write instructions in the form of an algorithm using pseudocode.
- Describe the purpose of variables and assignment operations.
- Write simple arithmetic and boolean expressions.

Introduction

A computer program is a sequence of instructions written in a programming language to meet a set of requirements. As a programmer you must learn to write clear and accurate instructions since a computer has no way to guess your intentions or ask for clarification. The process of developing instructions for a computer application is not so different from giving instructions to people. We will therefore begin this chapter by reviewing some important characteristics of human instructions and see how these apply to software design. We will then work through the design process required to develop some simple Web applications, including the application that was presented in Chapter 2.

As you work through this chapter you will acquire some useful tools to evaluate program requirements and learn to write instructions in the form of **pseudocode** in order to create an **algorithm**. By the end of the chapter you will be ready to learn how to convert instructions into a programming language in order to produce a working application. Take time to think about what you are learning in this chapter. You may be impatient to start coding but the ideas presented here are fundamental to the work of software design and application development.

What Are Instructions?

How many times have you been asked to provide instructions? Perhaps you have given directions, or instructed someone to use a machine, repair something, play a game, cook some food, or perform a calculation? Perhaps you have had to write down these instructions. And how many times have you tried to follow someone else's instructions, to install a printer, perform a task at work, assemble a child's toy, replace a filter, repair a faucet, use a new tool, play a game, bake a cake, learn to swim, or submit an assignment? How often have you been frustrated by instructions that are poorly worded or that miss some vital piece of information, for example when the assembly instructions for that new toy you bought for your child don't clearly explain exactly how the parts should fit together?

We all follow instructions many times every day, sometimes instructions that we learned a long time ago, sometimes instructions that are new to us. It takes skill to design and write instructions that are clear and understandable. This skill is not very well recognized or rewarded, and the instructions that we try to follow are often not as good as they might be. We pay quite a high price for this. When we use poorly written instructions we may be unable to complete a task, or we may damage something, or we may need to request clarification. The same applies to the instructions that make up a computer program. A poorly written program may generate high costs in terms of money, stress, and time.

Common Characteristics of Instructions

A computer program delivers a set of instructions to the computer to perform a task of some kind. These instructions must of course be in a form that the computer can understand, but instructions of all kinds share certain characteristics, whether intended to be performed by human beings or by a computer. For example when we are asked for directions, we are being asked to deliver a set of instructions. Look at the street map in Figure 3-1 and imagine that someone has just asked you for directions to the library from the corner of Queen Street and Martin Luther King Boulevard (in this example, Rose Avenue and Sycamore Lane are one-way streets while the other streets are two-way streets).

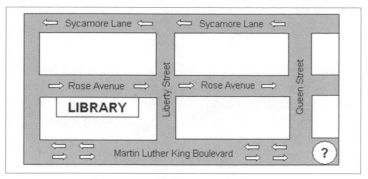

Figure 3-1: How do I get to the library?

Before you begin to design a solution for this or any problem, always take time to be sure that you completely understand the problem requirements. Exactly what is being asked? Consider this carefully and ask questions until you are sure what is needed with no assumptions on your part. For example, which library is this person looking for? We might assume the local library on Rose Avenue when he or she is completely unaware of that library and was actually asking for directions to the main city library a few miles away! Is this person walking or driving? If walking then the one-way streets don't matter. If you do misunderstand the requirements then your instructions may be terrific but they will solve the wrong problem! Asking questions helps ensure that you fully understand the requirements. This applies to instructions of any kind: understanding requirements is important when giving directions and important when developing computer programs.

Once you have a clear idea of the requirements, you can develop a solution and provide instructions. Here is one example of instructions that give directions to the library:

If you are driving: turn right on Queen Street. Continue on Queen Street for two blocks, then turn left on Sycamore Lane. Continue on Sycamore Lane for two blocks then turn left on Franklin Street. Drive one block then turn left on Rose Avenue. The library is on your right.

If you are walking: Walk one block along Martin Luther King Boulevard then turn right on Liberty Street. Walk one block and turn left on Rose Avenue. The library will be on your left.

A good set of instructions will be **understandable**, **correct**, **unambiguous**, and efficient. When we develop set of instructions we should measure them against each of these criteria before being satisfied with our work.

Instructions must be understandable.

Instructions must use terms and language that are understandable to the person (or computer) that is receiving them. In order to give effective instructions we must use a recognizable language. It is not useful to give directions in French if the person receiving them does not speak French! And an instruction to "turn right at the intersection with the sycamore tree" is not useful if the person does not know what a sycamore tree is.

Similarly, in order to write instructions that a computer can execute we must learn the terms and grammar of a programming language so that our instructions can be interpreted correctly. Programming instructions that do not use the programming language correctly are said to contain syntax errors. A computer cannot execute a program that contains **syntax errors**.

Instructions must be correct.

This may seem obvious but it is easy to make a mistake even when giving simple directions. For example we may say "turn right" when we meant to say "turn left". For this reason we should be careful to test our instructions very carefully before we apply them. Not only must each individual instruction be correct, but the entire set of instructions must also be **ordered** correctly. If you change the order of the sentences in your directions to the library then the individual might never reach the library.

In computer programming, instructions that are **understandable** but not **correct** are said to contain **logical errors**. The computer can execute the instructions but will not perform as expected. This is actually a more dangerous type of error than a syntax error. In the case of a syntax error, the program cannot execute so that it is obvious that there is a problem. In the case of a logical error the program executes and it may not be clear that it is doing something wrong, for example performing a calculation incorrectly.

Instructions must be unambiguous.

If you just say "turn on Queen Street" instead of "turn right on Queen Street", the instruction will be ambiguous since the person will not know which way to turn. Ambiguous instructions create uncertainty and the individual who is carrying out the instructions must either ask for clarification or else make their own decision.

A computer cannot interpret an ambiguous instruction so ambiguous instructions are treated as syntax errors that prevent a program from executing.

Instructions must be efficient.

We can provide very understandable, correct and unambiguous directions that are not very efficient. For example when asked for directions to the library, you could respond as follows:

If you are driving: turn right on Queen Street. Continue on Queen Street for two blocks, then turn left on Sycamore Lane. Drive one block, then turn left on Liberty Street. Continue on Liberty Street for two blocks then turn right on Martin Luther

> *King Boulevard. Drive one block then turn right. Take the next right on Rose Avenue. The library is on your right.*

These instructions are understandable, correct and unambiguous but they are not as efficient as the previous set of instructions. Now consider the following directions to the library:

> *Go to the airport. Fly to Paris, France. Stay in Paris until you find someone to marry. Get married then move to Italy. Find a job and stay for three years. Then fly back here. At the airport hail a taxi and ask the driver to bring you to the library. The taxi driver will know where it is.*

These instructions may be understandable, correct and unambiguous but they are certainly not very efficient (although they may make for an interesting life)!

Last, here is a set of instructions that are more efficient than any of the instructions that have been provided so far:

> *Continue along Martin Luther King Boulevard for two blocks then turn right. Take the next right on Rose Avenue. The library is on your right.*

It is important to recognize that, for many problems, you cannot know whether or not your solution uses the most efficient instructions that could be applied. Often there may be any number of acceptable solutions. Some of these will be more efficient than others, while some will be quite similar to others in terms of efficiency. If you look at the map again you will see that there are many ways to get to the library. If you really think about it you will realize that there are actually an **infinite** number of ways to get to the library!

This is an important point because many beginning programmers think that there is a "right answer" to a programming requirement when in fact there are many possible solutions. Different programmers are likely to solve the same problem in different ways. A good programmer knows this and is always ready to consider a different approach. As you become more skilled your solutions will become more efficient. Programmers often work in teams to brainstorm and consider many different solutions before deciding on a particular approach. Even so, since we are always working under time constraints, we often discover more efficient solutions after our software application is already in production. This is one of the reasons that new software versions are released.

It is also important to notice that efficiency can mean different things to different people. In the case of the library, somebody who is disabled may benefit by taking a backstreet route to the library with less obstacles, while somebody who is in a hurry might want the fastest route. Similarly, good software designers take account of the needs of different types of users when developing effective instructions. They also take account of the systems on which the programs will execute. For example a programmer may need to decide whether to use instructions that make the least use of memory, instructions that perform the fastest, or instructions that provide the most user-friendly interface.

Sequence, Selection and Repetition Structures

You may be surprised to learn that any instructions can be written using combinations of just three basic statement structures: **sequential statements, selection statements,** and **repetition (or loop) statements.** We used all three of these structures when we gave directions of the library. Here is a description of each type of statement:

Sequential Statements

These are instructions that simply follow each one after another and must be performed in order. The following statements are sequential:

```
Turn right on Queen Street
Turn left on Rose Avenue
```

Selection Statements

These are instructions which provide a choice of instructions to follow based on a test condition. Here is an example of a selection statement:

```
IF you are driving
    ..instructions to follow if the test condition is true..
```

In this example the test condition is **IF you are driving**. The instruction following the test condition will only be performed if the test is true.

Repetition (Loop) Statements

These are instructions that may be repeated, either a prescribed number of times or until some condition changes. Here is an example of a repetition statement:

```
Continue on Queen Street for two blocks
```

This instruction requires the individual to perform an action (drive a block) two times.

All computer programs consist of combinations of sequence, selection and repetition instructions as needed to meet the specific requirements of the application. For a while we will work with sequential instructions only. In later chapters we will explore the use of selection and repetition structures.

A Programming Example

Let's look at the steps you will take to develop instructions for a simple computer program. Here are the requirements for the circle application that you created in Chapter 2:

Circle requirements:

Write a program that asks the user for the radius of a circle. The program should calculate the circle's circumference and area, and display the radius, circumference and area.

These are simple requirements but we will use them to introduce the process of developing an application.

First we will want to consider the requirements carefully to be sure that we understand them. Are you clear about what this program needs to do?

A computer program can include instructions to perform three types of action:
- Receive **input** from user interfaces, microphones, files, databases, communications and other devices.
- **Process** data by performing assignments, conversions, calculations, comparisons, etc.
- Send **output** to user interfaces, printers, files, databases, communications and other devices.

It helps to evaluate your requirements in terms of input, processing and output. **Inputs** are the data values that the program must **receive** in order to perform its task. Processes are the operations, or actions, that the program must **perform** on the data. **Outputs** are the data values that the program **delivers** before it terminates.

Always look over your application requirements carefully. What input is required? Are the inputs to come from the user? From a file? From a combination of sources? What outputs are required? Are the outputs to be displayed on the screen? Sent to a printer? Looking over our Circle requirements, we can see that the program requires the radius of a circle as input, and this will be provided by the user. The program will deliver the radius, area and circumference of the circle as output and this output will be displayed to the user.

Now identify the actions that must be performed. These will indicate the instructions that your program must execute. In our Circle requirements, the actions are "ask the user for the radius of a circle", "calculate the circle's circumference", "calculate the circle's area", "display the radius", "display the circumference", and "display the area".

If you cannot clearly determine the required inputs, processing and outputs from the requirements, you will want to request clarification. It is never a good idea to guess the requirements that were intended!

Creating an Input, Processing, Output (IPO) chart

It helps to write the program's inputs, processes and outputs as a list or table, often referred to as an **Input/Processing/Output (IPO) chart**. An IPO chart makes it easier to think about the design for your algorithm. For example here is an IPO chart for your Circle requirements:

```
IPO listing for Circle:
Inputs:   radius
Processing:
     receive the radius from the user
     calculate the area
     calculate the circumference
     display the radius, area and circumference
Outputs:  radius, area and circumference
```

Designing the User Interface

Once we have an idea of the inputs, outputs and processes, the next step is usually to design the user interface (also known as storyboarding). Designing the interface helps us to plan our algorithms since it is common to design different parts of a program (the program modules) around each screen of an interface. Different interfaces can mean quite different approaches to the application design so it's a good idea to sketch out some different ideas for your interface before settling on a specific solution. Figure 3-2 shows the proposed design for our Circle Calculation interface.

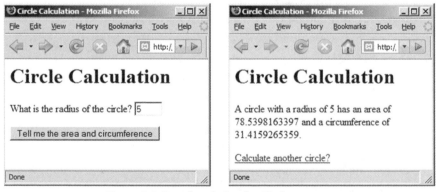

Figure 3-2: Interface design for Circle program

This design could simply be sketched out using a pencil and paper. For this application we have designed two screens. The first screen is a Web page that provides a heading, prompt, input box to obtain the user input (the radius), and a submission button. When the submission button is pressed, the data is submitted and processed by a program that performs the calculations and generates a second Web page containing the output.

This is a basic client/server design: the client submits a request and the server receives and processes the request, then generates a response which is sent back to the client.

For more complex applications, the design phase is extensive. Programs will be broken down into a large number of different modules and screens. The work of software design is usually undertaken by senior programmers while junior programmers develop the design into working code.

Once you have a clear idea of your interface, it is often useful to go back to your customer and review the requirements. That's because people can often think more clearly about what they want when they begin to see what the product will look like. Frequently customers will clarify their needs once they see your interface design.

Developing an Algorithm

An **algorithm** is the general term used to describe a set of instructions that perform a task of some kind. When we design an application we usually write our algorithms in a rather stylized form of English that is easy for a programmer to convert into any programming language. We call this style of writing **pseudocode** since it is "halfway" between English and actual program code. There are no precise rules for writing instructions in pseudocode, you will quickly get a feel for a style that works for you.

We designed our circle program in two components so we will develop the algorithm for each component separately. Here are the instructions for the first screen (circle.html) that provides as a form for the user:

```
circle.html algorithm:
   Prompt the user for radius
   Get the radius
   Submit the radius to circle.php for processing
END
```

In this pseudocode example we use a combination of Prompt and Get instructions to indicate each input that the application needs to receive from the user. The **Prompt** instruction tells the programmer that the user must be provided with a message in order to know what to do. The **Get** instruction tells the programmer to provide some way for the input to be received (for example the user must be provided with an input box or a drop-down list or some other way to select a radius).

We also use a **Submit** instruction to indicate that, once the input has been received, it must be submitted to **circle.php** (the program that will process the radius).

Here is an algorithm for the PHP program (**circle.php**) that processes the radius submitted by the user, performs the required calculations, and displays the results:

```
circle.php algorithm:
  Receive the radius from circle.html
  area = PI * square (radius)
  circumference = 2 * PI * radius
  Display radius, area, circumference
END
```

This program uses a **Receive** instruction to tell the programmer that code will be required to receive the radius from **circle.html**. The next two instructions indicate the code that is needed to calculate the area and circumference. The **Display** instruction tells the programmer that code is required to display the results. This program contains input (the data received from the form), processing (the calculations), and output (the values that are displayed to the user).

These algorithms are not written in any specific programming language, and do not tell the programmer exactly what to do. The pseudocode provides a general design and step-by-step outline for the application so that the programmer can more easily write the code to meet the requirements. The individual who translates the requirements into screens and algorithms is functioning as a software designer and may or may not be the same person as the programmer who develops the actual code.

The order of these instructions is important! Instructions in a computer program are executed one at a time, in the order that they are encountered. Consider the following instructions:

```
circle.php algorithm:
  area = PI * square (radius)
  Receive the radius from circle.html
  Display radius, area, circumference
  circumference = 2 * PI * radius
END
```

Clearly the area cannot be calculated before the radius has been received! And the circumference cannot be displayed before the circumference has been calculated!

Look at the two calculations in our algorithm:

```
area = PI * square (radius)
circumference = 2 * PI * radius
```

These statements contain **program variables**, **assignments** and **arithmetic expressions**. These are all new concepts so let's look at each in turn.

Variables

As humans, when we receive a piece of information, we store it in our memory and then retrieve it later when we need it. That's true even if we need it only a second later (for example when someone tells us his or her name, and we immediately use their name when we reply). The strange thing about human memory is that we don't actually know exactly where in our memory we store each piece of information. Which raises the question—how do we know where to find it? Don't think about that too much, you may lose your amazing memorization skills!

Just like humans, computer programs must store any piece of data in memory so that the program can access it later, even if "later" means the very next instruction! But a computer program must have a way to find each piece of information that has been stored. Unlike human memory, every storage location in a computer's memory is identified by a unique numeric address. Rather than refer to these addresses directly, programming languages allow programmers to create **variables**. Each variable has a name that represents the location in memory where a specific data value is stored. We use the variable name to refer to this location.

In our **circle.php** algorithm we indicate three variables. The value that is received from the user is stored in the variable named **radius**. The instruction **area = PI * square (radius)** tells the program to multiply the value of PI by the square of the value stored in the variable named **radius**, and to store the result in a variable named **area**. The instruction **circumference = 2 * PI * radius** tells the program to multiply 2 by the value of PI by the value stored in the variable named **radius**, and to store the result in a variable named **circumference**. The instruction **Display radius, area, circumference** tells the program to display the values that have been stored in these three memory locations.

Variable names should be meaningful so that the name clearly indicates the type of value that the variable contains. Often a single English word is not sufficient to accomplish this and a variable name might contain multiple English words. However programming languages cannot allow spaces in variable names since this will create ambiguity (is it one variable or two?). Programmers therefore follow certain naming conventions to combine multiple English words into a single variable name. The most common conventions are:

- Use underscores between each English word in a variable name to represent the spaces, for example **hourly_wage** and **hours_worked**.
- Use an uppercase letter to begin each English word in a variable name, for example **hourlyWage** and **hoursWorked**. This approach is termed **camelback** notation.

PHP programmers follow either convention, however programmers in most current languages use camelback notation and that is the convention that we will follow in this book.

Another important naming convention is that the **first** letter of a variable name should always be lower-case.

Assignment Operations

An instruction to store a value in a variable is known as an **assignment operation**, or **assignment statement**. Assignment statements are written by listing the name of the variable that is to receive a value on the left side of the **assignment operator**, which is usually represented by the = sign. The value (or an expression that will evaluate to a value) that is to be stored in the variable appears on the right side of the assignment operator. The statements **area = PI * square (radius)** and **circumference = 2 * PI * radius** are examples of assignments statements. Here are two more examples of assignment statements:

```
weeklyWage = hourlyWage * hoursWorked
weeklyWage = hourlyWage * 40
```

The first statement instructs the program to multiply the value stored in a variable named **hourlyWage** by the value stored in a variable named **hoursWorked** and store the result in a variable named **weeklyWage**. The second statement instructs the program to multiply the value stored in **hourlyWage** by **40** and store the result in the **weeklyWage** variable.

Remember: in an assignment statement, the variable that is to receive a value is always placed on the **left** of the assignment operator, and the **value** to be stored (or the **expression** that generates this value) is located on the **right** hand side of the assignment operator.

Arithmetic and Logical Expressions

An **arithmetic expression** is simply an arithmetic operation that generates a numeric result. For example, **2 + 3** is an arithmetic expression and so is **(2 + 3) * 20**. When writing computer programs, arithmetic expressions can also include the names of variables that are being used to store numbers. So **hourlyWage * hoursWorked** is an arithmetic expression. We can also write arithmetic expressions that combine variables and literal numbers, for example **hourlyWage * 40**.

Logical expressions (also called **Boolean** expressions) allow us to **compare** values, for example **hoursWorked < 40** is a **logical** expression that tests whether the value stored in **hoursWorked** is less than **40**. Unlike arithmetic expressions, which have a numeric result, logical expressions have a **true** or **false** result. We will explore the use of both arithmetic and logical expressions in later chapters.

A Smoking Calculator

Now consider the requirements for a program that will conduct a short smoking survey and give the person who is taking the survey some feedback concerning their smoking history:

Smoking requirements:

Write a program that prompts the user for their first and last names, the number of years they have smoked and daily average number of cigarettes they have smoked during this time. Calculate the approximate number of cigarettes they have smoked in their life by multiplying the number of years they have smoked by 365 by the daily average. The program should display all of the input data and the total in a short report.

Here is an IPO listing, developed from the requirements:

```
IPO listing for Smoking:
    Inputs:         first name, last name, years smoked, average
                    smoked daily
    Processing:     Obtain the four inputs from the user
                    Calculate the total smoked
                    Display the outputs
    Outputs:        last name, first name, years smoked,
                    average smoked daily, total smoked
```

Figure 3-3 shows the interface design.

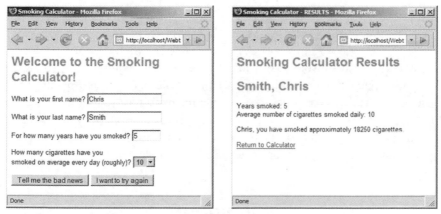

Figure 3-3: Interface for the Smoking application

Here is the algorithm for the first screen (an HTML document named **smoking.html** that contains the form that is displayed to obtain the user inputs):

```
smoking.html algorithm:
    Prompt for firstName
    Get firstName
    Prompt for lastName
    Get lastName
    Prompt for yearsSmoked
    Get yearsSmoked
    Prompt for smokedDaily
```

```
    Get smokedDaily
      Submit firstName, lastName, yearsSmoked, smokedDaily to
        smoking.php
  END
```

Here is the algorithm for the PHP program (**smoking.php**) that processes the input from the form and generates the second page:

```
  smoking.php algorithm:
    Receive firstName, lastName, yearsSmoked, smokedDaily from
        smoking.html
    totalSmoked = yearsSmoked * 365 * smokedDaily
    Display firstName, lastName, yearsSmoked, smokedDaily,
        totalSmoked
  END
```

Once again our algorithms do not give exact details of how the instructions are to be coded. They simply indicate the overall design and outline the steps that must be performed. The details will be developed by the programmer who converts the algorithm into a specific programming language.

Coding the Application

Once you have developed your algorithms to meet a set of requirements, you are ready to code your application. The following chapters will take you step-by-step through the process of creating Web pages that include forms to receive user input, and writing PHP applications that process user input and generate results. As you work through each chapter you will learn additional procedures and control structures that will enable you to handle increasingly sophisticated requirements.

Summary

A computer program delivers a set of instructions to the computer to perform a task of some kind. These instructions must be in a form that the computer can understand.

Instructions of all kinds share certain characteristics, whether intended to be performed by human beings or by a computer. A good set of instructions will be **understandable**, **correct**, **unambiguous**, and **efficient**. When we develop a set of instructions we should measure them against each of these criteria.

Computer instructions that are **understandable** but not **correct** are said to contain **logical errors**. Computer instructions that are not **understandable** (or **ambiguous**) are said to contain **syntax errors**.

Instructions may be **understandable** and **correct** but still may not be efficient.

A computer program is basically capable of three types of instruction: input, processing, and output. It is common practice to develop IPO (Input, Processing, Output) charts in order to better understand requirements. **Inputs** are the data values that the program needs to **receive** in order to perform its task. **Processes** are the actions or operations that the program must **perform. Outputs** are the data values that the program must **deliver** before it terminates.

It is common to design different parts of a client/server program (the program modules) around each screen of an interface.

An algorithm is a set of instructions to meet a set of requirements. Algorithms are constructed using combinations of three basic structures: **sequential statements, selection statements**, and **repetition (or loop) statements**.

Programmers usually write algorithms in a rather stylized form of English know as **pseudocode.** Algorithms written in pseudocode can easily be translated into a specific programming language (such as PHP) to create a working application.

Computer programs use **variables** to store data while the program is running. A variable references the address of a memory location where a data value is stored. The value can be accessed or modified within a program by using the variable name.

Variables names should be meaningful. Variable names that incorporate multiple English words make used of **underscores** to represent spaces or **camelback notation** (where an upper-case letter is used to begin each English word). By convention the first letter of a variable name is always lower-case.

An **assignment** operation is used to store a value in a variable. The syntax for an assignment operation requires that the variable name appears to the **left** of the **assignment operator.** The assignment operator is often represented by the = symbol. The value (or expression that generates the value) that is to be stored in the variable appears to the **right** of the assignment operator.

An **arithmetic expression** is an arithmetic operation that generates a numeric result. Arithmetic expressions can include the names of variables that are being used to store numbers. Arithmetic expressions can also combine variables and literal numbers.

A **logical expression** (also called **Boolean** expressions) **compares** values, and generates a **true** or **false** result.

Chapter 3 Review Questions

1. Consider the following instructions carefully. What is wrong?

   Prompt for startingOdometerReading
   Get startingOdometerReading
   Prompt for endingOdometerReading
   Get endingOdometerReading
   Display distanceTraveled
   distanceTraveled = endingOdometerReading – startingOdometerReading

   a. The instructions are not efficient
   b. The instructions are not correctly ordered
   c. The instructions are ambiguous
   d. The instructions are not understandable
   e. There is nothing wrong with these instructions

2. Consider the following instructions carefully. What is wrong?

   Face the audience
   Place your left leg forward
   Hold out your right hand over your head
   Extend your hand out from your shoulder

   a. The instructions are not efficient
   b. The instructions are not correct
   c. The instructions are ambiguous
   d. The instructions are not understandable
   e. There is nothing wrong with these instructions

3. In programming, instructions that are not understandable because they do not use the language correctly are said to contain:
   a. Logical errors
   b. Sequential statements
   c. Syntax errors
   d. Iteration statements
   e. Sequential statements

4. In programming, instructions that are understandable but not correct are said to contain:
   a. Logical errors
   b. Sequential statements
   c. Syntax errors
   d. Iteration statements
   e. Selection statements

5. Which of the following questions need to be more specific in order to answer it correctly?
   a. What is the sum of 23 and 45?
   b. Can you tell me your age?
   c. Which traffic light color means STOP?
   d. Can you tell me how to get to the store?
   e. What was the year of the first moon walk?

6. Consider the following instructions carefully. What is wrong?

   Take your rental car key to the parking lot
   Try all the cars until you find the car it fits — that's your rental car

   a. The instructions are not efficient
   b. The instructions are not correctly ordered
   c. The instructions are ambiguous
   d. The instructions are not understandable
   e. There is nothing wrong with these instructions

7. What is an algorithm?
   a. Instructions with input
   b. Instructions that are always repeated one or more times
   c. A set of clearly written, unambiguous instructions to perform a task
   d. Instructions that combine English with the structure and syntax of programming languages
   e. Instructions that provide a choice between two or more actions

8. What is pseudocode?
   a. Instructions with input
   b. Instructions that are always repeated one or more times
   c. A set of clearly written, unambiguous instructions to perform a task
   d. Instructions that combine English with the structure and syntax of programming languages
   e. Instructions that provide a choice between two or more actions

9. What is a selection statement?
   a. Instructions with input
   b. Instructions that are always repeated one or more times
   c. A set of clearly written, unambiguous instructions to perform a task
   d. Instructions that combine English with the structure and syntax of programming languages
   e. Instructions that provide a choice between two or more actions

10. How many assignment operations do you see in this algorithm?

age = 20
yearsToRetire = 65 − age
Display yearsToRetire

a. 0
b. 1
c. 2
d. 3
e. 4

11. How many **different** variables do you see in this algorithm?

age = 20
yearsToRetire = 65 − age
Display yearsToRetire

a. 0
b. 1
c. 2
d. 3
e. 4

12. What will be displayed if this algorithm is executed?

age = 20
yearsToRetire = 65 − age
Display yearsToRetire

a. 0
b. 20
c. 45
d. 65
e. 20, 45 and 65

13. What will be displayed if this algorithm is executed?

```
Set count to 0
REPEAT
   call in the next student
   ask the student for their GPA
   IF the student's GPA is greater than 3.2
     Add 1 to the count
UNTIL all students have been called
Display count
```

a. Displays 0
b. Displays the total number of students
c. Displays the number of students with a GPA less than 3.2
d. Displays the number of students with a GPA of 3.2 or greater
e. Displays the number of students with a GPA above 3.2

14. What does this algorithm display when it is executed?

```
Set count to 0
REPEAT
    call in the next student
    ask the student for their GPA
    Add 1 to the count
    IF the student's GPA is greater than 3.2
      Congratulate the student
UNTIL all students have been called
Display count
```

a. Displays 0
b. Displays the total number of students
c. Displays the number of students with a GPA less than 3.2
d. Displays the number of students with a GPA of 3.2 or greater
e. Displays the number of students with a GPA above 3.2

15. What does this algorithm display when it is executed?

```
Set count to 0
REPEAT
    call in the next student
    ask the student their GPA
    IF the GPA is greater than 3.2
      Congratulate the student
UNTIL all students have been called
Display count
```

a. Displays 0
b. Displays the total number of students
c. Displays the number of students with a GPA less than 3.2
d. Displays the number of students with a GPA of 3.2 or greater
e. Displays the number of students with a GPA above 3.2

16. How many inputs are included in the following requirement?

REQUIREMENT: *Write a program that asks the employee for their age. The program must subtract the age from 65, and display the age, followed by the number of years left to retirement.*

---

    a. 0
    b. 1
    c. 2
    d. 3
    e. 4

17. How many outputs are included in the following requirement?

REQUIREMENT: *Write a program that asks the employee for their age. The program must subtract the age from 65, and display the age, followed by the number of years left to retirement.*

---

    a. 0
    b. 1
    c. 2
    d. 3
    e. 4

18. Which variable name is an example of **camelback** notation?
    a. sales commission
    b. salesComission
    c. sales_commission
    d. SALESCOMISSION
    e. salescommission

19. What type of operation is used to store a value in a variable?
    a. Assignment operation
    b. Logical operation
    c. Arithmetic operation
    d. Sequential operation
    e. Repetition (loop) operation

20. What type of operation is used to compare two values?
    a. Assignment operation
    b. Logical operation
    c. Arithmetic operation
    d. Sequential operation
    e. Repetition (loop) operation

Chapter 3 Code Exercises

In Chapter 3 we learn how to analyze requirements and develop algorithms. Most of our Web-based applications will contain two components: an HTML document that contains the form to receive the user input and a PHP program that processes the input received from the form. These exercises will help you to develop algorithms for each component.

Your Chapter 3 code exercises can be found in your **Chapter03** folder. This folder is included in your customized XAMPP installation at the following location:

xampplite\htdocs\WebTech\coursework\Chapter03

Type your name and the date in the **Author** and **Date** sections of each file as you work on each exercise.

NOTE: Since you are just developing algorithms in this chapter you will not need to actually run the Web server. Each exercise is stored in a text file — just fix, modify or create each file as directed.

Debugging Exercises

Your **Chapter03** folder contains a number of "FixIt" text files. Each file contains an algorithm that has an error of some kind. Open the file in a text editor and read the comment section in the file to see what to do to fix them.

Code Modification Exercises

Your Chapter03 folder contains a number of "Modify" text files. Each file contains an algorithm that needs to be modified to meet a revised requirement. Modify the algorithms as needed.

Algorithm Creation Exercises

1. Develop the algorithms for **paintEstimate.html** and **paintEstimate.php** based on the following requirements:

Requirements for PaintEstimate: Write a Web-based application for the King Painting company. The page provided by paintEstimate.html should ask the user for the length, width and height of a room. These inputs will be submitted to paintEstimate.php for processing .

This program will use these inputs to perform a series of calculations: the area of each of the two long walls, the area of each of the two wide walls, the area of the ceiling, and the total area of the ceiling and the four walls combined. The program should then calculate the cost of paint, cost of labor, and the total cost, based on *the following charges: a gallon of paint costs $17.00 and covers 400 square feet; labor costs 25.00 an hour and it takes 1 hour to paint every 200 square feet. The program should output the length, width, height, and total area of the room, followed by the paint cost, labor cost, and the total cost.*

For example if the user inputs 20, 15 and 8 for the length, width and height, the area of each of the two long walls will be 20 * 8 = 160, the area of each of the two wide walls will be 15 * 8 = 120. The area of the ceiling will be 20 * 15 = 300. The area of the four walls and ceiling combined will be 160 + 160 + 120 + 120 + 300 = 860.

The coverage will be 860/400 = 2.15, and the paint cost will be 2.15 * 17.00 = 36.55. The labor will be 860/200 = 4.3 hours, and the labor cost will be 4.3 * 25.00 = 107.50. The total cost will be 36.55 + 107.50 = 144.05.

2. Develop the algorithms for **softwareOrder.html** and **softwareOrder.php** based on the following requirements:

   Requirements for softwareOrder: Write a Web-based application that allows a customer to order any number of copies of your amazing SaveTheWorld software. The page provided by softwareOrder.html should ask the user for the number of copies and the required operating system. These inputs will be submitted to software-Order.php for processing.

   This program should calculate: the subtotal for the order (each copy sells for 35.00); a 7% tax (which is 0.07 times the subtotal); the shipping and handling charge, which is 1.25 for each copy; and the total cost (the subtotal plus the shipping/handling charge plus the tax). The program should display the operating system, the number of copies ordered, the sub-total, the tax, the shipping/handling, and the total cost.

   For example if the user inputs 5 copies, the subtotal will be 5 * 35.00 = 175.00, the tax will be 12.25, the shipping/handling will be 6.25, and the total cost will be 193.50.

3. Develop the algorithms for **travel.html** and **travel.php** based on the following requirements:

   Requirements for travel: Write a Web-based application that allows a customer to order a package trip to Rome. The page provided by travel.html should ask the user for the number of people traveling and the number of nights to reserve. These inputs will be submitted to travel.php for processing.

   This program should calculate: the cost of the airline tickets ($875 per person), the cost of the hotel ($110 a person for each night), and the total cost. The program should display the number of people traveling, the number of nights, the cost of the airline tickets, the cost of the hotel, and the total cost.

For example if the user inputs 2 travelers for 4 nights the air travel will cost 2 * 875 = 1750 and the hotel cost will be 2 * 110 * 4 = 880, for a total cost of 2630.

4. Develop the algorithms for **gameIntro.html** and **gameIntro.php** based on the following requirements:

Requirements for gameIntro: Write a Web-based application that allows a player to create a game character and purchase some experience, health, and supplies before the game begins. The page provided by gameIntro.html should ask for a character name, character type, the number of experience tokens to be purchased, number of health tokens to be purchased, and number of supply tokens to be purchased. These inputs will be submitted to gameIntro.php for processing.

This program should calculate the cost of the purchases in gold pieces. Every 10 health tokens costs 1 gold piece. Every 2 experience tokens costs 1 gold piece. Every 25 supply tokens costs 1 gold piece. For now, don't worry about the total evaluating to a fractional number of gold pieces (for example the total may be 8.5 gold pieces). The program should display the character's name and type, the number of each token purchased, and the total cost.

For example if the player purchases 20 health tokens, 10 experience tokens, and 25 supplies tokens, the cost will be 20 / 10 + 10 / 2 + 25 / 25 = 2 + 5 + 1 = 8 gold pieces.

5. Develop the algorithms for **event.html** and **event.php** based on the following requirements:

Requirements for event: Write a Web-based application that processes a ticket request for a performance. The page provided by event.html should ask the user for a name, phone number, and number of tickets. These inputs will be submitted to event.php for processing. This program should calculate the cost of the tickets ($35.00 each). For example if the user requests 10 tickets the cost will be 10 * 35, which is 350.

The program should display the name, phone number, number of tickets, and cost of the tickets.

6. Develop algorithms for **fuelCost.html** and **fuelCost.php** based on the following requirements:

Requirements for fuelCost: Write a Web-based application that will calculate and display the fuel costs for a trip. The page provided by fuelCost.html should ask the user for his or her car's usual fuel consumption (mpg), the miles traveled, and the *fuel cost per gallon. These inputs will be submitted to fuelCost.php for processing. This program should calculate and display the cost of the trip based on these inputs. For example if the user submits 20 as the mpg, 100 as miles traveled, and 3.00 as the cost per gallon the program would calculate the cost as 100 / 20 * 3.00 which is $15.00. You are only required to write the algorithms. You will write the code in chapters 4 and 5.*

Chapter 4

Basics of Markup — Creating a User Interface with HTML

Intended Learning Outcomes

After completing this chapter, you should be able to:

- Explain the purpose of markup languages.
- Identify the three technologies that enabled the creation of HTML.
- Identify the basic protocols of the Internet and World Wide Web.
- Create a simple Web page using common HTML tags and attributes, including titles, paragraphs, headings, emphasized text, links to other pages, and images.
- Create an HTML table to display a list in columns and rows.
- Create an HTML table to layout a simple Web page.
- Explain the purpose of style sheets.
- Create and modify a simple Cascading Style Sheet (CSS).
- Explain the purpose of HTML forms and the role of a form's **action** attribute.
- Create simple HTML forms that include text boxes, drop down lists, submit and reset buttons.
- Explain the role of the **name** attribute to submit HTML form input for processing.

Introduction

You only have to look around to see that we live in a world of information. Take a moment to recognize that every piece of information that you receive has an **appearance**. Consider the appearance of information in books, on Web sites, on posters, in newspapers, on product packages, in e-mail messages, on electronic displays, on billboards. The term commonly used for organizing and formatting information to look a certain way is **rendering**. Consider what you are reading right now. How is this text rendered? Are you reading it on a printed page? On a screen? As an audio stream? What type and size of font is used? What color is the text? What color is the background? What do you think about the layout? Could it be presented some other way? Better? Worse?

We usually think of programming as the work of writing instructions to **process** information, but we must also write instructions to **render** that information, so that it will have a certain appearance. Information may need to be delivered as a display on a computer monitor, as a document for printing or archiving, as an e-mail or text message, as a Web page, or in some special format such as an electronic invoice.

Markup languages provide instructions that allow us to specify how data should be rendered for a particular document or purpose. You are working with a markup language when you use your word-processing software. When you select a piece of text in a word-processing document and click the **Bold** button or the **Indent** button, or choose a different font or color, you are applying markup instructions to your text. A word-processing program essentially provides a friendly interface for combining text with markup instructions. When you print or view your document, the appearance is defined by the markup instructions.

The appearance of Web pages is also defined by markup instructions. Each Web page contains a combination of text and markup. The standard markup language used to render the appearance of Web pages is **HTML**, or **Hypertext Markup Language**. Now that the Web is being used as an interface for an increasing range of software applications, programmers are learning to combine HTML instructions (to render the interface) with programming language instructions (to process the data). This is the approach we will take here.

We will begin with an introduction to markup languages. In this chapter you will learn a brief history of HTML and discover how HTML instructions are used to render text. You will design and create Web pages using common HTML commands and correct HTML syntax. You will also learn how **style sheets** are used to control the formatting of markup instructions, and how HTML can be used to create interactive user interfaces for Web applications. This work will not only prepare you for subsequent study if you plan to become proficient in markup, but will also introduce you to the process of writing and debugging instructions that must be syntactically correct and unambiguous.

Remember that this textbook is not intended to teach you the HTML language in detail but only to introduce the role of markup in application logic and interface design. Once you are comfortable with using basic HTML to render data as Web pages, you will be ready to use the PHP programming language to write the instructions required to **process** data.

As you read this chapter, consider: does the process of designing effective ways to render information interest you? There are many related professional fields, for example writing, editing, technical communications, digital media, graphic design, Web design, interface design, animation, and computer programming.

A Short History of HTML

Hypertext Markup Language (HTML) is a markup language that is widely used to specify how data is to be rendered by a **Web browser**. A Web browser is a program that interacts with remote Web servers over the Internet using a transmission protocol called **http** (**Hypertext Transmission Protocol**). HTML was developed from an idea into a language between 1989 and 1991, and the first Web browsers appeared in 1993 (they were named **lynx** and **Mosaic**). HTML made use of three existing technologies: **SGML**, **hyper-text**, and the **Internet**.

SGML

The general syntax of HTML was based on an existing markup language known as **SGML (Standard Generalized Markup Language)**. SGML was developed in the 1970's and is still used mainly in publishing fields to manage and deliver large and complex documents. Many of the tags used in HTML markup are actually a subset of the much more extensive markup instructions defined by SGML. The syntax of HTML has evolved greatly since 1991. The latest version of HTML is named HTML5, and includes features to handle audio and video, 2D drawing, local storage, form controls, and new elements to handle specific page content.

Hyper-text

Hypertext was invented in the 1940s. Hypertext is basically the idea of providing links through words and phrases within a document to obtain additional resources that are not contained in the document itself. This allows information to be interrelated on a global scale, and for users to explore an infinitely rich and multi-dimensional information landscape.

The Internet

The Internet was developed in the 1960s and allows computers to establish connections with other computers world-wide. Once connected, computers can communicate using various Internet protocols, or services. Essential Internet services include **ftp** (**File Transfer Protocol**) to transfer files, **telnet** to issue commands on a remote computer, **ping** to test the availability of a remote server, and **mail** to send and receive messages. In order to process HTML documents, a new Internet protocol was added: **http** (**Hypertext Transmission Protocol**). The http protocol allows the transfer of formatted text and multimedia that can be rendered and displayed by Web browsers. The addition of http to the Internet created the **World Wide Web**. When you specify **http://** in your URL, you are telling the browser that the data that is being requested is to be handled as a Web page.

Introducing HTML Tags

Markup languages define a set of **markup tags** that are used to control how information is to be handled . HTML tags are few in number and follow some simple rules. Let's begin with a hands-on example. The file **myWeb1.html**, is located in your **samples** folder. Figure 4-1 shows what you will see if you open this page in your Web browser. First be sure that your Web server is running and then open **myWeb1.html** by typing the following URL in your browser's address window:

http://localhost/WebTech/samples/myWeb1.html

Figure 4-1: myWeb1.html

This information for this page is stored in the **myWeb1.html** file which contains a combination of text and markup instructions (HTML code). When the Web browser opens the file, it displays the text according to the markup instructions. Let's look at the content of **myWeb1.html**. The file is located in the following folder (the exact location of the xampplite folder depends on where you installed your software):

xampplite\htdocs\WebTech\samples\myWeb1.html

Open this file in your text editor and look at the code.

```
<!DOCTYPE html>

<!-- Author: Mike O'Kane
     Date: August 13, 2013
     File: myWeb1.html
     Purpose: HTML Example - introducing some basic HTML tags
-->
<html>
<head>
   <title>HTML Example</title>
</head>
```

```
<body>
  <h1>My First Web Page</h1>

  <p>Hi! My name is <strong>Mike O'Kane</strong>. Let me tell you
  a little bit about myself.</p>
  <p>I enjoy hiking, kayaking, painting, writing, cooking (and
  eating!) and gardening. Sometimes I even like to program!</p>

</body>
</html>
```

Code Example: myWeb1.html

The first thing to notice about this file is that some of the text in the file is enclosed in < and > characters and this enclosed text is not displayed when you view the file in a browser. Any text that appears between < and > symbols in an HTML file is interpreted as an **HTML markup instruction**, commonly referred to as an **HTML tag**. These tags specify how the text in the document is to be rendered by the browser.

The very first line in the file is <**!DOCTYPE html**>. This is a special declaration that tells the browser which version of HTML is being used. This particular DOCTYPE declaration is used to specify HTML5. The DOCTYPE declaration should always appear as the first line of your HTML files, before any other text in the file. This declaration will be omitted from most of the printed examples in this book but you will see it in the actual files in your samples folder.

Now look at the rest of the text in the file. Do you see that the tags are usually in pairs? For example <**body**> and </**body**>, <**h1**> and </**h1**>, <**p**> and </**p**>, <**strong**> and </**strong**>. These are opening and closing tags for each markup instruction and the closing tag for each markup instruction includes a / forward slash. Any text that appears between a pair of tags is formatted according to the tag's purpose. The opening tag indicates where a format starts to apply, and the closing tag indicates where the format no longer applies. For example <**p**> indicates the beginning of a paragraph and </**p**> marks the end of the paragraph, whereas <**strong**> marks the beginning of bold formatting and </**strong**> indicates the end of the bold formatting. Also note that the tags can be **nested**, in other words the opening and closing tags for one instruction can be located inside the opening and closing tags of other instructions. In this example the <**strong**> and </**strong**> tags are located inside a pair of <**p**> and </**p**> tags.

Let's examine the purpose of each tag in **myWeb1.html**:

Comment Tags

The <!-- and --> are special symbols that tell the browser that any text within these tags is be treated as a **comment**. Comments are not part of the content that is displayed by the browser — the browser ignores everything that appears between the <!-- and the --> tags. Comment sections are used to provide important information that can be read by programmers who may need to maintain or modify the file contents. Comments are a form of **documentation**, which is an important component of every software project and a part of every programmer's job. In **myWeb1.html**, the comment section includes the programmer's name, the date the file was created, the name of the file and the purpose of the file.

NOTE: to save space, the comment sections will not be shown in the code examples throughout the remainder of this book, however these sections are included in the sample files on your disk.

HTML Tags

The <html> and </html> tags simply indicate the beginning and end of the HTML data in the file. The HTML data within these tags is located inside two major sections, the <head> and the <body> sections.

Head Tags

Certain tags can be included between the <**head**> and </**head**> tags in order to provide information about the page as a whole. In this example, we use the <**head**> section to produce a page title using the <**title**> and </**title**> tags. In this case the title is "**HTML Example**". Can you see where this is displayed when you view the page? Right—it shows up in the **title bar** at the top of the window.

Body Tags

Everything that you want to actually display in the browser window must be located between the <**body**> and </**body**> tags.

Heading Level Tags

The <**h1**> and </**h1**> tags are used to indicate a Heading Level 1. You can set various heading levels in HTML, with Level 1 as the highest level. You can specify headings anywhere in your document as needed. Note that the text that appears between these tags is displayed as a heading.

Paragraph Tags

The <**p**> and </**p**> tags are used to indicate the beginning and end of paragraphs. Notice that you can use these tags as often as you want, for every paragraph in the page.

Strong Tags

The <**strong**> and </**strong**> tags are used to indicate bold text. Once again these tags can be used as often as needed in an HTML document.

Ignoring White Space

A web browser ignores **white space** (except single spaces between words) when formatting an HTML document for display. **White space** refers to any multiple spaces, blank lines, tabs or indentations that were used to create the file. The browser formats your Web page based on the HTML tags only. To understand this, take a look at the code for **myWeb2.html**. This code is the same as **myWeb1.html** except that the <p> and </p> tags have been removed. Now view this in your Web browser. Even though the text is organized into paragraphs in your editor window, it is no longer displayed as paragraphs in the browser! That's because the browser only applies formatting according to the markup tags. A new paragraph is displayed whenever the browser finds a <p> tag.

More HTML Tags

Let's add a few more tags so that we can include images and links to our Web page. Take a look at **myWeb3.html** in your **samples** folder (see Figure 4-2).

Figure 4-2: myWeb3.html

Let's explore the code for **myWeb3.html**:

```
<!DOCTYPE html>

<html>
<head>
   <title>HTML Example</title>
   <link rel="stylesheet" type="text/css" href="sample.css" />
</head>
<body>
   <h1>My First Web Page</h1>

   <img src="okanepic.jpg" alt="image of Mike" />

   <p>Hi! My name is <strong>Mike O'Kane</strong>. Let me tell you
   a little bit about myself.</p>

   <p>I enjoy hiking, kayaking, painting, writing, cooking (and
   eating!) and gardening. Sometimes I even like to program!</p>

   <p>Here are some useful Web sites for this course:</p>

   <p><a href="http://www.w3c.org">The World Wide Web
   Consortium</a><br />
   <a href="http://www.php.net">PHP Home Page</a><br />
   <a href="http://www.w3Schools.com">W3Schools - Programming
      Tutorials</a><br /></p>
   <p><a href="welcome.html">Welcome to the course!</a><br />
   <a href="quoteGenerator.php">Quote for the day</a><br /></p>
</body>
</html>
```

Code Example: myWeb3.html

Image Tags

Look at the following line:

```
<img src="okanepic.jpg" alt="image of Mike" />
```

The <**img**> tag allows you to include images in your Web document. Many HTML tags can include **attributes** that provide additional specifications that are to be applied to the tag, and professional HTML developers need to become familiar with the various attributes that can be applied to each tag. Attributes are listed **inside** the opening tag, and each attribute has the general form **attribute** = "**value**". In this example, the <**img**> tag includes two **attributes**. The first attribute is the **src** attribute which is used to indicate the name and location of the image. The image file is named **okanepic.jpg**. Since this file is located in the same folder as **myWeb3.html**, the attribute is simply **src** = "**okanepic.jpg**". If the image was stored in a sub-folder named **images** inside the current folder, the attribute would be **src** = "**images/okanepic.jpg**". Appendix B provides other examples showing how relative file paths can be used to indicate the location of a file in a different folder on the same disk. You can also refer to an image located elsewhere on the Web, for example **src** = "**http://www.mikeokane.com/images/okanepic.jpg**"

The second attribute is the alt attribute which used to indicate what text to display if the browser is not capable of displaying images, so **alt** = "**image of Mike**" specifies that the message "image of Mike" can be used as an alternative to the image. Consider someone who is visually impaired who may be viewing your Web page with software that reads the contents of the page aloud. Since the software cannot display the image, it reads the message from the **alt** attribute instead.

Anchor Tags

Look at the following line:

```
<a href="http://www.w3c.org">The World Wide Web Consortium</a>
```

Now this looks interesting! This is the **anchor** tag, which allows you to place links on your page to other files. The <**a**> tag includes an **href** attribute which is used to indicate the URL that the link points to. The text between the <**a**> and </**a**> tags contains the phrase that appears on the current page—if the user clicks this text the browser submits a request for the page indicated in the **href** attribute and displays this page when it is received. Note that this example provides an **absolute address**—a complete URL to another Web page.

You can also specify **relative addresses**—links to other pages on the same disk as the current page. The simplest example of a relative address is the address of a file in the same folder. In this case, you can simply provide the file name, for example the last two anchor tags provide links to files in the same folder as **myWeb1.html**. The first of these is <**a href** = "**welcome.html**">Welcome to the Course!</a>. Since the **welcome.html** file is in the same folder as **myWeb3.html**, only the file name is provided. The second of the relative links is <**a href** = "**quoteGenerator.php**">Quote for the day</a>. Note that this link specifies a PHP program named **quoteGenerator.php** in the same folder.

Relative addresses can be used to provide links to files in sub-folders of the current folder, in parent folders, etc., without providing a complete URL. For a more complete discussion of the use of absolute and relative addresses refer to **Appendix B**.

Break Tags

Did you notice the <**br /**> tag? This is a line break. It simply tells the browser to move to the next line before displaying whatever comes next. This is a little unusual because there is no closing tag. Under the current HTML standard, tags that do not require any text between the opening and closing tag can simply include a closing / before the > of the opening tag. In other words **
** is actually shorthand for **
</br>**. You may have noticed that the **<img />** tag is another tag that can be used without a closing tag since it does not require text between the opening and closing tags.

Introducing HTML Tables

Web designers often use **HTML tables** to align output neatly in rows and columns. HTML tables are created using the following tags:

<table> and </table> indicate the beginning and end of the entire table. We can include a **border** attribute to include a border of any width, for example **<table - border="2">**. When the border attribute is set to "0" or simply left out, the table is displayed with no border, which can be very useful when we simply want to layout text without adding lines around it.

<tr> and </tr> indicate the beginning and end of each **row** in the table (**tr** stands for **table row**)

<td> and </td> indicate the beginning and end of each **column** in a row (**td** stands for **table data**).

<th> and </th> indicate column **headings** (**th** stands for **table heading**). By default, table heading are are usually displayed centered and in bold.

The primary purpose of the table tags is to display information neatly, in columns and rows. Let's compare two web pages, first without, and then with tables in order to see the difference. The document **annualTemps1.html** displays a list of average monthly temperatures for the city of Asheville, North Carolina, but the information for each month is simply displayed on separate lines **without** using an HTML table. Here is the code for **annualTemps1.html**:

```
<html>
<head>
  <title>Weather data with NO table</title>
</head>
<body>
  <h1>Monthly Temperatures</h1>
  <h2>Asheville, North Carolina</h2>
  <p>(This table displays the monthly averages)</p>
  <p>
  January: 25.8 (low) - 45.9 (high) <br />
  February: 28.0 (low) - 50.0 (high) <br />
  March: 34.9 (low) - 57.7 (high) <br />
  April: 41.8 (low) - 66.5 (high) <br />
  May: 50.6 (low) - 73.5 (high) <br />
```

```
    June: 58.3 (low) - 80.0 (high) <br />
    July: 62.7 (low) - 83.3 (high) <br />
    August: 61.8 (low) - 81.7 (high) <br />
    September: 55.4 (low) - 76.0 (high) <br />
    October: 43.3 (low) - 67.1 (high) <br />
    November: 35.3 (low) - 57.4 (high) <br />
    December: 28.8 (low) - 49.3 (high) <br />
    </p>
  </body>
</html>
```

Code Example: annualTemps1.html

(Note the use of the <h1></h1> and <h2></h2> tags to display the headings, and the <br /> tag to provide line breaks.)

This document is displayed as the first screen shot in Figure 4-3. You will see that the information does not line up very nicely.

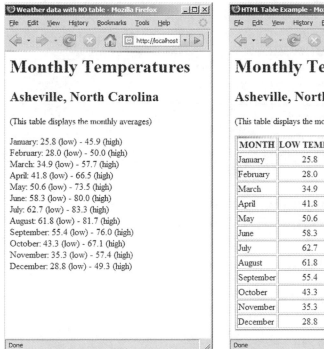

Figure 4-3: annualTemps1.html and annualTemps2.html screenshots

The document **annualTemps2.html** contains the same information but this time formatted using an HTML table. This document is displayed as the second screenshot in Figure 4-3. Clearly the layout looks **much** better!

Here is the HTML code for **annualTemps2.html**—notice the use of the table tags.

```
<html>
<head>
  <title>HTML Table Example</title>
  <link rel="stylesheet" type="text/css" href="sample.css" />
</head>
<body>
  <h1>Monthly Temperatures</h1>
  <h2>Asheville, North Carolina</h2>
  <p>(This table displays the monthly averages)</p>
  <table border="2">
    <tr> <th>MONTH</th>
         <th>LOW TEMP (F)</th>
         <th>HIGH TEMP (F)</th>
    </tr>
    <tr> <td>January</td>
         <td class="center">25.8</td>
         <td class="center">45.9</td>
    </tr>
    <tr> <td>February</td>
         <td class="center">28.0</td>
         <td class="center">50.0</td>
    </tr>
    <tr> <td>March</td>
         <td class="center">34.9</td>
         <td class="center">57.7</td>
    </tr>
    <tr> <td>April</td>
         <td class="center">41.8</td>
         <td class="center">66.5</td>
    </tr>
    <tr> <td>May</td>
         <td class="center">50.6</td>
         <td class="center">73.5</td>
    </tr>
    <tr> <td>June</td>
         <td class="center">58.3</td>
         <td class="center">80.0</td>
    </tr>
    <tr> <td>July</td>
         <td class="center">62.7</td>
         <td class="center">83.3</td>
    </tr>
    <tr> <td>August</td>
```

```
            <td class="center">61.8</td>
            <td class="center">81.7</td>
        </tr>
        <tr> <td>September</td>
            <td class="center">55.4</td>
            <td class="center">76.0</td>
        </tr>
        <tr> <td>October</td>
            <td class="center">43.3</td>
            <td class="center">67.1</td>
        </tr>
        <tr> <td>November</td>
            <td class="center">35.3</td>
            <td class="center">57.4</td>
        </tr>
        <tr> <td>December</td>
            <td class="center">28.8</td>
            <td class="center">49.3</td>
        </tr>
    </table>
  </body>
  </html>
```

Code Example: annualTemps2.html

The entire table is identified using the <**table**> and </**table**> tags, and the table is given a border using the **border** attribute. Each row is identified using the <**tr**> and </**tr**> tags. The column headings are identified using the <**th**> and </**th**> tags. The weather data to be displayed in each column is identified using the <**td**> and </**td**> tags: the first column in each row is left aligned and displays the month, the second column is center-aligned and displays the low temperature, and the third column is also center-aligned and displays the high temperature.

You may notice that some of the <td> tags are actually written <td class="center"> and that in these case the displayed text is centered in the column. Also notice that the <head> section of our file includes a new statement: <**link rel="stylesheet" type="text/css" href="sample.css"** />. We will learn how these two features work together to add special formatting to the tags in the section on **style sheets** later in this chapter.

Using HTML Tables to Layout Web Pages

Displaying data in rows and columns is an obvious use of an HTML table, but tables can also be used to layout Web pages. Take a look at the page displayed by **myWeb4.html** (Figure 4-4).

Figure 4-4: myWeb4.html screenshot

Note that the introductory paragraph and four of the links are now positioned to the **right** of the image. How is this accomplished? Look at the code for **myWeb4.html**:

```
<html>
<head>
   <title>HTML Example</title>
   <link rel="stylesheet" type="text/css" href="sample.css" />
</head>
<body>
   <h1>My First Web Page</h1>

   <table>
   <tr>
      <td> <img src="okanepic.jpg" alt="image of Mike" /> </td>
      <td><p>Hi! My name is <strong>Mike O'Kane</strong>. Let me
      tell you a little bit about myself. I enjoy hiking,
      kayaking, painting, writing, cooking (and eating!) and
      gardening. Sometimes I even like to program! Here are some
      useful Web sites for this course:</p>
      <p>
      <a href="http://www.w3c.org">The World Wide
      Web Consortium</a> <br />
      <a href="http://www.php.net">PHP Home Page</a> <br />
      <a href="http://www.w3Schools.com">W3Schools -
         Programming Tutorials</a><br />
```

```
        <a href="welcome.html">Welcome to the course!</a> <br />
        </p></td>
     </tr>
     </table>

     <p><a href = "quoteGenerator.php">Quote for the day</a> </p>
</body>
</html>
```

Code Example: myWeb4.html

Look for the various table tags. In this example a table containing just one row with two columns is used to modify the layout of the page. The image is placed in the **first** column of this row. The introductory paragraph and four links are **all** located within the **second** column of the same row. The link to the "Quote for the day" is located **after** the table. Note that table does not have a border in this example since it is just being used to layout components of the Web page.

This example only scratches the surface with regard to the use of tables for Web page design. Take a look at the Web page of a major news organization or retailer. Many of these sites use tables within tables to achieve a sophisticated layout. The table tags can also be customized by a range of attributes to provide precise layout instructions.

Other HTML Tags

HTML includes a wide range of tags for different formatting purposes, and each tag may be customized by a large number of attributes. It is not our goal to provide a comprehensive overview of HTML. We are learning just enough to be able to write Web applications that implement your algorithms. You will learn some additional HTML tags later in this chapter and Appendix E provides additional HTML references.

Deprecated HTML Tags

The specifications for HTML have evolved steadily. Many tags and attributes that were developed early on have since been **deprecated**, which means they have been replaced by more efficient solutions (in particular the use of style sheets which we shall learn about below). As you explore HTML you will often find references to tags that have been deprecated. Although the most widely used browsers all continue to recognize deprecated tags, at some point in the future, deprecated tags may no longer be recognized, so you should avoid using these tags. Examples of deprecated tags are <**u**> (underline), <**center**>, and <**font**>. Examples of deprecated attributes are **align**, **bgcolor**, and **width**.

(NOTE: we are using tables to control the layout of our simple Web pages. The use of tables for this purpose has now been replaced by the use of style sheets to position elements very precisely. Although style sheets are introduced in this chapter, the use of style sheets for positioning is beyond the scope of this book.)

Introducing Style Sheets

A Web browser determines how your text should be rendered based on your use of HTML markup tags. The browser applies default fonts, font sizes, colors, and many other formatting features for each tag, but what if you would like to apply a different rendering? What if you would like your paragraph text to be displayed in the Arial font? What if you want your <h1> headings to be displayed in red with a size of 18 point?

Consider also that a single Web site may contain a large number of Web pages. These pages should usually have a **consistent look and feel**. This is an important design consideration—visitors should expect to see the same fonts and color schemes and layouts on every page. Imagine that a decision is made to change the design of an entire Web site, consisting of any number of HTML documents. Perhaps the color scheme must be changed, or the fonts and font sizes. Changes will have to be made to every document! How much time will this take? How many errors are likely to occur? And how often might the site need to be changed?

Style sheets are used to define customized styles for HTML tags. Once created, a style sheet can be referenced by any number of HTML documents. When the Web browser opens any of these documents it refers to the style sheet in order to determine what style to apply to each tag. When the style sheet is changed the changes are automatically applied to all HTML documents that refer to it.

A style sheet specification that is frequently used with HTML documents is known as a **Cascading Style Sheet (CSS)**. Here is an example of a cascading style sheet named **sample.css**, which is located in your **samples** folder:

```
body    { background: white }

h1    { font-family: Arial, Helvetica, Sans-serif; font-size:18pt;
          color:red; font-weight:bold; }

h2    { font-family: Arial, Helvetica, Sans-serif; font-size:12pt;
          color:black; font-weight:bold; }

p { font-family: Arial, Helvetica, Sans-serif; font-size:10pt;
      color:black; }

p.alert { font-style: italic; color:red; }

table    { font-family: Arial, Helvetica, Sans-serif; font-size:10pt;
              color:black; }
```

```
td.center { text-align: center; }

select { font-family: Arial, Helvetica, Sans-serif; font-size:10pt;
         font-weight: bold; color:blue; background: lightBlue; }

option { font-family: Arial, Helvetica, Sans-serif; font-size:10pt;
         color:black; background: silver; }
```

Code Example: The sample.css style sheet

This style sheet is providing formatting information for a number of HTML tags. Note the general syntax of the style sheet. Each tag name is referenced on the left (the CSS reference to a tag is known as a **selector**). The list of formatting requirements for each tag is enclosed within curly braces { and }. Each requirement in the list consists of a **property** and a **value**, separated by a **colon**. A list can include any number of property:value pairs, separated by **semi-colons**.

For example the style sheet indicates that everything inside the <**body**> tags (in other words the entire document) is to be displayed with a **white** background. Text enclosed between <**h1**></**h1**> tags is to be displayed as **Arial, 18 point, red** and **bold** (and if Arial is not available, use Helvetica, and if Helvetica is not available, use **any** sans-serif font). Text enclosed between <**h2**></**h2**> tags is to be displayed as **Arial, 12 point, black** and **bold**. Text enclosed in <**p**></**p**> tags will be displayed as **Arial, 10 point, black**. Text in a table will be also displayed as **Arial, 10 point, black**.

The **sample.css** style sheet also includes other selectors that will be discussed later in this chapter.

If a style sheet does not list a tag, the browser will simply apply its own default style for that tag.

Multiple Styles for a Single Tag

Sometimes you may want to format the same tag differently in different parts of your document. For example, perhaps you want the text in **some** paragraphs on your Web pages to stand out because they are intended to alert the user about something important. You decide to call these paragraphs "alert" paragraphs and you want to display them in **red** and **italic**. The <**p**> tag can include a **class** attribute to identify that a particular paragraph needs special attention of some kind. For example, here's how we might identify certain paragraphs that will display "alert" messages:

```
<p class="alert">Be sure to save your files before you close down
   the computer!</p>
```

Now that you have identified these paragraphs in your HTML code using the class attribute, you can include special formatting instructions in your style sheet for these special paragraphs as follows:

```
p.alert { font-style: italic; color:red; }
```

We add the name that we created to identify these special paragraphs to the **p** selector, using a period as a separator. As a result, any text inside paragraphs tags that include the **class="alert"** attribute will be displayed in red and italics.

Note that the formats specified in the **p.alert** selector do not duplicate the formats that were previously specified for the <**p**> tag in the **p** selector entry, but only indicates formats that are **different** from the previous entry. The other formats that were previously defined for all paragraphs remain the same. This is true generally. For example the **body** selector could specify the default font-family for the entire page. Since the <**body**> tag applies to the entire Web page, the other selectors would then only need to specify the font-family if a different font was to be used for a specific tag.

The **class** attribute can be applied to a number of other HTML tags for similar purposes. Refer back to the HTML code for **annualTemps2.html**. This page uses the sample.css style sheet and you will notice that some of the <td> tags are written <td class="center">. If you refer to your sample.css file you will see that it includes the formatting instruction:

```
td.center {text-align:center;}
```

This instruction specifies that the content of <td> tags with a class attribute "center" will be centered.

HTML also provides two tags that can be used to apply formatting to different sections of your documents. These are the <**div**> and <**span**> tags and you will want to research the use of these tags if you are interested in learning more about page layout and formatting.

Selecting Colors for Fonts and Backgrounds

You may be wondering what colors you can use to change the appearance of your fonts and backgrounds. Traditionally 216 colors have been accepted as **Web safe**, meaning that these colors are guaranteed to display consistently on any system. However this restriction is no longer relevant since most computers are now capable of displaying millions of colors

Most browsers recognize a lengthy list of color **names** that you can use when specifying colors, however only sixteen names are accepted as completely standard (these are: aqua, black, blue, fuchsia, gray, green, lime, maroon, navy, olive, purple, red, silver, teal, white, and yellow). Many more (over 16 million) colors can be referenced using their hexadecimal value, for example the color named as teal can be represented as **#008080**, while the color named as **purple** has the value **#800080**. Each pair of digits in the hexadecimal value defines the strength of one of the primary colors of light: red, green and blue in that order, so teal contains no red (00), while purple contains a red value of 80.

Here is how we would add an entry in our style sheet to format our paragraph text to Arial (or Helvetica), 10pt, with the color set to #302B54 (presidential blue):

```
p { font-family:Arial, Helvetica; font-size:10pt; color:#302B54; }
```

You can use the Web to easily look up color charts and obtain the hexadecimal values that you need, for example search on "**html color chart**".

Referencing a Style Sheet in Your HTML Document

How do you specify which style sheet a Web document should use? Did you notice the additional line in the <**head**> section of **myWeb3.html**?

```
<head>
   <title>HTML Example</title>
   <link rel="stylesheet" type="text/css" href="sample.css" />
</head>
```

The line <**link rel="stylesheet" type="text/css" href="sample.css"** /> uses the <**link**> tag to tell the browser that a cascading style sheet is to be referenced in order to determine how to handle the tags in this document. The **href** attribute indicates that this style sheet is called **sample.css**, and that the style sheet is located in the same folder as the current document (since no file path or URL is specified).

You will want to include this line in every file that you develop in this course, exactly as it is written here, in order to apply the **sample.css** style sheet to your documents. You are welcome to copy and modify **sample.css** for your purposes. Don't change the copy in the **samples** folder however, that way you can always refer back to it if you need the original version.

We have seen that the **same** style sheet can be chosen for many different documents in order to provide a consistent look and feel. **Different** style sheets can be chosen for a single document so that the information can be presented in different ways for different purposes. To see an example, open **myWeb5.html** in your browser window. This file is exactly the same as **myWeb3.html** except that it uses a style sheet named funky.css. Quite a difference! Compare the content of the funky.css file with sample.css.

Applying a Style Sheet to Multiple Pages

When a Web browser displays any HTML document that references **sample.css**, the styles listed in this style sheet will be applied to the appropriate tags. Since most of the files in your samples folder refer to sample.css, any changes that you make to this style sheet will change the appearance of all these files.

For example if you change the first line in **sample.css** from **body** {background: white} to **body** {background: yellow} then every HTML page that uses this style sheet will be displayed with a background color of yellow. Try making other changes to **sample.css**. Use your Web browser to open various documents in the **samples** folder to see what happens to their appearance. Do you see how useful this is to manage a large Web site? If you wish to change a color or font or other formatting feature you can make the change in a single style sheet instead of modifying every file!

The code in **sample.css** is intended just to give you an idea of the power and value of style sheets, with enough style examples to get you started. You can define styles for any HMTL tag, and each style can include many more formatting properties than those listed here. Appendix E provides additional references, and you will want to explore these to learn more about creating style sheets for your own purposes.

Interactive User Interfaces

A program that interacts with a human user requires a **user interface**. User interface design is a career within the software industry. This type of work appeals to people who combine an understanding of logic and software design with sensitivity to the ways that different people think and respond. The field attracts people from a range of backgrounds including graphic design, digital media, psychology, anthropology, technical communications, and computer programming.

A **graphical user interface** usually provides a fairly standard set of visual components that allow the user to make choices and enter data using the mouse or keyboard. Web-based interfaces often make use of **HTML forms** to provide the user with input options such as **submit** and **reset buttons, prompts** and **text input boxes, password boxes, drop down lists, radio buttons** and **check boxes**. The Web browser displays an HTML page containing a form, which is designed to obtain **input** from the user. When the user completes the form and presses the Submit button, the browser submits the input from the form to a server-based program for processing. The program processes the input and generates a new Web page containing a suitable response. This new page is returned to the user's Web browser for display. This is an example of a client/server application.

We will now learn how to create HTML documents that contain forms for user input. In later chapters we will learn to write the programs (using the PHP language) that process the input from these forms and generate an appropriate response to the user.

Creating HTML Forms

The simplest HTML form contains nothing more than a **submit button** that the user can click in order to have some task performed. When the button is clicked the request is sent to a server which executes the program that the form specifies. The program performs the task and usually generates a new Web page containing the results of the operation. This new page is returned to the browser for display to the user.

Consider the following program requirements:

Wage1 requirements:

Write a program that allows the user to submit a request to calculate the weekly pay and display the hours worked, hourly wage, and weekly pay for an employee who works 19 hours and earns $15.75 an hour.

For this program we will develop two documents. The first (**wage1.html**) will display a form containing a Submit button. When the uses clicks this button the form will generate a request to the server to run a PHP program (**wage1.php**) that performs the calculation, then generates a Web page that displays the requested information. Figure 4-5 shows the screens for this application.

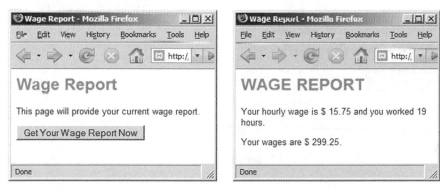

Figure 4-5: wage1.html and wage1.php screenshots

Here is the algorithm for the **wage1.html** document that displays the form:

```
wage1.html algorithm:
   Display Submit button to execute Wage1.php
END
```

And here is the algorithm for the program (**wage1.php**) that processes the request:

```
wage1.php algorithm:
   hourlyWage = 15.75
   hourlyWage = 19
   hourlyWage = hourlyWage * hoursWorked
   Display hourlyWage, hourlyWage, hourlyWage
END
```

In this chapter we are only concerned with creating the **wage1.html** document that displays the form. In Chapter 5 we will learn how to create the **wage1.php** program that performs the processing.

In your samples folder you will find the **wage1.html** file. In order to view this form first be sure that your **Web server** is running and then open **wage1.html** by typing the following URL in your browser's address window:

http://localhost/WebTech/samples/wage1.html

The form in **wage1.html** document simply provides a message and a Submit button with no additional input required from the user. If you press the **"Get Your Wage Report Now"** button a PHP program called **wage1.php** executes, and this program generates a second page.

Here is the HTML code for **wage1.html**:

```
<html>
<head>
   <title>Wage Report</title>
   <link rel="stylesheet" type="text/css" href="sample.css" />
</head>
<body>
   <h1>Wage Report</h1>
   <p>This page will provide your current wage report.
   <form action="wage1.php" method="post">
     <input type="submit" value="Get Your Wage Report Now" />
   </form>
   </p>
</body>
</html>
```

Code Example: wage1.html

As you can see most of the tags this document are similar to those you have already seen. What is new is the section containing a <**form**> tag and an <**input**> tag:

```
<form action="wage1.php" method="post">
  <input type="submit" value="Get Your Wage Report Now" />
</form>
```

The <**form**> tag includes two attributes:

action = **"wage1.php"** — the **action** attribute indicates the action that the Web server is to take when this form is submitted. Here the action specifies that a program named **wage1.php** is to be processed when the **Submit** button is pressed. In this example the **wage1.php** file is assumed to be in the same folder as **wage1.html** since only the file name is provided.

method = **"post"**—the method attribute specifies the manner in which any user input is passed to the receiving program. Two methods may be used: "post" and "get". Without getting into details here, in this course we will always specify **method** = **"post"** in our forms (this provides greater security and allows larger amounts of data to be submitted).

Between the <**form**> and </**form**> tags is an <**input**> tag:

```
<input type="submit" value="Get Your Wage Report Now" />
```

This defines the **submit** button. Since the button is a component of the form, the <input> tag **must** be located between the beginning and ending <**form**> tags. This <**input**> tag includes two attributes:

type = **"submit"**—the type attribute is used to specify what type of input is to be provided. **type** = **"submit"** tells the browser that this is a **submit** button. When this button is pressed the action specified in the <**form**> tag is passed back to the Web server to be processed (this particular form will submit a request to run the **wage1.php** program).

value = **"Get Your Wage Report Now"**—the **value** attribute tells the browser what message to display on the **Submit** button. You can provide any message you wish.

The <input> tag does not need a closing tag and instead includes a closing /> at the end of the tag.

Using HTML Forms to Obtain User Input

The form that we created in **wage1.html** does nothing but provide a submit button to run the **wage1.php** program. Since **wage1.php** requires no special input, we do not actually require a form to run the program. We could run **wage1.php** directly simply by typing the URL in the browser's address window, or by providing a link from a Web page. More often, you will use forms to write programs that require user input. Consider the following requirement:

Wage2 requirements:

Write an application that allows the user to submit their hours worked and hourly wage. The program should calculate the weekly pay and display the hours worked, hourly wage, and weekly pay.

Figure 4-6 shows a page design for a Web application that meets these requirements.

Figure 4-6: wage2.html and wage2.php screenshots

What is different from the Wage1 application?

The previous application generated a wage report based on an hourly wage of **$15.75** and **19** hours worked. That program was executed by a form that simply contained a submit button. This new version is much more powerful. The form provided by **wage2.html** includes input boxes that allow the user to enter **any** hourly wage and number of hours worked. Once the user enters the required data into the form, he or she presses the Submit button and the input is sent to **wage2.php** for processing. The form also includes a clear button so the user can easily clear the input boxes and start again. Here are the algorithms for **wage2.html** and **wage2.php**:

```
wage2.html algorithm:
   Prompt user for hourly wage
   Get hourlyWage
   Prompt user for hours worked
   Get hoursWorked
   Submit hourlyWage, hoursWorked to wage2.php
END
```

```
wage2.php algorithm:
   Receive hourlyWage, hoursWorked from wage2.html
   weeklyWage = hourlyWage * hoursWorked
   Display hourlyWage, hoursWorked, weeklyWage
END
```

Here we are only concerned with learning how to create the form in **wage2.html**. In Chapter 5 we will learn how to write the programming code for **wage2.php**. Here is the code for **wage2.html**:

```
<html>
<head>
   <title>Wage Report</title>
   <link rel="stylesheet" type="text/css" href="sample.css" />
</head>
```

```
<body>
  <h1>Wage Report</h1>
  <form action="wage2.php" method="post">
    <p>Please enter your hourly wage:
    <input type="text" size="20" name="hourlyWage" /></p>

    <p>And the hours you have worked:
    <input type="text" size="20" name="hoursWorked" /></p>

    <p><input type="submit" value="Get Your Wage Report Now" />
    <input type="reset" value="Clear and start again" /></p>

  </form>
</body>
</html>
```

Code Example: wage2.html

Compare this form with the form in **wage1.html**. The **action** attribute specifies **wage2.php** as the program that is to process the form when the submit button is pressed. There are now four <**input**> tags. Note that all four tags are located between the <**form**> and </**form**> tags. This is required since they are all components of the form. Let's look at the purpose of each <input> tag in turn:

```
<p>Please enter your hourly wage:
<input type="text" size="20" name="hourlyWage" />
</p>
```

This input tag provides a text box that allows the user to type in some data. Notice that a prompt ("Please enter your hourly wage:") is provided before this tag in order to tell the user what to enter. This tag contains three attributes:

type = "**text**"—tells the browser that this input tag is intended to display a text box to receive user input.

size = "**20**"—tells the browser how wide the text box should be.

name = "**hourlyWage**"—tells the browser what name to associate with the data that the user enters into the text box. This is VERY IMPORTANT. Whatever name you provide here will be passed to the program that will process the input (in this case wage2.php). Each input from the form will be uniquely identified by the name that you provide using the name attribute. Your names should not include spaces or begin with a number.

```
<p>And the hours you have worked:
<input type="text" size="20" name="hoursWorked" />
</p>
```

This <**input**> tag provides another textbox. A prompt is included before the text box so that the user knows what to type (**"And the hours you have worked:"**). The data that the user enters into this textbox will be associated with the name **hoursWorked**.

Note that this name must be different than the name provided for the first text box so that each value entered by the user will be submitted with a different name. Also notice that the names are **meaningful** and relate to the purpose of the input.

```
<input type="submit" value="Get Your Wage Report Now" />
```

This input tag is a submit button. In this example, the button contains the message Get **Your Wage Report Now.** When the button is pressed the **wage2.php** program will be executed since this the action indicated in the **action** attribute of the <**form**> tag.

```
<input type="reset" value="Clear and start again" />
```

The last input tag is a **reset** or **clear** button . When this button is pressed, all of the input boxes are cleared or reset to their default options so the user can start over. In this example, the reset button is given the message **Clear and Start Again**.

Using HTML Tables to Line Up
Prompt and Input Boxes

Take another look at Figure 4.6. Can you see that the input boxes do not line up with each other? Recall that a table can be used to display text and images in rows and columns. Tables can work very well to lay out forms since most forms use a combination of a prompt and input box (or drop down) to request each item of information from the user. We can use a table row for each prompt/input box combination so that each row contains two columns. The first column contains the prompt and the second column contains the input box or drop down list. Here is a revised version of the form in wage2.html, this time using a table:

```
<form action="wage2.php" method="post" >
<table>
<tr><td>Please enter your hourly wage:</td>
   <td><input type="text" size="20" name="hourlyWage" /></td></tr>
<tr><td>And the hours you have worked:</td>
   <td><input type="text" size="20" name="hoursWorked" /></td></tr>
<tr><td><input type="submit" value="Get Your Wage Report Now" />
</td>
<td><input type="reset" value="Clear and start again" /></td></tr>
</table>
</form>
```

The paragraph tags have now been replaced with a table with three rows and two columns. The first and second rows each contain a prompt in the first column and an input box in the second column. The third row contains the Submit button in the first column and the reset button in the second column. Note that the table does not have a border (since it is just being used for layout), and also that the opening and closing <**table**> and </**table**> tags both appear within the opening and closing <**form**> and </**form**> tags.

You can see these changes in the **wage2_Improved.html** file in your samples folder. Open this file in your Web browser. You will see that the prompts and input boxes now line up nicely. Each form is different. Sometimes it is best to use a table to line up just a part of your form (for example prompts and input boxes), and use paragraph or other tags to format other parts of the form (for example instructions or submit buttons).

Experiment with tables to lay out your forms when you complete the chapter exercises.

Problems with Form Submission

If the Web server cannot process the action that your form has requested, you will receive an error message. For example if you specify a **.php** file and the server cannot find the file you would get a message similar to the following (the actual message depends on which browser you are using):

> **Not Found**
> **The requested URL /htdocs/WebTech/samples/wage2.php was not found on this server.**

Often you will develop your HTML forms before you develop the PHP programs that process them. If you were to display **wage2.html** and press the submit button before **wage2.php** had been created you would receive an error message. You will also get an error if you press the submit button and the name of the **.php** program has been mistyped in the <**form**> tag, or if the path to the **.php** program is incorrect.

Drop Down Lists

So far we have seen how to create **text boxes**, **submit** buttons and **reset** buttons in your HTML forms. There are other ways to obtain user input. For example **drop down lists** allow the user to choose a value from a pre-defined list. Let's consider a form that allows the user to rate dogs and cats as pets. The user is asked to give ratings of **0** to **5** to indicate their preference for each animal. Of course we could just use textboxes to get these ratings but that would allow the user to enter anything! What if the user types 10 or "dogs are best!"?

In order to be sure that the user can only enter numbers from 1 to 5 we can use a drop down list that only contains these five options. The use of a drop down list **constrains** the user in order to ensure valid input.

Figure 4-7 shows the interface provided by **comparePets.html**.

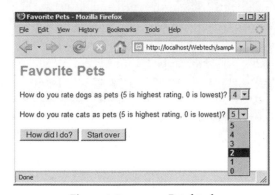

Figure 4-7: comparePets.html

In order to specify drop down lists in our forms we use the **<select>** and **</select>** tags to specify a drop down list and **<option>** and **</option>** tags to specify each value within the list. Here is the code for **comparePets.html**:

```
<html>
<head>
  <title>Favorite Pets</title>
  <link rel="stylesheet" type="text/css" href="sample.css" />
</head>
<body>

  <h1>Favorite Pets</h1>

  <form action="comparePets.php" method="post" >

    <p>How do you rate dogs as pets (5 is highest rating, 0 is
       lowest)?
    <select name="dogRating">
    <option>5</option>
    <option>4</option>
    <option>3</option>
    <option>2</option>
    <option>1</option>
    <option>0</option>
    </select>
    </p>

    <p>How do you rate cats as pets (5 is highest rating, 0 is
       lowest)?

    <select name="catRating">
    <option>5</option>
    <option>4</option>
    <option>3</option>
```

```
<option>2</option>
<option>1</option>
<option>0</option>
</select>
</p>

<p><input type="submit" value="How did I do?" />
<input type="reset" value="Start over" /></p>

    </form>
</body>
</html>
```

Code Example: comparePets.html

This example contains two drop down lists, and each list is enclosed in <**select**> and </**select**> tags. Note that each <**select**> tag includes the attribute name similar to input text boxes. In the <**select**> tag for the first drop down list, the attribute **name = "dogRating"** specifies that the name **dogRating** will be associated with the specific value that the user selects from the list of options. Similarly **catRating** is the name specified for the value selected from the second list.

Within the <**select**> and </**select**> tags, we include as many <**option**></**option**> tags as we need, one for each option that we wish to appear in the list. In this case the options are all numbers, but they can also be text, for example a list of movie titles could be used as options.

Combining Textboxes and Drop Down Lists

Now let's create an HTML page (**smoking.html**) that obtains the input needed for a program that conducts a short smoking survey (Figure 4-8).

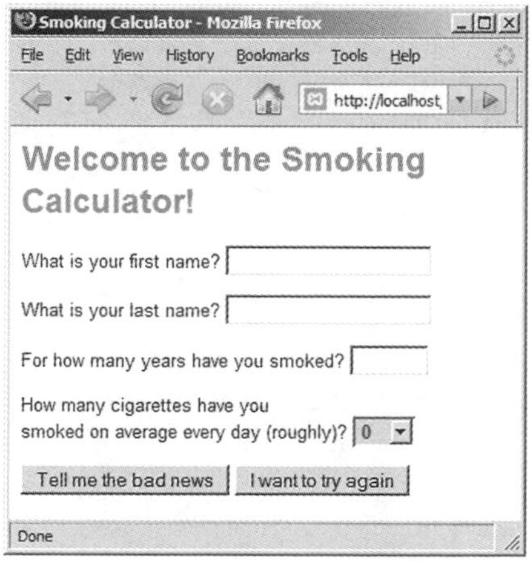

Figure 4-8: smoking.html

We will use text boxes for the first and last names and number of years, but we will use a drop down list for the number of cigarettes smoked daily. This is to provide a limited number of options (0, 1, 2, 5, 10, 20, 30, 40) to simplify the survey and so that the user does not have to figure this out too carefully.

When the **submit** button is pressed, input data will be submitted to a program named **smoking.php** for processing. Here is the code for **smoking.html**:

```
<html>
<head>
   <title>Smoking Calculator</title>
   <link rel="stylesheet" type="text/css" href="sample.css" />
</head>
<body>
   <h1>Welcome to the Smoking Calculator!</h1>
   <form action="smoking.php" method="post" >

      <p>What is your first name?
      <input type="text" size="20" name="firstName" />
      </p>

      <p>What is your last name?
      <input type="text" size="20" name="lastName" />
      </p>

      <p>For how many years have you smoked?
      <input type="text" size="5" name="yearsSmoked" />
      </p>

      <p>How many cigarettes have you <br \>
      smoked on average every day (roughly)?
      <select name="smokedDaily" >
         <option>0</option>
         <option>1</option>
         <option>2</option>
         <option>5</option>
         <option>10</option>
         <option>20</option>
         <option>30</option>
         <option>40</option>
      </select>
      </p>

      <p><input type="submit" value="Tell me the bad news" />
      <input type="reset" value="I want to try again" /></p>

   </form>
</body>
</html>
```

Code Example: smoking.html

Other Types of Input

There are other ways to receive user input in HTML forms: **password boxes** (which show only asterisks when the user types), **text areas** (for larger text entries), **radio buttons**, and **checkboxes**. Refer to Appendix E for references to additional HTML tags.

Look through the **.html** files in the **samples** folder. View these files in your browser and look over the code to get used to the general layout and syntax. Don't worry about the **.php** files just yet. These contain the programs that process the data from the forms and we will review these in later chapters.

Stylesheets and Forms

Style sheets can be used with the various form-related tags just as any other HTML tags. For example, you could add an **input** selector to your style sheet to change the appearance of your input boxes and submit buttons:

```
input {font-family: Arial, Helvetica, Sans-serif; font-size:10pt;
    font-style: italic; color:blue; background: lightBlue}
```

The **sample.css** style sheet provides formatting properties for drop down lists (<**select**> and <**option**> tags):

```
select { font-family: Arial, Helvetica, Sans-serif;
    font-size:10pt; font-weight: bold; color:blue;
    background: lightBlue}

option { font-family: Arial, Helvetica, Sans-serif;
    font-size: 10pt; color: black; background: silver}
```

The **option** selector modifies the appearance of **all** the options in the list. The **select** selector modifies the appearance of the **currently selected** option.

Summary

Markup languages provide syntax for instructions to render information for a specific purpose. HTML is a markup language that uses a syntax of **tags** and **attributes** to render information for display in a Web browser. HTML tags come in pairs, for example <**p**> and </**p**>, which open and close a format around the text that is to be formatted. In cases where no text is required between the opening and closing tag, the two tags can be combined into a single tag (for example the opening and closing break tags <**br**></**br**> can be simplified to <**br** />). Attributes appear inside opening tags and provide additional specifications concerning the tag. Useful tags include the <**img**> tag for including images, the <a> (anchor) tag for adding hypertext links, and the table tags (<**table**>, <**tr**>, and <td>) for tables with rows and columns. HTML tables are also often used to layout Web pages.

Style sheets make it easy to separate standard design specifications from individual pages so that the same specifications can be applied to multiple documents. Style sheets can also be used to render the same document in different ways for different purposes.

Interactive **user interfaces** allow users to control a program and provide any input needed for processing. Web interfaces can make use of HTML forms to obtain user input and submit this input to be processed by programs running on a Web server. The <form> tag includes an **action** attribute to indicate the program that is to process the form input.

The simplest Web form contains a button to submit the form with no additional input needed. Forms can contain **submit** and **reset buttons, prompts** and **text input boxes, password boxes, drop down lists, radio buttons** and **check boxes**. Each input field must be associated with a unique name since this is how the program that receives the form data will identify each input.

Drop down lists constrains the choices of the user in order to ensure valid input.

Chapter 4 Review Questions

1. Which word refers to the process of organizing and formatting text to appear a certain way?
    a. Rendering
    b. Compiling
    c. Interpreting
    d. Browsing
    e. Algorithm

2. Which is the earliest markup language?
    a. HTML
    b. SGML
    c. XML

3. Which of the following Web browsers was the first to appear?
    a. Mosaic
    b. Internet Explorer
    c. AOL
    d. Netscape
    e. Mozilla Firefox

4. Which of the following statements is true?
    a. The http protocol added the Internet to the World Wide Web
    b. The http protocol added the World Wide Web to the Internet

5. What symbols are used to indicate the beginning and end of a comment in HTML?
    a. <!--and-->
    b. /* and */
    c. <comment> and </ comment >
    d. <html> and </html>
    e. <head> and </head>

6. What is the purpose of a **comment**?
    a. Instructions to the Web browser showing how text is to be displayed
    b. Instructions to mark the beginning and end of the HTML document
    c. Instructions to emphasize certain text on the page
    d. Documentation intended for someone viewing the page in a Web browser
    e. Documentation intended for someone reading the file — not displayed by the browser

7. How many columns will be displayed by this table?

```
<table border="1">
<tr><td>France</td><td>Paris</td></tr>
<tr><td>England</td><td>London</td></tr>
<tr><td>Italy</td><td>Rome</td></tr>
</table>
```

   a. 1
   b. 2
   c. 3
   d. 4
   e. 5

8. How many paragraphs will the following HTML code display?

```
<p>This a <strong>test</strong>of your understanding of HTML tags.
</p><p>I wonder how many paragraphs this block of text will dis-
play?</p><p>I wonder ... </p>
```

   a. 1
   b. 2
   c. 3
   d. 4
   e. 6

9. What is white space?
   a. Text that is included in comment sections
   b. Multiple spaces, tabs, blank lines, blank areas or indentations in a text document
   c. The text that is not included inside HTML tags
   d. The text that is included inside HTML tags
   e. All areas of a Web page background that are colored white

10. What does the following code achieve? <img src = "test.jpg" alt="Test image" />
    a. Displays an image stored in a file named test.jpg or else displays the message "Test image" if the browser is configured not to display images
    b. Displays an image stored in a file named test.jpg with the message "Test image" below the image.

11. Which of the following is an example of an anchor tag that is using an **absolute** address?
    a. <a href="welcome.html">Welcome!</a>
    b. <a href="welcome.php">Welcome!</a>
    c. <a href="http://www.w3c.org/welcome.html">Welcome!</a>

12. Which of the following is an example of an anchor tag that is using a **relative** address?

    a. <a href="welcome.html">Welcome!</a>
    b. <a href="http://localhost/WebTech/samples/welcome.html">
          Welcome!</a>
    c. <a href="http://www.w3c.org/welcome.html">Welcome!</a>

13. What is the purpose of the <br /> tag?

    a. It renders text as bold
    b. It renders text as brown
    c. It renders text as bright red
    d. It creates a brown background
    e. It creates a line break

14. What does **css** stand for?

    a. Cascading Style Sheet
    b. Character Style Sheet
    c. Consistent Style Sheet
    d. Character Syntax Specification
    e. Character Symbolic Standard

15. What is the purpose of a css file?

    a. Provides a standard style that can be applied to multiple HTML documents
    b. Provides a standard style that can be only be applied to a single HTML document

16. Which of the following will correctly create a form that contains a Submit button, and will run a program named Test.php when the Submit button is pressed?

    a. <form action="submit" method="post">
       <input type="Test.php" value="submit" />
       </form>
    b. <form action="Test.php" method="post">
       <input type="submit" value="submit" />
       </form>
    c. <input type="submit" value="submit" />
       <form action="Test.php" method="post">
       </form>
    d. <form action="Test.php" method="post">
       </form>
       <input type="submit" value="submit" />
    e. <form action="post" method="Test.php" />
       <input type="submit" value="submit" />
       </form>

17. Look at the following form. What is the name of program that will be executed when this form is submitted?

```
<form action="calc.php" method="post" >
<p>What is your answer?
<input type="text" size="20" name="someInput" />
</p>
<p><input type="submit" value="Process The Form" /></p>
</form>
```

   a. calc.php
   b. post
   c. someInput
   d. submit
   e. Process The Form

18. Look at the following form. What type of input is the form using to receive the user's age?

```
<form action="calculate.php" method="post">
<p>What age are you?
<select name="age">
<option>Less than 18</option>
<option>18 - 65</option>
<option>Above 65</option>
</select>
</p><p><input type="submit" value="Calculate" /></p>
</form>
```

   a. Input Box
   b. Drop Down List
   c. No input

19. Look at the following form. What type of input is the form using to receive the user's age?

```
<form action=" calculate.php" method="post">
<p> What age are you?
<input type="text" size="5" name="age" />
</p><p><input type="submit" value="Provide listings" /></p>
</form>
```

   a. Input Box
   b. Drop Down List
   c. No input

20. What is wrong with this HTML code segment? <h1>This is a test <h1>
    a. The first <h1> tag should be </h1>
    b. The second <h1> tag should be </h1>
    c. Both <h1> tags should be </h1>
    d. The code should be <h1 This is a test /h1>
    e. Nothing is wrong with this code

Chapter 4 Code Exercises

Your Chapter 4 code exercises can be found in your **Chapter04** folder. This folder is included in your customized XAMPP installation at the following location:

xampplite\htdocs\WebTech\coursework\Chapter04

   Type your name and the date in the **Author** and **Date** sections of each file as you work on each exercise.

Debugging Exercises

Your **Chapter04** folder contains a number of **Fixit** files. Each file contains code with an error of some kind. Open the file in a text editor and read the comment section in the file to see what to do to fix them.

Code Modification Exercises

Your **Chapter04** folder contains a number of **Modify** files. Each file contains code with a comment section that indicates a revised requirement. Your job is to modify the code in each file to meet the new requirements.

Code Completion Exercises

1. You are developing a small Web site for a team of house painters: John and Mary King. The file **kingPainting.html** already contains the text to display a home page but it has not been formatted. Add the HTML code to this file to render the page as shown in Figure 4-9 (note that the words "customized" and "high quality" are bold, the address does not include any blank lines, and the link on this page should link to a file named **paintEstimate.html**).

Figure 4-9: kingPainting.html

2. Create an HTML document named **paintEstimate.html** based on the input requirements outlined in the paintEstimate exercise at the end of Chapter 3. Use an HTML table to line up the three prompts and input boxes. The form should be designed to execute a program named **paintEstimate.php** (you will have a chance to code this at the end of the next chapter). The three input fields should be named **roomLength**, **roomWidth**, and **roomHeight**. Note that clicking the Submit button will generate an error since **paintEstimate.php** does not exist yet.

Figure 4-10 shows how your form should appear.

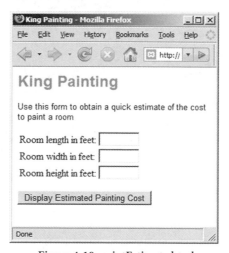

Figure 4-10: paintEstimate.html

3. You have developed an excellent educational computer game called **SaveTheWorld**. Create an HTML document named **softwareOrder.html** based on the input requirements outlined in the softwareOrder exercise at the end of Chapter 3. The form should be designed to execute a program named **softwareOrder.php (you will have a chance to code this at the end of the next chapter).** Use a drop down list to obtain the choice of operating system (Linux, Macintosh, Windows), and a textbox

for the number of copies. The names for the drop down selection should be **os**, and the name for number of copies should be **numCopies**. Figure 4-11 shows the layout for your form.

Figure 4-11: softwareOrder.html

4. Create an HTML document named **travel.html** based on the requirements outlined in the travel exercise at the end of Chapter 3. The form should be designed to execute a program named **travel.php** (you will have a chance to code this at the end of the next chapter). Use text boxes for the two input fields. The names for the two fields should be **numTravelers** and **numNights**. Figure 4-12 shows the layout for your form.

Figure 4-12: travel.html

5. Create an HTML document named **gameIntro.html** based on the requirements outlined in the gameIntro exercise at the end of Chapter 3. The form should execute a program named **gameIntro.php** (you will have a chance to code this at the end of the next chapter). The form should allow the user to type a **name** for the character, choose the **type** of character from a drop down list (Dwarf, Elf, Human, or Wizard), choose the number of **health tokens** to be purchased from a drop down list (0, 10, 20, or 30), choose the number of **experience tokens** to be purchased from a drop down list (0, 2, 4, 6, 8, or 10), and choose the number of **supply tokens** to be purchased from a drop down list (0, 25, 50, 75, or 100). The form should be designed to execute a program named gameIntro.php. Use these names for the input fields: **charName, charType, healthTokens, expTokens, supplyTokens**. Figure 4-13 shows

how the form should appear but feel free to play with the exact appearance of the form and if you prefer you can come up with your own character types.

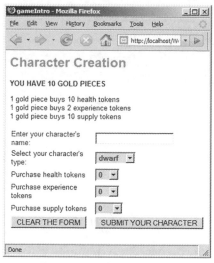

Figure 4-13: gameIntro.html

6. Your **chapter04** folder contains a folder named **story**. The **story** folder contains three .html pages named **scene1.html**, **scene2.html**, and **scene3.html**. Open scene1.html in your Web browser and click the links provided until you see how the three scenes work together. Figure 4-14 shows two scenes. Now look at the code for these three files. A table is used in each case to display an image, a description, and two URL's that provide the user with choices where to go next.

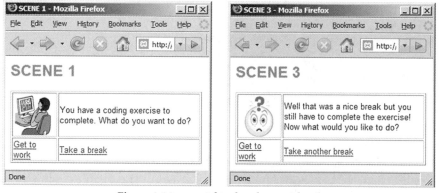

Figure 4-14: scene1.html and scene3.html

Come up with a story of your own. Change the three scenes and add one or two more scenes to make it interesting. Your scenes could constitute an adventure, a series of quiz questions, a journey, a collection of family photos, or something that only your imagination can come up with! If you need some clipart, a good site for free images is: **http://office.microsoft.com/en-us/clipart/default.aspx**

Your images may be larger than those shown in the example, but keep your images small enough so that the user does not need to scroll down to see the entire page, Also, whatever images you use, make them consistent in size that your scenes do not jump around each time you click on a new page. You may want to change the width of the table to accommodate your image size. Have fun!

7. Your **chapter04** folder contains a folder named **maze**. This folder provides the file for a simple maze game: **maze.jpg**, and 17 **.html** files named **Maze0.html**, **Maze1.html**, **Maze2.html**, etc. **Maze0.html** provides the entrance to the maze and displays a map of the maze (see Figure 4-15). The maze consists of 16 locations. **Maze1.html** is the upper left location, **Maze2.html** is the location to right (east) of **Maze1.html**. **Maze5.html** is the location below (to the south of) **Maze1.html**, and so on. Each file displays a different location in the maze, from left to right, top to bottom. The goal of the player is get to Maze 13.

View **Maze0.html** in your Web browser to get started. As you move through the maze you will discover that there is a problem—four of the files need to be completed: **Maze3.html**, **Maze7.html**, **Maze11.html**, **Maze12.html**. These files are missing links to connect them to the rest of the maze. Your job is to complete these files so that the game can be completed. You can figure out what to add to these files by looking at the code for the other .html files, and referring to the map. Feel free to change **maze13.html** to achieve a more interesting ending!

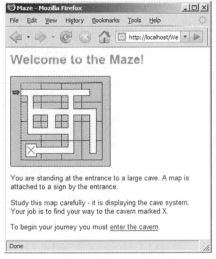

Figure 4-15: maze0.html

8. Complete the code in **event.html** based on the input requirements outlined in the event exercise at the end of Chapter 3. Be sure to save this to your Chapter04 folder. The event.html page should use an <h1> heading at the top and a paragraph to describe the performer. You can choose the performer and write a short description. Follow this with an <h2> tag to display a heading "To Purchase Tickets" followed by a form that requests a first name, phone number, and number of tickets (the

prompt for number of tickets should also indicate that the tickets are $35 each). Use the names firstName, phone, and numTickets for these inputs, and use <br /> tags so that each prompt and input field appears on a separate line. The form should be designed for submission to event.php which you will create in the next chapter. Run your Web server and test that this page displays correctly by opening a Web browser and using the URL:

http://localhost/Webtech/coursework/Chapter04/event.html

9. Complete the code in **fuelCost.html** so that it meets the input requirements outlined in the fuelCost exercise at the end of Chapter 3. Be sure to save this to your Chapter04 folder. Use these names for your form inputs: mpg, miles, costPerGallon. Run your Web server and test that this page displays correctly by opening a Web browser and using the URL:

http://localhost/Webtech/coursework/Chapter04/fuelCost.html

(note that submitting the form will generate an error since you have not yet created the fuelCost.php program that processes the form—we will do that in the next chapter).

Chapter 5

Creating a Working Program — Basics of PHP

Intended Learning Outcomes
- Distinguish between markup languages and programming languages.
- Develop .php files that combine PHP instructions with HTML tags.
- Write PHP instructions that correctly apply basic PHP syntax.
- Create and use variables in PHP instructions.
- Write instructions that use the $_POST array to receive input from an HTML form.
- Create expressions that perform basic arithmetic in PHP.
- Create expressions that use common PHP functions to perform calculations.
- Use print statements to generate HTML output from PHP code.
- Use the PHP number_format() function to format numeric output.

Introduction

In Chapter 3, you learned how to read program requirements, design an interface, and develop program instructions in the form of algorithms. In Chapter 4, you learned to create HTML documents to render information that can be viewed in a Web browser, and how to create forms that permit input from the user. It is now time to learn how to use a programming language to write code that is capable of retrieving user input, processing data and generating results. We will use the PHP programming language.

You may be confused concerning the difference between HTML and PHP. Why are you learning two languages anyway? Recall that HTML is a markup language and not a programming language. Markup languages, such as HTML, are used to describe or **render** data. We have learned how to use HTML tags for this purpose. Programming languages are used to **process** data, in other words, to execute instructions that operate on existing data to produce results.

For example, you can use HTML to **display** a form that will receive someone's hourly wage and the hours worked but you cannot use HTML to **process** this input. You need a programming language to **retrieve** the hourly wage and hours worked from the form, **multiply** these numbers to calculate the weekly pay, and **generate** new HTML to display the results. These are **data processing** operations.

Computer programs contain processing instructions that make use of variables, assignment operations, arithmetic and logical expressions and input/output operations. In this chapter you will learn sufficient PHP syntax to perform basic data processing. In later chapters you will build on these skills to develop applications that can work with files, perform tests, and repeat instructions.

Please note that this book is not intended to provide a complete course in PHP and many important features of the language are not covered here. Our purpose is to introduce you to a programming language in sufficient detail to give you an understanding of the programming process and to introduce you to the fundamentals of program logic and design. However, just as with HTML, you **will** learn sufficient PHP to develop many useful applications and prepare you for more advanced study. And hopefully you will have some fun in the process. Appendix D will help you debug your PHP code, and Appendix F provides additional material and useful PHP references.

Why PHP?

Why use PHP when there are so many other programming languages to choose from? Programming languages generally break down into two types: the more traditional **system programming languages** (such as C, C++, and Java) tend to be used for large scale application development and for creating major application components, while **scripting languages** (such as perl, PHP and Python) are increasingly used for rapid development of relatively smaller scale applications such as Web applications, and for "gluing together" code components.

PHP is especially designed for use with HTML to develop Web applications. Learning to program with PHP will serve anyone interested in developing proficiency in Web programming since a great percentage of Web sites around the world are written in this language. PHP is also quite easy to learn which makes it ideal for learning the basics of programming. And since the general syntax is quite similar to many current system programming languages such as Java and C++, your experience with PHP will prepare you for learning these languages.

Working with HTML and PHP

You have learned to develop HTML pages with forms designed to obtain user input and submit this data to a PHP programs for processing. Now it's time to develop those PHP programs! Let's start with the Wage1 example that we developed in Chapter 4. Here again are the algorithms for **wage1.html and wage1.php**:

```
wage1.html algorithm:
   Display Submit button to execute wage1.php
END
```

```
wage1.php algorithm:
   hourlyWage = 15.75
   hoursWorked = 19
   weeklyWage = hourlyWage * hoursWorked
   Display hourlyWage, hoursWorked, weeklyWage
END
```

You will recall that the form in wage1.html simply supplies a submit button. The form is designed to submit a request to run wage1.php when this button is pressed:

```html
<form action="wage1.php" method="post">
   <input type="submit" value="Get Your Wage Report Now" />
</form>
```

Here is the PHP code for **wage1.php**:

```php
<html>
<head>
   <title>Wage Report</title>
   <link rel="stylesheet" type="text/css" href="sample.css" />
</head>
<body>
   <h1>WAGE REPORT</h1>
   <?php
      $hourlyWage = 15.75;
      $hoursWorked = 19;
      $wage = $hourlyWage * $hoursWorked;

      print("<p>Your hourly wage is $$hourlyWage and you worked
         $hoursWorked hours.</p>");

      print("<p>Your wages are $$wage.</p>");
   ?>
</body>
</html>
```

Code Example: wage1.php

The first thing to notice is that this file contains a lot of HTML! PHP files can include HTML code as well as PHP code, however they are processed differently, and must be kept separate. Your PHP code **must** be located between PHP tags:

```
<?php
    ... php code is here ...
?>
```

If you include PHP instructions outside the PHP tags, this code will be treated as plain text and the instructions will simply be displayed on the Web page!

Similarly, HTML code **cannot** be directly included **between** the PHP tags. If you include HTML within the PHP tags, an error message will be generated when the file is processed since the processor expects PHP instructions within these tags.

When the PHP processor opens **wage1.php**, it begins to dynamically build a new document that will be sent back to the user's browser for viewing. When the processor encounters HTML code, this is added to the new document exactly as it is written. When the processor encounters a PHP section, the PHP instructions are processed. If output must be added to the new document from **within** a PHP section, this output must be generated using PHP **print** statements.

As the processor works through **wage1.php**, the first lines in the file are standard HTML:

```
<html>
<head>
  <title>Wage Report</title>
  <link rel="stylesheet" type="text/css" href="sample.css" />
</head>
<body>
  <h1>WAGE REPORT</h1>
```

These lines are simply directly added to the new document that is being generated.

The processor then reaches the <?**php** tag. The processor recognizes all statements between the <?**php** and ?> as PHP programming instructions that must be executed line by line. So the PHP instructions in **wage1.php** are:

```
<?php
  $hourlyWage = 15.75;
  $hoursWorked = 19;
  $wage = $hourlyWage * $hoursWorked;

  print("<p>Your hourly wage is $$hourlyWage and you worked
     $hoursWorked hours.</p>");
  print("<p>Your wages are $$wage.</p>");
?>
```

Note that there are five instructions (or **program statements**), separated by semi-colons. Every PHP instruction must end with a semi-colon. Let's examine this code one instruction at a time.

```
$hourlyWage = 15.75;
```

The first PHP instruction creates a variable named $hourlyWage and stores 15.75 in this variable. In PHP all variable names must begin with a $ sign. The = sign is the assignment operator, and so this is an instruction to assign the value 15.75 to $hourlyWage. Another way of saying this is that 15.75 is stored in the variable $hourlyWage (remember that a variable is simply a user-defined name for a storage location).

```
$hoursWorked = 19;
```

The second PHP instruction creates a variable called $hoursWorked and assigns the value 19 to this variable.

```
$wage = $hourlyWage * $hoursWorked;
```

The third PHP instruction first multiplies the value stored in $hourlyWage by the value stored in $hoursWorked, then creates a variable called $wage and stores the result of the multiplication in the $wage variable.

```
print("<p>Your hourly wage is $$hourlyWage and you worked
    $hoursWorked hours.</p>");
```

This instruction uses the PHP **print** statement. Recall that HTML code cannot be directly included **inside** a PHP section, and PHP code cannot be included **outside** PHP sections. However we often need to create HTML code for our new document that includes values that are generated in our PHP statements.

The **print** statement allows us to generate HTML output from within our PHP sections. In this case the statement will add the following to the new document: "**<p>Your hourly wage is $**", followed by the value stored in **$hourlyWage**, followed by "**and you worked**", followed by the value stored in **$hoursWorked**, followed by "**hours </p>**". In other words this print instruction is putting together five pieces of data, three literal character strings and the contents of two variables.

If you are wondering why "**$$hourlyWage**" includes two $ symbols, the first $ symbol is intended to be displayed as part of the output, while the second $ symbol is identifying **$hourlyWage** as a PHP variable.

The variable **$hourlyWage** contains the value 15.75 and the variable **$hoursWorked** contains the value 19, so this print instruction will generate the following string and add this to the text that is already part of the new HTML document:

```
<p>Your hourly wage is $15.75 and you worked 19 hours.</p>
```

The fifth PHP instruction also uses a print statement to generate output:

```
print("<p>Your wages are $$wage.</p>");
```

In this case, the statement is used to display a paragraph that includes the value stored in the $wage variable. The statement generates the string "<p>Your wages are $", followed by the value stored in the variable **$wage**, followed by the string ".</p>". Since the variable **$wage** contains the value **299.25**, the actual output that is added to the new HTML document is:

```
<p>Your wages are $299.25.</p>
```

That is the last PHP instruction but it is not the end of the wage1.php file. So far the processor has constructed a new document that contains the HTML from wage1.php that preceded the PHP code, and also the text that was generated inside the PHP section by the two print statements. The processor now adds the remaining two lines of HTML that are located after the PHP section:

```
</body>
</html>
```

Now that the processor has processed the entire file the new HTML document contains the following:

```
<html>
<head>
  <title>Wage Report</title>
  <link rel="stylesheet" type="text/css" href="sample.css" />
</head>
<body>
  <h1>WAGE REPORT</h1>
  <p>Your hourly wage is $15.75 and you worked 19 hours.</p>
  <p>Your wages are $299.25.</p>
</body>
</html>
```

Code Example: HTML output generated by wage1.php

The Web server now sends this document back to the Web browser to be displayed to the user. Notice that there is **no** PHP code in this new document. There is only the HTML code that was originally included in **wage1.php**, combined with the HTML code that the PHP section generated when the **print** statements were processed.

Important Features of Client/Server Programs

To help understand this, let's review, without getting into much detail, the process by which a PHP program executes and generates a new Web document.

When the **submit** button on an HTML form is pressed, an action is submitted to a Web server. If the action specifies a PHP program the Web server looks for the requested **.php** file and processes the content of the file line by line in order to generate a new document to send back to the browser. Any text in the **.php** file that is located **outside** <?php and ?> tags is added to the new document exactly as it is written. Each time that the processor finds a PHP code section in the file, this section is processed and if the code includes any **print()** instructions, the output from these instructions is added to the new document. When the end of the file is reached, the new document is sent back to the browser for display.

The two screens in Figure 5-1 show the original HTML document (**wage1.html**) that contains the form used to execute **wage1.php**, and the new document that is created on the server when **wage1.php** is processed and that is returned to the client.

Figure 5-1: wage1.html and wage1.php screenshots

What is exciting about this is that, while **.html** files are **static** files that are stored on the Web server and simply sent to the Web browser on request, **.php** files are **dynamic**. These files are also located on the Web server but when a **.php** file is requested the file is **processed**. As a result of the processing a new document is created and sent to the Web browser. The content and appearance of this document will depend on the PHP instructions in the file and may be different each time a user submits a request.

This is how Web sites provide you with information that is customized for your request. PHP is not the only language that can be used for this purpose. Dynamic web pages can be generated using any number of scripting languages. The process is very similar in all cases.

Consider two very important characteristics of client/server programming. First, the PHP program is located on a server, not on the user's computer. There is no need to install any software on the user's computer other than the Web browser. This means that software does not need to be distributed and that only a single copy is needed. This code can be easily maintained and modified with no need to change anything on the user's computer. Second, note that the user cannot access the PHP code. If the user clicks the **View Source** option from the browsers menu bar, he or she will only see the HTML document that was created. So the PHP code is **secure** and cannot be viewed or modified by the end user.

Receiving Input from a Form — wage2.php

Now let's convert our Wage2 example — recall that this example included user input. Here are the algorithms for **wage2.html** and **wage2.php**:

```
wage2.html algorithm:
   Prompt user for hourly wage
   Get hourlyWage
   Prompt user for hours worked
   Get hoursWorked
   Submit hourlyWage, hoursWorked to wage2.php
END
```

```
wage2.php algorithm:
   Receive hourlyWage, hoursWorked from wage2.html
   weeklyWage = hourlyWage * hoursWorked
   Display hourlyWage, hoursWorked, weeklyWage
END
```

First let's review the code for wage2.html (this contains the HTML form that allows the user to input value for the hourly wage and hours worked):

```
<html>
<head>
   <title>Wage Report</title>
   <link rel="stylesheet" type="text/css" href="sample.css" />
</head>
<body>
   <h1>Wage Report</h1>
   <form action="wage2.php" method="post">
      <p>Please enter your hourly wage:
      <input type="text" size="20" name="hourlyWage" />
      </p>
      <p>And the hours you have worked:
      <input type="text" size="20" name="hoursWorked" />
      </p>
      <input type="submit" value="Get Your Wage Report Now" />
```

```
      <input type="reset" value="Clear and start again" />
   </form>

</body>
</html>
```

Code Example: wage2.html

Note that this form (see Figure 5.2) is designed to receive input from the user in text boxes, and that the input will be associated with the names **hourlyWage** and **hoursWorked**. The values that are entered by the user will be associated with these names and submitted for processing by **wage2.php** when the Submit button is pressed.

Now let's look at the PHP code in the **wage2.php** file:

```
<html>
<head>
   <title>Wage Report</title>
   <link rel="stylesheet" type="text/css" href="sample.css" />
</head>
<body>
   <h1>Wage Report</h1>

   <?php
      $hourlyWage  = $_POST['hourlyWage'];
      $hoursWorked = $_POST['hoursWorked'];

      $wage = $hourlyWage * $hoursWorked;

      print("<p>Your hourly wage is $$hourlyWage and you worked
         $hoursWorked hours.</p>");

      print("<p>Your wages are $$wage.</p>");
   ?>
</body>
</html>
```

Code Example: wage2.php

Note that this program is very similar to **wage1.php** except that **wage2.php** does not contain the first two assignment statements that were included in **wage1.php**:

```
$hourlyWage = 15.75;
$hoursWorked = 19;
```

Instead, **wage2.php** includes the following two statements:

```
$hourlyWage  = $_POST['hourlyWage'];
$hoursWorked = $_POST['hoursWorked'];
```

Recall that each of two textboxes in the form provided by **wage2.html** included a **name** attribute. The name of the first textbox was **hourlyWage** and the name of the second textbox was **hoursWorked**. When the form is submitted, the server receives these two names along with the values that the user typed into each textbox. The server provides this information to the PHP program in a structure known as a **$_POST** array. The detailed structure of the $_POST array will be explained in Chapter 11. For now, you only need to understand how to use the $_POST array to retrieve values from HTML forms.

The $_POST array contains every value that was sent to the server when the user submitted the form. Each value is identified by the name that was specified in the form's input field. For example if the name used in the form's input field was 'hourlyWage' then the value is stored in **$_POST['hourlyWage']**. So the PHP program can obtain any of the submitted values simply by referencing the $_POST array, using the name of the appropriate input field. In our example we assign each value from the $_POST array to a PHP variable for use in subsequent program statements.

Whenever your PHP program needs to obtain values that were submitted from an HTML form using the "post" method, your code will need to include statements that extract the values from the **$_POST** array. Be careful to use the correct syntax. The name **$_POST** must be followed by square brackets containing the name of the appropriate form field in single or double quotes. The name of the form field should not begin with a $ sign since this is not a PHP variable name.

It is not necessary for the variable that stores the value from the $_POST array to have the same name as the form's input field. For example **$employeeHourlyWage = $_POST['hourlyWage'];** would work just as well as **$hourlyWage = $_POST['hourlyWage'];**. In that case, of course, the variable **$employeeHourlyWage** should be used throughout the remainder of the program instead of **$hourlyWage**.

Now that the values have been received from the form and stored in **$hourlyWage** and **$hoursWorked**, the third line of PHP code simply multiplies the values stored in these two variables and stores the result in the **$wage** variable, similar to **wage1.php**:

```
$wage = $hourlyWage * $hoursWorked;
```

The program then generates text to be added to the HTML document.

```
print("<p>Your hourly wage is $$hourlyWage and you worked
    $hoursWorked hours.</p>");

print("<p>Your wages are $$wage.</p>");
```

These statements are identical to those used in **wage1.php**.

To see what happens here, let's just assume that the user had entered **10.75** for an hourly wage and **25** for hours worked on the form that was then submitted to this program. In that case by the time the processor reaches these print statements, the values stored in **$hourlyWage**, **$hoursWorked** and **$weeklyWage** will be **10.75, 25** and **268.75** respectively. So the print statements will insert the following into the new HTML document:

```
<p>Your hourly wage is $10.75 and you worked 25 hours.</p>
<p>Your wages are $268.75.</p>
```

The entire new document will therefore look like this:

```
<html>
<head>
   <title>Wage Report</title>
   <link rel="stylesheet" type="text/css" href="sample.css" />
</head>
<body>
   <h1>WAGE REPORT</h1>
   <p>Your hourly wage is $10.75 and you worked 25 hours.</p>
   <p>Your wages are $268.75.</p>
</body>
</html>
```

Code Example: HTML output generated by wage2.php

The actual values for the hourly wage, hours worked and wage will of course depend on the values for the hourly wage and hours worked that were entered by the user.

Figure 5-2 illustrates a sample interaction using these user inputs.

Figure 5-2: wage2.html and wage2.php screenshots

Processing the Smoking Survey — smoking.php

Now let's convert the Smoking Calculator program. Here are the algorithms for smoking.html and smoking.php:

```
smoking.html algorithm:
  Prompt for firstName
  Get firstName
  Prompt for lastName
  Get lastName
  Prompt for yearsSmoked
  Get yearsSmoked
  Prompt for smokedDaily
  Get smokedDaily
  Submit firstName, lastName, yearsSmoked, smokedDaily to
    smoking.php
END
```

```
smoking.php algorithm:
  Receive firstName, lastName, yearsSmoked, smokedDaily from smok-
ing.html
  totalSmoked = yearsSmoked * 365 * smokedDaily
  Display firstName. lastName, yearsSmoked, smokedDaily, to-
talSmoked
END
```

Here is the code for **smoking.html**:

```html
<html>
<head>
  <title>Smoking Calculator</title>
  <link rel="stylesheet" type="text/css" href="sample.css" />
</head>
<body>
  <h1>Welcome to the Smoking Calculator!</h1>
  <form action="smoking.php" method="post" >

    <p>What is your first name?
    <input type="text" size="20" name="firstName" /></p>

    <p>What is your last name?
    <input type="text" size="20" name="lastName" /></p>

    <p>For how many years have you smoked?
    <input type="text" size="5" name="yearsSmoked" /></p>
```

```
      <p>How many cigarettes have you <br \>
      smoked on average every day (roughly)?
      <select name="smokedDaily" >
        <option>0</option>
        <option>1</option>
        <option>2</option>
        <option>5</option>
        <option>10</option>
        <option>20</option>
        <option>30</option>
        <option>40</option>
      </select></p>

      <p><input type="submit" value="Tell me the bad news" />
      <input type="reset" value="I want to try again" /></p>
    </form>
  </body>
</html>
```

Code Example: smoking.html

Recall that this form contains four input fields. Three of these are text boxes, named firstName, lastName and yearsSmoked. The fourth is a drop down list, named smoked-Daily. When the Submit button is pressed the input from these fields will be passed to the Web server for processing by smoking.php.

Here is the code for smoking.php:

```
<html>
<head>
  <title>Smoking Calculator - RESULTS</title>
  <link rel="stylesheet" type="text/css" href="sample.css" />
</head>
<body>
<?php
  $yearsSmoked = $_POST['yearsSmoked'];
  $smokedDaily = $_POST['smokedDaily'];
  $firstName = $_POST['firstName'];
  $lastName = $_POST['lastName'];

  $totalCigarettes = $yearsSmoked * 365 * $smokedDaily;

  print ("<h1>Smoking Calculator Results</h1>");
  print ("<h1>$lastName, $firstName</h1>");
  print("<p>Years smoked: $yearsSmoked<br />");

  print("Average number of cigarettes smoked daily:
    $smokedDaily</p>");
```

```
print ("<p>$firstName, you have smoked approximately
    $totalCigarettes cigarettes.</p>");

print ("<p><a href=\"smoking.html\">Return to Calculator
    </a></p>");
?>
</body>
</html>
```

Code Example: smoking.php

The server receives the names of the form fields firstName, lastName, yearsSmoked and smokedDaily, as well as the values that the user entered into these fields, and delivers these to the PHP program in the $_POST array. The program retrieves the values from the $_POST array and assigns these to PHP variables by referencing the names of the form's input fields:

```
$yearsSmoked = $_POST['yearsSmoked'];
$smokedDaily = $_POST['smokedDaily'];
$firstName = $_POST['firstName'];
$lastName = $_POST['lastName'];
```

The next PHP instruction multiplies the value stored in $yearsSmoked by 365 by the value stored in $smokedDaily and stores the result in a new variable $totalCigarettes:

```
$totalCigarettes = $yearsSmoked * 365 * $smokedDaily;
```

The remaining statements create text that becomes part of the new HTML document.

Note that in this example print() statements are used to create the two headings:

```
print (" <h1>Smoking Calculator Results</h1>");
print (" <h1>$lastName, $firstName </h1>");
```

Although the first heading could have been listed before the PHP section as simple HTML, the second heading must be included in the PHP section because this heading displays the last and first names and these are stored in PHP variables **$firstName** and **$lastName**. We can only refer to these variables within our PHP code section, and we can only generate HTML within PHP code sections using the PHP **print()** function.

Figure 5-3 shows a sample interaction. The second screen shows the document created by **smoking.php** after processing data submitted from the form supplied by **smoking.html**.

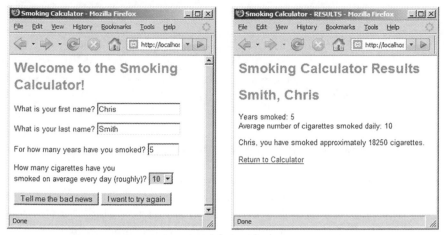

Figure 5-3: smoking.html and smoking.php screenshots

PHP — General Guidelines and Syntax

You are now ready to develop PHP code to process input from your own forms. First let's review some important guidelines and syntax rules to help you get started writing PHP.

All PHP statements must end with a semi-colon

If you leave out a semi-colon the processor will generate an error message.

Variable names must follow PHP naming rules

The first character of a PHP variable name must always be a $ sign.

The second character must be a letter a–z, A–Z, or else an underscore.

After the first two characters, any combination of numeric digits and other characters are allowed. **However spaces are not allowed anywhere in a variable name.**

Here are some examples of **valid** variable names:

```
$userName
$employee1
$averageSalary
```

Here are some examples of **invalid** variable names:

```
$My Salary (spaces are not allowed)
$1stProgram (2nd character cannot be a digit)
salary3 (1st character must be a $)
```

PHP is case-sensitive

For example variables named **$salary**, **$Salary** and **$SALARY** will be considered to be three entirely different variables! So be careful not to mistype the name of a variable when you refer to it more than once — copying and pasting variable names helps to avoid this problem.

Variable names should be meaningful

The use of meaningful variable names makes it easy for another programmer to understand how a variable is being used. For example, **$averageSalary** and **$userPassword** are good variable names because it is obvious what they are being used for. However **$c1** and **$hgTER34** are poor variable names because it is not clear what they might contain.

The first letter of a PHP variable name should be lower-case

By convention in PHP the first letter in a variable name is lower-case. Underscores or upper-case letters are included in the variable if it contains multiple English words, for example, **$distanceToMoon** or **$distance_to_moon**. Notice that either of these are much easier to read than **$distancetomoon**. Using an uppercase letter to begin each English word within a variable name is referred to as **camelback** notation.

PHP variables are created the first time that they appear in the code

In PHP a variable is created the first time that the variable name appears in the code. You can create as many variables as you want. Once a variable has been created, your code can refer to it as often as necessary. If a numeric variable is used in a calculation or **print**() function before it has been assigned a value, the processor automatically assigns the value 0 to the variable. This can lead to trouble! Here's an example where the programmer mistypes a variable name:

```
$hourlyWage = 15.75;
$hoursWorked = 19;
$weeklyWage = $hourlyWage * $housrWorked;
```

In this example the value stored in **$weeklyWage** will be 0. Why? Because **$hoursWorked** has been mistyped as **$housrWorked** in the last statement. The processor thinks that this is a new variable and since it has no value it is assigned 0, and this is used in the calculation. The best protection against mistyping variable names is to copy and paste and avoid retyping a variable name! It is also important to test your programs carefully to ensure your calculations are working correctly.

PHP allows you to mix data types

PHP assumes that you know what you are doing with your variables and this can get you into trouble if you're not careful. For example PHP will allow the following:

```
$firstName = "Mary";
$age = 30;
$result = $firstName * $age;
```

The third statement appears to multiply the character string "Mary" by 30! In fact the processor sets the integer value of **$firstName** to 0 in order to perform the calculation so the result is that 0 is stored in the **$result** variable. It is up to you to protect your code against these type of errors. Later we will look at ways to validate input to help avoid these problems.

Variables can receive data from forms

As you saw in the **wage2.php** example, when form data is submitted to a PHP program for processing, the server provides a **$_POST** array which contains the values submitted to the form, indexed by the names of the form's input fields. These values can be extracted from the **$_POST** array by referencing the appropriate field name (for example **$_POST['hourlyWage']**). In this textbook we will make it a practice to assign all of the values received in the **$_POST** array to PHP variables with the same name as the form names.

Values are assigned to variables using the assignment operator

As we saw in our examples, assignment statements are used to stored values in variables. Assignments statements use the = sign as an **assignment operator**. The syntax is always in the form

```
<variable> = expression;
```

where the variable on the left of the assignment operator will receive a value. The expression on the right side of the operator will be calculated and the resulting value assigned. Note that the expression is evaluated **before** a value is assigned to the variable on the left of the assignment operator. The following examples are all valid assignments:

```
$retailPrice = 20.56;
$tax = $retailPrice * 0.07.
$total = $retailPrice + $tax;
$firstName = "Mary";
$lastName = "Jones";
$fullName = "$firstName $lastName";
```

In the last statement the **$fullName** variable receives the string contained in **$firstName** followed by a space followed by the string contained in **$lastName**.

Values stored in variables can be replaced by new values

You can replace the value that is stored in a variable, for example:

```
$retailPrice = 20.56;

(... other code here ...)

$retailPrice = 75.50;
```

In this example, 20.56 is stored in **$retailPrice**, then later on the program **75.50** is stored in the same variable. Before this second assignment, **$retailPrice** contains **20.56**, but after this statement **$retailPrice** contains **75.50** and the previous value is lost.

A variable can appear on BOTH sides of an assignment

You can also modify the value stored in a variable and store the result back into the same variable, replacing the old value. This can be very useful, for example, when we need to accumulate a total:

```
$total = 225.25;
$nextPurchase = 14.75;
$total = $total + $nextPurchase;
```

In this example, **225.25** is stored in **$total**, then **14.75** is stored in **$nextPurchase**. The next statement adds the value stored in **$total** to the value stored in **$nextPurchase**, and stores the result back into **$total**. So **$total** now contains the value **240.00** and the previous value (**225.25**) has been lost.

We often find it useful to use a variable to count something. In these cases we need to increment (or decrement) the value that is currently stored in a variable. For example, if we are using a variable named **$numberOfStudents** that is being used to count, we could **increment** the value currently stored in this variable with the statement:

```
$numberOfStudents = $numberOfStudents + 1;
```

This increment operation is so common that most languages, including PHP, provide a shorthand operator ++. So the last statement can simply be written

```
$numberOfStudents++;
```

which means add 1 to the value currently stored in the **$numberOfStudents** variable.

Similarly variables are often used to count **down**, or **decrement**. We can decrement the value currently stored in **$numberOfStudents** as follows:

```
$numberOfStudents = $numberOfStudents - 1;
```

This statement can also be written:

```
$numberOfStudents--;
```

Note that the increment and decrement operators must not include spaces.

Special note: assigning different data types to a variable

If you have previous experience programming in other languages, you may be surprised to see that PHP variables do not need to be defined to contain specific data types. PHP determines the appropriate data type for a variable at the time that a value is assigned or used in an expression. Chapter 13 discusses the significance of data types in more detail.

Arithmetic Expressions

Let's look more carefully at arithmetic expressions. The **arithmetic operators** are:

+ (addition)	- (subtraction)
* (multiplication)	/ (division)
% (modulus)	

When the processor encounters an arithmetic expression, **multiplication** and **division** operations are evaluated first in order from left to right, then **addition** and **subtraction** operations are evaluated in order from left to right. For example 1 + 2 * 3 - 4 first evaluates to 1 + 6 - 4 which evaluates to 7 - 4 which evaluates to 3.

Parentheses can be used to change the **precedence** of an expression. Any part of the expression that is enclosed in parentheses is evaluated first. For example (1 + 2) * (3 - 4) evaluates to 3 * (3 - 4) which evaluates to 3 * -1 which evaluates to -3.

If parentheses are nested the expressions inside the innermost parentheses are evaluated first, followed by the expressions inside the next innermost parentheses, and so on. For example (1 +2) * (3 / (4 - 1)) evaluates to (1 +2) * (3 / 3) which evaluates to (3) * (3 / 3) which evaluates to 3 * 1 which evaluates to 3.

Arithmetic can include any combination of literal values and variables, for example the following calculation includes two variables and the literal value **40** (note that this assumes that **$hourlyWage** and **$deductions** have already been assigned values otherwise **0** will be assigned to **$weeklyWage!**):

```
$weeklyWage = ($hourlyWage * 40) - $deductions;
```

The **modulus operator %** is a **division** operator that calculates the remainder of a division. For example the result of **5 % 3** is **2** since 3 divides into 5 once with a remainder of 2. Similarly the result of **15 % 4** is **3** since 4 divides into 15 three times with a remainder of 3.

Using Arithmetic Functions

Most programming languages, including PHP provide a number of useful arithmetic **functions**. A function provides pre-written code to perform a useful task. Most programming languages provide a library of standard functions that can be called as needed by your programs. In a later chapter you will also learn how to create your own functions.

Functions do not just simplify the programmer's task. By using functions that have already been developed and thoroughly tested, the programmer does not run the risk of introducing errors by writing new code unnecessarily. It is considered good programming practice to always use existing functions when these are available. This practice aligns with the general principle of **reusability**.

In most languages, including PHP, functions are represented in code statements by specifying the function name followed by a pair of parentheses. If the function requires any arguments (values that the function needs in order to perform its task) then these are included within the parentheses in the order that the function expects. Multiple arguments must be separated by commas.

Here is a list of some common arithmetic functions in PHP, along with examples of their use:

pow()

The **pow()** function is used to raise a value to an exponent, for example **pow(2, 3)** will calculate the value of 2 cubed, while **pow(5, 17)** will calculate the value of 5 to the power of 17. The pow() function requires two arguments, the value to be raised, followed by the exponent. Variables can be used as arguments, so for example if you want to square the value stored in **$number** and store the result in a variable named **$square**, you could write:

```
$square = pow($number, 2);
```

and if you wanted to raise the value stored in **$number** by the value stored in **$exponent** and store the result in a variable named **$result**, you could write:

```
$result = pow($number, $exponent);
```

pi()

The **pi()** function simply delivers an accurate value for PI. If you need to use PI in a calculation this is a much better approach than typing in a value directly. For example if the radius of a circle is stored in **$radius**, you could calculate and store the circumference as follows:

```
$circumference = 2 * pi() * $radius;
```

To calculate the area you could use the **pi()** and **pow()** functions in your expression:

```
$area = pi() * pow($radius, 2);
```

Note that, unlike the pow() function, the pi() function does not have any arguments. The parentheses are still required however to indicate that pi() is a function.

round()

The **round()** function can be used to round a number to the nearest integer value. For example **round(3.8)** will generate the value **4**, while **round(3.2)** will generate the value **3**. The **round()** function can also be directed to round off to any number of places by adding a second argument that indicates the required number of decimal places, for example **round(3.828, 2)** will generate the value **3.83**.

ceil()

The **ceil()** function is similar to the **round()** function except that it always rounds up for positive numbers or down for negative numbers. For example **ceil(3.8)** will generate the value **4**, while **ceil(3.2)** will also generate the value **4**. This is useful for certain calculations. Consider a program that must calculate the number of gallons of paint needed to paint a wall at the rate of 200 square feet a gallon. If we divide the area of the wall by 200 we always want the result to be rounded up in order to know how many gallons of paint we need to be purchase, for example:

```
gallonsOfPaint = ceil($wallArea / 200);
```

floor()

The **floor**() function is also similar to the **round**() function except that it always rounds down for positive numbers or up for negative numbers. For example **floor(3.8)** will generate the value **3**, while **floor(3.2)** will also generate the value **3**. This is useful for certain calculations. Consider a program that contains a variable **$months** and that the value in this variable needs to be broken down into years and months. If we divide **$months** by **12**, we will get the number of years, but this may include a decimal value (for example if **$months** contains **28**, this will generate **2.33333..**). We round down to the actual number of years using the **floor**() function:

```
$years = floor($months / 12);
$monthsLeftOver = $months % 12;
```

Note that, in this example, once we have figured out the number of years, we need to calculate the number of months left over. We can do this using the modulus operator to get the remainder after dividing the value stored in **$months** by 12). For example if **$months** contains **28**, $years will contain **2** (the rounded down result of dividing **28** by **12**), and **$monthsLeftOver** will contain **4** (the remainder from dividing **28** by **12**).

sqrt()

The **sqrt**() function will return the square root of a value. For example sqrt(16) will generate a value of **4**.

rand()

The **rand**() function is useful for many purposes. This function can be used to generate a random number in any range, for example **rand(1, 10)** will generate a random number between **1** and **10**. If **rand**() is used with no arguments, it will generate a decimal value between **0** and **1**.

There are many other arithmetic functions available for your use. Appendix F provides useful references.

White Space in PHP Files

The PHP processor ignores white space (extra blank spaces, tabs, new lines) except in output statements. That means that the previous code examples could be written much less neatly! For example, **wage1.php** could be written like this:

```
<html><head>          <title>Wage Report</title><link rel
="stylesheet" type="text/css" ref
="sample.css" /></head><body><h1>WAGE REPORT</h1><?php $hourlyWage
=
15.75; $hoursWorked = 19; $wage
= $hourlyWage * $hoursWorked; print("<p>Your hourly wage is
$hourlyWage." and you worked $hoursWorked hours.</p>");
print("<p>Your wages
are $$wage.</p>");?></body></html>
```

This code will actually produce the same results as the previous version but obviously this is much harder to read and that is why we type in our code neatly!

There are two important reasons to write code neatly and using a standard layout. First you will often need to refer back to your own code in order to make corrections or modifications. Second, other programmers will need to reference your code, for example, if you leave a position. A programmer can lose significant time trying to read poorly written code, especially in the case of large applications. Many software companies require their programmers to follow certain conventions in code layout.

Generating HTML Output from PHP

As we saw in our three code examples, a **.php** file is often used to dynamically generate a return page in response to a request from a user. The **.php** file can contain sections of HTML code and sections of PHP code. The processor assembles the return document by working through the **.php** file line by line. Whenever it reads a section of HTML code, this is added to the return document exactly as it appears in the **.php file**. Whenever it finds a section of PHP code, the processor processes the PHP instructions. If the PHP code includes **print**() statements, the output from these statements is added to the new document.

The general syntax for the **print**() functon is:

```
print (" ... your HTML output here ...");
```

Note the parentheses and the double quotes (the parentheses are actually optional in PHP but we will use them in this book so that our syntax is more consistent with other languages). You can place any character string that you wish to output between the quotes. A character string is simply a sequence of characters that can be read as text. For example "How are you?" is a character string, and so is "123 Main Street" and "Please enter your first name: " and "Italy" and "dfge+%*?f12&". In fact the text of the book you are reading is also one very long character string! Character strings can include HTML tags, so for example "<p>Hello, how are you today?</p>" is a character string that includes opening and closing paragraph tags. That means that we can include strings that contain HTML tags in our print statements and these tags will be added to the return document along with the other text in the string.

PHP also allows you to include variables within the quotes as part of your character string, in which case the value of the variable is displayed, for example:

```
print ("<p>Hello, $firstName, how are you today?<p>");
```

Be careful! Remember to include the $ symbol before your variable name, otherwise the PHP processor will think your variable name is just part the character string that is to be displayed! For example, consider this version of the previous print statement:

```
print ("<p>Hello, firstName, how are you today?<p>");
```

Since there is no $ to indicate a variable, this statement will simply assume that the word "firstName" is part of the string and display this word literally (try it).

And if you require spaces, commas, periods or symbols (such as the $ symbol) to appear before or after the value of the variable in your output, be sure to include these in your character strings!

Including Double Quotes in Character Strings

Although it is not always required in PHP, most programming languages require you to indicate character strings in your code by enclosing them in quotes. This allows the language processor to distinguish between literal text that is to be treated as-written, and text that is part of the actual programming code. In this book we follow the standard convention of enclosing character strings in double quotes since that is a requirement for most languages. But using double quotes to surround our literal strings creates a problem: what if you need to display a double quote as **part** of the character string? If you need to include a double quote in your output, you must use \" instead of ". The **back slash** character tells the print statement that this quote is to be included as part of the character string, otherwise the processor will assume that the double quote indicates the end of the character string. For example:

```
print("<p>I said \"How are you today?\"<p>");
```

will generate:

```
I said "How are you today?"
```

The back slash is known as an escape character and is used to print a number of special characters (not just the double quote) that would otherwise be difficult to output. The use of escape characters is covered in more detail in the next chapter.

You can include HTML tags in your print() statements. For example:

```
print("<p>You wages are $$wage.</p>");
```

You can include HTML tags with attributes in your print() statements but remember to use \" when typing your attribute values since these are enclosed in double quotes. For example:

```
print("<a href=\"someFile.html\">Return to someFile</a>");
```

NOTE: PHP allow you to use either single OR double quotes to surround character strings. This means that you can use single quotes around a string that contains double quotes, in which case you no longer need to use \" in your string. Similarly, a string that contains a single quote can be surrounded by double quotes. However this will not work in all cases, for example some strings may include both single and double quotes. Also this will not work in many other languages. For these reasons, this book uses \" whenever a double quote is to be included within a character string.

Using Multiple PHP Sections

You can include as many PHP sections in your document as you want, as long as each PHP section contains only PHP instructions. The processor simply processes each PHP section in turn and adds any output from the **print** statements to the HTML code that is located outside the PHP sections, in order. This allows you to use simple HTML throughout your page except in places where the HTML must be generated by PHP code. A .php file might contain many small PHP sections sandwiched between HTML code.

You can even place your <?**php** and ?> at the very beginning and very end of the document! In that case ALL of the HTML code would have to be generated using **print** statements! However since it is easier to type HTML directly whenever you can, the more common practice is to mix PHP sections with HTML sections, and use print statements only when your HTML output must be generated by PHP code (for example when the HTML is generated from PHP variables, functions, or control structures). You will get a feel for this as you develop your own code. Always ensure that your HTML sections contain only HTML tags, and that any HTML generated in your PHP sections is generated in print statements.

Using the number_format() Function to Display Numbers to a Specific Number of Places

Often you want your program's numeric output to be formatted to display a specific number of decimal places. For example an employee's pay is a dollar amount and should always be displayed to exactly two places. However a calculation to multiply an hourly wage by hours worked may generate a value that contains more or less than two decimal places. The **number_format**() function allows you to display a value to a fixed number of places without changing the value itself. For example **number_format($wage, 2)** will generate a character string with the value of the **$wage** variable rounded to two places, so if the variable contains **250.5**, this will generate "**250.50**", and if the variable contains **250.575**, this will generate "**250.58**". The **number_format**() function takes two arguments, a value and the number of decimal places to be displayed. The actual value stored in **$wage** is not changed.

Including Calls to PHP Functions inside PHP print Statements

We can use PHP functions such as number_format() in our print statements but we need to be careful how we do this. At first glance you might think that instead of:

```
print("<p>Your wages are $$wage.</p>");
```

you could simply use the following

```
print("<p>Your wages are $number_format($wage, 2).</p>");
```

But this will **not** work since PHP will assume you want to display the character string "number_format" exactly as written, as part of the output text, so, for example, if **$wage** contains the value **456.78**, this will generate:

```
<p>Your wages are $number_format(456.78, 2).</p>");
```

This is definitely **not** what we want! We want PHP to understand that we are calling the **number_format**() function in order to round and display the value stored in **$wage** to 2 places.

To accomplish this, we must **separate** the call to the function from the character strings in our print statement. We do this as follows:

```
print("<p>Your wages are $".number_format($wage, 2).".</p>");
```

We need to consider the syntax of this statement carefully. This **print** statement now consists of three items: a character string ("**<p>Your wages are $**"), followed by a call to the **number_format**() function, followed by another character string ("**.</p>**"). The two character strings are enclosed in quotes to indicate that these contain literal text, while the call to the **number_format**() function is **not** enclosed in quotes to indicate that this is a PHP instruction that must be executed in order to obtain a value. There are periods between the two character strings and the call to the **number_format**() function. These periods are required and tell the **print** statement to **join** these three items (the first character string, the string returned by the call to the function, and the remaining character string) to create a single complete output string.

String Concatenation and the Concatenation Operator

This process of combining a number of strings into a single string is termed concatenation. In PHP the strings to be concatenated must be connected by periods and the period is known as the concatenation operator (some other languages use the + operator instead of the period to concatenate strings). Concatenation is very useful to programmers since it is often important to add different strings together. For example your program might need to create a variable to contain a person's full name by joining the content of a variable containing a first name with a space followed by the content of a variable containing a last name:

```
$fullName = $firstName." ".$lastName;
```

If **$firstName** contains "**Chris**" and **$lastName** contains "**Smith**", **$fullName** now contains "**Chris Smith**". Do you see the importance of the " " string in this concatenation of strings? Without it, **$fullName** would contain "**ChrisSmith**" with no space between the two names.

You can use the concatenation syntax whenever you wish to concatenate calls to PHP functions with literal character strings, for example:

```
print("<p>The cube of 34 is ".pow(34, 3)."</p>");
```

or (this example assumes that $streetAddress, $city, $state and $zip already contain values):

```
print("<p>I live at ".$streetAddress.", ".$city.", ".
   $state." ".$zip."</p>");
```

Look at that last example carefully to see how commas and spaces are included in the address.

Variables can also be concatenated with strings although, as we have seen, this is not necessary in PHP since variables can be included directly in character string. However in most programming languages, variables can never be included directly within character strings and must always be concatenated. For this reason, some PHP programmers consider it good practice to always concatenate their variables, for example:

```
print("Hello, ".$firstName.", how are you today?");
```

instead of:

```
print("Hello, $firstName, how are you today?");
```

and

```
print("<p>Your hourly wage is $".$hourlyWage." and you worked
    ".$hoursWorked." hours.</p>");
```

instead of:

```
print("<p>Your hourly wage is $$hourlyWage and you worked
    $hoursWorked hours.</p>");
```

In this textbook, the variables are included directly inside the character strings to keep the code samples as simple as possible.

The PHP echo Statement

In addition to the print statement that has been applied in this book, PHP also offers the echo statement. The two are almost identical in operation, for example:

```
print ("Hello, $firstName, how are you today?");
```

could be written:

```
echo "Hello, $firstName, how are you today?";
```

Users of the echo statement usually leave out the opening and closing parentheses since parentheses do not work when concatenation is included in an echo statement. Most programmers simply choose one over the other. We use the print statement with parentheses simply because this is closer to the syntax of output statements in other languages.

Finding Syntax Errors

Syntax errors are errors that prevent the processor from running the program. If the PHP processor is unable to understand an instruction it will generate an error message and stop executing. For example, you may forget semi-colons, mistype a variable name, include HTML within a PHP section without using a **print**() statement, refer to a variable or function outside a PHP section, forget to close a PHP section with ?> , etc.

Don't think is it unusual if you create a number of errors, or if you find it difficult to find some errors. The process (and frustration) of debugging code is an important and normal part of programming. **Appendix D** will help you find and resolve many common errors, and hopefully save you some frustration.

Finding Logical Errors

Often the most difficult errors to find are **logical errors**. Logical errors occur when the program executes but does not work as expected. For example the program may generate incorrect output. Logical errors can be the result of incorrect arithmetic expressions, statements that are out of order, or use of the wrong variables in expressions or print statements. In PHP, errors may also occur as a result of incorrect variable names since if you mistype a variable name, the processor creates a new variable with your "new" name.

The only way to catch logical variables is to test your program carefully. Review your program requirements and consider what tests may be needed to ensure that your program is running correctly. When a program requires user input, run it with various input values so that you can check the results.

When we add selection and loop structures we will need to test code much more thoroughly—this will be covered in later chapters.

Summary

PHP is a programming language that allows you to covert your algorithms into working Web programs. A PHP file may contain a combination of HTML code and PHP code. When the file is processed, the PHP processor reads the file line by line and generates a new document. Any HTML code is written directly into the new document. Any PHP code sections are processed and if these generate output from **print**() statements, this output is inserted into the new document. The print statements can include any combination of text, HTML tags and values from PHP variables and expressions. When the processor reaches the end of the file, the content of the new document is returned to the Web browser.

Character strings, variables and values returned by PHP functions such as number_format() can be joined together by a process known as **concatenation**, using the **concatenation operator** (which is a period in PHP).

A PHP program can receive input from an HTML form. The values from the form are submitted along with the names specified in the form for each input field. The server passes these values and the names to a PHP **$_POST** array. Each value can be extracted from the **$_POST** array by specifying the appropriate name.

Syntax errors will prevent the processor from processing PHP code and will generate error messages that must then be debugged.

Logical errors will not be caught by the processor and will not generate error messages. These are errors in the logic of the program and require testing to find.

Chapter 5 Review Questions

1. PHP is an example of a:
   a. System programming language
   b. Scripting language

2. Which statement is true?
   a. HTML files can contain HTML tags, text and PHP code
   b. PHP files can contain PHP code but not HTML tags
   c. PHP files can contain HTML tags, text and PHP code
   d. PHP files can contain PHP code and text but not HTML tags
   e. PHP files can contain HTML tags but no PHP code

3. Where must the PHP code be located inside a .php file?
   a. Between <?php and ?>
   b. Between <php> and </php>
   c. Between <? and ?>
   d. Between <php? and ?php>
   e. Between <php?> and </? >

4. Every PHP statement must end with:
   a. A period .
   b. A closing bracket >
   c. A double quote "
   d. A semi-colon ;
   e. An equals sign =

5. PHP variables must begin with:
   a. A lower-case letter
   b. An upper-case letter
   c. Either a lower-case letter or an upper-case letter
   d. A number
   e. A dollar sign $

6. Which one of the following is an acceptable name for a PHP variable?
   a. $this one
   b. thisOne
   c. this1
   d. $thisOne
   e. $1ofThese

7. Which one of the following correctly stores the result of 15 * 25 in a PHP variable?
   a. $result = 15 * 25;
   b. 15 * 25 = $result;
   c. result = 15 * 25;
   d. 25 * 15 = result;
   e. 15 * $result * 25;

8. What HTML code is generated after the following statements are executed?

```
$wage = 230.75;
print ("<p>Your wages are wage</p>");
```

   a. <p>Your wages are 230.75</p>
   b. <p>Your wages are 230.75;</p>
   c. <p>Your wages are $230.75</p>
   d. <p>Your wages are </p>
   e. <p>Your wages are wage</p>

9. Look at the following HTML form, then decide which one of the following statements is correct.

```
<form action="zipIt.php" method="post">
<p>Please enter your zip code:
<input type="text" size="20" name="zipCode" /></p>
<input type="submit" value="Submit your zip code" />
</form>
```

   a. When the processor executes zipIt.php, the zip code submitted by the
      user can be extracted from $_POST['zipIt']
   b. When the processor executes zipIt.php, the zip code submitted by the
      user can be extracted from $_POST['$zipIt']
   c. When the processor executes zipIt.php, the zip code submitted by the
      user can be extracted from $_POST['zipCode']
   d. When the processor executes zipIt.php, the zip code submitted by the
      user can be extracted from $_POST['$zipCode']
   e. When the processor executes zipIt.php, the zip code submitted by the
      user can be extracted from $_POST['zip code']

10. The following HTML form passes a value to sleepyTime.php with the name sleep-Hours. Which PHP statement would correctly receive this value and assign it to a PHP variable named $sleepHours?

```
<form action="sleepyTime.php" method="post">
<p>How many hours do you sleep each night:
<input type="text" size="20" name="sleepHours" />
</p>
<input type="submit" value="Can I sleep now?" />
</form>
```

   a. $_POST[$sleepHours] = 'sleepHours';
   b. $_POST['sleepHours'] = $sleepHours;
   c. sleepHours = $_POST[$sleepHours];
   d. $sleepHours = $_POST['sleepHours'];
   e. $sleepHours = $_POST[$sleepHours];

11. What is wrong with the following PHP code segment?

```
$discount = 2.50;
$itemCost = 10.50;
$reducedCost - $itemCost - $discount;
print ("<p>REDUCED FOR QUICK SALE!!
     Your cost is only $$itemCost!</p>");
```

   a. The first and second statements are in the wrong order
   b. The second and third statements are in the wrong order
   c. The third and fourth statements are in the wrong order
   d. The wrong variable is included in the print statement
   e. The value stored in $reducedCost will be 10.50 when it should be 8.00

12. What is wrong with the following PHP code segment?

```
$discount = 2.50;
$reducedCost = $itemCost - $discount;
$itemCost = 10.50;
print ("<p>REDUCED FOR QUICK SALE!!
     Your cost is only $$reducedCost!</p>");
```

   a. The first and second statements are in the wrong order
   b. The second and third statements are in the wrong order
   c. The third and fourth statements are in the wrong order
   d. The wrong variable is included in the print statement
   e. The value stored in $reducedCost will be 10.50 when it should be 8.00

13. What is wrong with the following PHP code segment?

```
$discount = 2.50;
$itemCost = 10.50;
$reducedCost = $itemCost - $Discount;
print ("<p>REDUCED FOR QUICK SALE!!
        Your cost is only $$reducedCost!</p>");
```

    a. The first and second statements are in the wrong order
    b. The second and third statements are in the wrong order
    c. The third and fourth statements are in the wrong order
    d. The wrong variable is included in the print statement
    e. The value stored in $reducedCost will be 10.50 when it should be 8.00

14. What value is stored in $savings after these three PHP instructions are executed?

```
$savings = 500.00;
$deposit = 200;
$savings = $savings + $deposit;
```

    a. 200.00
    b. 500.00
    c. 700.00
    d. 1200.00
    e. Error! you cannot use the same variable on both sides of the = operator.

15. What value is stored in $result after this PHP instruction is executed?

```
$result = 2 + 3 * 5 - 1;
```

    a. 14
    b. 16
    c. 20
    d. 24
    e. 28

16. What value is stored in $result after this PHP instruction is executed?

```
$result = (2 + 3) * (5 - 1);
```

    a. 14
    b. 16
    c. 20
    d. 24
    e. 28

17. The value 2.4 will be stored in $gallonsNeeded after these three PHP instructions are executed. Which PHP function should you use to figure out how many gallon cans of paint you will need to buy (hint: you would need 3 cans)?

```
$areaToPaint = 1200;
$coveragePerGallon = 500;
$gallonsNeeded = $areaToPaint / $coveragePerGallon ;
```

    a. $gallonCansNeeded = round ($gallonsNeeded);
    b. $gallonCansNeeded = floor ($gallonsNeeded);
    c. $gallonCansNeeded = ceil ($gallonsNeeded);
    d. $gallonCansNeeded = pow ($gallonsNeeded);
    e. $gallonCansNeeded = sqrt ($gallonsNeeded);

18. What will the following print statement generate?

```
print("<p>She said \"You're hired!\" </p>");
```

    a. She said \"You're hired!\"
    b. <p>She said \"You're hired!\" </p>
    c. She said "You're hired!" </p>
    d. <p>She said "You're hired!" </p>
    e. You cannot include quotes in a print statement!

19. The arithmetic is wrong in following PHP statement (should be 65 - $age). Is this a syntax error or a logical error?

```
$yearsToRetire = $age - 65;
```

    a. Syntax error
    b. Logical error

20. The following print statement is missing a closing quote. Is this a syntax error or a logical error?

```
print ("<p>I guess I have an error - I'm melting!</p>);
```

    a. Syntax error
    b. Logical error

Chapter 5 Code Exercises

Don't be surprised if you find these exercises a little frustrating as you get used to PHP syntax. Don't feel bad if you struggle to get your programs working—this is a normal part of the programming process and all programmers experience it. Developing the algorithms first helps minimize the pain! It is always a good idea to take your time, step away from the computer if you get stuck, come back and look through your code carefully.

Your Chapter 5 code exercises can be found in your **Chapter05** folder. This folder is included in your customized XAMPP installation at the following location:

> xampplite\htdocs\WebTech\coursework\Chapter05

Type your name and the date in the **Author** and **Date** sections of each file as you work on each exercise.

Debugging Exercises

Your **Chapter05** folder contains a number of "FixIt" files. Each of these files contains PHP code that has an error of some kind. The type of error is indicated. You will need to run each program in order to see the errors, and to debug and test the code to see if it works correctly. For example to run **fixIt1.php**, first run the Web server, then use the URL:

> http://localhost/WebTech/coursework/Chapter05/fixIt1.php

Code Modification Exercises

Your Chapter05 folder contains a number of "Modify" files. Each pair of files contains HTML and PHP code that needs to be modified to meet a requirement. The requirements are included in each file. Modify the algorithms as specified, being careful to make changes to the .html and .php files as directed.

Code Completion Exercises

1. Create a PHP program named **paintEstimate.php** based on the processing requirements outlined in the paintEstimate exercise at the end of Chapter 3. The complete code for paintEstimate.html has been provided in the **Chapter05** folder, along with some code for **paintEstimate.php** to save you some time. Your job is to add the necessary PHP code to **paintEstimate.php**. Be careful to use the same names and case to receive the input values from **paintEstimate.html**.

IMPORTANT: Use the **ceil**() function to round up the number of gallons of paint needed to cover the room to the next whole number, and also to round up the number of hours of labor. You can't buy gallons in fractions, and we will assume the labor is paid in hourly increments. Also use the **number_format**() function to display your currency outputs to two decimal places.

In order to test your code, you will need to start your Web server if it is not already running, and then open **paintEstimate.html** in a browser window (be sure you are using a URL and not a Windows address). Enter test input into the form, and then submit for processing by **paintEstimate.php**. Use the sample data listed in the exercise at the end of Chapter 3 to test your results (room length = 20, room width = 15, room height = 8). Using this sample data, since you have rounded up the paint coverage, your paint cost will now be 3 * 17.00 = 51.00, and your labor cost will now be 5 * 25 = 125.00, so the total cost will be 176.00.

2. Create a PHP program named **softwareOrder.php** based on the processing requirements outlined in the **softwareOrder** exercise at the end of Chapter 3. The complete code for **softwareOrder.html** has been provided in the **Chapter05** folder, along with some code for **softwareOrder.php** to save you some time. Your job is to add the necessary PHP code to **softwareOrder.php**. Be careful to use the same names and case to receive the input values from **softwareOrder.html**.

In order to test your code, you will need to start your Web server if it is not already running, then open **softwareOrder.html** in a browser window (be sure you are opening the file using a URL and not a Windows address). Enter test input into the form, and then submit for processing by **softwareOrder.php**. Use the sample data listed in the exercise at the end of Chapter 3 to test your results.

3. Create a PHP program named **travel.php** based on the processing requirements outlined in the travel exercise at the end of Chapter 3. The complete code for **travel.html** has been provided in the **Chapter05** folder, along with some code for **travel.php** to save you some time. Your job is to add the necessary PHP code to **travel.php**. Be careful to use the same names and case to receive the input values from travel.html.

In order to test your code, you will need to start your Web server if it is not already running, then open **travel.html** in a browser window (be sure you are opening the file using a URL and not a Windows address). Enter test input into the form, and then submit for processing by **travel.php**. Use the sample data listed in the exercise at the end of Chapter 3 to test your results.

4. Create a PHP program named **gameIntro.php** based on the processing requirements outlined in the gameIntro exercise at the end of Chapter 3. The complete code for **gameIntro.html** has been provided in the **Chapter05** folder, along with some code for **gameIntro.php** to save you some time. Your job is to add the necessary PHP code to **gameIntro.php**. Be careful to use the same names and case to receive the input values from **gameIntro.html**.

In order to test your code, you will need to start your Web server if it is not already running, then open **gameIntro.html** in a browser window (be sure you are opening the file using a URL and not a Windows address). Enter test input into the form, and then submit for processing by **gameIntro.php**. Use the sample data listed in the exercise at the end of Chapter 3 to test your results (after purchasing 20 health tokens, 10 experience tokens, and 25 supply tokens, the character should have spent 8 gold pieces). An example of the output is shown in Figure 5-4. Note that the character's name and type should be displayed in the heading.

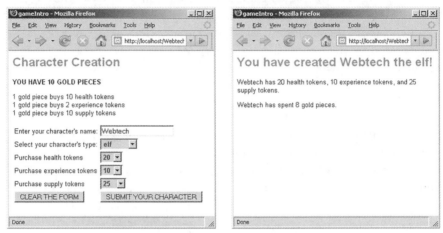

Figure 5-4: gameIntro.html and gameIntro.php screenshots

5. Copy your **event.html** file from your Chapter04 folder to your Chapter05 folder. Now create a PHP program named **event.php** based on the processing requirements outlined in the event exercise at the end of Chapter 3. Test your code by starting your Web server if it is not already running, opening a Web browser, and entering the URL:

    http://localhost/Webtech/coursework/Chapter05/event.html

    Enter any test input into the form, and then submit for processing by event.php. For example if you enter 10 for the number of tickets the program should display a total cost of 350.

6. Copy your **fuelCost.html** file from your Chapter04 folder to your Chapter05 folder. Now create a PHP program named **fuelCost.php** based on the processing requirements outlined in the fuelCost exercise at the end of Chapter 3. Test your code by starting your Web server if it is not already running, opening a Web browser, and entering the URL:

    http://localhost/Webtech/coursework/Chapter05/fuelCost.html

    Enter 20 as the mpg, 100 as miles traveled, and 3.00 as the cost per gallon. This should generate a result of 15.0. Test two or three times using numbers of your own and make sure that the program is working correctly.

Chapter 6

Persistence —
Saving and Retrieving Data

Intended Learning Outcomes

After completing this chapter, you should be able to:

- Distinguish between transient and persistent data.
- Describe the advantages of a client/server design that includes remote data storage.
- Contrast the use of text files with a RDBMS for data storage.
- List the basic operations that can be performed on a text file.
- Utilize the fopen(), fgets(), and fclose() functions to read data from a text file.
- Utilize the fopen(), fputs(), and fclose() functions to write data to a text file.
- Recognize and utilize escape characters in text output.
- Utilize the fopen(), fputs(), and fclose() functions to append data to a text file.
- Explain the process of parsing a character string that contains a data record.
- Utilize the explode() and list() functions to parse a character string.
- Apply PHP file-handling functions to process multiple files.

Introduction

In order to be useful, a program must usually receive input, perform processing tasks, and generate output. So far our programs have received input from HTML forms submitted by the user, and generated output as new HTML pages to be viewed by the user. The pages containing the forms and the pages displaying the program's response constitute a **user interface**.

Input and output is not restricted to interactions with a user. Programs may also interact with various devices in order to: issue and receive **instructions** (for example to control a machine); send and receive **messages** (for example to conduct transactions with other programs); and **store and retrieve data** (for example to create, query or update files or database tables). These devices be local or remote and may include disk drives, network servers, microphones, cameras, scanners, printers, robots, or machines of any kind.

In order to interact with any device, a program must typically: (1) open a connection; (2) perform the required input and/or output operations; and (3) close the connection.

In this chapter you will learn to distinguish between temporary (transient) data and data that is stored (persistent data), and compare the use of text files and databases for persistent data storage. You will learn the basic operations needed to process text files, and implement these operations using PHP file-handling functions to read, write and append text files located on a Web server. You will also learn how to extract (parse) multiple data values from a single line that has been read from a text file.

The Difference Between Persistent and Transient Data

As human beings, we receive and generate data of all kinds every moment of our lives, eating, sleeping, walking, talking, listening, making phone calls, working, playing. Much of this data is not recorded and is easily forgotten. For example, you may be out walking and someone asks you for directions. You respond with appropriate instructions. No record is kept and so the data associated with this event is lost.

Other kinds of data is not lost. If you read a book or listen to a CD, or make a list, you are working with data that you (or someone else) can access again at a later date. That's because the data is **stored** in some form or another.

In the world of computing, data that is used and then forgotten is known as **transient** data. More precisely transient data refers to data that is produced while an application is running and lost when the application ends. Keyboard input and display output are examples of transient data because keyboards and monitors do not "remember" the data once it has been transmitted. Data that is stored in a program's variables is also transient since variables are created while an application is running and disappear when the application ends. Input that is received as a stream of data from devices such as a microphone or satellite or scanner is also transient. Similarly output that sends data to a dynamic Web page is transient.

Data whose life extends beyond the lifetime of any of the programs that process it is known as **persistent data**. Persistent data is **stored** so that it can be accessed and modified by programs as needed. Persistent data is commonly stored in files and databases, located on fixed disks, optical disks, tapes, or other storage media. If your application reads data from a storage medium, or writes data to a storage medium, then the application is working with persistent data.

Many programs work with a combination of transient and persistent data. For example, you might write a program that asks the user for information of some kind and then stores the information in a file for later use. In this case the user inputs and screen displays may be considered transient data, while the data that the program writes to the file is persistent since it will remain in the file after the program ends. Or you may write a program that reads data from a file, then displays the information to the user. In this case the input is derived from persistent data stored in the file, and the output to the screen is transient data.

Persistent data stored in files or databases may be used by many different programs, for many different purposes. Consider a data file that contains weekly timesheet data for employees (for example the first name, last name, hours worked and hourly pay for each employee). Four different programs might process this file for different purposes. Program **A** might allow a clerical worker to type an employee's timesheet information into a form, then add this information to the timesheet file. Program **B** might read all the timesheets in the timesheet file, calculate the weekly wage for each employee, and print paychecks. Program **C** might read the timesheet file and develop useful statistics for a payroll manager (for example the total wages, the average wage, highest wage, lowest wage, etc). Program **D** might provide a planning tool (for example the program might read the hourly pay of all employees and create a new file showing what each employee will earn if they receive a 10% raise).

In a client/server environment, the employee data file can be located on a server and the various programs that operate on the file can be located on the same server. Client programs can then interact with the appropriate server programs as needed (Figure 6-1).

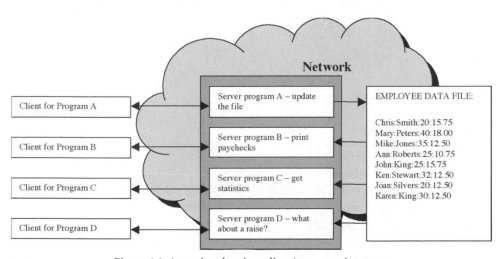

Figure 6-1: Accessing data in a client/server environment

Here are some the advantages of a network-based design when working with stored data:

- The data file is stored in one secure, central location (the server) and can be easily backed up and maintained. Just imagine if each program or each user worked with their own copy of this file! What would happen if a new employee needed to be added, or other changes had to be made?
- The only programs with direct access to the data file are also stored on the server, so these programs can be easily modified without any need to change programs running on client computers. Similarly new programs can be added without any need to change existing programs, for example a new program could be added to compare the hourly wages of male and female employees.
- Client interfaces can be designed for specific users to allow access to appropriate programs on the server. For example a manager might need a client interface that provides access to Program C and Program D, while an administrative assistant may only have access to Program A.

Files and Databases

Files may be used to store data in many different formats. **Text files** contain data as a series of lines of plain text. Text files may be used to contain small and large data sets, from a few lines that contain, for example, the current status of a game when a user hits the Save button, to thousands of lines that contain for example, hourly readings from weather stations all across the country. In either case, each line in the file is handled as a character string and can be processed by an application or viewed in a text editor.

Data is often stored in the form of **records**. A record is simply a grouping of related data. In our timesheet example, an employee's timesheet record consists of four data items: the employee's first name, last name, hours worked and hourly pay.

Text files may be used for storing records (usually one record on each line) but this approach is not very efficient when it comes to storing large amounts of data that must be processed quickly and efficiently. Any program that processes a file of records must provide all the instructions necessary to perform any required data operations such as inserting, updating, or adding records, sorting the contents of the file, or searching the file for specific information. The use of text files is also not very secure since text files can be easily viewed by any person or program with access to the file.

Databases provide a much more sophisticated solution for storing data records. The most widely used type of database is a **relational database**, which allows an organization to store data in database **tables** consisting of rows (**records**) and columns (**fields**). Table 6-1 shows an example of a relational database table to store timesheet records with four fields in each record.

firstName	lastName	hoursWorked	hourlyWage
Chris	Smith	20	15.75
Mary	Peters	40	18.00
Mike	Jones	35	12.50
Ann	Roberts	25	10.75
John	King	25	15.75
Ken	Stewart	32	12.50
Joan	Silvers	20	12.50
Karen	King	30	12.50

Table 6-1: Example of a relational database table

Database tables can be related to one another to avoid duplication of information and simplify management. Databases incorporate many useful functions that facilitate table creation, data updates and deletions, data queries, and report creation. A **Relational Database Management System (RDBMS)** is software that provides a full range of management tools for working with databases. This greatly simplifies software development since other programs can call the functions provided by the RDBMS rather than providing their own functions. A RDBMS also implements sophisticated security so that access by people or programs to various tables and even individual fields can be controlled, based on ID's and passwords.

If you write programs that interact with databases, you will need to learn the language that the RDBMS uses to receive instructions. The most commonly used language for this purpose is **Structured Query Language** (SQL). There are various versions of SQL, used for working with different RDBMS systems.

Files and databases are both extremely important mechanisms for data storage, and the PHP language is designed to work effectively with both. In this chapter, we will explore basic procedures associated with text file processing as an introduction to working with persistent data. Later, in Chapter 14, we will learn how to use PHP to connect to a MySQL database.

Working with a Text File

In order to work with a text file, a program must first **open** the file. There are basically three ways to open a text file:

Opening a File for Read Operations

This allows the program to read data from the file, in other words to use the file as a source of input. Assuming the file exists, this operation opens the file and positions a **read pointer** at the beginning of the file. Once the file has been opened for read operations, the program may issue instructions to read data from the file one line at a time.

After each read instruction, the read pointer advances so that the next read operation will access the next line in the file.

Opening a File for Write Operations

This allows the program to write to the file, in other words to use the file for output. This operation always creates a new file even if a file with the same name already exists in the folder location. If a file with the same name already exists in the folder location, it is replaced by the new file so be very careful when using this operation!

Once the new file has been created it is opened for writing and the write marker is located at the beginning of the file. Each time data is added to the file, it is added to the location of the write marker and the write marker is advanced to the end of the data, ready for the next write operation.

You will open a file for **write** operations when you want to **replace** data in an existing file with new data. This is useful for example when saving the most recent status of a game (player name, score, position, etc), or when you want to store your most recent list of employees. In these cases you want to replace a file containing older data with a file containing the current data. Any program or person that needs to read this data can open the file confident that the file contains the latest data.

Opening a File for Append Operations

This allows the program to write data to the end of an existing file. If the specified file does not already exist in the folder location, the file is created just as if the file had been opened for writing. The write marker is positioned at the end of any existing data ready for the next write operation.

You will open a file for **append** operations when you want to **add** data to an existing file. This is useful, for example, when adding a survey response to a file that contains a list of previous responses, or adding the latest hourly reading of weather data (temperature, precipitation, humidity, etc.) to a file that already weather readings for the previous hours of the day. In these cases it's important to add, and not replace, data, so that **all** of the data that has been stored in the file remains available.

Closing a Text File

When a program that has opened a file no longer needs to access it, the file should be **closed.** The close operation places an **End-Of-File** (EOF) marker at the end of the file and releases the file for access by other programs. This is very important. If the file is not closed properly, it may be corrupted and the contents lost.

As we have seen, a single file may serve multiple programs that need to access the file for different purposes or different users. Files should therefore be opened and closed as efficiently as possible, since an open file may not be accessible by other programs waiting to use it. Good programming practice is to: open a file only when the program is ready to work with it; close the file as soon as the program has finished using it. This is especially important in the case of network programming where hundreds or thousands of programs may need to access the same file within a short period of time (for example on a busy Web site).

Reading Data from a Text File

Let's start with an example where we open a text file, read data from the file, close the file, and then process the data. Consider a file named **scores.txt** that contains five scores on separate lines as follows:

89
77
92
69
87

Here is a program requirement to process the **scores.txt** file:

averageScore requirement:

Read the five scores from the scores.txt file, then calculate and display the average score.

Here is a solution algorithm for **averageScore.php**:

```
averageScore.php algorithm:
  Open scores.txt as scoresFile for reading
  Read score1, score2, score3, score4, score5 from scoresFile
  Close scoresFile
  avgScore = (score1 + score2 + score3 + score4 + score5) / 5
  Display averageScore
END
```

Note that we are using some new words in our pseudocode.

Open

Use **Open** to indicate that the program must open a file and specify whether the file is to be opened for reading, writing or appending. We indicate that we are opening the

scores.txt file as **scoresFile**, since programs use variables to represent the data connection (sometime called the **file handle**) to sources such as text files. Notice that, once the file has been opened, the remaining instructions in the algorithm refer to the variable **scoresFile**, and not the actual file named **scores.txt**.

Read

Use **Read** to indicate that the program must read a value from a file into a variable. In this example, we read the values from five lines of the file into five program variables. The program then uses the values stored in these variables to calculate the average score.

Close

Use **Close** to indicate that the program must close a file. Note that our algorithm is designed to close the file as soon as the required data has been read from the file into program variables. The algorithm would be just as correct if the close operation was left until **after** the instructions to calculate and display the average score, but this would not be good programming practice. As mentioned previously, it is good practice to close a file as soon as the program no longer needs it.

PHP Functions to Read Data from a Text File

Here is the PHP code for the averageScore algorithm (this program is available as **averageScore.php** in the **samples** folder):

```
<html>
<head>
  <title>AVERAGE SCORE</title>
  <link rel="stylesheet" type="text/css" href="sample.css" />
</head>
<body>
  <?php
    $scoresFile = fopen("scores.txt","r");

    $score1 = fgets($scoresFile);
    $score2 = fgets($scoresFile);
    $score3 = fgets($scoresFile);
    $score4 = fgets($scoresFile);
    $score5 = fgets($scoresFile);

    fclose($scoresFile);
```

```
    $avgScore = ($score1 + $score2 + $score3 + $score4 +
        $score5) / 5;

    print ("<h1>AVERAGE SCORE</h1>");

    print("<p>The average score is $avgScore.</p>");

    print ("<p><a href=\"averageScore.html\">Return to
        averageScore form</a></p>");
  ?>
</body>
</html>
```

Code Example: averageScore.php

Let's review this code line by line.

```
$scoresFile = fopen("scores.txt","r");
```

This instruction uses the PHP **fopen**() function to open a file. The first parameter "**scores.txt**" indicates the name of the file to open. The second parameter "**r**" indicates how the file is to be opened. In this case the file is to be opened for reading ("**r**"), with the read pointer set to the beginning of the file.

The **fopen**() function provides a file reference (known as a **file handle**) that the program can use to refer to its connection with the file data in subsequent statements. This reference is stored in the **$scoresFile** variable—note that the **fgets**() and **fclose**() functions both use the **$scoresFile** variable to refer to the file. Always follow this practice—refer to the file variable and not the actual file name once the file has been opened.

```
$score1 = fgets($scoresFile);
```

The **fgets**() function reads and returns the next line from the file. The data stored in this line (in this case the value 89) is assigned to the **$score1** variable. The **fgets**() function always reads the **entire** next line in a file.

When you use the **fgets**() function you must specify the variable that refers to the file (in this case, **$scoresFile**). This is important: since a program is capable of processing multiple files at the same time, the processor must know which file to read each time a program statement calls the **fgets**() function.

Once a line has been read from the file, the read marker advances to the start of the next line.

```
$score2 = fgets($scoresFile);
$score3 = fgets($scoresFile);
$score4 = fgets($scoresFile);
$score5 = fgets($scoresFile);
```

In each of these lines, the **fgets**() function reads and returns the next line from the file, and the content of the line is then assigned to a score variable. After each read operation, the read marker is advanced to the next line. In this way the program processes the file, one line at a time.

```
fclose($scoresFile);
```

The **fclose**() function is used to close the file. It is good programming practice to close a file as soon as your program has finished using it. This ensures that the file is available for processing by other programs as soon as possible.

```
$avgScore = ($score1+$score2+$score3+$score4+$score5) / 5;

print("<p>The average score is $avgScore. </p>");
```

This is more familiar code. The average is calculated and stored in **$avgScore**. The **print**() function outputs the average score in HTML format. Figure 6-2 shows how the program's output will appear as a Web page. The first screen shows **averageScore.html** which is used to provide the user with a **submit** button to run **averageScore.php** and the second screen shows the results after **averageScore.php** has been processed.

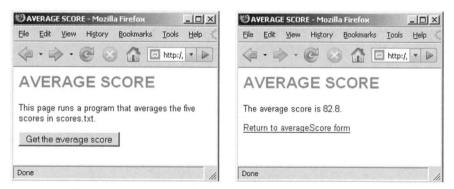

Figure 6-2: averageScore.html and averageScore.php screenshots

You may have a number of questions at this time, for example "What if the file contains hundreds of line of data?", or "What if I don't know how many lines might be in the file when the program executes?" These are great questions. In this chapter we will learn basic operations on files. In later chapters we will learn how to use loop structures to process larger files and files of unknown length.

Writing Data to a Text File

Now consider the following requirement:

WriteScores requirement:

Write a program that asks the user for five student scores and the name of a file to store them. The program should receive the scores, write them to the file that the user specified (each score on a separate line) and report back to the user.

For this requirement we will first create an HTML document (**writeScores.html**) that contains a form to receive the five scores and the name of the file that the scores are to be written to. Then we will create a PHP file (**writeScores.php**) that will receive the scores and file name, write the scores to the file, and report back to the user.

Here is the algorithm for **writeScores.html**:

```
writeScores.html algorithm:
   Prompt the user for score1, score2, score3, score4, score5
   Get score1, score2, score3, score4, score5
   Prompt the user for the name of the file to store the scores
   Get fileName
   Submit score1, score2, score3, score4, score5, fileName to
      writeScores.php
END
```

Here is the code for **writeScores.html** (we are using a table to line up the prompts and input boxes nicely):

```
<html>
<head>
   <title>Save Your Scores</title>
   <link rel="stylesheet" type="text/css" href="sample.css" />
</head>
<body>
   <h1>Save Your Scores</h1>
   <p>
   <form action="writeScores.php" method="post">
     <table border="1">
     <tr><td>Score #1: </td><td><input type="text" size="5"
       name="score1" /></td></tr>
     <tr><td>Score #2: </td><td><input type="text" size="5"
       name="score2" /></td></tr>
     <tr><td>Score #3: </td><td><input type="text" size="5"
       name="score3" /></td></tr>
```

```
<tr><td>Score #4: </td><td><input type="text" size="5"
   name="score4" /></td></tr>
<tr><td>Score #5: </td><td><input type="text" size="5"
   name="score5" /></td></tr>
</table>

<p>Enter the name of the file to store the scores. (WARNING:
if this file already exists, the data in the file will be
lost). Include the file extension, for example myscores.txt.
</p>
<p>File name: <input type="text" size="20" name="fileName" />
</p>
<p>
<input type="submit" value="Save the Scores" />
<input type="reset" value="Clear and Start Again" />
</p>
</form>
</p>
</body>
</html>
```

Code Example: writeScores.html

Note that the page includes careful instructions to the user with regard to creating a file name. This is important since our PHP program will attempt to create a file with the name that the user provides.

Here is the algorithm for **writeScores.php**:

```
writeScores.php algorithm:
   Receive score1, score2, score3, score4, score5, fileName from
      writeScores.html
   Open fileName as scoresFile for writing
   Write score1, score2, score3, score4, score5 to scoresFile
   Close scoresFile
   Display "File Created" message to user
END
```

Note that we use the word **Write** when we wish to indicate an instruction to write data to a file in pseudocode.

PHP Functions to Write Data to a Text File

The process of writing to files in PHP is similar to that of reading files. First we need to open the file for writing using the **fopen**() function, except that we now specify "**w**" instead of "**r**". If the file does not exist the file is created. If the file already exists it is replaced, so be careful how you use the "**w**" option!

Once the file has been opened for writing we can use the **fputs**() function as needed to write data to the file. When we are finished writing to the file, we close it using the **fclose**() function.

Here is the code for **writeScores.php**:

```
<html>
<head>
  <title>Save Your Scores</title>
  <link rel="stylesheet" type="text/css" href="sample.css" />
</head>
<body>
  <?php

    $fileName = $_POST['fileName'];

    $score1 = $_POST['score1'];
    $score2 = $_POST['score2'];
    $score3 = $_POST['score3'];
    $score4 = $_POST['score4'];
    $score5 = $_POST['score5'];

    $scoresFile = fopen("$fileName","w");

    fputs($scoresFile, "$score1\n");
    fputs($scoresFile, "$score2\n");
    fputs($scoresFile, "$score3\n");
    fputs($scoresFile, "$score4\n");
    fputs($scoresFile, "$score5\n");

    fclose($scoresFile );

    print (" <h1>The following scores have been stored in
        $fileName:</h1>");
    print("<p>$score1<br />$score2<br />$score3<br />
        $score4<br />$score5</p>");
    print ("<p><a href=\"writeScores.html\">Return to
        writeScores form</a></p>");
  ?>
</body>
</html>
```

Code Example: writeScores.php

Let's review the PHP code carefully:

```php
$fileName = $_POST['fileName'];
$score1 = $_POST['score1'];
$score2 = $_POST['score2'];
$score3 = $_POST['score3'];
$score4 = $_POST['score4'];
$score5 = $_POST['score5'];
```

These six statements extract the values that were input by the user from the PHP $_POST array (the five scores and the name of the file that the user wants the scores to be written to).

```php
$scoresFile = fopen("$fileName","w");
```

This statement opens a file for writing. We can also specify a file name directly in our fopen() function, for example **fopen("scores.txt", "w")**, but here we open a file that has the name supplied by the user. That file name was received from the form and stored in the variable **$fileName**. Be careful: if you are using a variable that contains a filename, use the variable name including the $ symbol. If you are specifying a file name directly, include the file extension and do **not** use the $ symbol!

If the file to be opened for writing already exists, it is overwritten. If it does not exist, the file is created.

```php
fputs($scoresFile, "$score1\n");
fputs($scoresFile, "$score2\n");
fputs($scoresFile, "$score3\n");
fputs($scoresFile, "$score4\n");
fputs($scoresFile, "$score5\n");
```

The **fputs()** function is used to write data to a file. The first argument is the variable that refers to the file (in this case the variable **$scoresFile**) and the second argument is a string containing the data that is to be written to the file.

Note that, in each case, the output consists of a variable (for example **$score1**) followed immediately by **\n**. The **fputs()** function does not automatically add a new line after writing data to the file. The **\n** represents **the new line** character and is an example of an **escape character**. Escape characters are explained in more detail below. If you do **not** include newline characters in these statements, all five **fputs()** instructions will add data to the same line (try it).

You can include multiple **new line** characters in a single **fputs()** statement, so instead of writing the five scores using five **fputs()** statements, you could actually write this using a single **fputs()** instruction:

```
fputs($scoresFile,"$score1\n$score2\n$score3\n$score4\n$score5\n");
```

Notice that the value from each variable is written to the file followed by a new line marker, so the values are written on five separate lines.

```
fclose($scoresFile);
```

The **fclose**() function closes the file. As always it is important to close a file once the program is done using it.

```
print(" <h1>The following scores have been stored in
    $fileName:</h1>");

print("<p>$score1<br />$score2<br />$score3<br />
    $score4<br />$score5</p>");

print(" <p><a href=\"writeScores.html\">Return to writeScores
    form</a></p> ");
```

This PHP code generates some HTML that informs the user that the file was created. Note the use of the break <br /> tags to list the scores on separate lines.

Figure 6-3 shows a sample interaction.

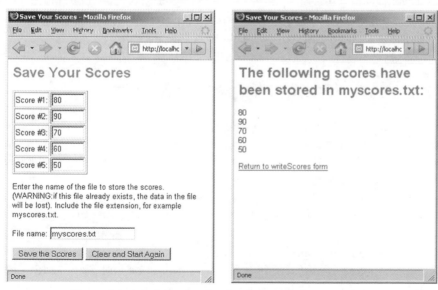

Figure 6-3: writeScores.html and writeScores.php screenshots

In this example the user types the name **myscores.txt** as the name of the file to write to. Here is the content of **myscores.txt** after this program has executed:

```
80
90
70
60
50
```

Try running this program a few times and type in different scores each time, using the same file name. Now try typing the same scores each time, using a different file name. Check the contents of the files that you create as you do this. Every time you specify a different file name, the PHP program creates a new file. Every time you specify the same file name, the old file is replaced.

Be Careful to Avoid Security Holes!

The idea of asking the user to supply a file name that will be used to open a file for writing is acceptable **only** when working with trusted users under secure conditions (for example for testing purposes). This would be quite dangerous under most conditions—do you see why? Since the user can enter any file a name and path, and since opening a file for write operations will replace an existing file with the same name, you are essentially giving a user the power to delete any file that your program can access! This is an example of a **security hole**, where an application contains a feature that allows a malicious user to perform some inappropriate action.

Using Escape Characters

As we just learned, when you are writing data to a text file, you sometimes need to specify when to begin a new line. We do this using the new line character **\n**. This is an example of an **escape character**. Escape characters are two-character sequences to represent characters that could not otherwise be included in output statements. Each escape sequence consists of a back slash \ followed by another keyboard character that indicates the actual character that is to be generated, for example **\n**.

Another useful escape character is \" which represents a double quote. Why can't we just type the double quote directly when we need this character in our output? Since double quotes are used to indicate the beginning and end of the entire character string, we have to use an escape character if the text actually contains a double quote, otherwise the processor would assume that this double quote indicates the end of the character string.

Here are the most commonly used escape characters:

```
\t    generates a tab
\n    starts a new line
\"    generates a double quote "
\'    generates a single quote '
\\    generates a back slash \
```

Note that, since the back slash is used to indicate an escape character, we must use a **double** back slash if we wish to output the back slash character itself!

Here is an output example showing the use of a number of escape characters:

```
fputs($someFile, "He said \"That\'s fine,\"\n\tand then
   left.\n\nThe End.");
```

would store the following text in the file (note the quotes, new line and tab):

```
He said "That's fine,"
   and then left.

The End.
```

Note that to end a line and then generate a second blank line you will use two new line characters consecutively: \n\n.

Escape Characters and HTML Tags

Do not confuse the use of escape characters such as the \n newline character that is used to add new lines to text output with HTML tags such as the <br /> or <p> tags. HTML tags are used to instruct the Web browser how to format text on a Web page. The newline character is used to add new lines to strings of text. We have seen how a newline character can be used to add a new line to text that is written to a text file by the **fputs**() function. You can also include a new line character in a PHP **print** statement but this will only add a line break in the HTML code that is being generated, just as if you were typing the HTML code in a text editor and pressed the Enter key. Using a newline character in a print statement will not produce a line break in the Web page that that the browser displays to the user, for this you must use the appropriate HTML tag.

Using PHP to Append Data to Files

Appending data to files is similar to writing data to files except that, with an append operation, if the file already exists the data will be **added** to the end of the existing file content. In other words existing files are not lost with append operations.

Append operations are useful whenever you need to add data to an existing file. This is a very common requirement. For example **log files** are files that keep track of some kind of activity. A print server application might append a message to a **print** log file each time a printer is used. A business owner might use an application that appends the mileage of each business trip to a **mileage** log file. A program that is processing a file of scores might append a message to an **error** log file each time a score is found that is out of range.

When data is appended to a file, any data already stored in the file is preserved. The file grows over time as new data is added.

Let's use the mileage log example to learn how to append data to a file. Many small business owners must keep track of the miles that they travel on each business-related trip for tax purposes. Consider the following requirement:

MileageLog requirement:

Write a program that allows a small business owner to submit travel mileage for a business trip. The program should receive the mileage and append this to a text file named mileageLog.txt, then inform the user that the data has been added.

The user can use the form to submit mileage as often as needed.

According to this requirement, when a user enters a mileage amount into the form and presses the Submit button, the input will be appended to the **mileageLog.txt** file.

Here is the pseudocode for the HTML document that will receive and submit the mileage:

```
mileageLog.html algorithm:
   Prompt for mileage
   Get mileage
   Submit mileage to mileageLog.php
END
```

Here is the code for **mileageLog.html**:

```
<html>
<head>
   <title>Mileage Log</title>
   <link rel="stylesheet" type="text/css" href="sample.css" />
</head>
```

```
<body>
  <h1>Mileage Log</h1>

  <form action="mileageLog.php" method="post">
    <p>Enter your mileage:
      <input type="text" size="5" name="mileage" /></p>
    <p><input type="submit" value="Submit mileage" /></p>
  </form>
</body>
</html>
```

Code Example: mileageLog.html

Here is the pseudocode for the PHP program that will receive the user input and append the data to the **mileageLog.txt** file:

```
mileageLog.php algorithm:
  Receive mileage from mileageLog.html

  Open mileageLog.txt as logFile for appending
  Write mileage to logFile
  Close logFile

  Display "Mileage has been recorded" message to the user
END
```

PHP Functions to Append Data to a Text File

We use the same PHP functions to **append** to a file that we use to **write** to a file. The only difference is that we use "**a**" for append rather than "**w**" for write in our **fopen**() function. Here is the PHP code for **mileageLog.php**:

```
<html>
<head>
  <title>Mileage Log</title>
  <link rel="stylesheet" type="text/css" href="sample.css" />
</head>
<body>
  <?php
    $mileage = $_POST['mileage'];

    $logFile = fopen("mileageLog.txt","a");
    fputs($logFile, "$mileage\n");
    fclose($logFile);
```

```
    print(" <h1>Your mileage submission ($mileage) has
        been recorded:</h1>");
    print(" <p><a href=\"mileageLog.html\">Submit
        another mileage</a></p>");
  ?>
</body>
</html>
```

Code Example: mileageLog.php

Let's review the PHP code line by line:

```
$mileage = $_POST['mileage'];
```

Here we extract the input from the PHP $_POST array and assign the value to a variable.

```
$logFile = fopen("mileageLog.txt","a");
```

This statement opens a file named **mileageLog.txt** for appending ("**a**"). If the file does not exist it is created. If the file does exist, the write marker is moved to the **end** of the existing data in the file.

```
fputs($logFile, "$mileage\n");
```

The **fputs**() function is used to write the mileage amount to the file. This function is used in exactly the same way whether a file is opened for write or append operations. Since the file was opened for appending, the data will be added to the end of any data that is already stored in the file.

It is important to include the **new line** character at the end of the output string so that the next time a mileage amount is added, it will appear on the next line of the file and not on the same line.

```
fclose($scoresFile );
```

The **fclose**() function closes the file. As always it is important to close a file once the program is done using it. The file can then be reopened when another survey is submitted, or when it is time to process the surveys in the file.

Figure 6-4 shows a sample interaction.

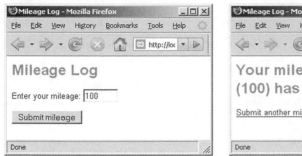 

Figure 6-4: mileageLog.html and mileageLog.php screenshots

Open **mileageLog.html** yourself a few times and add new mileage amount each time. Each time you do this, check the contents of **mileageLog.txt** and observe that a new line is added to this file each time a new amount is submitted. For example here is how the content of **mileageLog.txt** might appear after submitting three mileage amounts:

```
100
45
234
```

Processing Files that Contain Complete Records on Each Line

Consider the following program requirement:

wageReport1 requirement:

Write a program that reads an employee timesheet record from a file named timesheet.txt. The file contains the employee's first name, last name, hours worked and hourly wage on a single line, for example:

Mike:Smith:20:12.55

The program should calculate and display the weekly wage.

What makes this requirement different from our previous file-processing examples?

Previously each line in our data files have contained only a single data value (for example a score or a mileage amount). As a result, each **fgets**() instruction retrieved a **single** value. Often, however, each line of a data file contains a **record** of some kind. Recall that a record is a grouping of related data items. A line that contains an entire record will include **multiple** data items. In this case, a single line in **timesheet.txt** contains a timesheet record with four values (first name, last name, hours worked and hourly wage).

Storing an entire record on a single line is a common practice since a single file can then easily contain any number of records, each record stored on a separate line. We introduce this topic by considering how to process a file that contains a single record.

Note that the four data values are separated by colons. When multiple values are stored on a single line, we need to some way to **separate** each value, otherwise a program that reads the data from the file will have no way to identify each value. Imagine for example if, instead of:

```
Mike:Smith:20:12.55
```

the line in the file looked like this:

```
MikeSmith2012.55
```

Can you see the problem? How can a program decide where each value ends and the next value begins?

To avoid this problem, standard practice is to add **separators** or **delimiters** between each value. The separator can be any character, as long as it will not appear in the values themselves. You may have heard the phrase "comma-delimited file" or "tab-delimited file". These phrases indicate a file where the values on each line are separated by commas or tabs respectively. Any program that is designed to read the data from the file must know what delimiter was used in order to know how to retrieve the separate values (we will learn how to do this shortly).

In our example we are using colons as delimiters.

PHP Functions to Parse a Delimited Character String

Recall that the PHP **fgets**() function reads an entire line from a text file. When we use **fgets**() to read a line containing a record with multiple values, the entire record is read from the file as a single character string. So if we use **fgets**() to read the line

```
Mike:Smith:20:12.55
```

and store this in a variable, the variable will contain a character string with the entire contents of the line, in other words: "Mike:Smith:20:12.55".

We need to extract the four values from this string in order to work with each value individually. The process of extracting values from a larger data string is known as **parsing**. We must parse the string "Mike:Smith:20:12.55" in order to extract the employee's first name, last name, hours worked this week, and hourly rate of pay. Once we have extracted the four values and stored these in separate variables, we can perform the required processing.

Here is the pseudocode for **wageReport1.php**:

```
wageReport1.php algorithm:
   Open timesheet.txt as timesheetFile for reading
   Read employeeRecord from timesheetFile
   Close timesheetFile

   Get firstName, lastName, hours, payRate from employeeRecord
   pay = hours * payRate
   Display lastName, firstName, pay
END
```

The algorithm instructs the program to open the timesheet file, read the first line from the file and store this in a variable named **employeeRecord**, and close the file. The algorithm then use the word **Get** to indicate that the program must extract the four values from the character string stored in the **employeeRecord** variable, and store these values in the variables **firstName**, **lastName**, **hours** and **payRate,** respectively. Once the values have been stored in separate variables, the program then performs the required calculation and displays the results.

How do we convert this algorithm to PHP code? Remember that **fgets**() reads an entire line from a file, so we can easily obtain the employee record from the file as follows:

```
$timesheetFile = fopen("timesheet.txt","r");
$employeeRecord = fgets($timesheetFile);
fclose($timesheetFile);
```

The **$employeeRecord** variable now contains the entire line of data from **timesheet.txt**. The question is: how can we parse the contents of this variable to get the values we need for **$firstName, $lastName, $hours** and **$payRate?**

PHP provides two useful functions that we can use in combination to parse our line of data. The PHP **explode**() function extracts data values from a character string based on a delimiter of some kind. To use the **explode**() function we must indicate the character that we are using as a delimiter (in this case the colon character), and we must specify the character string that is to be parsed (in this case the string is stored in **$employeeRecord**):

```
explode(":", $employeeRecord)
```

The **explode**() function extracts the values between the colons. and provides these in a special data structure called an array (arrays are explained in Chapter 11). If

$employeeRecord contains the character string "Mike:Smith:20:12.55", the array will contain the values "Mike", "Smith", "20", and "12.55".

The PHP **list**() function is designed to retrieve a list of values from an array and store these in separate variables. Here is a line of PHP code that shows how the **list**() function receives the values returned by the **explode**() function, and stores these values into four newly created variables:

```
list($firstName, $lastName, $hours, $payRate) = explode (":",
    $employeeRecord);
```

The four arguments supplied to the **list**() function are variables. Each variable will receive one of the values extracted from the character string by the **explode**() function. The extracted values will be assigned to these variables in order. If **$employeeRecord** contains the character string "Mike:Smith:20:12.55", the variable **$firstName** will contain "Mike", the variable **$lastName** will contain "Smith", the variable **$hours** will contain 20, and the variable **$payRate** will contain 12.55.

Once we have used the **explode**() and **list**() functions to extract the values from the line and store these in variables, we can then calculate and output the weekly wage. Here is the complete PHP code for **wageReport1.php**:

```
<html>
<head>
  <title>EMPLOYEE WEEKLY WAGE REPORT</title>
  <link rel="stylesheet" type="text/css" href="sample.css" />
</head>
<body>
  <?php
    $timesheetFile = fopen("timesheet.txt","r");
    $employeeRecord = fgets($timesheetFile);
    fclose($timesheetFile);

    list($firstName, $lastName, $hours, $payRate) =
      explode (":", $employeeRecord);
    $pay = $hours * $payRate;

    print ("<h1>EMPLOYEE WEEKLY WAGE REPORT </h1>");
    print("<p>$lastName, $firstName: $ $pay.</p>");

    print (" <p><a href=\"wageReport1.html\">Return to
      wageReport1 form</a></p> ");
  ?>
</body>
</html>
```

Code Example: wageReport1.php

Note that we closed the file before parsing the line of data. That's because we only need the file open to read the line from the file and store the content in a program variable. The process of parsing the line is performed on the variable and not on the file.

Note that the explode() and list() functions are used for a variety of purposes, not only to parse records from a file, and not always in combination with one another. The use of these two functions is explained more completely in chapter 11.

Processing a File with Multiple Records

Now let's look at a requirement to process a file that contains **multiple** records:

---

wageReport2 requirement:

Write a program that reads an employee timesheet from a file named timesheets.txt. The file contains three lines. Each line contains one employee's first name, last name, hours worked and hourly wage, for example:

Mike:Smith:20:12.55

Mary:King:40:17.50

Chris:Jones:35:9.50

The program should calculate and display the weekly wage for each employee and also calculate and display the total wages.

Each line in the **timesheets.txt** file contains a single employee record and each record contains four data fields: the employee's first name, last name, hours worked this week, and hourly rate of pay. The data fields are separated by colons. There are three records in the file.

This problem is not very different from the previous problem except that we need to process **three** lines instead of one, and we need to calculate and display the total pay in addition to the pay for each employee. Here is the algorithm:

```
wageReport2.php algorithm:

    Open timesheets.txt as timesheetFile for reading
    Read employeeRecord1 from timesheetFile
    Read employeeRecord2 from timesheetFile
    Read employeeRecord3 from timesheetFile
    Close timesheetFile

    Get firstName1, lastName1, hours1, payRate1 from employeeRecord1
    Get firstName2, lastName2, hours2, payRate2 from employeeRecord2
    Get firstName3, lastName3, hours3, payRate3 from employeeRecord3
```

```
    pay1 = hours1 * payRate1
    pay2 = hours2 * payRate2
    pay3 = hours3 * payRate3
    totalPay = pay1 + pay2 + pay3


    Display lastName1, firstName1, pay1
    Display lastName2, firstName2, pay2
    Display lastName3, firstName3, pay3
    Display totalPay
END
```

This looks complicated but if you look through this carefully you will see that the algorithm really breaks down into four groups of instructions. The first group instructions open the file, read the three lines of data into variables and then close the file. The second group of instructions extract the first name, last name, hours worked and pay rate from the three variables. The next group of instructions performs the calculations. The last group of instructions generates the output. Here is the code for **wageReport2.php**:

```
<html>
<head>
  <title>EMPLOYEE WEEKLY WAGE REPORT</title>
  <link rel="stylesheet" type="text/css" href="sample.css" />
</head>
<body>
  <?php
    $timesheetFile = fopen("timesheets.txt","r");
    $employeeRecord1 = fgets($timesheetFile);
    $employeeRecord2 = fgets($timesheetFile);
    $employeeRecord3 = fgets($timesheetFile);
    fclose($timesheetFile);

    list($firstName1, $lastName1, $hours1, $payRate1) =
        explode(":",$employeeRecord1);
    list($firstName2, $lastName2, $hours2, $payRate2) =
        explode(":", $employeeRecord2);
    list($firstName3, $lastName3, $hours3, $payRate3) =
        explode(":", $employeeRecord3);

    $pay1 = $hours1 * $payRate1;
    $pay2 = $hours2 * $payRate2;
    $pay3 = $hours3 * $payRate3;
    $totalPay = $pay1 + $pay2 + $pay3;

    print("<h1>EMPLOYEE WEEKLY WAGE REPORT </h1>");
    print("<p>$lastName1, $firstName1: $ $pay1.");
    print("<br />$lastName2, $firstName2: $ $pay2.");
```

```
    print("<br />$lastName3, $firstName3: $ $pay3. </p>");
    print("<p><strong>TOTAL PAY: $ $totalPay.</strong></p>");
    print(" <p><a href=\"wageReport2.html\">Return to
       wageReport2 form</a></p>");
 ?>
</body>
</html>
```

Code Example: wageReport2.php

Figure 6-5: wageReport2.html and wageReport2.php screenshots

Figure 6-5 shows the output from **wageReport2.html** and **wageReport2.php**.

Perhaps you are wondering "This works fine for three records, but what if the file contains the records for 20, or 2,000 or 20,000 employees? What if you do not even know how many records will be stored in the file?" These problems are not as difficult as they sound. In fact they can be solved quite easily using program loops. In Chapter 10 we will see how we can process files with any number of records.

Appending Records to a File

We must often create programs that **write** or **append** lines that contain entire records. For example consider an online survey, where each submission constitutes a single survey response that must be appended to a file of survey responses. Here is such a requirement for our smoking survey:

SmokingSurvey requirement:

Write a program that prompts the user for their first and last name, the number of years they have smoked and daily average number of cigarettes they have smoked during this time. The program should receive the input and append this as a single line to a file named smoking_survey.txt, then inform the user that the data has been added.

Each value should be separated by colons.

According to this requirement, when a user completes the form and presses the Submit button, the input will be appended to the **smoking_survey.txt** file. This is a simple but powerful program. Many different people can submit a survey simply by accessing the form with their own Web browser. Each submitted survey will be added to the file which eventually may contain hundreds or thousands of surveys Another program can be designed to read the **smoking_survey.txt** file, process the survey data, and report the results (we will develop this program in a later chapter).

Here is the pseudocode for the HTML document that we will use to receive the input from someone who wishes to submit a survey:

```
smokingSurvey.html algorithm:
  Prompt for firstName
  Get firstName
  Prompt for lastName
  Get lastName
  Prompt for yearsSmoked
  Get yearsSmoked
  Prompt for smokedDaily
  Get smokedDaily

  Submit firstName, lastName, yearsSmoked, smokedDaily
    to smokingSurvey.php
END
```

Here is the code for **smokingSurvey.html**:

```
<html>
<head>
  <title>Smoking Survey</title>
  <link rel="stylesheet" type="text/css" href="sample.css" />
</head>
<body>
  <h1>Smoking Survey</h1>

  <form action="smokingSurvey.php" method="post" />
    <p>What is your first name?
    <input type="text" size="20" name="firstName" /></p>

    <p>What is your last name?
    <input type="text" size="20" name="lastName" /></p>

    <p>For how many years have you smoked?
    <input type="text" size="5" name="yearsSmoked" /></p>

    <p>How many cigarettes have you <br \>
```

```
    smoked on average every day (roughly)?
    <select name="smokedDaily">
      <option>0</option>
      <option>1</option>
      <option>2</option>
      <option>5</option>
      <option>10</option>
      <option>20</option>
      <option>30</option>
      <option>40</option>
    </select></p>

    <p><input type="submit" value="Submit survey data" />
    <input type="reset" value="Clear the survey form" /></p>
  </form>
</body>
</html>
```

Code Example: smokingSurvey.html

Here is the pseudocode for the PHP program that will receive the user input and append the data to the **smoking_survey.txt** file:

```
smokingSurvey.php algorithm:
  Receive firstName, lastName, yearsSmoked, smokedDaily from
    smokingSurvey.html
  Open smoking_survey.txt as surveyFile for appending
  Write firstName, lastName, yearsSmoked, smokeDaily to surveyFile
  Close surveyFile
  Display "Data has been added" message to user
END
```

Here is the PHP code for **smokingSurvey.php**:

```
<html>
<head>
  <title>Smoking Survey</title>
  <link rel="stylesheet" type="text/css" href="sample.css" />
</head>
<body>

  <?php
    $yearsSmoked  = $_POST['yearsSmoked'];
    $smokedDaily  = $_POST['smokedDaily'];
    $firstName    = $_POST['firstName'];
    $lastName     = $_POST['lastName'];
```

```
$surveyFile = fopen("smoking_survey.txt","a");

fputs($surveyFile,
   "$firstName:$lastName:$yearsSmoked:$smokedDaily\n");

fclose($surveyFile);

print("<h1>Thank you for participating!</h1>");

print("<p>Your data has been added to our survey.</p>");

print (" <p><a href=\"smokingSurvey.html\">Return to the
   Survey form </a></p> ");
?>
</body>
</html>
```

Code Example: smokingSurvey.php

Let's review the PHP code line by line:

```
$yearsSmoked = $_POST['yearsSmoked'];
$smokedDaily = $_POST['smokedDaily'];
$firstName = $_POST['firstName'];
$lastName = $_POST['lastName'];
```

Here we extract the inputs from the PHP $_POST array and assign these to variables.

```
$surveyFile = fopen("smoking_survey.txt","a");
```

This statement opens a file named **smoking_survey.txt** for appending ("**a**"). If the file does not exist it is created.

```
fputs($surveyFile, "$firstName:$lastName:$yearsSmoked:$smokedDaily\n");
```

The **fputs**() function is used to write a string of data to a file (the file referenced by the variable **$surveyFile**). Since the file was opened for appending, the data will be added to the end of any data that is already stored in the file.

In this example, we want our **fputs**() statement to add a single line to the file so that each line contains the data for an entire survey submission. We therefore include all four variables that contain input from the user **without** adding **new line** characters between each variable since we want all four values to be written to a **single** line. We provide a new line character at the **end** of the string so that the next survey that is submitted will be written to a new line in the file.

Notice also the colons between each of the variables. We are using the colons to separate the four values, so that they can be parsed easily by any program that reads the file. The colons will simply be written to the file along with the values of each variable, in the order indicated. If the four variables contained the values "John", "Smith", "2" and "20" our **fputs**() statement will append "John:Smith:2:30" to **smoking_survey.txt**.

```
fclose($scoresFile);
```

The **fclose**() function closes the file. As always it is important to close a file once the program is done using it.

Figure 6-6 shows a sample interaction. Open **smokingSurvey.html** yourself a few times and add new survey data each time. Each time you do this, check the contents of **smoking_survey.txt** and observe that a new line is added to this file each time a new survey is submitted. Now imagine thousands of people submitting their own data. Every submission is processed by our PHP code and appended to the file.

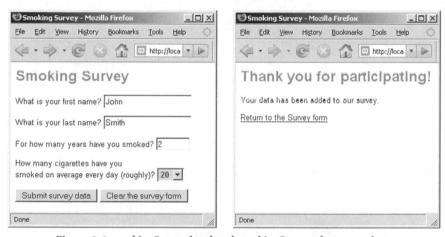

Figure 6-6: smokingSurvey.html and smokingSurvey.php screenshots

Working with Multiple Files

A program can open multiple files at the same time. Some files may be opened for reading, others for writing, others for appending, depending on the program requirements. As always each file should be opened when the program needs to use it and closed when the program is finished using it. It is easy to see why our file-related functions such as **fopen**(), **fgets**(), **fputs**() and **fclose**() all need an argument that references the file that they are intended to work with, for example **fclose($scoresFile)** will close the file referenced by the $scoresFile variable, while **fclose($surveyFile)** will close the file referenced by the $surveyFile variable. An example of a program that reads from one file and writes to another is included in the samples folder: **wageReport3.html** and **wageReport3.php**.

Summary

Files and databases permit programs to work with **persistent** data—data with a life that extends beyond the time that a program is actually running.

Files must be **opened** and **closed** for use by a program. When a text file is opened it is necessary to specify whether the purpose is to **read**, **write** or **append** data.

If a file that does not already exist is opened for writing or appending, the file is created. If a file that already exists is opened for writing, the current file is **replaced** by the new file. If a file that already exists is opened for appending, any data that is written to the file is **added** to the end of the existing file content.

In PHP the function to open a file is fopen(). The value returned by the open operation provides a connection to the data associated with the file and is termed the **file handle**. The file handle should be assigned to a program variable—this variable is then used in subsequent program instructions to refer to the file.

The PHP function to read a line from the file is **fgets()**. The variable representing the file handle should be used as an argument. The function returns the content of the next line in the file. The **read marker** is then advanced to the start of the next line.

The PHP function to write a line from the file is **fputs()**. This function takes two arguments: the variable that represents the file handle, and the character string to be written to the file. Once the string has been written to the file the **write marker**, is advanced to the position immediately following the last character in the file.

Escape characters are used to specify characters within character strings that could not otherwise be included. Escape characters consist of the \ character followed by a character that indicates character to be included in the string. An example of an escape character is **\n** which indicates the new line character.

When writing to a file, the new line character must be indicated in the output string wherever you wish a new line to be added to the file.

Text files may include multiple values (data **records**) on each line. In such case, each value is usually separated by special character, such as a comma, tab, or space. This character is termed the **separator** or **delimiter** and cannot occur within the values themselves.

In order to process lines that contained multiple values, the first step is to read the line. The contents of the line can then be parsed to extract the various values based on the delimiter. The PHP **explode()** function performs this task, and the PHP **list()** function can be used to receive the resulting list of values and store these values in individual variables.

The function to close a file is **fclose()**. File should always be closed when the program no longer needs access to the file. It is good practice to open, process and close files as quickly as possible so that the file has the greatest availability for other purposes.

A program can process multiple files at the same time.

Chapter 6 Review Questions

1. A program asks the user for their age and calculates and displays the numbers of years that they have until they retire. What type of data is this program working with?
   a. Transient data
   b. Persistent data
   c. A combination of transient and persistent data

2. A program asks the user for their ID and password, reads a file to determine their bonus, then displays the bonus to the screen. What type of data is this program working with?
   a. Transient data
   b. Persistent data
   c. A combination of transient and persistent data

3. How can a data file be accessed by a PHP program?
   a. Read data from the file
   b. Write data to the file
   c. Append data to the file
   d. Read or write as needed but not append
   e. Read, write or append as needed

4. Tables, records and fields are the basic elements of:
   a. Data files
   b. Relational Databases
   c. PHP programs
   d. Client/Server applications
   e. HTML documents

5. What happens if you open a text file for write operations and the file already exists?
   a. An error message is generated automatically
   b. The file is replaced by a new file and the content of the old file is lost
   c. The file is replaced by a new file and a backup is made of the old file
   d. The existing file is opened and any new output is added to the end of the current file content
   e. A new file is created so there are now two files with the same name in the same folder

6. What happens if you open a text file for append operations and the file already exists?
   a. An error message is generated automatically
   b. The file is replaced by a new file and the content of the old file is lost
   c. The file is replaced by a new file and a backup is made of the old file
   d. The existing file is opened and any new output is added to the end of the current file content
   e. A new file is created so there are now two files with the same name in the same folder

7. Which is the better programming practice?
   a. Open a file as soon as your program begins and close the file just before your program ends
   b. Open a file only when the program needs to work with it and close the file as soon as the program no longer needs it

8. What is wrong with this algorithm?

   ```
   Open scores.txt as scoresFile for reading
   Close scoresFile
   Read score1, score2, score3, score4, score5 from scoresFile
   ```

   a. The file should have been opened for append operations
   b. The file should have been opened for write operations
   c. You must read the data from the file before opening the file
   d. You must read the data from the file before closing the file
   e. You can only read one value from a file

9. What is wrong with this code?

   ```
   $scoresFile = fopen("scores.txt","w");
   $score1 = fgets($scoresFile);
   $score2 = fgets($scoresFile);
   $score3 = fgets($scoresFile);
   fclose($scoresFile);
   ```

   a. The code is designed to read data but the program has been opened for write operations
   b. The code is designed to write data but the program has been opened for read operations
   c. In lines 2, 3 and 4, fgets($scoreFile) should be written fgets(scores.txt)
   d. The close($scoresFile) statement should be the second statement
   e. The close($scoresFile) statement should be close(scores.txt)

10. Consider the following code:

```
$someFile = fopen("somefile.txt","r");
$someValue = fgets($someFile);
fclose($someFile);
```

Assume somefile.txt contains the following text on two lines:

```
2005
2004
```

What does $someValue contain after these statements are executed?
   a. 2005
   b. 2004
   c. 4009
   d. 20052004
   e. An error is generated since there is too much data in the file

11. Consider the following code:

```
$someFile = fopen("somefile.txt","r");
$someValue = fgets($someFile );
fclose($someFile);
```

Assume somefile.txt contains the following text on two lines:

```
Chris:Smith:2005
Mary:Jones:2004
```

What does $someValue contain after these statements are executed?
   a. Chris
   b. Chris:Smith:2005
   c. Chris:Smith:2005:Mary:Jones:2004
   d. Mary:Jones:2004
   e. An error is generated since there is too much data in the file

12. Assume somefile.txt contains the following text on two lines:

```
Chris-Smith-2005
Mary-Jones-2004
```

What is being used as a delimiter in this file?
   a. firstName, lastName, and year
   b. The colon :
   c. The dash –
   d. The new line marker
   e. The year

13. Assume that a variable named $currentRecord has already been used to read a line of text from a file and contains the string "Chris:Smith:2005". Which of the following lines of code will correctly parse the string and store the three values into variables $firstName, $lastName, and $year?
   a. fgets($firstName, $lastName, $year) = explode(":", $currentRecord);
   b. list(":", $currentRecord) = explode($firstName, $lastName, $year);
   c. explode(":", $currentRecord) = list($firstName, $lastName, $year);
   d. list($firstName, $lastName, $year) = explode(":", $currentRecord);
   e. list($firstName, $lastName, $year) = fgets(":", $currentRecord);

14. Which statement is true?
   a. A program can only open one file during the program's execution
   b. A program can open any number of files during the program's execution but only one file can be open at a time
   c. A program can open any number of files at the same time as long as they are all open for reading, or else all open for writing or else all open for appending
   d. A program can open any number of files at the same time for any operations as needed (reading, writing or appending)
   e. A program cannot open files

15. Which of the following instructions will write the message "This is a test" to a file referenced by the variable $someFile?
   a. fopen($someFile, "This is a test");
   b. fgets($someFile, "This is a test");
   c. fputs($someFile, "This is a test");
   d. list($someFile, "This is a test");
   e. explode($someFile, "This is a test");

16. How many lines will this statement store in the file referenced by the variable $someFile?

```
$fputs($someFile, "Testing..One\nTwo..Three\n");
```

   a. 0
   b. 1
   c. 2
   d. 3
   e. 4

17. How many lines will this statement store in the file referenced by the variable $someFile?

```
$fputs($someFile, "Testing..\n\nOne\nTwo\nThree\n");
```

   a. 1
   b. 2
   c. 3
   d. 4
   e. 5

18. Assume somefile.txt contains the following text on two lines:

```
Washington, USA
Paris, France
```

   What will the file contain after the following instructions are executed?

```
$someFile = fopen("someFile.txt","a");
fputs($someFile, "London, England\n");
fputs($someFile, "Rome, Italy\n");
fclose($someFile);
```

   a. Washington, USA
      Paris, France
      London, England
      Rome, Italy
   b. London, England
      Rome, Italy
   c. London, England
   d. Rome, Italy
   e. London, England
      Rome, Italy
      Washington, USA
      Paris, France

19. Assume somefile.txt contains the following text on two lines:

> Chris:Smith:2005
> Mary:Jones:2004

What will the file contain after the following instructions are executed?

```
$someFile = fopen("someFile.txt","w");
fputs($someFile, "Mark:Jones:2003\n");
fputs($someFile, "Anne:Silvers:2004\n");
fclose($someFile);
```

a. Chris:Smith:2005
   Mary:Jones:2004
   Mark:Jones:2003
   Anne:Silvers:2004
b. Mark:Jones:2003
   Anne:Silvers:2004
c. Anne:Silvers:2004
d. Mark:Jones:2003
   Anne:Silvers:2004
   Chris:Smith:2005
   Mary:Jones:2004
e. Chris:Smith:2005
   Mary:Jones:2004

20. Which operation might result in the loss of an existing file (assuming the file is opened and closed correctly)?
   a. Read operations only
   b. Write operations only
   c. Append operations only
   d. Write or append operations only
   e. Read, write or append operations

Chapter 6 Code Exercises

Your Chapter 6 code exercises can be found in your **Chapter06** folder. This folder is included in your customized XAMPP installation at the following location:

xampplite\htdocs\WebTech\coursework\Chapter06

Type your name and the date in the **Author** and **Date** sections of each file as you work on each exercise.

Debugging Exercises

Your **Chapter06** folder should contain a number of "FixIt" files. Each of these files contains PHP code that has an error of some kind. You will need to run each program in order to see the errors, and to debug and test the code to see if it works correctly. For example to run **fixIt1.php**, first run the Web server, then use the URL:

http://localhost/WebTech/coursework/Chapter06/fixIt1.php

Code Modification Exercises

Your **Chapter06** folder contains a number of "Modify" files. Each pair of files contains HTML and PHP code that needs to be modified to meet a requirement. The requirements are included in each file. Modify the algorithms as specified, being careful to make changes to the .html and .php files as directed.

Code Completion Exercises

1. Your **Chapter06** folder contains three files **paintReport.html, paintReport.php**. and **paintContracts.txt**. You do not need to change **paintReport.html**—this simply contains a form with a Submit button to run **paintReport.php**. The **paintContracts.txt file contains five numbers, each on a separate line, representing the income from this month's paint contracts.** Your job is to develop the code in **paintReport.php** in order to: open the **paintContracts.txt** file; read the five lines from the file; close the file; calculate the total income. The print statement to display the five payments and the total has been provided. Note the variable names!

2. Your **Chapter06** folder contains two files **submitOrder.html** and **submitOrder.php**. You will see that **submitOrder.html** is exactly the same as **softwareOrder.html** that you developed in Chapter 5. The form is used to submit the operating system and number of copies. Your job is to provide the code in **submitOrder.php** that will: open a file named **order.txt**; **write** the operating systems and number of copies received from the form to a single line in this file, separated by a colon; then close the file. For example if the user selected **Macintosh** and requested **10** copies, **submitOrder.php** should create the file **order.txt** and write the following data to the file (followed by a new line character): Macintosh:10.

3. Your **Chapter06** folder contains two files: **processOrder.html** and **processOrder.php**.

   You do not need to change **processOrder.html**—this simply contains a form with a Submit button to run **processOrder.php**. Your job is to develop the code in **processOrder.php** to: open the **order.txt** file; read the line from the file; close the file; then parse the line to obtain the operating system and number of copies. The code to calculate and display the order cost has already been provided to save you time. Be sure to use the same variable names in your own code!

Figure 6-7 shows sample screen shots if **order.txt** contains the line: **Macintosh:10**

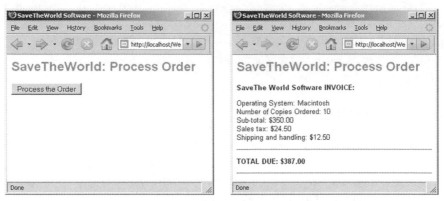

Figure 6-7: processOrder.html and processOrder.php screenshots

4. Your Chapter06 folder contains two files: travel.html and travel.php.

You do not need to change **travel.html** — this simply contains the same form that was used in the previous chapter to receive a travel submission from the user. Your job is to develop the code in **travel.php** to: open the **reservations.txt** file for **appending**; write the destination, number of travelers and number of nights to the file on a **single** line, separated by **colons**, and ending with a newline character; then close the file. The destination will always be "Rome", so if the user submits 3 travelers for 5 nights, your program should append the line: **Rome:3:5** to the file. Submit a few reservations to be sure that the program is appending each reservation to a new line in the file. You may want to delete the file a few times until you get the code working correctly.

5. Your **Chapter06** folder contains a file named **restoreGame.php, and a file named gameStatus.dat** (this is a simple text file — the .dat extension is often used instead of .txt to indicate that a file contains data). The **gameStatus.dat** file contains five lines of text: the first line contains the character's name; the second line contains the character's type; the third line contains the number of health tokens; the fourth line contains the number of experience tokens; and the fifth line contains the number of supply tokens.

Your job is to develop the code in **restoreGame.php** as follows: open the **gameStatus.dat** file for **reading**; read the five lines from the file; close the file. The code to display the information has been provided.

6. Copy **event.html** and **event.php** from your Chapter05 folder to your Chapter06 folder. This application processes ticket orders for a performance. Your Chapter06 folder contains a file named **ticketCount.txt** which contains a single line containing the number of tickets that have already ordered for the performance. You are

now going to modify your event.php program so that it will add the number of tickets that have just been ordered to the number already in the ticketCount.txt file. In other words the ticketCount.txt file will be updated every time a new ticket order is submitted, so that this file will always contain the count of ALL tickets purchased by ALL customers. Updating the number in the file requires a two-step procedure so read the following instructions carefully.

In order to add the tickets just purchased, we must: (1) open the ticketCount.txt file for read operations, read the previous count of tickets sold from the file into a program variable, then close the file; (2) add the number of tickets that were just ordered (the number received from the form) to the previous count that was read from the file (this will provide the new count); and (3) open the ticketCount.txt file again, this time for write operations, write the new count to the file, and close the file.

So for example if the user just requested 10 tickets, and ticketCount.txt previously contained 40, step (1) would read the 40 into a variable, step (2) would add 10 to this variable to make 50, and step (3) would write 50 back to the ticket-Count.txt file (which would replace the 40 previously in the file). So the file will now contain 50.

Test your program by using event.html to submit two or three orders. Use your text editor to open ticketCount.txt after each submission. You should see that the number in the file increases each time. We will make use of this file in future exercises.

7. For this exercise you will create a trip log that will keep track of your driving trips. Your Chapter06 folder includes a file named **tripLog.html**. This file contains a form that asks the user to submit the date and miles traveled, followed by four drop down lists to indicate whether or not the trip included breakfast, lunch, dinner, or a hotel (each of these allows the user to select **YES** or **NO**).

Your folder also includes tripLog.php which must process the form. This program is partially completed. Add the code to APPEND the values received from the form to a file named tripLog.txt. The values should be appended as a single line of text, using colons to separate each value. Add a newline \n character at the end of the line. Here's how a line might appear in the file:

```
3/15/2011:120:NO:YES:YES:YES
```

Be sure your program is appending each entry to the file so that new entries are added to the next line and do not over-write previous entries. Run your program a few times, entering trip information for different dates. Use your text editor to open tripLog.txt and check that your program is working correctly.

Chapter 7

Programs that Choose — Introducing Selection Structures

Intended Learning Outcomes

After completing this chapter, you should be able to:

- Explain the purpose of a selection structure.
- Determine the result of a Boolean expression.
- Identify the relational operators.
- Evaluate a simple truth table.
- Distinguish between an IF and IF..ELSE structure.
- Choose an appropriate selection structure based on requirements.
- Design and code an application containing an IF structure.
- Design and code an application containing an IF..ELSE structure.
- Compare two strings without regard for case.
- Construct a string whose content is partially dependent on a selection structure.

Introduction

Until now all of our algorithms have consisted of a series of sequential instructions that are to be executed, one after the other, one instruction at a time. We are now ready to design applications that can perform tests while the program is running, and choose between different instructions based on the result of these tests. In other words, we are ready to write programs that make decisions.

We often make decisions based on tests in our own lives. For example, here are in-structions for an attendant at a theater to check theater goers for tickets:

```
Ask the next party for their tickets
IF this party has valid tickets
   Direct them to their seats
ELSE
   Direct them to the ticket desk
```

In this case, the test is **this party has valid tickets**. The result of this test will always generate a **true** or **false** result. If the test is **true**, one set of instructions is performed (**Direct them to their seats**). If the test is **false**, a different set of instructions is performed (**Direct them to the ticket desk**).

This example demonstrates a **selection control structure,** also known as a **decision structure.** In programming, selection control structures allow us to design applications that can choose between different groups of program instructions by performing a test that will generate a **true** or **false** result. We can use selection control structures for many different purposes. Here are some common examples:

Selective Updates

Applications may need to selectively update data values based on some criterion. For example we might need to write a program that tests whether or not an employee's hourly wage is less than $8 an hour. If the test is true the hourly wage is updated to $8, otherwise the hourly wage is unchanged.

Selective Calculations

Applications may need to perform different calculations depending on some test condition. For example, a program designed to calculate bonuses might be required to test whether an employee has worked at least 35 hours. If the test is true, the program will assign and calculate a $50.00 bonus, otherwise the program will assign and calculate a $25.00 bonus.

Security

A common application requirement is to perform a process only if a valid ID/password combination is provided. The program would be designed to test an ID and password to see if these are valid. If the test is true, the program would fulfill the request, otherwise the program would issue some kind of error response.

Selective Response

Applications may need to be designed to respond to a user's input based on an evaluation of the input. For example, a user may be given a quiz question and the program must evaluate the answer and provide an appropriate response.

Input Validation

It is always important to ensure that all input is valid before performing any required processing. For example we might need to test that the user entered a positive number when asked for the hours that they have worked. If the test is true the program would go ahead and process the input according to the program requirements. If the test is false the program would generate an error message instead.

A program that finds an error may be designed to terminate without further processing, but sometimes a program is designed to simply ignore invalid input and continue to process valid input. For example a program designed to find the average of a list of scores in a file might test each score to ensure that it is valid (for example between 0 and 100). If the test is true, the score would be included in the average, otherwise it would be ignored (and perhaps a message would be appended to a log file for future reference).

Data Cleaning

Often data stored in files and databases contains errors, inconsistencies or omissions that need to be corrected before the data can be processed correctly. As an example of correctable errors, consider a file containing misspelled city names. As an example of inconsistencies, consider a list of medical doctors titles are variously entered as "Dr", "Dr" and "Doctor". As an example of omissions, consider an address list where zip codes are missing from some addresses.

Often the quality of stored data can be significantly improved by "cleaning" operations, where a program reads the data, performs various tests, and replaces "dirty" data with corrected ("clean") values.

Selective Reporting

Applications may need to perform statistics on data that requires selective reporting. For example, a program might be designed to read a file of scores and count the number of passing (scores that are 60 or higher) and failing scores. This program would need to read each score and test if the score is at least 60 (or whatever value indicates a passing grade). If the test is true the number of passing scores would be increased, otherwise the number of failing scores would be increased.

Selective Searching:

Consider a requirement to search a file of employees and display the hourly pay of all employees named "Smith". The program would need to read through all of the employee records in the file and test each one to see if the last name is "Smith". If the test is true, the employee's hourly pay would be displayed, otherwise the program would not display anything for that record.

Sorting Data

A more advanced use of selection control structures is to sort data according to some sort criterion, for example, sort a list of employee records by last name. Sorting algorithms require constant testing of data values in order to determine the correct order.

In this chapter we will develop applications that use selection control structures to perform operations related to the first four of the examples listed here. In subsequent chapters we will learn how to develop algorithms that illustrate many of the other examples.

As you work through this chapter, take time to fully understand the logic. You are learning the fundamental structures of computer programming and it is important that you can apply these structures effectively when you develop your own applications.

Introducing IF and IF..ELSE Structures

In **Chapter 5** we created a simple wage processing application that required user input (**wage2.html** and **wage2.php** in your **samples** folder). In order to gain an understanding of selection structures, we will now develop three different versions of this application by adding selection structures to:

1. Update the wage of anyone earning less than 8.00 an hour
2. Assign a bonus based on the number of hours worked.
3. Obtain a password from the user and only process the wage if the password is correct.

We will develop our algorithms using two fundamental selection structures that are provided by every programming language: IF structures and IF..ELSE structures. The basic syntax of an IF structure written in pseudocode is:

```
IF (..a suitable test that might be true or false )
   Instructions to perform if the test is true
ENDIF
```

The basic syntax of an IF..ELSE structure written in pseudocode is:

```
IF (..a suitable test that might be true or false )
   Instructions to perform if the test is true
ELSE
   Instructions to perform if the test is false
ENDIF
```

Introducing Flow Charts

To more easily understand the way that selection structures work, we will make use of another useful design tool known as a **flow chart.** Programmers draw flow charts to better visualize the logical execution of their program instructions. Until now our programs instructions have simply executed in sequence, one instruction after another. Figure 7-1 provides a general illustration that shows how a simple sequence of instructions might appear in a flow chart.

Flow charts use different symbols to indicate the various statements and control structures that determine the logical execution of program code. Usually **rectangles with curved corners** are used to indicate the beginning and end of the code segment that is displayed in the flow chart, and **rectangles with square corners** are used to display each program statement. The arrows between the program statements indicate the flow of the program. The arrows in Figure 7-1 show us that each program statement is executed in order

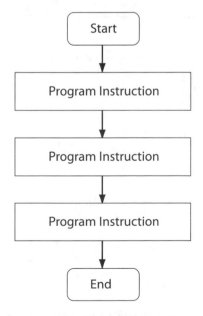

Figure 7-1 General-purpose Flow Chart showing a sequence of instructions

In this first example, the phrase "Program instruction" is used to indicate an instruction of some kind. As we shall see shortly, each rectangle will usually contain a more specific program instruction, such as "Print Welcome message" or "pay = wage * hoursWorked".

Now let's see how a flow chart can help us understand the logic of different selection control structures. Figure 7-2 provides an example of a generic flow chart that includes an **IF** structure. Note that this flow chart indicates some program instructions and then uses a **diamond** symbol to indicate a test. When the program performs this test it will "choose" between two paths depending on whether the test is true or false and the flow chart helps us to see this visually. In this case, we can see that if the test is **true**, the program will branch and execute a block of program instructions before moving on to the program instructions that appear in the next part of the program, but if the test is **false** the program will **skip** this block of instructions and just move on to the next instructions.

The diamond shape is a standard symbol in flow charts. It is used to indicate a decision point in the code, a test that will be true or false. Two arrows branch from a di-

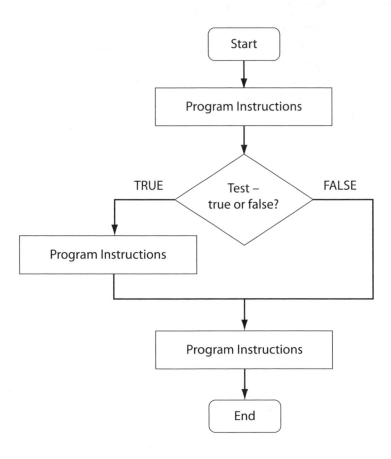

Figure 7-2 General-purpose Flow Chart showing an IF structure

amond symbol in order to display visually what happens if the test is true and what happens if the test is false.

Figure 7-3 provides an example of a flow chart for an **IF..ELSE** structure. This flow chart begins the same way as the **IF** structure example in Figure 7-2. However this time the chart shows us that the program will branch to one of two different blocks of instructions before moving on, depending on whether the test is true or false. So this is different from the IF structure where the program simply skipped to the next part of the program if the test was false.

Compare these two flow charts to the pseudocode examples of IF and IF..ELSE structures that were listed earlier. Which is easier for you to understand? If you are a visual thinker, you may find it useful to draw your own flow charts as you work out the logic of your own programs.

Note that these examples are intended as an introduction only. We will use more specific examples of flow charts as we learn how to use selection structures to meet actual program requirements.

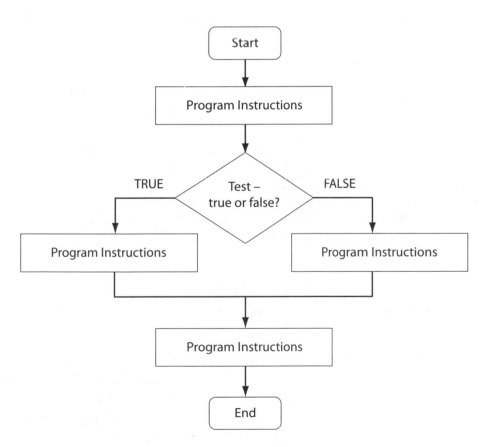

Figure 7-3 General-purpose Flow Chart showing an IF..ELSE structure

Boolean Expressions and Relational Operators

We have seen that **IF** and **IF..ELSE** structures are based on tests that have a **true** or **false** result. Before we can develop algorithms that include these structures we must first learn how to construct our tests. True/false tests are known as **Boolean expressions** (after the English mathematician George Boole) and the operators used to create Boolean expressions are known as relational operators. Table 7-1 shows how the standard **relational operators** are specified in the PHP language (and in most programming languages):

Relational Operation	Operator
Less than or equal to	<=
Less than	<
Equal to	==
Greater than	>
Greater than or equal to	>=
Not equal to	Either <> or !=

Table 7-1: The relational operators

Note that the **Equal to** operator is == and not = as you might expect. This is because most current programming languages use the = operator to assign values to variables. PHP allows the use of either <> or != to represent **Not equal to**. Most current languages use the != representation and we will use that in this book.

Assume that we are testing a variable named **$hourlyWage** that happens to contain the value 8.00. Here are the results of tests that use the various relational operators:

```
$hourlyWage < 8.00 is false      $hourlyWage <= 8.00  is true
$hourlyWage > 8.00is false       $hourlyWage >= 8.00  is true
$hourlyWage == 8.00 is true      $hourlyWage != 8.00  is false
```

When you develop an algorithm you must determine which operator you need to use to create a test that will meet your program requirements correctly. Always consider your tests very carefully, because the wrong test will cause your program to produce incorrect results. For example, does your program requirement specify that (a) employees with wages **below** $8.00 an hour receive a wage increase or (b) employees with wages **not more than** $8.00 an hour receive a wage increase? If the answer is (a) then you would use the < operator in your test (for example **$hourlyWage** < **8.00**) but if the answer is (b) then you will need to use the <= operator (for example **$hourlyWage** <= **8.00**).

It is very easy to get confused between = and ==. A very common programming error is to write **if ($hourlyWage = 8.00)** instead of **if ($hourlyWage == 8.00)** which will cause an unwanted assignment operation and an incorrect test result. Remember that the = operator is an **assignment** operator, used to store a value in a variable. The expression **$hourlyWage = 8.00;** stores **8.00** in the variable **$hourlyWage**. The == operator is a **relational** operator and is used to compare two values and return a true or false result. The expression (**$hourlyWage == 8.00**) will be **true** if $hourlyWage contains the value **8.00**, or **false** otherwise.

Selection Using the IF Structure

Consider the following requirement:

Wage3 requirement:

Write a program that asks the employee for an hourly wage and the number of hours worked.

If the hourly wage is below 8.00 it should be changed to 8.00. No change is needed if the hourly wage is already at least 8.00.

The program should then calculate and display the hourly wage, hours worked, and weekly wage.

To meet this requirement we need a selection structure to test if the hourly wage is less than 8.00, and, if the test is **true**, update the wage to 8.00. But what if the test is **false** (if the wage is already 8.00 or above)? In this case, our program does not need to do anything and the wage is left unchanged. When our requirement does not require any special action if a test is false, we can use an IF structure.

To meet these requirements, we first need to receive the hourly wage and hours worked from the user. Here is the algorithm for **wage3.html** (the HTML page that will use a form to receive the user input and submit the input to **wage3.php**):

```
wage3.html algorithm:
  Prompt for hourly wage
  Get hourlyWage
  Prompt for hours worked
  Get hoursWorked
  Submit hourlyWage and hoursWorked to wage3.php
END
```

Here is the HTML code for this document:

```
<html>
<head>
  <title>Wage Report</title>
  <link rel="stylesheet" type="text/css" href="sample.css" />
</head>
```

```
<body>
  <h1>Wage Report</h1>
  <p><form action="wage3.php" method="post">
    <p>Please enter your hourly wage:
      <input type="text" size="20" name="hourlyWage" />
    </p>
    <p>And the hours you have worked:
      <input type="text" size="20" name="hoursWorked" />
    </p>
    <input type="submit" value="Get Your Wage Report Now" />
    <input type="reset" value="Clear and start again" />
  </form></p>
</body>
</html>
```

Code Example: wage3.html

Now let's develop the algorithm to process the input according to our requirement document. We will use an **IF** structure to update the hourly wage if the wage that was input by the user is less than 8.00. Here is the algorithm for **wage3.php:**

```
wage3.php algorithm:
  Receive hourlyWage, hoursWorked from wage3.html
  IF (hourlyWage < 8.00)
    hourlyWage =8.00
  ENDIF
  weeklyWage = hourlyWage * hoursWorked
  Display heading
  Display hourlyWage, hoursWorked, weeklyWage
END
```

After receiving the user input, the algorithm tests the value stored in the **hourlyWage** variable (the value received from the user). If this value is less than 8.00 then the test will be **true** so the statements inside the IF structure will be executed. In this case we only need a single statement in the if structure which updates the value stored in **hourlyWage** to 8.00. If the test is **false** then the statements inside the IF structure will be skipped and the value stored in the **hourlyWage** variable will be left unchanged.

Next the program processes the statement **following** the IF structure. The value stored in **hourlyWage** (which may or may not have just been updated) is multiplied by the value stored in **hoursWorked** and the result is stored in **weeklyWage**. The program then displays a heading and the values of the three variables.

Figure 7-4 shows this algorithm as a flow chart, slightly simplified to focus on the selection structure. Examine this carefully so that you can see that the flowchart follows the same logic as the pseudocode but displays the logic visually. They say that a picture is worth a thousand words and perhaps you will agree that the algorithm much easier to understand when it is presented this way.

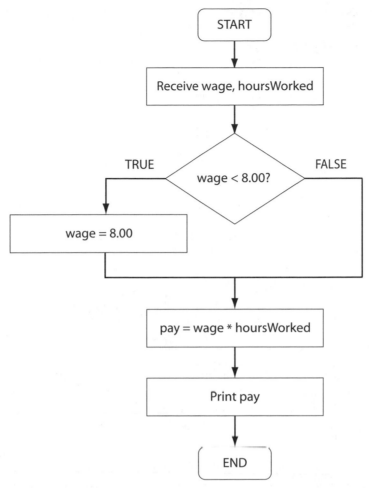

Figure 7-4: Flow Chart showing the algorithm for wage3.php

Here is the PHP code for **wage3.php** that implements this algorithm:

```
<html>
<head>
  <title>Wage Report</title>
  <link rel="stylesheet" type="text/css" href="sample.css" />
</head>
<body>
  <?php
    $hourlyWage = $_POST['hourlyWage'];
    $hoursWorked = $_POST['hoursWorked'];

    if ($hourlyWage < 8.00)
    {
      $hourlyWage = 8.00;
    }
```

```
    $weeklyWage = $hourlyWage * $hoursWorked;

    print("<h1>Wage Report</h1>");
    print("<p>Your hourly wage is $$hourlyWage and you worked
        $hoursWorked hours.</p>");
    print("<p>Your wages are $$weeklyWage.</p>");

    print ("<a href=\"wage3.html\">Return to form</a>");
  ?>
</body>
</html>
```

Code Example: wage3.php

Notice that the IF structure is coded differently in PHP than in pseudocode. Here is the syntax for writing an IF structure in PHP:

```
if (test condition)
{
   // statements to perform if the test is true
}
```

The test in the heading of the IF structure should be enclosed in parentheses. Note the use of curly braces to enclose the block of statements that are to be executed if the test is **true** (there is no ENDIF instruction in PHP). Any statements **between** the curly braces will be executed only if the test is true. Any statements that **follow** the closing curly brace are not part of the IF structure, so these will be executed regardless of the test.

Never include a semi-colon directly following the test condition in the heading of the IF structure! A semi-colon indicates the end of a program instruction and the heading (first line) of a control structure is not considered to be an instruction. If you write **if ($hourlyWage > 0);** the processor will mistakenly assume that, if the test is true, the program should execute the instruction that comes before the semi-colon, which in this case is no instruction at all!

Testing Threshold Values

Since there are two paths through this code depending on the value of the hourly wage, you should test the application at least **twice:**

```
Test 1:     Enter an hourly wage less than 8.00
Test 2:     Enter an hourly wage 8.00 or above
```

When testing to ensure that a selection structure will work as expected, it is especially important to test the **threshold values**. These are the two values closest to your test condition that should generate a true and false result if your test is correctly designed). Good threshold values in this case would be 7.99 and 8.00 since 7.99 should generate a true result and 8.00 should generate a false result.

Selection Using the IF..ELSE Structure

Take a look at the following program requirement:

Wage4 requirement:

Write a program that asks the employee for an hourly wage and the number of hours worked.

If the hours worked is at least 35, the program should assign a bonus of 50.00, otherwise the program should assign a bonus of 25.00.

The program should calculate and display the hourly wage, hours worked, bonus and weekly wage (including the bonus).

To meet this requirement we must design a program that will test the hours worked. Based on this test we want our program to either assign a 50.00 bonus or else assign a 25.00 bonus. In other words we want our program to choose between **two** different groups of statements depending on the result of the test. This requires the use of an IF..ELSE structure. Here is the algorithm for **wage4.php**:

```
wage4.php algorithm:
  Receive hourlyWage, hoursWorked from wage4.html
  IF (hoursWorked >= 35)
    bonus = 50.00
  ELSE
    bonus = 25.00
  ENDIF
  weeklyWage = hourlyWage * hoursWorked + bonus
  Display heading
  Display hourlyWage, hoursWorked, bonus, weeklyWage
END
```

This program will receive values for the **hourlyWage** and **hoursWorked** variables from the HTML form submitted by **wage4.html** (included in your **samples** folder). The program first performs a test: **IF (hoursWorked >= 35)**. This test will have a **true** or **false** result. If the test is **true**, then the statements between the IF and the ELSE are executed and the statements between the ELSE and ENDIF are skipped. If the test is **false**, then the statements between the IF and the ELSE are skipped and the statements between the ELSE and ENDIF are executed.

Figure 7-5 shows a slightly simplified version of this algorithm as a flow chart.

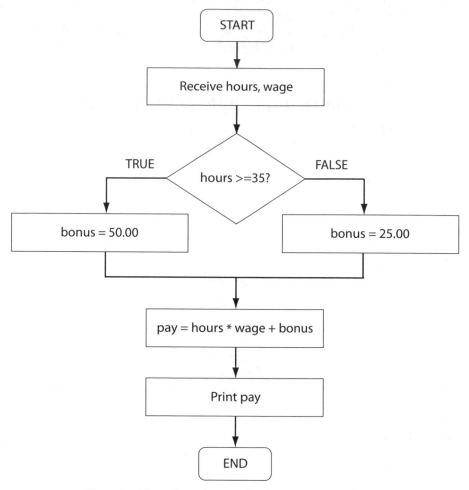

Figure 7-5: Flow Chart showing the algorithm for wage4.php

It is important to understand that each time this program runs, only one of these two blocks of statements will execute. In other words there are two possible paths through the program and only one path will be chosen each time the program runs.

Once the program has executed the IF..ELSE structure, it will have assigned either 50.00 or 25.00 to the **bonus** variable. The statements that **follow** the ENDIF are not part of the IF..ELSE structure. These statements will be executed whether the test was true or false. In this example, the next statement calculates the wage. This calculation includes the value stored in the **bonus** variable, which may be 50.00 or 25.00. The program then displays the values stored in the four variables.

Here is the PHP code for **wage4.php**:

```
<html>
<head>
   <title>Wage Report</title>
   <link rel="stylesheet" type="text/css" href="sample.css" />
```

```php
</head>
<body>
  <?php

    $hourlyWage = $_POST['hourlyWage'];
    $hoursWorked = $_POST['hoursWorked'];

    if ($hoursWorked >= 35)
    {
      $bonus = 50.00;
    }
    else
    {
      $bonus = 25.00;
    }

    $weeklyWage = $hourlyWage * $hoursWorked + $bonus;

    print("<h1>Wage Report</h1>");
    print("<p>Your hourly wage is $$hourlyWage and you worked
      $hoursWorked hours.</p>");
    print("<p>Your bonus is $$bonus.</p>");
    print("<p>Your weekly wage is $$weeklyWage.</p>");
    print("<a href=\"wage4.html\">Return to form</a>");
  ?>
</body>
</html>
```

Code Example: wage4.php

Just as with **wage3.php**, notice the use of **curly braces** { and }. A pair of braces is used to enclose the statements that are to be executed if the test condition is **true** (the statements between the IF and the ELSE. A second pair of braces is used to enclose the statements that are to be executed if the test condition is **false** (following the ELSE). In this example, there is just one statement in each of these two blocks.

In PHP, **IF..ELSE** statements have the following general form:

```php
if (test condition)
{
  // statements to perform if the test is true
}
else
{
  // statements to perform if the test is false
}
```

Always think carefully what statements need to appear **before** the **IF..ELSE** structures, which statements need to be included between the { and } braces of the IF section, which statements need to be included between the { and } braces of the ELSE section, and which statements need to be **follow** the **IF..ELSE** section. If you place a statement in the wrong location, your program logic will be incorrect and your program will not work as intended.

Since there are two paths through this code depending on the value of the hours worked, you should test the application at least **twice:**

Test 1:	hours worked at least 35
Test 2:	hours worked less than 35

If we run the program using 35 for the hours worked and then a second time using 34 for the hours worked, this will ensure that these threshold values generate the expected results. Figure 7-6 shows the result if the user enters 35 when prompted for the hours worked.

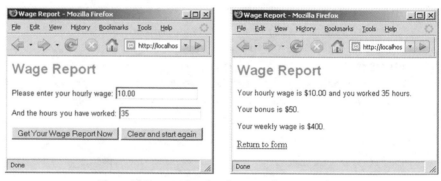

Figure 7-6: wage4.html and wage4.php screenshots

Figure 7-7 shows the result if the user enters 34.

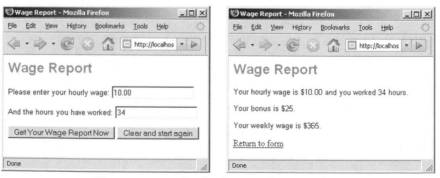

Figure 7-7: wage4.html and wage4.php screenshots

When to Use Braces in IF..ELSE Statements

As previously mentioned, **braces** are used to tell the processor which statements are part of the IF block and which statements are part of the ELSE block. Braces are actually only needed if there is more than one statement in the block. Here is a variation of the **wage4.php** code which is acceptable only because each of the sections contains a single statement:

```php
<?php

    $hourlyWage = $_POST['hourlyWage'];
    $hoursWorked = $_POST['hoursWorked'];

    if ($hoursWorked >= 35)
       $bonus = 50.00;
    else
       $bonus = 25.00;

    $weeklyWage = $hourlyWage * $hoursWorked + $bonus;

    print("<h1>Wage Report</h1>");
    print("<p>Your hourly wage is $$hourlyWage and you worked
       $hoursWorked hours.</p>");

    print("<p>Your bonus is $$bonus.</p>");
    print("<p>Your weekly wage is $$weeklyWage.</p>");

    print ("<a href=\"wage4.html\">Return to form</a>");

?>
```

Code Example: Alternative version of wage4.php

In this example no braces are used for either the IF section or the ELSE section because there is only a single statement to be executed in either case. You can still include braces if you prefer. The rule is that if you have more than one statement in either the IF section or in the ELSE section, then you **must** use braces for that section. **Not including braces when they are needed is a very common programming error.**

Some programmers prefer to **always** use braces.

Comparing Strings — Testing for a Correct Password

Our examples so far have used selection structures to test numeric values stored in variables. We can just as easily compare character strings, for example a password that has been submitted by the user. Recall that a character string may contain any sequence of text characters. The following are all examples of character strings:

"John"	"123 Main Street"	"A123-HFC"
"123-45-6789"	"Enter your password:"	"Price: $10.75"

Consider the following requirement:

Wage5 requirement:

Write a program that asks the employee for an hourly wage, the number of hours worked, and a password.

If the password is correct, the program should calculate the weekly wage and display the hourly wage, hours worked, and weekly wage. Otherwise the program should display an error message.

For testing purposes, the correct password is "employee".

To meet this requirement, we must design an algorithm for a program that will perform quite differently based on the value stored in a password variable. First, here is the algorithm that we will use to create a form for **wage5.html**:

```
wage5.html algorithm:

    Prompt for hourly wage
    Get hourlyWage
    Prompt for hours worked
    Get hoursWorked
    Prompt for password
    Get userPassword
    Submit hourlyWage, hoursWorked, password to wage5.php
END
```

Here is the HTML code for this document:

```
<html>
<head>
    <title>Wage Report</title>
    <link rel="stylesheet" type="text/css" href="sample.css" />
</head>
<body>
```

```
    <h1>Wage Report</h1>
    <p><form action="wage5.php" method="post">
      <p>Please enter your hourly wage:
        <input type="text" size="20" name="hourlyWage" />
      </p>
      <p>And the hours you have worked:
        <input type="text" size="20" name="hoursWorked" />
      </p>
      <p>Please enter your password:
        <input type="password" size="20" name="userPassword" />
      </p>
      <input type="submit" value="Get Your Wage Report Now" />
      <input type="reset" value="Clear and start again" />
    </form></p>
</body>
</html>
```

Code Example: wage5.html

The form now includes a prompt and input box to receive a password. Usually we want passwords and other secure data entries to appear as **asterisks** when typed by the user. We achieve this by using an HTML <**input**> tag in our form with the type set to be "**password**" instead of "**text**":

```
    <p>Please enter your password:
      <input type="password" size="20" name="userPassword" />
    </p>
```

Here is the algorithm for **wage5.php**:

```
wage5.php algorithm:
    Receive hourlyWage, hoursWorked, password from wage5.html
    Display "Wage Report" heading
    IF (password == "employee")
      weeklyWage = hourlyWage * hoursWorked
      Display hourlyWage, hoursWorked, weeklyWage
    ELSE
      Display "Incorrect Password" message
      Display "Please try again"
    ENDIF
END
```

Here is the PHP code for **wage5.php**:

```
<html>
<head>
  <title>Wage Report</title>
```

```
    <link rel="stylesheet" type="text/css" href="sample.css" />
  </head>
  <body>
    <?php
      $hourlyWage = $_POST['hourlyWage'];
      $hoursWorked = $_POST['hoursWorked'];
      $userPassword = $_POST['userPassword'];

      print("<h1>Wage Report</h1>");
      if ($userPassword == "employee")
      {
         $weeklyWage = $hourlyWage * $hoursWorked;

         print("<p>Your hourly wage is $$hourlyWage and you worked
            $hoursWorked hours.</p>");
         print("<p>Your wages are $$weeklyWage.</p>");
      }
      else
      {
         print("<p><strong>YOU ENTERED AN INVALID
            PASSWORD!</strong></p>");
         print("<p>Please try again</p>");
      }
      print ("<a href=\"wage5.html\">Return to form</a>");
    ?>


  </body>
  </html>
```

Code Example: wage5.php

Note the use of the == operator to test whether the value stored in **$userPassword** is equal to **"employee"**. Be very careful not to use the = assignment operator by mistake, for example **if ($userPassword = "employee")**. If you make this mistake the processor will assume that you wish to store the value **"employee"** in the $userPassword variable, rather than test whether the variable contains this value.

For this algorithm, the **"Wage Report"** heading for the HTML must be displayed **before** the IF..ELSE structure. This will then be followed by either the output generated in the IF section or else the output generated inside the ELSE section. If the instruction to output the heading was located **inside** either the IF or the **ELSE** section, it might not be displayed. If the instruction was located **after** the entire IF..ELSE section, the heading would appear **following** the wage information or error message. An alternative would be to include the **print("<h1>Wage Report</h1>");** instruction in **both** the IF section **and** the ELSE section. This is considered bad programming practice since it requires code duplication. This increases the chance of typing errors, and also makes it harder to update code, for example if the heading needs to be changed. **As a general rule, if you find that you have duplicated a line of code, you should probably rethink your program logic.**

Since there are two paths through this code depending on the value of the password, you should test the application at least **twice:**

```
Test 1:   enter "employee" as the password
Test 2:   enter an incorrect password
```

Try entering "**EMPLOYEE**" as the password. Does the program accept passwords that do not use the correct case?

Ignoring the Case of a Character String

Our program will only accept "employee" as the correct password if the user enters this in lower-case characters. This may appropriate in this case, but sometimes when we test character strings we want to **ignore** the case. For example we may want to accept "employee" as a password whether the user types "employee", EMPLOYEE" or even "EmPloYEe". Instead of testing for every possible combination it is much easier to first convert the user's input to all lower-case and then compare this with "employee". We could just as well convert the input to all upper-case and compare this with "EM-PLOYEE".

Most programming languages, including PHP, provide a number of useful **string-processing** functions that make it easy to perform common operations on character strings. PHP provides the **strtolower()** and **strtoupper()** functions to convert a string to either lower or upper case. If we want to allow our program to accept the user's password without regard to case, we can add the following statement before the IF..ELSE section:

```
$userPassword = strtolower($userPassword);
```

This statement passes the value currently stored in **$userPassword** (the password that was entered by the user) to the **strtolower()** function. The function converts the password to all lower-case and returns the new version. This lower-case version of the password is then stored back in **$userPassword**, replacing the original version. Now when the program compares $userPassword with "employee" it will generate a true result even if the user submitted a password that included upper-case letters.

NOTE: In this example we actually changed the value stored in the **$userPassword** to lower-case. As an alternative we could leave the value unchanged and simply use the **strtolower()** function in the test itself:

```
if (strtolower($userPassword) == "employee")
```

Here the string is converted to lower-case in order to perform the test but the converted string is not assigned to **$userPassword** and so this variable still contains the original version of the string. In some applications it may be important that the original value is preserved.

The **strtolower()** and **strtoupper()** can be used on character strings that include non-alphabetical characters such as numbers or special characters. Non-alphabetical characters are unchanged.

Providing a Selective Response

Consider the following requirement:

Quiz1 requirement:

Write a program that provides the user with a quiz question using a drop down box with a list of possible answers. The program should display an appropriate response based on the user's input.

If the user provides the wrong answer the program should display the correct answer.

For test purposes, ask the question: What symbol is used to test whether two values are equal in PHP? Provide these possible answers: =, ==, and !=.

In this case we want to provide a selective response based on the user's answer to a question. Here is the algorithm for the HTML document that will provide the input form (**quiz1.html**):

```
quiz1.html algorithm:
   Prompt for the answer to the quiz question
   Get userAnswer
   Submit userAnswer to quiz1.php
END
```

We can test user input from a drop down list just as easily as input from an input box, and in this case we want to restrict the user's input to some specific choices. Here is the code for **quiz1.html**:

```
<html>
<head>
   <title>ADDITION QUIZ</title>
   <link rel="stylesheet" type="text/css" href="sample.css" />
</head>
<body>
   <h1>PHP QUIZ</h1>
```

```
<form action="quiz1.php" method="post">
  <p>What symbol is used to test whether two values are equal
     in PHP?

  <select name="userAnswer">
  <option>=</option>
  <option>==</option>
  <option>!=</option>
  </select>
  </p>

  <p><input type="submit" value="Submit your answer" /></p>
  </form>
</body>
</html>
```

Code Example: quiz1.html

Here is the algorithm for the PHP program that will process the input (**quiz1.php**):

```
quiz1.php algorithm:

  Receive userAnswer from quiz1.html
  Display "PHP QUIZ" heading
  correctAnswer = "=="
  IF (userAnswer == correctAnswer)
    Display "That is correct!"
  ELSE
    Display "That is incorrect!"
    Display correctAnswer
  ENDIF
END
```

Note once again the use of the = operator to assign a value to a variable (for example **correctAnswer** = "=="), and the use of the == operator to compare two values, for example **userAnswer** == **correctAnswer**. In this case the value stored in the **userAnswer** variable is compared to the value stored in the **correctAnswer** variable.

Here is the code for **quiz1.php**:

```
<html>
<head>
  <title>ADDITION QUIZ</title>
  <link rel="stylesheet" type="text/css" href="sample.css" />
</head>
<body>
  <?php
```

```
    $userAnswer = $_POST['userAnswer'];

    print("<h1>ADDITION QUIZ</h1>");

    $correctAnswer = "==";

    if ($userAnswer == $correctAnswer)
      print("<p>That is correct!</p>");
    else
    {
      print("<p>That is incorrect!</p>");
      print("<p>The correct answer is $correctAnswer</p>");
    }

  ?>
</body>
</html>
```

Code Example: quiz1.php

In this case, we are comparing the string that the user selected from the drop down list with the string stored in the **$correctAnswer** variable. Note that when processing input from a drop down list we never need to worry about the case, since we know exactly what text is listed inside each of the **<option>** **</option>**tags.

Note that the IF section contains only a **single** instruction and so curly braces are not needed. On the other hand the ELSE section contains **two** instructions and so these must be enclosed in braces.

Why did we assign the value "==" to the variable **$correctAnswer** instead of referring to it directly in our code? This avoids duplication. If we were to change our quiz to handle a different question with a new correct answer, we would only have to change the instruction **$correctAnswer** = "=="; to store the new correct answer in this variable. The rest of the code would then work correctly with no additional changes. Otherwise we would have to search through the code for every occurrence of the correct answer and change each one.

Using Selection to Construct a Line of Output

Often when a program generates output, some parts of the output will depend on the result of tests and must be included in selection structures, while other parts of the output will be the same regardless of any testing. These conditions may even apply to various parts of a sentence or paragraph. Consider the following requirement:

Grade1 requirement:

Write a program that asks the user to enter three exam scores. The program will calculate the average score and determine whether the average constitutes a passing or failing grade. A passing grade is 60 or higher.

The program should display the three scores followed by a line that begins "OVERALL GRADE: ", followed by "Pass" or "Fail".

This requires us to create a line that begins the same no matter what the score (with the phrase "OVERALL GRADE: "), but ends with either "**Pass**" or "**Fail**" depending on the result of a test.

Here is the algorithm for the HTML document that will provide the input form (**grade1.html**):

```
grade1.html algorithm:
    Prompt for the score for Exam 1
    Get exam1
    Prompt for the score for Exam 2
    Get exam2
    Prompt for the score for Exam 3
    Get exam3
    Submit exam1, exam2, exam3 to grade1.php
END
```

Here is the HTML code for **grade1.html**:

```
<html>
<head>
    <title>EXAM GRADE</title>
    <link rel ="stylesheet" type="text/css" href="sample.css" />
</head>
<body>
    <h1>EXAM GRADE</h1>

    <form action="grade1.php" method="post">
    <p>Enter score for Exam 1:
        <input type="text" size="10" name="exam1" /></p>
    <p>Enter score for Exam 2:
        <input type="text" size="10" name="exam2" /></p>
    <p>Enter score for Exam 3:
        <input type="text" size="10" name="exam3" /></p>
    <p><input type="submit" value="Submit your scores" /></p>
    </form>
</body>
</html>
```

Code Example: grade1.html

Here is the algorithm for the PHP program that will process the input (**grade1.php**):

```
grade1.php algorithm:
   Receive exam1, exam2, exam3 from grade1.html
   Display "EXAM GRADE"
   Display exam1, exam2, exam3
   Display "OVERALL GRADE: "
   averageScore = (exam1 + exam2 + exam3) /3

   IF (averageScore >= 60)
     Display "Pass"
   ELSE
     Display "Fail"
   ENDIF
END
```

Here is the PHP code for **grade1.php**:

```php
<html>
<head>
   <title>EXAM GRADE</title>
   <link rel="stylesheet" type="text/css" href="sample.css" />
</head>
<body>
   <?php
     $exam1 = $_POST['exam1'];
     $exam2 = $_POST['exam2'];
     $exam3 = $_POST['exam3'];

     print("<h1>EXAM GRADE</h1>");
     print("Exam 1 score: $exam1<br />");
     print("Exam 2 score: $exam2<br />");
     print("Exam 3 score: $exam3<br />");
     print("<p><strong>OVERALL GRADE: ");
     $averageScore = ($exam1 + $exam2 + $exam3) / 3;

     if ($averageScore >= 60)
       print("Pass</strong></p>");
     else
       print("Fail</strong></p>");

     print ("<p><a href=\"grade1.html\">Return to form</a></p>");
   ?>
</body>
</html>
```

Code Example: grade1.php

In order to display the word "**Pass**" or "**Fail**" on the same line as "**OVERALL GRADE** "
we first used a print statement before the IF..ELSE structure to begin a paragraph with
the words "**OVERALL GRADE:** ". We complete the paragraph in one of two different
ways depending on the result of the test (**$averageScore >= 60**).

It is possible to take another approach here and that is to progressively add (concatenate) all the output from the program to a single variable, and then simply print
the contents of this variable in a single instruction once all required output has been
added. Here is the relevant code from **grade2.php** which demonstrates this approach:

```php
<?php
    $exam1 = $_POST['exam1'];
    $exam2 = $_POST['exam2'];
    $exam3 = $_POST['exam3'];

    $report = "<h1>EXAM GRADE</h1>
        Exam 1 score: $exam1<br />
        Exam 2 score: $exam2<br />
        Exam 3 score: $exam3<br />
        <p><strong>OVERALL GRADE: ";

    $averageScore = ($exam1 + $exam2 + $exam3) / 3;

    if ($averageScore >= 60)
        $report = $report."Pass</strong></p>";
    else
        $report = $report."Fail</strong></p>";

    $report = $report."<p><a href=\"grade2.html\">
        Return to form</a></p>";
    print("$report");
?>
</body>
</html>
```

Here the variable **$report** is first assigned all of the output content that must appear
before the output from the IF..ELSE structure. Then the appropriate string from the
IF..ELSE structure is added to the previous content of the variable using the concatenation operator (this is a **period** in PHP). Following the IF..ELSE structure the last
line of required output is added to the variable. Now that the **$report** variable con-
tains all the required output, the program requires only a single **print**() statement.

This is an especially useful approach when the same text may need to be output to
multiple locations, for example to a file and also to a Web page. As always, it is important for you as the program designer to consider carefully what you need to accomplish
and assemble your logic in a way that meets the requirements correctly and efficiently. A
good designer designs an application in a way that also anticipates **future** requirements.

Summary

This chapter has introduced selection control structures which allow programs to make decisions. A decision is based on the result of a test that may be either **true** or **false**. Tests that have true or false results are known as Boolean expressions, and are based on comparisons using the relational operators (==, <, <=, >=, >, and !=).

The two most commonly used control structures are: IF structures which provide a series of statements to be executed if the result of a test is **true**, and where no special action is needed if the result of the test is **false**; and IF..ELSE structures, which provide a series of statements to be executed if the result of a test is **true**, and an alternative series of statements to be executed if the result of the test is **false**.

General purpose algorithms generally use the words **IF** and **ENDIF** to indicate the beginning and end of an IF structure, and **IF**, **ELSE** and **ENDIF** to indicate the parts of an IF..ELSE structure.

In PHP curly braces { and } are used to surround the block of statements in the IF section of an IF or IF..ELSE structure, and to surround the block of statements in the ELSE section of an IF..ELSE structure. In either case, if there is just a single instruction to be performed, the braces can be left out.

The test that controls the selection structure should always be enclosed in parentheses.

A common programming error is to use = instead of == when comparing values for equality. Another common error is to include a semi-colon immediately following the test at the start of the IF structure.

Programs that include selection structures should be tested thoroughly with a test case for each possible path through the program. Programs with a single IF structure or a single IF..ELSE structure will require two tests, once where the test has a true result, and once where the test has a false result. Effective tests will use threshold values (values that are closest to the test condition). For example if the test is (**wage < 8.00**) the threshold values will be 7.99 and 8.00).

The **strtolower()** and **strtoupper()** functions allow you to convert the case of character strings. This is useful when you wish to test two strings without regard for case.

Chapter 7 Review Questions

1. A test that evaluates to true or false is known as
   a. An arithmetic expression
   b. A Boolean expression
   c. A relational expression
   d. An assignment operation
   e. An algorithm

2. A selection control structure can contain
   a. An IF structure without an ELSE
   b. An IF structure with an ELSE
   c. An ELSE structure without an IF
   d. Either A or B but not C
   e. Either A or C but not B

3. What is wrong with the following piece of PHP code?

```
if ($answer = 4)
    print("<p>That's the correct answer!</p>");
```

   a. There must be an else section
   b. A semi-colon is missing at the end of the first line
   c. The = should be ==
   d. Curly braces must be included here
   e. There is nothing wrong with the code as written

4. What is wrong with the following piece of PHP code?

```
if ($carsSold <= 10);
    print("<p>If you sell more than 10 you get a bonus!</p>");
else
    print("<p>Good job - you sold more than 10 cars!</p>");
```

   a. The test should not be in parentheses
   b. There should not be a semi-colon at the end of the first line
   c. Curly braces must be included around the statement between the if
      and else
   d. Curly braces must be included around the statements after the else
   e. There is nothing wrong with the code as written

5. What is wrong with the following piece of PHP code?

```
if ($carsSold <= 10)
    print("<p>If you sell more than 10 you get a bonus!</p>");
else
    print("<p>Good job - you sold more than 10 cars!");
    print("You will receive a $500 bonus!</p>");
```

   a. The test should not be in parentheses
   b. There should be a semi-colon at the end of the first line
   c. Curly braces must be included around the statements between the if
      and else
   d. Curly braces must be included around the statements after the else
   e. There is nothing wrong with the code as written

6. Which of the following is NOT a relational operator
    a. =
    b. <
    c. <=
    d. !=
    e. >=

7. If a variable named $carsSold contains the value 10, what is the result of this test?

    ```
    if ($carsSold <= 10)
    ```

    a. True
    b. False

8. If a variable named $carsSold contains the value 20, what is the result of this test?

    ```
    if ($carsSold != 10)
    ```

    a. True
    b. False

9. What HTML output will be generated by the following PHP code?

    ```
    $age = 55;
    $retirementAge = 65;
    $yearsToRetire = $retirementAge - $age ;
    if ($yearsToRetire >= 10)
       print("<p> You have a long way to go yet..</p>");
    else
        print("<p> You have $yearsToRetire years to retire..</p>");
    print("<p>It will be here before you know it!</p>");
    ```

    a. <p> You have a long way to go yet..</p>
    b. <p> You have a long way to go yet..</p>
       <p>It will be here before you know it!</p>
    c. <p> You have 10 years to retire..</p>
    d. <p> You have 10 years to retire..</p>
       <p>It will be here before you know it!</p>
    e. <p> You have a long way to go yet..</p>
       <p> You have 10 years to retire..</p>
       <p>It will be here before you know it!</p>

10. Which of the following code segments shows the correct use of curly braces?
    a. if ($carsSold <= 10)

```
        print("<p>You did not sell many cars this month");
        print("<p>If you sell more than 10 you get a
          bonus!</p>")
      else
        print("<p>Good job - you sold more than 10 cars!");
```

    b. if ($carsSold <= 10)

```
      {
        print("<p>You did not sell many cars this month");
        print("<p>If you sell more than 10 you get a
          bonus!</p>")
      }
      else
        print("<p>Good job - you sold more than 10 cars!");
```

    c. if ($carsSold <= 10)

```
        print("<p>You did not sell many cars this month");
        print("<p>If you sell more than 10 you get a
          bonus!</p>")
      else
      {
        print("<p>Good job - you sold more than 10 cars!");
      }
```

    d. if ($carsSold <= 10)

```
      {
        print("<p>You did not sell many cars this month");
        print("<p>If you sell more than 10 you get a
          bonus!</p>")
      else
        print("<p>Good job - you sold more than 10 cars!");
      }
```

    e. if ($carsSold <= 10)

```
        print("<p>You did not sell many cars this month");
        print("<p>If you sell more than 10 you get a
          bonus!</p>")
      {
      else
        print("<p>Good job - you sold more than 10 cars!");
      }
```

11. Which would be good **threshold** values to use as inputs to test a selection structure with the heading if ($carsSold <= 10)?
    a. 0 and 10
    b. 9 and 10
    c. 10 and 11
    d. 0 and 100
    e. 0 and -1

12. What is wrong with the following algorithm?

```
hourlyWage = 12.00
hoursWorked = 40
IF (totalWage < 200.00)
   bonus = 100.00
ELSE
   bonus = 50.00
ENDIF
totalWage = hourlyWage * hoursWorked
Display totalWage, bonus
```

    a. The IF..ELSE structure should be listed first
    b. Curly braces are missing
    c. The ENDIF should appear before the ELSE
    d. The calculation for totalWage should appear before the IF test
    e. The Display statement should appear before the IF test

13. What value will be stored in $cityName after the following statement is executed?

```
$cityName = strtoupper("New York City");
```

    a. New York City
    b. NEW YORK CITY
    c. newYorkCity
    d. new york city
    e. NEWYORKCITY

14. What value is stored in $result after these PHP instructions are executed?

```
$value1 = 10;
$value2 = 20;
if ($value1 > $value2)
   $value2 = 50;
$result = $value1 + $value2;
print("<p>The result is $result</p>");
```

a. 0
b. 30
c. 50
d. 70
e. 80

15. What value is stored in $result after these PHP instructions are executed?

```
$value1 = 10;
$value2 = 20;
if ($value1 > $value2)
    $value2 = 50;
else
    $value1 = 30;
$result = $value1 + $value2;
print("<p>The result is $result</p>");
```

a. 0
b. 30
c. 50
d. 70
e. 80

16. What value is stored in $result after these PHP instructions are executed?

```
$value1 = 10;
$value2 = 20;
if ($value1 > $value2)
    $value2 = 50;
$value1 = 50;
$result = $value1 + $value2;
print("<p>The result is $result</p>");
```

a. 0
b. 30
c. 50
d. 70
e. 100

17. Which piece of code is correct to meet the following requirement:

Display "Good score" for scores above 85

---

    a. if ($score == 85)
        print ("<p>Good score</p>");
    b. if ($score <= 85)
        print ("<p>Good score</p>");
    c. if ($score < 85)
        print ("<p>Good score</p>");
    d. if ($score >= 85)
        print ("<p>Good score</p>");
    e. if ($score > 85)
        print ("<p>Good score</p>");

18. Which piece of code is correct to meet the following requirement:

Calculate and display the 7% sales tax if the purchase amount is positive, otherwise display an error message

---

    a. if ($purchaseAmount > 0)

```
        $salesTax = $purchaseAmount * 0.07;
        print ("<p>The sales tax is $salesTax</p>");
    print ("<p>Error: Purchase amount must be positive"</p>");
```

    b. if ($purchaseAmount > 0)

```
        $salesTax = $purchaseAmount * 0.07;
        print ("<p>The sales tax is $salesTax</p>");
    else
        print ("<p>Error: Purchase amount must be
          positive"</p>");
```

    c. if ($purchaseAmount > 0)

```
    {
        $salesTax = $purchaseAmount * 0.07;
        print ("<p>The sales tax is $salesTax</p>");
    }
    else
        print ("<p>Error: Purchase amount must be
          positive"</p>");
```

d. if ($purchaseAmount <= 0)

```
    {
       $salesTax = $purchaseAmount * 0.07;
       print ("<p>The sales tax is $salesTax</p>");
    }
    else
    {
       print ("<p>Error: Purchase amount must be
          positive"</p>");
    }
```

e. if ($purchaseAmount == 0)

```
    {
       $salesTax = $purchaseAmount * 0.07;
       print ("<p>The sales tax is $salesTax</p>");
    }
    else
       print ("<p>Error: Purchase amount must be
          positive"</p>")
```

19. How many possible paths are there through a program that includes a single IF..ELSE structure?
    a. 0
    b. 1
    c. 2
    d. 3
    e. 4

20. How many possible paths are there through a program that includes a single IF structure?
    a. 0
    b. 1
    c. 2
    d. 3
    e. 4

Chapter 7 Code Exercises

Your Chapter 7 code exercises can be found in your **Chapter07** folder. This folder is included in your customized XAMPP installation at the following location:

xampplite\htdocs\WebTech\coursework\Chapter07

Type your name and the date in the **Author** and **Date** sections of each file as you work on each exercise.

Debugging Exercises

Your **Chapter07** folder contains a number of "FixIt" files. Each of these files contains PHP code that has an error of some kind. You will need to run each program in order to see the errors, and to debug and test the code to see if it works correctly. For example to run **fixIt1.php**, first run the Web server, then use the URL:

http://localhost/WebTech/coursework/Chapter07/fixIt1.php

Code Modification Exercises

Your **Chapter07** folder contains a number of "Modify" files. Each pair of files contains HTML and PHP code that needs to be modified to meet a requirement. The requirements are included in each file. Modify the algorithms as specified, being careful to make changes to the .html and .php files as directed.

Code Completion Exercises

1. Your **Chapter07** folder contains modified versions of **paintEstimate.html** and **paintEstimate.php**. The code in **paintEstimate.html** does not need to be changed. The HTML form includes a drop down selection to ask the user if they are a first time customer. Note that the name for this input is **firstTime**, and the possible values are "**yes**" and "**no**". The PHP program should be modified to test the user's selection and, if the user chose "**yes**", should calculate a **10%** deduction to the **total** estimate and generate the following additional output: "<p>We want your service! Since you are a first time customer, we are offering a 10% deduction.</p><p>Your actual costs will be: $xxx</p>" where $xxx is their cost after the deduction. Make the changes to **paintEstimate.php** so that the program works as described. Should you use an IF or IF..ELSE structure when you modify **paintEstimate.php**?

Think carefully where your selection structure must appear in the code. Figure 7-8 shows examples of output where the user chose yes (first screen) and no

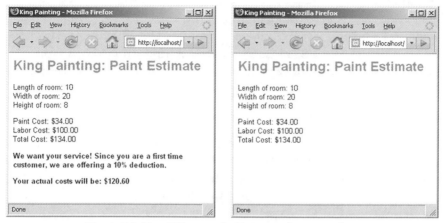

Figure 7-8: Two different paintEstimate.php screenshots

(second screen). In both cases the user entered 10, 20 and 8 for the length, width and height.

2. Your Chapter07 folder contains versions of **softwareOrder.html** and **software-Order.php**. The code in **softwareOrder.html** does not need to be changed. The PHP program should test the number of copies ordered. If there are **less than five copies** the shipping and handling charge is a standard **3.50** no matter how many copies, otherwise the shipping handling is **0.75** for each copy. Make the changes to **softwareOrder.php** so that the program works as described. Should you use an IF or IF..ELSE structure when you modify **softwareOrder.php**? Think carefully where your selection structure must appear in the code. Figure 7-9 shows output examples when either 4 or 5 is entered for the number of copies.

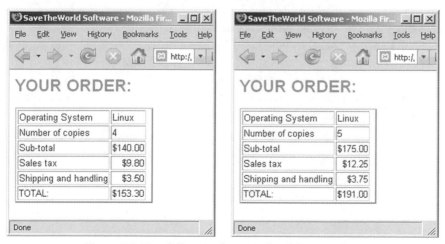

Figure 7-9: Two different softwareOrder.php screenshots

3. Your **Chapter07** folder contains modified versions of **travel.html** and **travel.php**. The code in **travel.html** does not need to be changed. This form now includes a choice of travel destinations. If the destination is Rome, the air fare is **$875** and the nightly hotel cost is **$110** (so for example a trip to Rome by two people for 5 nights would cost a total of $2850). If the destination is Tokyo, the air fare is **$1575** and the nightly hotel cost is **$240** (so for example a trip to Tokyo by two people for 5 nights would cost a total of $5550). Assume that each traveler has a separate room.

   Add the necessary selection structure. The PHP program already includes the code to perform the appropriate calculations and display the costs.

4. Your **Chapter07** folder contains previous versions of **gameIntro.html** and **gameIntro.php**. Change **gameIntro.html so that the user is also asked for a secret password in order to submit the character. The password is php123. The** PHP program should test the password and accept any combination of upper- or lower-case letters (for example PhP123 or pHP123 are both acceptable). If the password is accepted, the program calculates and displays the cost and other information, otherwise the program displays an error message: "<p>Sorry! That password is NOT correct! Please try again.</p>".

5. Copy **event.html** and **event.php** from your Chapter06 folder to your Chapter07 folder. Your Chapter07 folder already contains a file named **ticketCount.txt**. You are going to modify your event.php file so that, after receiving the form inputs, it will check the count of tickets sold (the number in ticketCount.txt) and then use an IF.. ELSE structure to either process the order or report that there are not enough seats available. Assume that the performance venue has seating for 100. You will need to think carefully about the order of your instructions and the placement of braces in your IF..ELSE structure.

   To check for available seats, after receiving the input from the form, your event.php program must: (1) open ticketCount.txt for read operations, read the count of tickets already sold, and close the file; (2) calculate the number of seats available (this will be 100 minus the count of seats already sold); and (3) use an IF..ELSE structure that tests whether the current order exceeds the number of available seats. If so, the program should simply notify the user that there are not enough tickets remaining to complete the order, otherwise the program should go ahead and process the order (this includes updating the ticketCount.txt file so that it contains the new count).

   Test your work to be sure that it works correctly in either situation. Does it work correctly if the number of seats being ordered is EXACTLY the number of available seats?

6. Copy **fuelCost.html** and **fuelCost.php** from your Chapter05 folder to your Chapter07 folder. Modify fuelCost.html by adding a drop down list with a prompt that asks whether or not the trip is work-related. Name this input '**workRelated**' and allow the user to select YES or NO from the drop down list.

Now modify fuelCost.php to receive this input in addition to the other inputs. The program should calculate the fuel cost in the same way as before, but should then use an IF.. ELSE structure to test whether or not the trip is work related. If the trip IS work related, the program should calculate the amount that will be reimbursed to you by your employer, at the rate of 0.35 a mile (so for example, if the trip was 100 miles you would be reimbursed 0.35 x 100 or $35.00). If the trip is not work related, the amount to be reimbursed will be 0.

Your program should then display the miles traveled, the fuel cost, whether or not the trip was work-related, and the amount to be reimbursed.

Chapter 8

Multiple Selection, Nesting, ANDs and ORs

Intended Learning Outcomes

After completing this chapter, you should be able to:

- Solve requirements that require multiple selection structures
- Include multiple but distinct selection structures in a single application
- Describe the importance of input validation
- Apply the trim() function to remove leading and trailing white space
- Recognize the syntax and use of the logical operator AND
- Recognize the syntax and use of the logical operator OR
- Chain together multiple selection structures using ELSEIF
- Apply top down design to solve more complex requirements
- Nest selection structures to meet requirements
- Describe the challenge of software testing

Introduction

In the last chapter we learned to create Boolean expressions and IF and IF..ELSE selection structures. Most real-world applications include multiple selection structures in order to meet requirements. In this chapter we will see that multiple IF and IF..ELSE selection structures can be included in a single application in various ways:

- Applications can include any number of **independent** selection structures, each serving a distinct and separate purpose.
- Selection structures may be **chained** together another so that the program can choose between more than two possible actions based on series of tests.

- Selection structures may be **nested** inside other selection structures. In these cases, the inner selection structures will only be processed under certain conditions.

We will also learn how to use the **AND** and **OR** operators to combine multiple true/false tests into **compound Boolean expressions** that generate a single true/false result.

There is no limit to the ways in which multiple selection structures and compound expressions can be combined, and large applications may contain hundreds or even thousands of selection structures in quite complex algorithms. Hopefully this chapter will give you a taste of what is possible, and provide sufficient syntax to help you apply these structures to meet any set of application requirements.

Creating a Program with Multiple but Independent Selection Structures

Let's combine two of the wage requirements that we developed in the last chapter:

Wage6 requirement:

Write a program that asks the employee for an hourly wage and the number of hours worked.

If the hourly wage is below 8.00 it should be increased to 8.00. No increase is needed if the hourly wage is already at least 8.00.

The program should assign a bonus based on the hours worked. If the hours worked is at least 35, the program should assign a bonus of 50.00, otherwise the program should assign a bonus of 25.00.

The program should calculate and display the hourly wage, hours worked, bonus and weekly wage (including the bonus).

The algorithm that meets this requirement must include two separate selection structures. One selection structure is needed to update the hourly wage if necessary. The other will be used to calculate the bonus. Here is the algorithm for **wage6.php**:

```
wage6.php algorithm:

   Receive hourlyWage, hoursWorked from wage6.html

   IF (hourlyWage < 8.00)
      hourlyWage = 8.00
   ENDIF

   IF (hoursWorked >= 35)
```

```
      bonus = 50.00
   ELSE
      bonus = 25.00
   ENDIF

   weeklyWage = hourlyWage * hoursWorked + bonus
   Display heading
   Display hourlyWage, hoursWorked, bonus, weeklyWage
END
```

Look through this algorithm carefully. Notice that the hourly wage that was entered by the user may or may not be increased, but a bonus will **always** be calculated. This is because the first selection is an IF structure, with no action taken if the test is **false**, while the second structure is an IF..ELSE structure, which provides actions for either a **true** result or a **false** result. In this algorithm these two structures just happen to directly follow one another, but selection structures can be included anywhere in your algorithm as needed.

Consider the order of the statements in this algorithm. Since the two selection structures are unrelated to one another, they could be included in your algorithm in either order. In other words, the structure to assign a bonus could appear before the structure that determines whether or not to increase the hourly wage. This is not always the case—later in this chapter we will look at requirements where multiple selection structures **must** be ordered correctly or even **nested** inside one another.

The weeklyWage calculation uses the hourly wage and the bonus, so this calculation **must** appear after both selection structures, otherwise the calculation will be performed before a possible change to the hourly wage, and before a bonus has been assigned. Similarly the output statements must appear after all variables have been assigned values by the program. Always remember that a computer program cannot "look ahead", and that statements are processed in the order that they are listed.

Here is the PHP code for **wage6.php**:

```
<html>
<head>
   <title>Wage Report</title>
   <link rel="stylesheet" type="text/css" href="sample.css" />
</head>
<body>
   <?php
      $hourlyWage = $_POST['hourlyWage'];
      $hoursWorked = $_POST['hoursWorked'];

      if ($hourlyWage < 8.00)
         $hourlyWage = 8.00;
```

```
      if ($hoursWorked >= 35)
         $bonus = 50.00;
      else
         $bonus = 25.00;

      $weeklyWage = $hourlyWage * $hoursWorked + $bonus;

      print("<h1>Wage Report</h1>");
      print("<p>Your hourly wage is $$hourlyWage and you worked
         $hoursWorked hours.</p>");
      print("<p>Your bonus is $$bonus.</p>");
      print("<p>Your weekly wage is $$weeklyWage.</p>");
      print ("<a href=\"wage6.html\">Return to form</a>");
   ?>
</body>
</html>
```

Code Example: wage6,php

How many tests are needed to test this code thoroughly? Note that there are **four** possible paths through this program: two paths through the **IF** structure, and two paths through the IF..ELSE structure. You should test for each possible path, as follows:

Test 1: *A value for hourlyWage that is less than 8.00, and a value for hoursWorked that is 35 or above*

Test 2: A value for hourlyWage that is less than 8.00, and a value for hoursWorked that is less than 35

Test 3: A value for hourlyWage that is 8.00 or higher, and a value for hoursWorked that is 35 or above

Test 4: A value for hourlyWage that is 8.00 or higher, and a value for hoursWorkedthat is less than 35

Do you see that all four tests are needed to be sure that all of the statements in the program are working correctly?

Validating User Input

The HTML form that we have used in our wage programs allows the user to enter an hourly wage and hours worked. However, until now we have not tested whether or not the user input is actually valid. As we will see there are a number of ways that the user might enter invalid input. As an example, Figure 8-1 shows what happens if a user enters -10 for an hourly wage and 0 for hours worked to our **Wage6** application:

Figure 8-1: Entering invalid input into the wage6 form

When this data is submitted to **wage6.php**, the program receives an hourly wage of −10.00 and hours worked of 0. Although this input is invalid the program goes ahead and processes a weekly wage. The first selection structure increases any wage less than 8.00, and since -10 is less than 8.00 the negative wage is increased to 8.00! The second selection structure assigns a bonus of $25 to anyone who works less than 35 hours, and since 0 is less than 35 a bonus of $25.00 is assigned.

When the statement **$weeklyWage = $hourlyWage * $hoursWorked;** is processed, PHP multiplies 8.00 (the new hourly wage) by 0 (the hours worked), and then adds 25.00 (the bonus). As a result, 25.00 is stored in **$weeklyWage**.

Clearly this is not what we want to happen here! Instead we want to inform the user that there was a problem with the input. To do that, we must **validate** the input before processing the weekly wage. If the input is not valid the program should display an error message. Ideally the program will identify various kinds of errors so that error messages can be customized to describe the exact problem that was found (this is an example of **user-friendliness**).

Here is a revised requirement for our Wage program that includes a requirement for input validation:

Wage7 requirement:

Write a program that asks the employee for an hourly wage and the number of hours worked. The program should validate these inputs and either generate appropriate error messages or process the inputs as follows:

If the hourly wage is below 8.00 it should be increased to 8.00. No increase is needed if the hourly wage is already at least 8.00.

The program should assign a bonus based on the hours worked. If the hours worked is at least 35, the program should assign a bonus of 50.00, otherwise the program should assign a bonus of 25.00.

The program should calculate and display the hourly wage, hours worked, bonus and weekly wage (including the bonus).

In order to write programs that handle invalid input we must first decide what type of input errors might occur. Here is a list of four possible input errors associated with this application:

1. The user might submit the form without entering data in either the hourly wage field or the hours worked field (or **both** fields might be empty).
2. The form might be submitted with **non-numeric data** in either the hourly wage field, the hours worked field, or in both fields. For example the user might enter "NOT ENOUGH" in the hourly wage field.
3. The form might be submitted with an hourly wage that is **below the minimum wage**.
4. The form might be submitted with a **value of 0 or less** in the hours worked field.

We will see how to include tests for these four conditions in turn. In the process we will learn how to create compound Boolean expressions and discover how to combine IF..ELSE structures in various ways.

Introducing the Logical Operators AND and OR

The first two types of input error (no data or non-numeric data) might apply to **either** or **both** user inputs (the hourly wage and hours worked) and so we will need to test both variables in each case. So far we have only tested a single variable to determine the action in each selection structure. However programming languages allow us to combine multiple tests using the **logical operators AND** and **OR**. Expressions that combine multiple true/false tests are often referred to as **compound Boolean expressions**. To understand this, first consider the following algorithm to decide whether or not to accept a job offer or keep your current job:

```
IF the salary is better AND the prospects for advancement are
good
   Accept the job offer
ELSE
   Keep your current job
ENDIF
```

This selection structure uses **two** tests, **each** of which may be **true** or **false**. The salary may or may not be better, and the prospects for advancement may or may not be good. The two tests are combined using the word **AND**, which indicates that **both** tests must be **true** in order to accept the job offer. If **either** or **both** tests are false, the decision is to keep your current job.

One way to understand the overall result of a compound expression is to construct a **truth table**. This is illustrated in Table 8-1.

Salary is better	Prospects are good	Overall result	Action
True	True	True	Accept job offer
True	False	False	Keep current job
False	True	False	Keep current job
False	False	False	Keep current job

Table 8-1: Truth table using the AND operator

As you can see, when two tests are combined using the AND operator, only one possible combination generates an overall true result, while three possible combinations generate an overall false result.

Now compare the previous algorithm to the following:

```
IF the salary is better OR the prospects for advancement are good
   Accept the job offer
ELSE
   Keep your current job
ENDIF
```

The only difference is that we have replaced the **AND** operator with the **OR** operator. Now the test instructs us to accept the job offer if the salary is better **OR** the prospects for advancement are good, or if **both** of these statements are true. Now we only keep our current job if **both** statements are **false**. Table 8-2 shows a truth table using the OR operator.

Salary is better	Prospects are good	Overall result	Action
True	True	True	Accept job offer
True	False	True	Accept job offer
False	True	True	Accept job offer
False	False	False	Keep current job

Table 8-2: Truth table using the OR operator

In this case, three possible combinations generate an overall true result, while only one possible combination generates an overall false result.

The **AND** and **OR** operators allow us to combine simple expressions into compound expressions in order to meet more complex requirements. Now let's see how we can apply these operators to our wage program.

Using the OR Operator to Validate Input

As a first step towards validating our form input, we want our Wage7 program to calculate and display the weekly wage only if the user actually types a value into both the hourly wage and hours worked fields. If **either** or **both** of these fields are empty the program should simply output an error message. Here is an algorithm to achieve this input validation:

```
wage7.php algorithm:

  Receive hourlyWage, hoursWorked from wage7.html

  IF (hourlyWage is empty OR hoursWorked is empty)
     display an "empty field" error message
  ELSE
     process the weekly wage
  ENDIF
END
```

Notice that here we are using a "high-level" algorithm to work out the general logic of our program without getting into too much detail. The statement "process the weekly wage" actually represents quite a number of instructions. This high-level approach is helpful when we just want to plan our overall program structure before focusing on the details. Once we are satisfied with the general logic we can create a more detailed algorithm (see below). The general term used to describe working from a high-level to a detailed design is **top down design**.

In this algorithm we use the **OR** operator to combine two tests into one compound expression. As we have seen, when we use the word **OR** between two tests, we are testing whether **EITHER** or **BOTH** tests are **true**. The truth table in Table 8-3 shows each possible true or false outcome for this compound expression.

hourlyWage is empty	hoursWorked is empty	Overall result	Action
True	True	True	Display error message
True	False	True	Display error message
False	True	True	Display error message
False	False	False	Process weekly pay

Table 8-3: Truth table using the OR operator to test for empty fields

For example if **hourlyWage** contains no data and hoursWorked contains **20**, we can see that the **hourlyWage is empty** test is **true** and the **hoursWorked > 0** test is false. Since we are using the OR operator to combine these tests, the overall result is **true**, and so the program will generate an error message. But if the **hourlyWage** is **10.00** and **hoursWorked** is **10**, the **hourlyWage is empty** test is **false** and the **hoursWorked is empty** test is also **false** so the overall result is **false**, and the program will skip to the ELSE section and process the weekly wage. When the **OR** operator is used to combine two tests, the overall result will only be **false** if **both** tests generate a **false** result. In our algorithm, the program will only execute the ELSE section if both tests are false.

Here is the complete algorithm, including the statements to process the weekly wage.

```
wage7.php algorithm:

  Receive hourlyWage, hoursWorked from wage7.html

  Display "Wage Report" heading

  IF (hourlyWage is empty OR hoursWorked is empty)
    display an "empty field" error message
  ELSE
    IF (hourlyWage < 8.00)
      hourlyWage = 8.00
    ENDIF
    IF (hoursWorked >= 35)
      bonus = 50.00
    ELSE
      bonus = 25.00
    ENDIF
    weeklyWage = hourlyWage * hoursWorked + bonus
    Display hourlyWage, hoursWorked, bonus, weeklyWage
  ENDIF
END
```

Note that we have moved the instruction **Display "Wage Report" heading** before the IF..ELSE structure. That is because we want the heading to be displayed whether the program generates an error message or calculates the weekly pay. As we add control structures we must be very careful to consider which statements should occur **before** the control structures, which should be contained **inside** the control structures, and which should appear **after** (or **between**) the control structures.

Note also that the statements in the ELSE section of the first IF structure actually include other selection structures! We will discuss this shortly.

PHP provides a useful function to test whether or not a variable is empty. You guessed it, the function name is **empty**()! Here is the PHP code for this algorithm:

```
<html>
<head>
  <title>Wage Report</title>
  <link rel="stylesheet" type="text/css" href="sample.css" />
</head>
<body>
  <?php
    $hourlyWage = $_POST['hourlyWage'];
    $hoursWorked = $_POST['hoursWorked'];
```

```
print("<h1>Wage Report</h1>");

if ( empty($hourlyWage) OR empty($hoursWorked) )
  print("ERROR: Input is missing!");
else
{
  if ($hourlyWage < 8.00)
    $hourlyWage = 8.00;

  if ($hoursWorked >= 35)
    $bonus = 50.00;
  else
    $bonus = 25.00;

  $weeklyWage = $hourlyWage * $hoursWorked + $bonus;

  print("<p>Your hourly wage is $$hourlyWage and you
    worked $hoursWorked hours.</p>");
  print("<p>Your bonus is $$bonus.</p>");
  print("<p>Your weekly wage is $$weeklyWage.</p>");
}

print ("<a href=\"wage7.html\">Return to form</a>");
?>
</body>
</html>
```

Code Example: wage7.php (first validation stage)

PHP allows us to use the word **OR** in our program code. We can alternatively use the characters || to represent the OR operator. Some programming languages require the use of || and the word **OR** cannot be used.

Nested Selection Structures

This code contains another important feature of program logic. The code in the ELSE section of the first IF..ELSE structure includes two additional selection structures: if (**$hourlyWage** < 8.00) and **if ($hoursWorked** >= 35). When a control structure is located inside another control structure we say that it is **nested**.

When a selection structure is nested inside the IF section of another selection structure it will only be processed if the test for the outside selection structure is **true**. Similarly when a selection structure is nested inside the ELSE section of another selection structure it will only be processed if the test for the outside selection structure is **false**.

Selection structures can be included inside the IF or ELSE sections of other selection structures just as any other program statements can be included in these sections. IF..ELSE structures can be nested inside other IF..ELSE structures that are nested inside other IF..ELSE structures and so on. Most applications of any kind of complexity will require multiple nested selection structures.

A flow chart can help us understand how nested structures are processed. Figure 8-2 shows a slightly simplified flow chart for this program. You can see that the visual nature of the flowchart makes it easier to understand the logic of this more complex structure. Take some time to compare this to the pseudocode version of the algorithm.

Use of Braces in Nested Selection Structures

Recall that the blocks of code inside IF and ELSE sections must be surrounded by opening and closing curly braces { and } unless the code consists of a single statement. When you use nested selection structures, you will need to be very careful to ensure that you are using opening and closing braces appropriately. For example, can you see the problem with the following code snippet?

```
if ( empty($hourlyWage) )
   print("ERROR: Input is missing!");
else
{
   if ($hourlyWage < 8.00)
   {
      $hourlyWage - 8.00;
      print("<p>Your hourly wage has been increased.</p>");

   print("<p>Your hourly wage is $$hourlyWage</p>");
}
```

A closing curly brace is missing between the two print statements. This missing brace indicates the end of the nested IF structure. The correct code looks like this:

```
if ( empty($hourlyWage) )
   print("ERROR: Input is missing!");
else
{
   if ($hourlyWage < 8.00)
   {
      $hourlyWage = 8.00;
      print("<p>Your hourly wage has been
               increased.</p>");
   }
   print("<p>Your hourly wage is $$hourlyWage</p>");
}
```

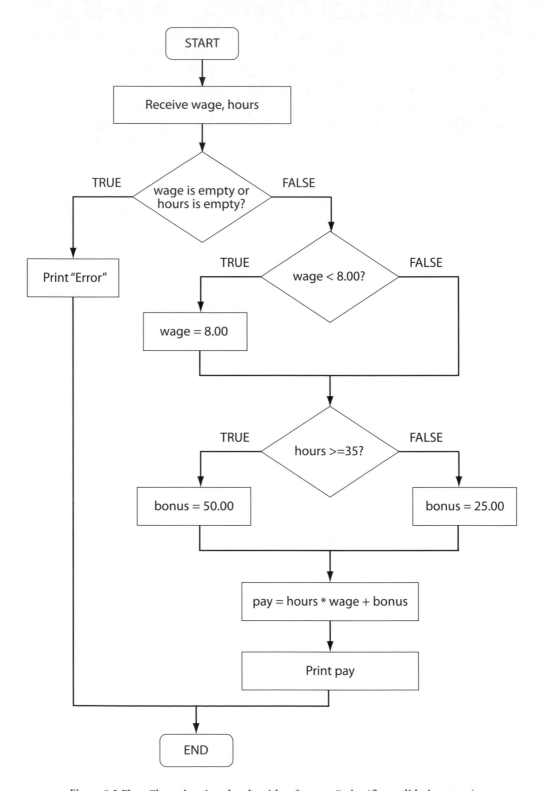

Figure 8.2 Flow Chart showing the algorithm for wage7.php (first validation stage)

This is a common programming error, and this type of error can often be hard to find and correct. The processor will report the location of the error incorrectly, on a line that occurs later in the program code (perhaps even the last line of your program).

To understand this, take another look at the code that contains the error. The processor will find the first opening brace and proceed to treat the code that follows as part of the ELSE section of the first IF..ELSE structure. The processor then encounters the next opening brace and treats the code following that brace as part of the IF section of the nested IF structure. When the processor finds the closing brace after the second **print**() statement it assumes that this indicates the end of the IF section of the **nested** IF structure! The processor will continue to look for the closing brace of the ELSE component of the first selection structure, and will generate an error message only when it is clear that this brace cannot be found, which may not be before the last line of your program. If that's the case, the error message will indicate that the error was found in the last line!

This is just one situation where the processor reports the wrong line number when an error is found. This makes it hard to find errors such as those caused by missing braces. Since every opening brace must be paired with a closing brace, it can help to simply count the number of opening and closing braces in your code. This at least tells you whether or not a brace is missing. Finding the exact location of a missing brace requires careful review of your algorithm and program logic.

Chaining Related Selection Structures

Our program now tests for empty fields but what about **incorrect** input? For example, what if the user enters "not enough" when asked for an hourly wage, or simply makes a typing error of some kind? The hourly wage and hours worked inputs must be numeric, otherwise the program should generate an error message instead of processing the weekly pay.

So we need to extend our program to choose between **three** different actions based on the user input:

- If the user submits empty fields, generate an "empty field" message
- If the user submits non-numeric input, generate an "non-numeric input" message
- Otherwise process the wage and display the results

How can we use IF..ELSE structures to choose between more than two possible actions? Look at the following algorithm carefully:

```
Algorithm for wage7.php
    Receive hourlyWage, hoursWorked from wage7.html

    Display "Wage Report" heading
```

```
IF (hourlyWage is empty OR hoursWorked is empty)
   display an "empty field" error message
ELSE IF (hourlyWage is not numeric OR hoursWorked is not numeric)
     display a "non-numeric input" error message
ELSE
   IF (hourlyWage < 8.00)
     hourlyWage = 8.00
   ENDIF

   IF (hoursWorked >= 35)
     bonus = 50.00
   ELSE
     bonus = 25.00
   ENDIF

   weeklyWage = hourlyWage * hoursWorked + bonus
   Display hourlyWage, hoursWorked, bonus, weeklyWage

 ENDIF
END
```

The ELSE section of the **first** IF..ELSE structure consists of a second IF..ELSE structure that tests for non-numeric input, and the ELSE section of the **second** IF..ELSE structure contains the code to actually process the wage.

If the first test (for an empty field) is **true**, the "empty field" error message is generated and the program skips the ELSE section. Since this section includes the second IF..ELSE structure, the second IF..ELSE structure is skipped entirely. If the first test is **false**, the program skips to the ELSE section, encounters the second IF..ELSE structure, and tests for non-numeric input. If this test is **true**, the program generates the "non-numeric input" error message and skips the second ELSE section. If the test for non-numeric input is **false**, the program will skip to the **second** ELSE section and will calculate and display the weekly pay. Note that this section includes the selection structure that determines whether or not to increase the hourly wage, and the selection structure to assign a bonus. Since these structures are nested inside the second ELSE section they will only be processed if the input is valid.

This example demonstrates how we can handle more than two possible actions by **chaining** multiple IF..ELSE structures. We achieve this by placing each IF..ELSE structure directly following the ELSE of the previous IF..ELSE structure. The program will continue through the chain until a test is true and will then perform the appropriate processing.

This chaining requirement is so common that we often replace each chained ELSE IF in our algorithm with the combined word ELSEIF. Here is the same algorithm once again, this time using the ELSEIF verb. Also note the single ENDIF at the end of the entire structure.

```
Receive hourlyWage, hoursWorked from wage7.html

Display "Wage Report" heading

IF (hourlyWage is empty OR hoursWorked is empty)
   display an "empty field" error message
ELSEIF (hourlyWage is not numeric OR hoursWorked is not numeric)
      display a "non-numeric input" error message
ELSE
   IF (hourlyWage < 8.00)
     hourlyWage = 8.00
   ENDIF
   IF (hoursWorked >= 35)
     bonus = 50.00
   ELSE
     bonus = 25.00
   ENDIF
   weeklyWage = hourlyWage * hoursWorked + bonus
   Display hourlyWage, hoursWorked, bonus, weeklyWage
ENDIF
END
```

Some languages, including PHP, provide the word **elseif** for ELSEIF sections. This word can be optionally used in place of the two words **else if** and we will use this in our examples.

Introducing the NOT Operator

In order to code the second IF..ELSE structure, we need to test that the user's input is non-numeric. PHP provides an **is_numeric**() function to test if a variable contains numeric data, for example **is_numeric($hoursWorked)**. However in our algorithm we do not want to test if our hourly wage and hours worked variables contain **numeric** data—we want to test whether these variables contains **non-numeric** data. That means checking whether the result of our **is_numeric($hoursWorked)** is **false.** We can accomplish this using the NOT operator.

The NOT operator simply reverses the logic of a test. In many current languages, including PHP, the NOT operator is written as an exclamation mark. So if we wish to test whether the variable $hoursWorked contains non-numeric data we can write **!is_numeric($hoursWorked)**. The NOT operator asks if the test result is **false**, rather than asking if the test is **true.** This may seem to just make the logic more difficult to understand but in cases such as this the NOT operator actually makes it easier to develop your algorithm. We will see other examples of this operator in later chapters.

Here is the PHP code that includes the test for non-numeric input, using the **is_nu-meric** function with the NOT operator:

```
<html>
<head>
   <title>Wage Report</title>
   <link rel="stylesheet" type="text/css" href="sample.css" />
</head>
<body>
   <?php
      $hourlyWage = $_POST['hourlyWage'];
      $hoursWorked = $_POST['hoursWorked'];

      print("<h1>Wage Report</h1>");

      if ( empty($hourlyWage) OR empty($hoursWorked) )
         print("ERROR: Input is missing!");
      elseif ( !is_numeric($hourlyWage) OR
                !is_numeric($hoursWorked) )
         print("ERROR: Non-numeric input found!");
      else
      {
         if ($hourlyWage < 8.00)
            $hourlyWage = 8.00;

         if ($hoursWorked >= 35)
            $bonus = 50.00;
         else
            $bonus = 25.00;

         $weeklyWage = $hourlyWage * $hoursWorked + $bonus;

         print("<p>Your hourly wage is $$hourlyWage and you worked
            $hoursWorked hours.</p>");
         print("<p>Your bonus is $$bonus.</p>");
         print("<p>Your weekly wage is $$weeklyWage.</p>");
      }

      print ("<a href=\"wage7.html\">Return to form</a>");
   ?>
</body>
</html>
```

Code Example: wage7.php (second validation stage)

Additional Input Validation

We have not yet completed our input validation requirements for the Wage7 application. We must also ensure that the user does not enter numbers that are **out of range**. The hourly wage should not be below the minimum wage (here we will assume that the minimum wage is 6.50). The hours worked should not be 0 or a negative number. We will test these two conditions separately so that we can display a customized message in each case. We now want the program to choose between five different actions:

- If the user submits empty fields, generate an "empty field" message
- If the user submits non-numeric input, generate an "non-numeric input" message
- If the user submits an hourly wage below 6.50, generate an "hourly wage must be at least 6.50" message
- If the user submits an hours worked of 0 or less, generate an "hours worked must be above 0" message
- Otherwise process the wage and display the results

Here is the revised algorithm for **wage7.php**:

```
wage7.php algorithm:

   Receive hourlyWage, hoursWorked from wage7.html

   Display "Wage Report" heading

   IF (hourlyWage is empty OR hoursWorked is empty)
      display an "empty field" error message
   ELSEIF (hourlyWage is not numeric OR hoursWorked is not
   numeric)
      display a "non-numeric input" error message
   ELSEIF (hourlyWage < 6.50)
      display an "hourly wage must be at least 6.50" error message
   ELSEIF (hourlyWorked <= 0)
      display an "hours worked must be above 0" error message
   ELSE
      IF (hourlyWage < 8.00)
         hourlyWage = 8.00
      ENDIF
      IF (hoursWorked >= 35)
         bonus = 50.00
      ELSE
         bonus = 25.00
      ENDIF
      weeklyWage = hourlyWage * hoursWorked + bonus
      Display hourlyWage, hoursWorked, bonus, weeklyWage
   ENDIF
END
```

We are now chaining **four** IF..ELSE structures together in order to allow the program to select between five actions based on the user's input. Note that we don't indent the IF..ELSE structures in this case since we would quickly run off the right margin of the page! The program will now only calculate and display the weekly pay if the tests fail in all four IF..ELSE structures.

Here is the complete code for wage7.php:

```
<html>
<head>
  <title>Wage Report</title>
  <link rel="stylesheet" type="text/css" href="sample.css" />
</head>
<body>
  <?php
    $hourlyWage = $_POST['hourlyWage'];
    $hoursWorked = $_POST['hoursWorked'];
    print("<h1>Wage Report</h1>");
    if ( empty($hourlyWage) OR empty($hoursWorked) )
      print("ERROR: Input is missing!");
    elseif ( !is_numeric($hourlyWage) OR
             !is_numeric($hoursWorked) )
      print("ERROR: Non-numeric input found!");
    elseif ($hourlyWage < 6.50)
      print("ERROR: Hourly wage is below minimum wage!");
    elseif ($hoursWorked <= 0 )
      print("ERROR: Hours worked is less than 0!");
    else
    {
      if ($hourlyWage < 8.00)
        $hourlyWage = 8.00;

      if ($hoursWorked >= 35)
        $bonus = 50.00;
      else
        $bonus = 25.00;

      $weeklyWage = $hourlyWage * $hoursWorked + $bonus;
      print("<p>Your hourly wage is $$hourlyWage and you worked
        $hoursWorked hours.</p>");
      print("<p>Your bonus is $$bonus.</p>");
      print("<p>Your weekly wage is $$weeklyWage.</p>");
    }
    print ("<p><a href=\"wage7.html\">Return to form</a></p>");
  ?>
</body>
</html>
```

Code Example: wage7.php (complete)

Review this carefully and notice which programming statements must appear before your selection structures, which should be included **inside** the various sections of your selection structures, and which should **follow** your selection structures. These decisions will depend on your program requirements.

Figure 8-3 shows an example of valid input.

Figure 8-3: wage7.html and wage7.php screenshots (valid input)

Figure 8-4 shows an example of invalid input.

Figure 8-4: wage7.html and wage7.php screenshots (invalid input)

Run this program yourself and try various combinations of valid and invalid input to see that the different types of invalid input are handled correctly.

More about Input Validation: Using the trim() Function

Input validation is a tedious process and as a programmer you will want to take advantage of any tools that can reduce the likelihood of input errors. When receiving input from the user, you can minimize errors by providing selection features such as drop down lists, radio buttons and checkboxes where the user does not have the option to submit any value other than those provided.

Often however your application must receive input that was **typed**, whether into a form, or a file, or a database record. A common problem with user input is that it may contain **leading** or **trailing white space**, in other words, spaces, tabs or new line characters that were added to the beginning or end of the input. These additional characters can become a problem when the input is processed.

For example consider a programs that must test a user's password. If the correct password is "xyz123" and the user enters " xyz123" (a space at the beginning) then a comparison between the user's input and the correct password will generate a false result. Similarly a test of a character string that has been read from a file may not yield a correct result if the string from the file contains an **end-of-line** marker.

PHP provides a **trim**() function which receives any character string and returns a modified version of the same string with any leading and trailing white space removed. If the original string did not contain any leading or trailing white space, the function returns the same string unchanged.

For example, if a variable named **$password** is used to receive a password from the user, we can ensure that the password does not contain any leading or trailing white space as follows:

```
$password = trim($password);
```

In this case the trimmed string will replace the previous string stored in the variable. As an alternative we could leave the value stored in the variable unchanged and instead apply the **trim**() function when testing the variable, for example:

```
if (trim($password) == "xyz123")
```

In this case the trim operation is performed as part of the test, and the actual string stored in **$password** is not changed.

When receiving a data value from the **$_POST** array, the **trim**() function can be used to trim the value **before** it is assigned to a program variable, for example:

```
$password = trim($_POST['password']);
```

Similarly a line from a file can be trimmed before being assigned a program variable:

```
$nextLine = (trim(fgets($someFile)));
```

It is usually good practice to trim character strings before they are processed. If you ever find that your string comparisons are not working as expected, this may be the problem. In this book we have not included the use of the **trim**() function in our examples to avoid unnecessary code complexity and to keep the focus on basic concepts and procedures.

Using the AND Operator to Assign a Bonus

We can also combine tests using the AND operator. The following requirement uses a new rule to calculate bonuses. This rule requires us to test both the hours worked and the hourly wage:

Wage8 requirement:

Write a program that asks the employee for an hourly wage and the number of hours worked. The program should validate these inputs and either generate appropriate error messages or process the inputs as follows:

If the hourly wage is below 8.00 it should be increased to 8.00. No increase is needed if the hourly wage is already at least 8.00.

The program should assign a bonus based on the hourly wage and hours worked. If the hourly wage is at least 25.00 and the hours worked is less than 35 a bonus of 25.00 should be assigned, otherwise a bonus of 50.00 should be assigned.

The program should calculate and display the hourly wage, hours worked, bonus and weekly pay (the weekly pay should include the bonus).

Two tests are now required to determine the bonus. The first is "**If the hourly wage is at least 25.00**" and the second is "**If the hours worked is less than 35**". Each of these two tests might generate a **true** or **false** result depending on the user input. According to the requirement, if the first test is true **AND** the second test is **true**, the employee is assigned a $25.00 bonus, otherwise the employee is assigned a $50.00 bonus.

The word **AND** here refers to a **logical operator** with a very precise meaning. When we use the word **AND** between these tests, we are testing whether or not **both** tests are **true**. If the first test is **true and** the second test is **true** then the overall result is **true** and person gets a $25.00 bonus. But if **either** or **both** tests are **false**, then the overall result is **false** and the person gets a $50.00 bonus. Table 8-4 shows the **truth table** for this example.

hourlyWage>=25.00	hoursWorked<35	Overall result	bonus
True	True	True	25.00
True	False	False	50.00
False	True	False	50.00
False	False	False	50.00

Table 8-4: Truth Table using the AND operator to test for a bonus

If the hourly wage is **25.00** and the hours worked is **10**, we can see that the first test is **true** and the second test is also **true** so the overall result is **true** and a **$25.00** bonus is assigned. If the hourly wage is **25.00** and the hours worked is **35** hours, the first test is **true** and the second test is **false**. The overall result is **false** so a **$50.00** bonus is assigned.

When the **AND** operator is used to combine two tests, the overall result will only be **true** if **both** tests generate a true result.

Here is the algorithm for **wage8.php**:

```
wage8.php algorithm:

    Receive hourlyWage, hoursWorked from wage8.html

    Display "Wage Report" heading

    IF (hourlyWage is empty OR hoursWorked is empty)
       display an "empty field" error message
    ELSEIF (hourlyWage is not numeric OR hoursWorked is not
             numeric)
       display a "non-numeric input" error message
    ELSEIF (hourlyWage < 6.50)
       display an "hourly wage must be at least 6.50" error message
    ELSEIF (hourlyWorked <= 0)
       display an "hours worked must be above 0" error message
    ELSE
       IF (hourlyWage < 8.00)
          hourlyWage = 8.00
       ENDIF

       IF (hourlyWage >= 25.00 AND hoursWorked < 35)
          bonus = 25.00
       ELSE
          bonus = 50.00
       ENDIF
       weeklyWage = hourlyWage * hoursWorked + bonus
       Display hourlyWage, hoursWorked, bonus, weeklyWage
    ENDIF
END
```

Note that the test to increase the hourly wage **must** now appear **before** the test to assign the bonus. Do you see why? The test to determine the bonus now uses the hourly wage and so any increase to the hourly wage must occur **before** the bonus is determined.

Here is the code for **wage8.php** that implements this algorithm (note that there are no braces in either the if or the else section since each section contains only a single statement):

```
<html>
<head>
  <title>Wage Report</title>
```

```php
    <link rel="stylesheet" type="text/css" href="sample.css" />
  </head>
  <body>
    <?php

      $hourlyWage = $_POST['hourlyWage'];
      $hoursWorked = $_POST['hoursWorked'];

      print("<h1>Wage Report</h1>");

      if (empty($hourlyWage) OR empty($hoursWorked))
        print("ERROR: Input is missing!");
      elseif (!is_numeric($hourlyWage) OR !is_numeric($hoursWorked))
        print("ERROR: Non-numeric input found!");
      elseif ($hourlyWage < 6.50)
        print("ERROR: Hourly wage is below minimum wage!");
      elseif ($hoursWorked <= 0)
        print("ERROR: Hours worked is less than 0!");
      else
      {
        if ($hourlyWage < 8.00)
          $hourlyWage = 8.00;

        if (($hourlyWage >= 25.00 AND $hoursWorked < 35)
          $bonus = 25.00;
        else
          $bonus = 50.00;

        $weeklyWage = $hourlyWage * $hoursWorked + $bonus;

        print("<p>Your hourly wage is $$hourlyWage and you worked
          $hoursWorked hours.</p>");
        print("<p>Your bonus is $$bonus.</p>");
        print("<p>Your weekly wage is $$weeklyWage.</p>");
      }

      print ("<p><a href=\"wage8.html\">Return to form</a></p>");
    ?>
  </body>
</html>
```

Code Example: wage8.php

Note that PHP allows us to use the word **AND** in our program code. We can alternatively use the characters **&&** to represent the **AND** operator. Some programming languages require the use of **&&** and the word **AND** cannot be used.

When to Use AND or OR?
Be Careful with Your Logic!

We have used the **OR** operator to combine two tests in order to validate user input, and we have used the **AND** operator to combine two tests for a requirement to assign a bonus. These are just examples and you can use either operator for any purpose when two or more true/false tests must be combined into a single compound expression.

Remember that two tests combined with the **AND** operator will **only** generate a **true** result if **both** tests are **true**. On the other hand, two tests combined with the **OR** operator will always generate a **true** result unless **both** tests are **false**. Consider very carefully whether you should use **AND** or **OR** in your solution algorithms to meet your program requirements. What happens if you accidentally use **OR** in the last algorithm instead of **AND** to calculate the bonus? Now employees who earn 25.00 or more an hour **OR** work less than 35 hours will get the 25.00 bonus, and only those who earn less than 25.00 and work at least 35 hours will get the 50.00 bonus. That will make a lot of employees unhappy and you may be out of a job! What if your incorrect algorithm was used to generate pay checks for thousands of employees?

Read program requirements very carefully to be sure that you understand what is needed. Software designers quickly learn to focus on the **business rules** within a requirement document, such as the rules for assigning a bonus. Always ask for clarification if there is **any** uncertainty concerning these rules.

The Challenge of Software Testing

It is important to test a program thoroughly before releasing it for production, but this is not a trivial task. How many times do you need to test our **wage8.php** code to be sure that it works correctly under all conditions? The various selection structures means that there are many different paths through this code! Let's consider some of the tests that must be made to verify that our code will work as intended. These tests provide numerous combinations to test different paths through the four selection structures. Here are the various values that will need to be tested:

Test 01:	*hourly wage field is empty*
Test 02:	*hours worked field is empty*
Test 03:	*hourly wage field is non-numeric*
Test 04:	*hours worked field is non-numeric*
Test 05:	*hourly wage field < 6.50*
Test 06:	*hours worked field <=0*
Test 07:	*hourly wage field >= 6.50 and < 8.00*
Test 08:	*hourly wage field > 8.00*

Test 09:	*hourlyWage field >= 25.00 AND hoursWorked field < 35*
Test 10:	*hourlyWage field >= 25.00 AND hoursWorked field >= 35*
Test 11:	*hourlyWage field < 25.00 AND hoursWorked field < 35*
Test 12:	*hourlyWage field < 25.00 AND hoursWorked field >= 35*

Does this mean only 12 tests are required? Not at all! These tests must be made in all **combinations** to ensure that every possible combination of input values will generate the expected result. For example Test 01 should be combined with Test 02, but also with Test 04, Test 06, etc.

If you consider how many tests are needed for this relatively small piece of code that contains four selection structures, consider how much testing is required for applications with hundreds, thousands, and millions of lines of code. There is a point that is reached quite quickly where it is literally impossible to test every possible path through a program and that is why there are so many bugs in software applications. This is one reason why pseudocode is important — it helps programmers to **walk-through** their algorithms before writing actual code which is much harder to debug. Other tools to minimize errors are:

- Reuse existing code as much as possible, code that has already been tested and is well understood.
- Develop the code in small pieces (modules) and test each module thoroughly before putting them all together.
- Work in teams so that other programmers review and test algorithms and code segments throughout the development process.
- Create large sets of test data and write testing programs that run this data against your applications in order to automate the testing process as much as possible.

A Special Case: The Switch Statement

Sometimes we need to test a single variable multiple times in order to determine an appropriate action. As an example, we might want to test a variable that contains the **number** of a month (for example 3) in order to display the appropriate **name** of the month (for example "March"). We can accomplish this using chained IF..ELSE statements:

```
IF (month == 1)
   display "January"
ELSEIF (month == 2)
   display "February"
ELSEIF (month == 3)
   display "March"
ELSEIF (month == 4)
   display "April"
and so on..
```

However most languages provide a specialized selection structure, known as a **switch** (or **case**) structure, that can be used in these situations where a single variable must be tested multiple times for different values. The switch statement is described, with examples, in Appendix G.

More Examples in the Samples Folder

For your interest and enjoyment a number of additional examples of applications that use selection structures are provided in the **samples** folder. These are intended to give you some ideas as you apply selection structures to your own applications. Here is a brief summary of these examples:

comparePets

The **comparePets.html** code uses two drop down lists that allow the user to rate dogs and cats as pets. The **comparePets.php** code uses an **if..elseif..else** structure to comment on the user's ratings.

mathProblem and mathSolution

It is common practice to use **.php** files instead of **.html** files to provide the HTML forms for user input. Sometimes this is necessary since the forms require some PHP processing. Here is an example where a PHP program is needed to generate the initial HTML form because the form includes two numbers that must be randomly generated using the PHP **rand**() function. The example also uses **hidden fields** in the form. (Hidden fields are used to send values that the use does not see to the receiving program. These values are sent in addition to the values that are provided by the user. In this case the two random numbers are sent as part of the form data so that the receiving program can compare the user's answer to the correct answer.) If you are interested in learning how to generate random numbers, take a look at this code.

quizProgram and quizResults

This example uses a PHP program (**quizProgram.php**) is required to generate the initial HTML form because the form contains three quiz questions that must be read from a file named **testbank.txt**. Each line of testbank.txt contains a question, three possible answers and the correct answer, separated by colons. These values are read from the file and then added to a form containing drop down lists with the possible answers. The user's answers are sent to **quizResults.php** along with the correct answers (the correct answers are sent as **hidden** fields) and **quizResults.php** calculates and displays the score.

jokester

The **jokester.html** code uses a drop down list to allow the user to select a joke, and **jokester.php** uses an **if..elseif..else** structure to display the appropriate joke.

artGallery

The **artGallery.html** code uses a drop down list to allow the user to select an artist. The **artGallery.php** code tests the character string received from the form and displays a brief artist biography and a painting (using the HTML **<img>** tag).

Some Words of Encouragement

It is easy for anyone to feel overwhelmed or panicked when confronted with a requirement that needs to be converted to an algorithm and then into working code. One reason for this is that we assume that we should be able to understand and solve problems quickly and move onto the coding process. We feel that we are wasting time if we are not able to start coding immediately.

The truth is that very few people can look at a problem, immediately understand the requirements, and quickly develop an effective algorithm. It takes time to do this and the more time that is spent considering the problem carefully the better! Software designers allocate considerable time (often weeks or months) to review program requirements and develop an effective design.

It helps to stay away from the computer when you are working out your algorithm. Even if your programming problem is quite small, you should follow this practice. Use pencil and paper to make notes, decide your inputs and outputs and processes, and outline your algorithm. Take a divide-and-conquer approach—break the problem down into parts until you can clearly understand all of the steps and calculations that are needed. Desk-check your algorithm by walking through it using some test data. Only begin to code when you are reasonably satisfied that your algorithm should work, and be prepared to come back to the algorithm if you run into problems.

Software designers and programmers spend a great deal of time working together, away from the computer. They use sticky notes, white boards, and other tools to brainstorm, experiment and walk through the problem definition and solution algorithm. If you understand that this is an important step that takes time you will save yourself a lot of stress, and will be in a better position to produce a high quality and well-designed solution.

Summary

In this chapter we learned how to develop algorithms that include multiple selection structures and compound Boolean expressions. Multiple selection structures may be distinct from one another or may be **nested** inside one another in order to meet the program requirements. If necessary, IF..ELSE structures can also be chained together (as many as needed) to permit more than two possible outcomes to a business rule, for example to assign a bonus that may have more than two possible values. The resulting IF..ELSE IF..ELSE structure can also be written in the form IF..ELSEIF..ELSE.

The **AND** and **OR** operators can be used to combine two or more simple Boolean expressions to produce a compound Boolean expression. When two expressions are combined using the **AND** operator, both tests must generate a **true** result in order for the combined test to be **true**. When two expressions are combined using the **OR** operator, either or both tests can generate a **true** result in order for the combined test to be **true**.

Input validation is an important component of software design to ensure that a program does not attempt to process bad data.

A **high-level design** (or **top down design**) approach is important when tackling more complex requirements. The designer develops the more general structure of the application before focusing on the details.

Programmers usually brainstorm **away** from the computer in order to work through requirements and develop effective algorithms.

Software testing is a complex and skilled task. Software can never be completely tested and this explains why there can often be so many bugs even after applications have been distributed.

Chapter 8 Review Questions

1. How many different paths are there through a program that contains one IF structure, followed by one (separate) IF..ELSE structure?
    a. 1
    b. 2
    c. 3
    d. 4
    e. 5

2. If $hourlyWage contains the value 10.00 and $hoursWorked contains the value 20, what value will $bonus contain after the following code is executed?

```
if ($hourlyWage > 10 or $hoursWorked < 20)
```

```
    $bonus = $25.00;
  else
    $bonus = $50.00;
```

a. 25.00
b. 50.00

3. If $hourlyWage contains the value 10.00 and $hoursWorked contains the value 20, what value will $bonus contain after the following code is executed?

```
  if ($hourlyWage > 10 or $hoursWorked <= 20)
    $bonus = $25.00;
  else
    $bonus = $50.00;
```

a. 25.00
b. 50.00

4. If $hourlyWage contains the value 10.00 and $hoursWorked contains the value 20, what value will $bonus contain after the following code is executed?

```
  if ($hourlyWage > 10 and $hoursWorked < 20)
    $bonus = $25.00;
  else
    $bonus = $50.00;
```

a. 25.00
b. 50.00

5. If $hourlyWage contains the value 10.00 and $hoursWorked contains the value 20, what value will $bonus contain after the following code is executed?

```
  if ($hourlyWage > 10 and $hoursWorked <= 20)
    $bonus = $25.00;
  else
    $bonus = $50.00;
```

a. 25.00
b. 50.00

6. If $hourlyWage contains the value 10.00 and $hoursWorked contains the value 20, what value will $bonus contain after the following code is executed?

```
  if ($hourlyWage >= 10 and $hoursWorked <= 20)
    $bonus = $25.00;
  else
    $bonus = $50.00;
```

    a. 25.00
    b. 50.00

7. Given the following requirements which would be the appropriate test to use?

> *A discount of 10% should be applied only when the following conditions **both** apply:*
>
>   *The customer has ordered at least 10 copies*
>
>   *The item cost is above 25.00*

    a. if ($numCopies > 10 and $itemCost > 25.00)
    b. if ($numCopies >= 10 and $itemCost >= 25.00)
    c. if ($numCopies >= 10 and $itemCost > 25.00)
    d. if ($numCopies >= 10 or $itemCost >= 25.00)
    e. if ($numCopies >= 10 or $itemCost > 25.00)

8. If a variable named $carsSold contains the value 8, what is stored in $bonus after this code is processed? (Are these structures separate or chained?)

```
if ($carsSold < 10)
    $bonus = 0.00;
elseif ($carsSold < 20)
    $bonus = 100.00;
else
    $bonus = 200.00;
```

    a. 0.00
    b. 100.00
    c. 200.00

9. If a variable named $carsSold contains the value 8 what is stored in $bonus after this code is processed? (Are these structures separate or chained?)

```
if ($carsSold < 10)
    $bonus = 0.00;
if ($carsSold < 20)
    $bonus = 100.00;
else
    $bonus = 200.00;
```

    a. 0.00
    b. 100.00
    c. 200.00

10. If a variable named $carsSold contains the value 8 and $yearsOnJob contains the value 2, what is stored in $bonus after this code is processed?

```
if ($carsSold < 10 and $yearsOnJob > 1)
```

```
     $bonus = 0.00;
  elseif ($carsSold < 20)
     $bonus = 100.00;
  else
     $bonus = 200.00;
```

a. 0.00
b. 100.00
c. 200.00

11. Consider the following code? Which employee will get a 750.00 bonus?

```
if ($yearsWorked < 5)
{
   if ($salary < 18000.00)
      $bonus = 500.00;
   else
      $bonus = 400.00;
}
else
   $bonus = 750.00;
```

a. Employees who have worked at least 5 years, no matter what their salary is.
b. Employees who have worked at least 5 years, with a salary of at least 18000.00.
c. Employees who have worked at least 5 years, with a salary less than 18000.00.
d. Employees who have worked less than 5 years, no matter what their salary is.
e. Employees who have worked less than 5 years, with a salary of at least 18000.00.

12. Consider the following code. What bonus will be assigned for an employee who has worked 5 years and earns 18000.00?

```
if ($yearsWorked < 5)
{
   if ($salary < 18000.00)
      $bonus = 500.00;
   else
      $bonus = 400.00;
}
else
```

```
$bonus = 750.00;
```

 a. 500.00
 b. 400.00
 c. 750.00

13. If a variable named $ticketsOrdered contains the value 50, and $maximumOrder contains the value 25 what is stored in $totalCost after this code is processed?

```
if ($ticketsOrdered > $maximumOrder)
   $ticketsOrdered = $maximumOrder;
if ($ticketsOrdered >= 10 )
   $totalCost = $ticketsOrdered * 4.00;
else
   $totalCost = $ticketsOrdered * 5.00;
```

 a. 0.00
 b. 100.00
 c. 125.00
 d. 200.00
 e. 250.00

14. How many different paths are there through the code segment in question 13?
 a. 1
 b. 2
 c. 3
 d. 4
 e. 8

15. Run compareMovies.html in the samples folder a few times. Take a look at compareMovies.php—how many paths are there through this code?
 a. 1
 b. 2
 c. 3
 d. 4
 e. 8

16. Run artGallery.html in the samples folder a few times then look at the code for artGallery.php. Which of the following descriptions of the control structures is most accurate?
 a. The code contains a single if structure
 b. The code contains a single if..else structure
 c. The code contains multiple if..else structures chained together
 d. The code contains multiple if..else structures that are entirely separate

from one another

e. The code contains a single if structure followed by a single if..else structure

17. What is the purpose of input validation?
    a. Check that the user's ID and password are valid
    b. Ensure that any data entered by the user is valid
    c. Process the user's data and display the results
    d. Test that any files needed by the program are actually on the disk
    e. Ensure that the file path of the PHP program is correct

18. The programmer made a mistake reading the requirements and used OR instead of AND in the following code! Will customers benefit or lose by this error?

```
if ($totalPurchases > 100.00 or $customerStatus ==
   "PREFERRED")
   $discount = 25.00;
else
   $discount = 0.00;
```

    a. The customers benefit — more customers will get a discount as a result of the error.
    b. The customers lose — less customers will get a discount as a result of the error.
    c. It makes no difference whether AND or OR is used here.

19. Dress shoes sell for 95.00, trail shoes sell for 75.00, and casual shoes sell for 55.00. Here's what a programmer wrote as a selection structure to display the price based on a user's style selection. The logic is incorrect since if the style is "Dress" two prices are displayed. What's wrong with the logic?

```
if ($style == "Dress")
   print ("<p>Price: $95.00</p>");
if ($style == "Trail")
   print ("<p>Price: $75.00</p>");
else
   print ("<p>Price: $55.00</p>");
```

    a. The second if should be an else.

    b. The else should be an elseif.

    c. The second if should be an elseif.

    d. Curly braces are needed around each print statement.

    e. The two == should each be =

20. Which statement is true?

    a. A program can include any number of if and if..else structures, which may be nested inside one another, chained together or entirely separate from one another, in any order, as required by the program logic.

    b. A program can include a maximum of two if structures and if..else structures.

    c. Multiple if..else structures must always be chained together.

    d. Multiple if..else structures must always be nested inside one another.

    e. If structures must always occur before if..else structures in a program.

Chapter 8 Code Exercises

Your Chapter 8 code exercises can be found in your **Chapter08** folder. This folder is included in your customized XAMPP installation at the following location:

    xampplite\htdocs\WebTech\coursework\Chapter08

    Type your name and the date in the Author and Date sections of each file as you work on each exercise.

Debugging Exercises

Your **Chapter08** folder should contain a number of "FixIt" files. Each of these files contains PHP code that has an error of some kind. You will need to run each program in order to see the errors, and to debug and test the code to see if it works correctly. For example to run **fixIt1.php**, first run the Web server, then use the URL:

    http://localhost/WebTech/coursework/Chapter08/fixIt1.php

Code Modification Exercises

Your **Chapter08** folder contains a number of "Modify" files. Each pair of files contains HTML and PHP code that needs to be modified to meet a requirement. The requirements are included in each file. Modify the algorithms as specified, being careful to make changes to the .html and .php files as directed.

Code Completion Exercises

1. Read this exercise carefully and take your time to work out the logic. Your **Chapter08** folder contains versions of **paintEstimate.html** and **paintEstimate.php**. The code in **paintEstimate.html** does not need to be changed. The HTML form includes a drop down selection to ask the user if they are a first time customer. The name for this input is **firstTime**, and the possible values are "**yes**" and "**no**". The HTML form also includes a drop down selection to ask the user what paint quality they want. The name for this input is **paint**, and the possible values are "**premium**" and "**regular**". Note that the first letter of each paint selection is lower-case.

   The PHP program already includes a calculation for the paint cost that assumes that the paint costs 17.00 for a gallon, however this is no longer correct. Replace this with a selection structure that will assign the paint cost as either **20.00** or **15.00** a gallon, depending on whether the user selected premium (**20.00**) or regular (**15.00**).

   The program must **also** apply a new test to determine whether or not a customer should receive a discount. If the user is a first time customer and their total cost is at least 200.00, the program should calculate a 10% deduction to the total estimate, and, **instead** of displaying the total cost, should generate the following output: "<p>We want your service! Since you are a first time customer and your order is over $200.00, we are offering a 10% deduction.</p><p> Your actual costs will be: $xxx</p>" where $xxx is their cost after the deduction. **Otherwise** the program should display the total cost as provided in the existing code.

   Make the changes to **paintEstimate.php** so that the program works as described. Think carefully where your two selection structures must appear in the code. Test your program carefully with various test input to be sure that your program is working correctly for first time and other customers, with initial total costs above and below 200.00, and choosing different choices of paint quality.

2. Read this exercise carefully and take your time to work out the logic. Your **Chapter08** folder contains a previous version of **softwareOrder.html** and **softwareOrder.php**. You do not need to change **softwareOrder.html**.

   The PHP program should now test the number of copies ordered. If the number of copies is less than 1, the program should display an error message and **should not calculate or display anything else** (the error message is already provided).

   The program **also** needs code to calculate the shipping and handling charge. If there are **less than five copies** the shipping and handling charge is a standard **3.50** no matter how many copies, otherwise if there are less than 10 copies, the shipping handling is **0.75** for each copy, otherwise the shipping handling is **0.85** for each copy.

   Make the changes to **softwareOrder.php** so that the program works as described. Think carefully where your selection structures must appear in the code, and how they need be associated with one another. Test your code carefully with different inputs until you are satisfied that the selections structures are working as expected and delivering the correct results.

3. Read this exercise carefully and take your time to work out the logic. Your **Chapter08** folder contains a modified version of **travel.html** and **travel.php**. You do not need to change **travel.html**. This form now allows the user to select among **five** travel destinations. The costs are as follows:

> Barcelona: the air fare is $875 and the hotel cost per night is $85
> Cairo: the air fare is $950 and the hotel cost per night is $98
> Rome: the air fare is $875 and the hotel cost per night is $110
> Santiago: the air fare is $820 and the hotel cost per night is $85
> Tokyo: the air fare is $1575 and the hotel cost per night is $240

You must add the code to assign appropriate airfare and hotel cost per night, depending on the selected destination. Use the same variables names that are provided in the existing code.

Also, if the destination is Tokyo, there is a special air fare discount of **$200 per traveler** if the party is staying at least 5 nights. You can use a nested IF structure to calculate this or you can use a compound Boolean expression.

To test your code, try entering 1 passenger for 1 night for each destination and compare your output with the values listed above. Then try entering 1 passenger for 5 nights to Tokyo (with the discount this should amount to $2575.00). Try one or two other tests to be sure your program is calculating correctly.

4. Read this exercise carefully and take your time to work out the logic. Your Chapter08 folder contains a modified version of **gameIntro.html** and **gameIntro.php**. You do not need to change **gameIntro.html**.

Do you remember that the player begins with 10 gold pieces? It is time to ensure that he or she did not overspend! If the total number of gold pieces spent is greater than 10, the program should only display an error message (this has been provided) and should not perform any additional processing or display any other output. Otherwise the program should assign bonus tokens to the character as follows:

> Wizards receive 2 extra experience tokens
> Humans and dwarfs receive 10 extra supply tokens
> Elves receive 5 extra health tokens

The program should also calculate the number of gold pieces left so that this amount can be displayed as part of the output (all of the output statements have been provided—note the variable names).

Be careful with the order of your statements and the location and organization of your selection structures. Test your code carefully. Be sure to test for overspending, and also test that the correct bonuses are assigned to each character type.

5. Copy **event.html** and **event.php** from your Chapter07 folder to your Chapter08 folder. You are now going to add another IF..ELSE structure that checks that the user actually entered the required information when submitting the form. This can be tested by using the empty() function to test whether the variables $firstName, $phone and $numTickets contain values. We can test all three variables together using the OR operator as follows:

```
if (empty($firstName) or empty($phone) or empty($numTickets))
```

Your job is to add an IF..ELSE structure that uses this test, so that if any of these variables are empty, the program displays an error message (and that is all it does), otherwise the program executes the code that you have previously developed to process the order (this includes the existing IF..ELSE structure that you developed in the Chapter07 exercise). Consider carefully where the heading of the new IF..ELSE structure must be located and where the opening and closing braces of the IF and ELSE sections must be located.

Take time to test your work to be sure that it works correctly in different cases, and to experience how sophisticated your program is now becoming.

6. Your Chapter08 folder already contains **busTravel.html** and **busTravel.php**. You do not need to change busTravel.html which provides the user with a form to submit business travel information for reimbursement. The form includes input fields for the date and miles traveled, followed by four YES/NO entries to indicate whether or not the travel included breakfast, lunch, dinner or hotel.

The busTravel.php file already contains code to receive the form input and to display the results has been provided (note the variable names). Your job is to insert the code to process the form input and calculate the reimbursement for the trip. The basic reimbursement will be the miles traveled * 0.35. If breakfast was included add 6.00 to the reimbursement. If lunch was included, add 8.50 to the reimbursement. If dinner was included, add 17.50 to the reimbursement. If a hotel was included, add 110.00 to the reimbursement. So for example if the user submitted 120 for the mile traveled, "NO" for breakfast, and "YES" for lunch, dinner and hotel, the complete reimbursement will be 120*0.35 + 8.50 + 17.50 + 110.00, which is $178.00.

Be sure to test your program a few times so that you are sure it works correctly with different submissions. Try choosing "NO" for all of the drop down lists, then "YES" for all of the lists, then try different combinations of "YES" and "NO".

Chapter 9

Programs that Count— Harnessing the Power of Repetition

Intended Learning Outcomes

After completing this chapter, you should be able to:

- Describe the purpose of loop structures.
- Identify standard loop structures.
- Explain the purpose of each component of a FOR loop heading.
- Trace the processing of a simple FOR loop.
- Design and code a FOR loop.
- Use variables to control a FOR loop.
- Apply the loop counting variable to perform processing within a FOR loop.
- Use a FOR loop with an HTML table to generate output.
- Use a FOR loop to accumulate a total.
- Use a FOR loop to find high and low values in a series.
- Use a FOR loop to process a data file.
- Nest selection structures within a FOR loop.
- Nest a FOR loop within a FOR loop.

Introduction

We have learned how to write programs to process relatively small amounts of data such as calculating the weekly pay for a single employee, or converting a temperature from Centigrade to Fahrenheit, but what about programs that must handle much larger data sets? What if we need to write an application that calculates wages for a **thousand** employees? Or an application that converts to Fahrenheit all of the Centigrade temperatures between 0 and 100 degrees? Or that determines the average rainfall from data in a file that contains rainfall readings for an entire year?

These may appear to be more complicated problems that require extensive coding but in fact they are not very complicated at all. This is because computer programs can easily be designed to **repeat** a sequence of instructions as many times as needed in order to process very large amounts of data.

Loop, or **repetition,** structures provide one of the more powerful tools available to a programmer. Just as a selection structure allows a program to **choose between** two different blocks of statements based on a test condition, so a loop structure allows a program to **repeatedly execute** a block of statements, where the number of repetitions is based on a test condition. Programs can use loop structures to process larger data sets for any purpose, for example to convert data values, perform statistical operations, generate graphs or tables, search the data, sort the data, etc.

Loop structures and selection structures can be combined in any number of configurations to meet the requirements of any application. Together these structures provide the basic processing tools underlying all software design and development. Most current programming languages, including PHP, provide four different loop structures as follows:

FOR loops are most often used where a program can determine the required number of repetitions before the loop executes. FOR loops are often referred to as **count-controlled** loops since the loop is controlled by a counting variable.

For example a FOR loop could be used to display the monthly rainfall for each month of the year since the loop will need to repeat exactly 12 times (once for each month).

WHILE loops are most often used where the program cannot determine the required number of repetitions before the loop executes. This will be the case when the number of repetitions will be determined by a condition that occurs while the loop is processing. WHILE loops are often referred to as **event-controlled** loops since they continue to repeat until an event occurs.

For example a WHILE loop can be used to process lines from a file of unknown length—the number of repetitions will depend on the number of lines in the file. The event in this case would be reaching the end of the file. WHILE loops may even repeat 0 times (for example if the loop processes an empty file).

REPEAT (or DO..WHILE) loops. These loops are similar to WHILE loops except that they always repeat at least once.

For example a REPEAT loop might be used to request a valid input from the user. If the user enters an invalid input the first time, the loop will repeat until the user submits an acceptable value.

FOREACH loops are a special type of counting loop, often used to simplify the processing of a list of values stored in a data structure known as an array.

In this chapter you will learn how to use FOR loops to repeat instructions using a counting variable, and how to include selection structures within a FOR loop to perform common processing operations. The other three loop structures will be explained in later chapters.

Controlling a Loop by Counting

As a first example of a FOR loop, consider the following algorithm:

```
Testing1.php algorithm:
  Display "This is a test"
  FOR (counter = 1 to 3)
    Display "Testing ..."
  ENDFOR
  Display "End of test"

END
```

This algorithm first displays a heading, and then defines a FOR loop. Any instructions located between the FOR loop heading and ENDFOR will be repeated—in this example there is just one instruction: **Display "Testing ...".** A FOR loop usually uses a counting variable to control the number of repetitions. In this algorithm a variable named **counter** is defined in the FOR loop heading to first receive the value 1, then the value 2, and then the value 3. For each value of the counter variable, the loop statements are executed, so this loop will run three times and the phrase "Testing ..." will display three times (see Figure 9-2). The counting variable is just a standard variable and can be given any name.

Figure 9-1 shows a flow chart for this algorithm. Notice how a flow chart can diagram the flow of a FOR loop structure. The test that controls the loop indicates that the loop control will be given successive values of 1, 2 and 3. Each time the loop repeats, the statements in the loop structure will be executed (in this case just one statement), and the program then returns to the loop test. When the loop test becomes false (after the third iteration), the program skips the loop structure and moves on to the next instruction following the loop.

Coding a FOR Loop in PHP

The syntax of a FOR loop is similar in most programming languages. Here is the PHP code (testing1.php) that implements our algorithm:

```
<html>
<head>
  <title>Testing ... </title>
```

```
    <link rel="stylesheet" type="text/css" href="sample.css" />
  </head>
<body>
  <?php
    print("<h1>This is a test</h1>");

    for ($counter = 1; $counter <= 3; $counter = $counter + 1)
    {
      print("Testing ... <br />");
    }

    print("<h1>End of test</h1>");
  ?>
</body>
</html>
```

Code Example: testing1.php

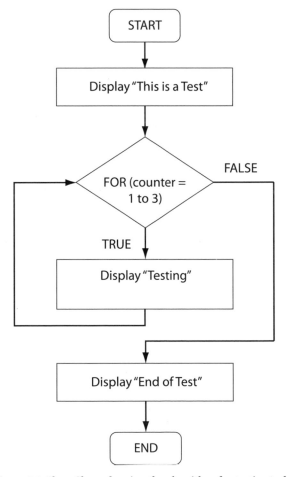

Figure 9.1 Flow Chart showing the algorithm for testing1.php

The loop heading looks a little different from our pseudocode. Let's look at this heading carefully:

```
for ($counter = 1; $counter <= 3; $counter = $counter + 1)
```

The heading of a FOR loop contains three sections, separated by two semi-colons:

- The **loop initialization section** appears before the first semi-colon and specifies the initial value for the variable that will be used to count the number of repetitions. In this example the variable is named **$counter** and the initialization statement is **$counter = 1**.
- The **loop condition section** appears after the first semi-colon and provides the test that determines whether or not the loop statements should continue to repeat. In this example the condition is **$counter <=3**.
- The **loop update section** appears after the second semi-colon and indicates how the value of the counting variable should be modified after each repetition of the loop statements. In this example the modification is **$counter = $counter + 1** which will add 1 to the value stored in **$counter** after each repetition.

The statements that are intended to execute repeatedly are listed below the loop heading and are enclosed within curly braces { and }. These statements are often referred to as the **body** of the loop. The braces are important since without these the processor will assume that only the first statement following the loop heading is to be repeated.

Let's look carefully at what happens when this loop is processed.

The first time that the program encounters the loop, the initialization statement is executed. In this case the **$counter** variable is created and assigned the value 1.

Next, the loop condition (**$counter <= 3**) is tested. Since **$counter** currently contains the value **1**, the test is **true** and so the instructions inside the loop are executed. In this example the loop contains only a single statement: **print("Testing ...
")**;

Once the statements in the loop body have been executed, the loop update section is processed. In this example, the result of the update is that 1 is added to the value of **$counter** so this variable now contains 2.

Following the update, the loop condition is re-tested. Since **$counter** contains the value **2**, the test is still **true** so the instructions inside the loop are executed. The loop update is again processed so the value of **$counter** is incremented to **3**.

The loop condition is again tested. Since $counter contains the value 3, the test is **true** so the instructions inside the loop are executed again. The loop update is again processed so the value of $counter is incremented to 4.

The loop condition is again tested. Since the counter variable contains the value **4**, the test is **false**. A **false** result causes the program to stop processing the loop and skip past the loop to the next statement that follows the closing brace of the loop structure. In this case the next statement is **print("<h1>End of test</h1>")**;.

The loop has therefore been designed to repeat three times, based on the initial vale of the counting variable, the loop condition, and the loop update. Figure 9-2 shows the output from this program.

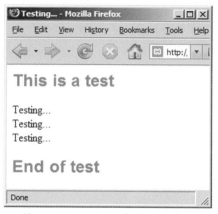

Figure 9-2: testing1.php screenshot

Run the program, and then modify it to get a feel how this works. Here are some suggested modifications:

1. Change $counter = 1; to $counter = 0; and run the program again. Why does the loop now repeat **4** times? Change the code back to its original form.
2. Change $counter = 1; to $counter = 10; and run the program again. Why does the loop now repeat **0** times? Change the code back to its original form.
3. Change $counter = $counter + 1; to $counter = $counter + 2; and run the program again. Why does the loop now repeat **2** times? Change the code back to its original form.
4. Change the loop test from ($counter <= 3) to ($counter < 3) and run the program again. Why does the loop now repeat **2** times? Change the code back to its original form.
5. Change the loop test from ($counter <= 3) to ($counter <= 100) and run the program again. Why does the loop now repeat **100** times? Change the code back to its original form.

General Syntax of a FOR Loop

You can use a FOR loop for many purposes, wherever you need a set of instructions to be repeated a predetermined number of times. In PHP (and most languages) the general syntax for writing a FOR loop is as follows:

```
for (loop initialization; loop condition; loop update)
{
    ... instructions to be repeated ...
}
```

Note that there is **no semi-colon** after the closing parenthesis at the end of the FOR loop heading! That's because headings of loop structures (just like headings of selection structures or any other structures) do not require semi-colons. This is very important — if you place a semi-colon at the end of the loop heading the statements in your loop structure will appear not to repeat! Since the semi-colon appears before the braces, the processor will assume that the loop consists of only a single statement, and that this statement is an instruction to do nothing each time the loop repeats!

Be sure that you understand how the different parts of the loop heading work together to control the loop. There is nothing magical about the way that a loop operates — the program simply processes the statements exactly as they are written. You have a lot of flexibility in how you decide to control a counting loop and this will depend on the details of your program requirement. You can specify any initial value for the loop counting variable, and you can increment the value of the variable by any amount each time through the loop.

Including the Counting Variable in Your Loop Statements

We have seen that the counting variable contains a different value each time that our loop is repeated. We can write statements within the loop structure that make use of this value. For example what if we want to display the value of the counter as a part of the output in our testing program? Take a look at Figure 9-3.

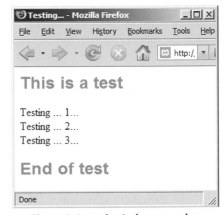

Figure 9-3: testing2.php screenshot

Here is **testing2.php** which performs similarly to **testing1.php** except that it displays the value of the **$counter** variable each time that the loop statements are executed:

```
<html>
<head>
   <title>Testing ... </title>
   <link rel="stylesheet" type="text/css" href="sample.css" />
</head>
<body>
  <?php
    print("<h1>This is a test</h1>");

    for ($counter = 1; $counter <= 3; $counter = $counter + 1)
    {
       print("Testing ... $counter ... <br />");
    }

    print("<h1>End of test</h1>");
  ?>
</body>
</html>
```

Code Example: testing2.php

The only difference is the line:

```
print("Testing ... $counter ... <br />");
```

The value of $counter is included in the output. The first time through the loop, the value is 1, the second time the value is 2 and the last time the value is 3. You can use the value of the counting variable inside the loop structure for any purpose that you choose. We will see some other examples shortly.

Using a Variable to Control the Loop Condition

Our two examples have been coded to repeat a loop three times. We used a literal value (in this case 3) to achieve this but it is often useful to write a program that uses a **variable** to control the number of times that the loop will repeat.

Let's consider an example where the user is asked to specify how many times the loop should repeat. Here is code for **testing3.html** which includes a form that obtains this information from the user:

```
<html>
<head>
```

```
    <title>Testing..</title>
    <link rel="stylesheet" type="text/css" href="sample.css" />
  </head>
<body>
    <h1>Testing..</h1>
    <form action="testing3.php" method="post">

      <p>How many times do you want the test to repeat?
        <input type="text" size="20" name="numTimes" />
      </p>

      <p><input type="submit" value="Run the test!" /></p>

    </form>
</body>
</html>
```

Code Example: testing3.html

Here is **testing3.php** which receives the user's input in a variable named **$numTimes** and uses this to control the number of times that the loop repeats. Note the use of **$numTimes** in the loop condition section:

```
<html>
<head>
   <title>Testing ... </title>
   <link rel ="stylesheet" type="text/css" href="sample.css" />
</head>
<body>
   <?php

     $numTimes = $_POST['numTimes'];

     print("<h1>This is a test ($numTimes repetitions)</h1>");

     for($counter = 1;$counter <= $numTimes;$counter = $counter+1)
     {
        print("Testing ... $counter ... <br />");
     }

     print("<h1>End of test</h1>");

   ?>
</body>
</html>
```

Code Example: testing3.php

The loop condition now indicates **$counter** <= **$numTimes**, so the loop will repeat the number of times that the user requested. Note that the code **also** uses the value stored in **$numTimes** in the **print**() statement that generates a heading. Figure 9-4 shows some sample input/output for this program.

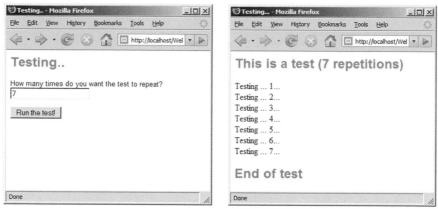

Figure 9-4: testing3.html and testing3.php screenshots

Converting from Celsius to Fahrenheit

Now let's see how we can use a FOR loop to generate a more useful table. Consider the following requirement:

TempConverter1 requirement:

Create a program that converts all Celsius temperatures between 0° and 100° to Fahrenheit and displays these. The conversion formula is: (9 / 5) * C + 32.

First take a moment to appreciate the difficulty of meeting this requirement without using a loop:

```
TempConverter1 algorithm (without a FOR loop):

   celsius = 0
   fahrenheit = (9 / 5) * celsius + 32
   Display celsius and fahrenheit
   celsius = 1
   fahrenheit = (9 / 5) * celsius + 32
   Display celsius and fahrenheit

   ... instructions here for all Celsius temperatures between 2
   and 98! ...

   celsius = 99
   fahrenheit = (9 / 5) * celsius + 32
```

```
    Display celsius and fahrenheit
    celsius = 100
    fahrenheit = (9 / 5) * celsius + 32
    Display celsius and fahrenheit
END
```

This algorithm only shows the instructions to convert and display the first two and last two temperatures — the complete algorithm would actually need 300 instructions! It is easy to see that this is not practical. In fact this approach is impossible for some requirements. What if the program was required to convert all temperatures in a range where the starting and ending temperatures were to be input by the user? Since the programmer does not know in advance what the user will choose, there is no way to know how many statements to include.

Now look at how easily the same requirement can be handled using a FOR loop:

```
TempConverter1.php algorithm:


    FOR celsius = 0 to 100
        fahrenheit = (9 / 5) * celsius + 32
        Display celsius and fahrenheit
    ENDFOR
END
```

In this algorithm the variable named **celsius** is used as the loop counting variable. The loop statements will execute **101** times. The first time the loop is executed, **celsius** will have the value **0**, and the last time the loop is executed, celsius will have the value **100**. For each repetition, the loop statements will: convert the current value of **celsius** to Fahrenheit; assign the result of the conversion to the **fahrenheit** variable; and display the two temperatures.

Here is the PHP code for this algorithm:

```
<html>
<head>
  <title>Temperature Conversions</title>
  <link rel ="stylesheet" type="text/css" href="sample.css" />
</head>

<body>
  <?php
    print("<h1>Temperature Conversions</h1>");

    for ($celsius = 0; $celsius <= 100; $celsius = $celsius + 1)
    {
      $fahrenheit = (9 / 5) * $celsius + 32;
```

```
        print("$celsius degrees Celsius = $fahrenheit degrees
           Fahrenheit<br />");
     }
  ?>
</body>
</html>
```

Code Example: tempConverter1.php

Figure 9-5 shows the first few lines of the HTML document that this program creates.

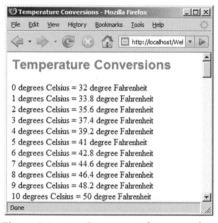

Figure 9-5: tempConverter1.php screenshot

Changing the Increment Value

Let's look at a modified requirement:

TempConverter2 requirement:

*Create a program that converts every 10th Celsius temperature (0° C., 10°C., 20°C., etc) between 0° and 100° to Fahrenheit and displays these. The conversion formula is: (9 / 5) * C + 32*

This is the same as the previous requirement except that the program should now only display every 10th conversion. We can do this easily by simply incrementing our counting variable by 10 instead of by 1. Here is a revised algorithm:

```
TempConverter2.php algorithm
   FOR celsius = 0 to 100 INCREMENT BY 10
      fahrenheit = (9 / 5) * celsius + 32
      Display celsius and fahrenheit
   ENDFOR
END
```

The INCREMENT BY 10 in the FOR loop heading indicates that the value of celsius is to be increased by 10 each time through the loop. We can code this in PHP as follows:

```
<html>
<head>
   <title>Temperature Conversions</title>
   <link rel="stylesheet" type="text/css" href="sample.css" />
</head>
<body>
   <?php

      print("<h1>Temperature Conversions</h1>");

      for ($celsius = 0;$celsius <= 100;$celsius = $celsius + 10)
      {
         $fahrenheit = (9 / 5) * $celsius + 32;
         print("$celsius degrees Celsius = $fahrenheit degrees
            Fahrenheit<br />");
      }
   ?>
</body>
</html>
```

Code Example: tempConverter2.php

Just as in the algorithm, the only difference is the loop heading:

```
for ($celsius = 0; $celsius <= 100; $celsius = $celsius + 10 )
```

The loop counting variable ($celsius) is incremented by 10 each time the loop statements are executed. The first time through the loop, the value of $celsius is 0, the next time, 10, the next time, 20, and so on until the value of $celsius is incremented to 110 and the loop condition test generates a false result. Figure 9-6 shows the output from this code.

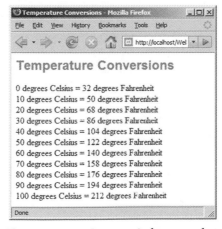

Figure 9-6: tempConverter2.php screenshot

Using Loops with HTML Tables

The output from our temperature conversion programs does not line up very nicely. You may be thinking that it would be much better to using an HTML table to display this output neatly in rows and columns. Loops can provide a very effective programming tool for creating HTML tables, since a new table row can be generated by each loop repetition.

Let's modify our temperature conversion program (**tempConverter3.php**) so that the output is formatted using table tags (Figure 9-7). Each row of the table contains two columns, one for the Celsius temperature and one for the Fahrenheit temperature. As you can see the appearance is much neater.

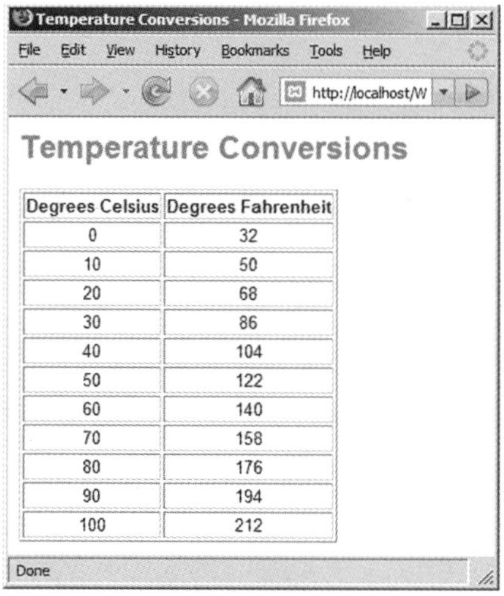

Figure 9-7: tempConverter3.php screenshot

Since we are using a loop to generate the table rows, coding this takes a little planning. Here is the PHP code for **tempConverter3.php**:

```
<html>
<head>
  <title>Temperature Conversions</title>
  <link rel ="stylesheet" type="text/css" href="sample.css" />
</head>
<body>
  <?php
    print("<h1>Temperature Conversions</h1>");

    print ("<table border=\"1\"> ");
    print ("<tr><td><strong>Degrees Celsius</strong></td>
      <td><strong>Degrees Fahrenheit</strong></td></tr>");
```

```
    for ($celsius = 0;$celsius <= 100;$celsius = $celsius + 10)
    {
      $fahrenheit = (9 / 5) * $celsius + 32;
      print("<tr><td class=\"center\">$celsius</td>
        <td class=\"center\">$fahrenheit</td></tr>");
    }

    print ("</table>");
  ?>
</body>
</html>
```

Code Example: tempConverter3.php

Take a good look at this PHP code. The print statements that generate the beginning <table> tag and the first <tr> row (the row that contains the row headings) are both located **before** the FOR loop structure. That's because we don't these elements to repeat. Similarly, the print statement that displays the closing </**table**> tag is located **after** the FOR loop structure.

The loop structure itself includes the statement to convert the temperature for the current Celsius value, and a **print**() statement that generates a new table row containing the Celsius and Fahrenheit values. Each time the loop repeats a new Celsius value will be converted and a new row added to the table.

A critical design decision when you are coding any loop is to determine which statements must occur **before** the loop structure, which statements are to be repeated **inside** the loop structure, and which statements should **follow** the loop structure. Can you see what would happen if, for example, the print statement that generates the table headings was located **inside** the loop structure?

Allowing the User to Control the Loop

Now consider a more general purpose requirement where the **user** selects the range of temperatures to be converted:

TempConverter4 requirement:

Create a program that asks the user for a starting and ending temperature, and an increment value n. The program should then convert every nth temperature between the starting and ending temperature to Fahrenheit and display these. The conversion formula is: (9 / 5) * C + 32

Now our loop counter must be designed to count from an initial temperature value to an ending temperature value provided by the user. This value is to be incremented after each repetition by a value also provided by the user. Let's look at the algorithm to solve this problem. Here is the algorithm for the HTML document designed to receive the user input:

tempConverter4.html algorithm:

```
Prompt user for startTemp
Get startTemp
Prompt user for endTemp
Get endTemp
Prompt user for increment
Get increment
Submit startTemp, endTemp, increment to TempConverter4.php
END
```

Let's also use an HTML table to line up the prompts and input boxes in our HTML form. Here is the code for **tempConverter4.html**:

```html
<html>
<head>
  <title>Temperature Conversions</title>
  <link rel="stylesheet" type="text/css" href="sample.css" />
</head>
<body>
  <h1>Temperature Conversions</h1>
  <form action="tempConverter4.php" method="post">
    <table>
    <tr> <td>Starting temperature (Celsius):</td>
      <td><input type="text" size="10" name="startTemp" />
    </td>
    </tr>

    <tr> <td>Ending temperature (Celsius): </td>
      <td><input type="text" size="10" name="endTemp" /></td>
    </tr>

    <tr> <td>Increment value: </td>
      <td><input type="text" size="5" name="increment" /></td>
    </tr>

    <tr>
      <td><input type="submit" value="Display Table" /></td>
      <td><input type="reset" value="Clear the form" /></td>
    </tr>
    </table>
  </form>
</body>
</html>
```

Code Example: tempConverter4.html

Here is the algorithm for **tempConvertor4.php** that will receive the inputs from **tempConvertor4.html** and generate the conversion table:

```
tempConverter4.php algorithm:
   Receive startTemp, endTemp, increment from tempConverter4.html
   FOR celsius = startTemp to endTemp INCREMENT BY increment
      fahrenheit = (9 / 5) * celsius + 32
      Display celsius and fahrenheit
   ENDFOR
END
```

Note that this algorithm is essentially the same as before except that the loop variable is now controlled by the user's input. Here is the code for **tempConverter4.php**:

```
<html>
<head>
   <title>Temperature Conversions</title>
   <link rel ="stylesheet" type="text/css" href="sample.css" />
</head>
<body>
   <?php
      $startTemp = $_POST['startTemp'];
      $endTemp = $_POST['endTemp'];
      $increment = $_POST['increment'];

      print("<h1>Temperature Conversions</h1>");
      print("<table border=\"1\"> ");
      print("<tr><td><strong>Degrees Celsius</strong></td>
        <td><strong>Degrees Fahrenheit</strong></td></tr>");

      for ($celsius = $startTemp; $celsius <= $endTemp;
           $celsius = $celsius + $increment )
      {
        $fahrenheit = (9 / 5) * $celsius + 32;
        print("<tr><td class=\"center\">$celsius</td>
           <td class=\"center\">$fahrenheit</td></tr>");
      }
      print ("</table>");
   ?>
</body>
</html>
```

Code Example: tempConverter4.php

Look carefully at the FOR loop heading (the only line that has been modified). The initial value for $celsius is the value of $startTemp which was received from the user. The loop test uses $endTemp, also supplied by the user. And the value of $celsius is incremented each time by the value stored in $increment, which also came from the user. Figure 9-8 shows some sample input and output (note that **both** pages use HTML tables).

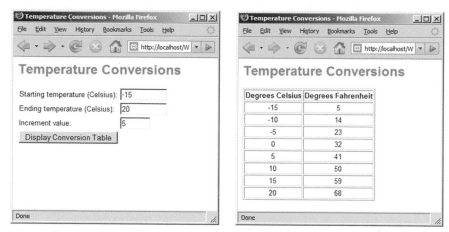

Figure 9-8: tempConverter4.html and tempConverter4.php screenshots

Improving Processing Efficiency

An experienced programmer is careful to design applications to minimize processing time wherever this can be achieved effectively. Since loop structures may repeat a series of processing instructions tens, hundreds, thousands or millions of times, it is always a good idea to examine the code within a loop structure to see if we can make it run more efficiently. For example our temperature conversion program contains a calculation to convert a Celsius temperature to Fahrenheit:

```
$fahrenheit = (9 / 5) * $celsius + 32;
```

This calculation must be processed every time that the program runs through the loop, using a different value stored in the **$celsius** variable. Is there anything that we can do to make this processing task more efficient?

The conversion formula includes the calculation (**9 / 5**). Every time the program loops with a new value of **$celsius**, the same division operation is repeated. What if we perform the **9 / 5** division **before** the loop and store the result in a variable. Now we can simply refer to the value stored in this variable every time a new temperature is calculated? In the example below we create a variable named **$conversionFactor** to store the result of **9 / 5** and then refer to this variable in the loop:

```
$conversionFactor = 9 / 5;
for ($celsius = $startTemp; $celsius <= $endTemp;
            $celsius = $celsius + $increment )
{
    $fahrenheit = $conversionFactor * $celsius + 32;
```

```
        print("<tr><td class=\"center\">$celsius</td>
          <td class=\"center\">$fahrenheit</td></tr>");
    }
```

Do you see how this works? We have now improved our program's processing efficiency. For example if the program repeats the instructions in the FOR loop 100 times, we have just saved the processor **99** division operations since the **9/5** calculation is now performed only once, before the loop.

Performing 100 divisions is of course a trivial task on a modern high-speed computer, but software designers should always pay attention to processing efficiency. This is especially true with regard to client/server applications, where an application running on a server may be regularly executed by thousands of users worldwide. Under these conditions, small inefficiencies can add up quickly to slower performance for everyone.

Using Loops to "Crunch Numbers"

We often refer to the work of processing large sets of numeric data values as **number crunching**. Some common examples of number crunching are:

- Generating daily, weekly or annual weather statistics based on data readings.
- Calculating the average, high and low scores from a set of student scores.
- Reducing a large data set so that it can be rendered effectively into a visual format, such as a chart or graph.
- Processing a file of timesheet records in order to generate pay checks.

Loop structures are an important tool for number-crunching large sets of data values. Some standard algorithms are widely used to perform common operations on data sets, such as obtaining the sum or average, finding the highest and lowest values, etc. Once you understand how these algorithms work, you can apply them to process many different data sets.

Using a Loop to Accumulate a Total

A requirement to calculate the total of a series of values is very straightforward when only two or three values are involved. For example a requirement to calculate and display the total of the values stored in three variables can be handled as follows:

```
    sum = number1 + number2 + number3
    Display total
```

But what if your program needs to sum 10, 100, 1,000, or 1,000,000 values? If your instinct is "Hmmm, this sounds like a job for a loop structure" then you are thinking like a programmer.

To understand how to accumulate a total, let's forget about computer programs for a moment. Consider how YOU might calculate the sum of 100 numbers if someone asked you to do this. Your first reaction might be "I can't add 100 numbers!" but in fact you can handle this task quite easily.

Ask the person to read out the numbers, one by one. In your head you start out with a total of 0. Each time a new number is provided, you add this to your total. To add 100 numbers you only need to deal with two numbers at a time — the total that you have already accumulated and the next number that needs to be added. With a little care and patience, you can easily add thousands of numbers — but you might not find this a very interesting activity!

Taking time to work out the steps to solve a problem is the way to figure out many pro-gramming tasks. Now that we have determined how **humans** accumulate a total, we can more easily develop an algorithm for a computer program to accomplish the same task.

Here is the algorithm to accumulate the sum of 100 numbers, using a FOR loop:

```
total = 0
FOR count = 1 TO 100
   Read nextNumber
   total = total + nextNumber
END FOR
Display total
```

The variable named **total** is first assigned the value **0**. The loop is designed to repeat 100 times. Each time through the loop, the program reads the next number, adds this to the value currently stored in **total** and stores the result in **total**, replacing the previ-ous value. By the time the loop has repeated 100 times, **total** will contain the sum of all of the values that have been read.

Let's walk through this for a count of 1 to 5, assuming that the five values are 5, 15, 12, 3, and 15:

```
total = 0

count = 1:  total = 0 + 5      total is now 5
count = 2:  total = 5 + 15     total is now 20
count = 3:  total = 20 + 12    total is now 32
count = 4:  total = 32 + 3     total is now 35
count = 5:  total = 35 + 15    total is now 50
```

When the loop has repeated five times, the total contains the value 50 which is the sum of the five values.

The instruction **total = total + nextNumber** may look confusing at first. How can total be equal to **total + number**? But remember that this is **not** a mathematical equa-tion — it is an **assignment** operation. The instruction is to add the value already stored in the **total** variable to the value stored in the **nextNumber** variable, and then store the result back into the **total** variable (replacing the previous value). In this way the total of all the numbers is being accumulated as the loop repeats.

The first instruction sets the **total** variable to **0**. Why do we need to do this? Consider the first time that the loop instructions are executed — the **total** variable must have an initial value so that **total = total + nextNumber** can be processed. We assign **0** to **total** before the loop so that this first calculation will work correctly. It would be a mistake to assign 0 to total **inside** the loop! Can you see what would go wrong if we did this? Right, the total would be reset to 0 every time the loop repeats!

Note that this algorithm can be used to accumulate the total of **any** list of numbers as long as you know in advance how many numbers are to be processed. In a subsequent chapter we will learn to use a similar algorithm that can be used when it is not known in advance how many numbers are to be processed.

Finding the Total and Average from a File of Numbers

Applications that use loops to perform more intensive processing of this kind will usually work with data that has been previously stored in files or databases. It is unlikely that we will want to ask the user to enter a long series of numbers in order to sum them or perform any other processing.

Consider the following requirement:

Rainfall1 requirement:

Write a program that processes a file named rainfall2007.txt. The file contains the year followed by 12 monthly rainfall amounts, each on a separate line. The program should display the year, total rainfall for the year and the average monthly rainfall.

Here's an example of the contents of the **rainfall2007.txt** file:

```
2007
3.21
3.61
2.84
1.06
0.16
0.04
0.02
0.11
0.45
0.52
2.03
2.20
```

In order to solve this problem we will need to read the year from the first line of the file, then use a loop to read each of the 12 rainfall amounts from the file and accumulate this in a total, just as we did in the previous example. Here is our algorithm:

```
Rainfall1.php algorithm:

   Open rainfall2007.txt as rainfallData for reading
   read year from rainfallData
   totalRainfall = 0
   FOR count = 1 TO 12
      read nextRainfall from rainfallData
      totalRainfall = totalRainfall + nextRainfall
   ENDFOR
   Close rainfallData
   avgRainfall = totalRainfall / 12
   Display year, totalRainfall, avgRainfall
END
```

As always it is important to consider what instructions need to occur **before** the loop structure, which instructions are to be repeated inside the loop structure and which instructions should be executed **after** the loop structure. It is important to open the file and read the first line containing the year **before** the loop because we do not want these instructions to repeat. On the other hand we need to read a line of data from the file and add this value to the total 12 times, so these instructions must be included **inside** the loop. The instructions to close the file, calculate the average and display the results should appear **after** the loop structure. Be sure that you understand this.

Here is the PHP code for **rainfall1.php**:

```
<html>
<head>
   <title>RAINFALL</title>
   <link rel ="stylesheet" type="text/css" href="sample.css" />
</head>
<body>
   <?php
      $rainDataFile = fopen("rainfall2007.txt","r");
      $year = fgets($rainDataFile);
      $totalRainfall = 0;
      for ($count= 1; $count <= 12; $count = $count + 1)
      {
         $nextRainfall = fgets($rainDataFile);
         $totalRainfall = $totalRainfall + $nextRainfall;
      }

      fclose($rainDataFile);
```

```
    $avgRainfall = $totalRainfall / 12;

    print("<h1>RAINFALL SUMMARY FOR $year</h1>");
    print("<p>TOTAL RAINFALL: $totalRainfall.</p>");
    print("<p>AVERAGE MONTHLY RAINFALL: $avgRainfall.</p>");
  ?>
</body>
</html>
```

Code Example: rainfall1.php

Figure 9-9 shows the output.

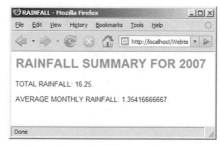

Figure 9-9: rainfall1.php screenshot

Finding the Highest and Lowest Values in a Series

Another common processing task is to find the highest and lowest values in a series. Once again, the easiest way to understand how to solve this problem is to consider how you would do it yourself. Let's first consider finding the highest value in a series of positive values.

Ask someone to read out a list of numbers. When the first number is read out, write this down as the highest number. Each time another number is read out, compare the new number with the number you have previously written down as the highest number. If the new number is higher, cross out your previous highest number and write the new number as the highest number. Repeat this procedure until all of the numbers have been read. At the end, you will have the highest value in the entire series.

Here is the algorithm for finding the highest number in a series of 100 positive numbers:

```
FOR count = 1 TO 100
   Read nextNumber
   IF count == 1 OR nextNumber > highestNumber
     highestNumber = nextNumber
   ENDIF
END FOR

Display highestNumber
```

This example shows a **selection** structure located **inside** a **loop** structure. Follow the logic carefully. Each time through the loop a new number is read into the **nextNumber** variable. The IF statement in the loop uses the OR operator to combine two tests. If this is the **first** number to be read (if the **count** variable contains **1**) then the value of **nextNumber** is assigned to the **highestNumber** variable. That's because the first time through the loop there is no previous value to compare so the first number must be the highest number at that point. The second test of the IF structure (**nextNumber > highestNumber**) compares the value of the number that has just been read with the value previously stored in **highestNumber**. If the new value is higher then the new value is assigned to highestNumber, replacing the previous value, and the loop repeats.

Since the IF structure contains no ELSE section, if the new value is **not** higher than the value already stored in the **highestValue** variable (and unless this is the first repetition), the loop simply repeats and the previous value of **highestNumber** is left unchanged. In this way the value of **highestNumber** will always contain the highest value that has been read so far.

A similar algorithm will find the **lowest** value in a series of numbers:

```
FOR count = 1 TO 100
  Read nextNumber
  IF count == 1 OR nextNumber < lowestNumber
    lowestNumber = nextNumber
  ENDIF
END FOR

Display lowestNumber
```

These examples demonstrate the use of an IF selection structure inside a loop structure. A loop structure might include any number of IF and IF..ELSE structures to meet the program requirements.

Performing Multiple Operations on a File of Numbers

Let's apply all of these algorithms to process our file of rainfall data, Here is a modified requirement:

Rainfall2 requirement:

Write a program that processes a file named rainfall2007.txt. The file contains the year followed by 12 monthly rainfall amounts, each on a separate line. The program should display the year, total rainfall for the year, the average monthly rainfall, highest monthly rainfall amount and lowest monthly rainfall amount.

Here is the algorithm that includes the procedures to calculate the total and also obtain the highest and lowest values from the file of rainfall amounts:

```
Rainfall2.php algorithm:
  Open rainfall2007.txt as rainfallData for reading
  read year from rainData
  totalRainfall = 0
  FOR count = 1 TO 12
    read nextRainfall from rainData
    totalRainfall = totalRainfall + nextRainfall
    IF count == 1 OR nextRainfall > highestRainfall
      highestRainfall = nextRainfall
    ENDIF
    IF count ==1 OR nextRainfall < lowestRainfall
      lowestRainfall = nextRainfall
    ENDIF
  ENDFOR
  Close rainData
  avgRainfall = totalRainfall / 12
  Display year, totalRainfall, avgRainfall, highestRainfall, low-
estRainfall
END
```

Here is the PHP code for **rainfall2.php:**

```
<html>
<head>
  <title>RAINFALL</title>
  <link rel="stylesheet" type="text/css" href="sample.css" />
</head>
<body>
  <?php
    $rainDataFile = fopen("rainfall2007.txt","r");
    $year = fgets($rainDataFile);

    $totalRainfall = 0;

    for ($count= 1; $count <= 12; $count = $count + 1)
    {
      $nextRainfall = fgets($rainDataFile);
      $totalRainfall = $totalRainfall + $nextRainfall;

      if ($count == 1 OR $nextRainfall > $highestRainfall)
        $highestRainfall = $nextRainfall;

      if ($count == 1 OR $nextRainfall < $lowestRainfall)
        $lowestRainfall = $nextRainfall;
    }
```

```
    fclose($rainDataFile);

    $avgRainfall = $totalRainfall / 12;

    print("<h1>RAINFALL SUMMARY FOR $year</h1>");
    print("<p>TOTAL RAINFALL: $totalRainfall.</p>");
    print("<p>AVERAGE MONTHLY RAINFALL: $avgRainfall.</p>");
    print("<p>HIGHEST MONTHLY RAINFALL:
            $highestRainfall.</p>");
    print("<p>LOWEST MONTHLY RAINFALL: $lowestRainfall.</p>");
  ?>
</body>
</html>
```

Code Example: rainfall2.php

Figure 9-10 shows the Web page generated by this program.

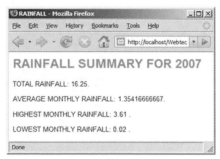

Figure 9-10: rainfall2.php screenshot

Nesting IF..ELSE Structures to Customize Output from a Loop

Consider the following requirement:

Rainfall3 requirement:

*Write a program that processes a file named rainfall2007.txt. The file contains the year followed by 12 monthly rainfall amounts, each on a separate line. The program should display the year and then list the **name** of each month, followed by the rainfall amount for the month.*

It is simple enough to use a loop to read the file and display the value of each month:

```
Rainfall3.php algorithm:
  Open rainfall2007.txt as rainfallData for reading
  read year from rainData
  FOR count = 1 TO 12
```

```
      read nextRainfall from rainData
      Display nextRainfall
   ENDFOR
   Close rainData
END
```

But how can we display the **name** of each month as well as the rainfall amount? To do this we must use a selection structure inside our loop to test the value of the count variable and display the appropriate month name for each repetition. Here is our revised algorithm:

```
Rainfall3.php algorithm:
   Open rainfall2007.txt as rainfallData for reading
   read year from rainData
   FOR count = 1 TO 12
      read nextRainfall from rainData
      if (count == 1)
         Display January:
      elseif (count == 2)
         Display February:
      elseif (count == 3)
         Display March:
      elseif (count == 4)
         Display April:
      elseif (count == 5)
         Display May:
      elseif (count == 6)
         Display June:
      elseif (count == 7)
         Display July:
      elseif (count == 8)
         Display August:
      elseif (count == 9)
         Display September:
      elseif (count == 10)
         Display October:
      elseif (count == 11)
         Display November:
      else
         Display December:
      ENDIF
      Display nextRainfall
   ENDFOR
   Close rainData
END
```

Each time the loop is processed:

1. The next value is read from the file and stored in the **nextRainfall** variable.
2. The program works through the nested IF..ELSEIF..ELSE structure, testing the value currently stored in the counting variable. When a **true** result is obtained, the appropriate month name is displayed.
3. The program then moves past any remaining tests in the selection structure and displays the value stored in the nextRainfall variable.

Let's convert this algorithm to PHP. In order to display the information neatly as an HTML document, we will use a table (see Figure 9-11).

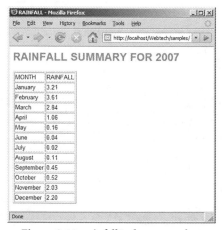

Figure 9-11: rainfall3.php screenshot

In order to produce this table correctly, the <**table**> tag and the row that contains the column headings must be generated **before** the loop structure. Each row that will contain the name and rainfall for a single month is generated **inside** the loop structure. Inside the loop, the next rainfall amount is read from the file, then the opening <**tr**> tag for the row is printed, followed by the IF structure which is used to print the first <**td**></**td**> tags that contain the appropriate month name. The IF structure is followed by another print statement that prints the second <**td**></**td**> tags that contain the monthly rainfall amount and also the closing </**tr**> tag to end the row.

Once all of the rainfall amounts have been read from the file and printed in rows, the FOR loop ends and a print statement after the loop is used to print the closing </**table**> tag.

Here is the PHP code for **rainfall3.php**:

```
<html>
<head>
  <title>RAINFALL</title>
  <link rel="stylesheet" type="text/css" href="sample.css" />
</head>
<body>
```

```php
<?php
   $rainDataFile = fopen("rainfall2007.txt","r");

   $year = fgets($rainDataFile);
   print("<h1>RAINFALL SUMMARY FOR $year</h1>");

   print("<table border=\"1\" >");
   print("<tr><td>MONTH</td><td>RAINFALL</td></tr>");

   for ($count= 1; $count <= 12; $count = $count + 1)
   {
     $nextRainfall = fgets($rainDataFile);
     print ("<tr>");
     if ($count == 1)
        print("<td>January</td>");
     elseif ($count == 2)
        print("<td>February</td>");
     elseif ($count == 3)
        print("<td>March</td>");
     elseif ($count == 4)
        print("<td>April</td>");
     elseif ($count == 5)
        print("<td>May</td>");
     elseif ($count == 6)
        print("<td>June</td>");
     elseif ($count == 7)
        print("<td>July</td>");
     elseif ($count == 8)
        print("<td>August</td>");
     elseif ($count == 9)
        print("<td>September</td>");
     elseif ($count == 10)
        print("<td>October</td>");
     elseif ($count == 11)
        print("<td>November</td>");
     else
        print("<td>December</td>");

     print("<td>$nextRainfall</td></tr>");

   }
   fclose($rainDataFile);
   print("</table>");
?>
</body>
</html>
```

Code Example: rainfall3.php

NOTE: The switch statement has already been mentioned in an earlier chapter. A switch statement provides an alternative to the use of chained IF..ELSE structures where a single variable is test for multiple values (as in this case, where the **$count** variable is tested for 12 possible values). Appendix G includes an example showing how a switch statement can be used to display the name of the month.

Loops within Loops—Creating a Bar Chart

Programmers are often required to develop code that displays numeric information visually. Charts and images are often much easier to understand than lists of numbers. Here is a revised requirement to display the monthly rainfall data:

Rainfall4 requirement:

Write a program that processes a file named rainfall2007.txt. The file contains the year followed by 12 monthly rainfall amounts, each on a separate line. The program should display the year and list the name of each month, followed by a colored bar that represents the rainfall amount for the month.

One way to create a colored bar that indicates the rainfall amount for each month is to display a series of colored squares. If the rainfall amount is 1 or less, we display just one square (■). If the amount is greater than 1 but less than 2, we display two squares (■ ■), and so on We can easily create an image of a colored square using any graphics package. We will use a red square stored as **InchOfRain.jpg** (this file is in your **samples** folder).

To determine how many squares to display for each month, we must first round **up** the current rainfall amount to the nearest whole number using the PHP **ceil()** function. We can then use our rounded number with a FOR loop to display our image the required number of times. For example, if the January rainfall amount is 3.21, this value rounds up to 4, so we will want our loop to display the image four times (■■■■).

Note that we round **up** rather than down so that rainfall amounts below 1 will be displayed as a single square rather than as 0 squares. Here is the algorithm:

```
chartLength = ceil(nextRainfall)
FOR numInches = 1 TO chartLength
   Display InchOrRain.jpg
ENDFOR
```

Figure 9-12 shows a table that includes bar charts for every month of the year.

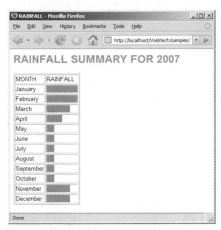

Figure 9-12: rainfall4.php screenshot

In order to produce a chart like this, that shows all the monthly rainfall amounts, we must include the FOR loop that generates a series of squares for each bar **inside** the FOR loop that counts through the months. Here is the algorithm for rainfall4.php:

```
Rainfall4.php algorithm:
  Open rainfall2007.txt as rainfallData for reading
  read year from rainData
  FOR count = 1 TO 12
    read nextRainfall from rainData
    if (count == 1)
      Display January:
    elseif (count == 2)
      Display February:
    elseif (count == 3)
      Display March:
    elseif (count == 4)
      Display April:
    elseif (count == 5)
      Display May:
    elseif (count == 6)
      Display June:
    elseif (count == 7)
      Display July:
    elseif (count == 8)
      Display August:
    elseif (count == 9)
      Display September:
    elseif (count == 10)
      Display October:
    elseif (count == 11)
      Display November:
```

```
        else
          Display December:
        ENDIF
        chartLength = ceil(nextRainfall)
        FOR numInches = 1 TO chartLength
          Display InchOrRain.jpg
        ENDFOR
      ENDFOR
      Close rainData
    END
```

It is important to understand that the loop that creates a new bar for each month must be nested **inside** the FOR loop that counts from 1 to 12. This ensures that the FOR loop that generates a bar is processed **completely** every time that the outer loop processes once. The inner loop will actually be used 12 times, once for each month.

Here is the PHP code for **rainfall4.php,** look over this carefully:

```php
<html>
<head>
  <title>RAINFALL</title>
  <link rel="stylesheet" type="text/css" href="sample.css" />
</head>
<body>
  <?php
    $rainDataFile = fopen("rainfall2007.txt","r");
    $year = fgets($rainDataFile);

    print ("<h1>RAINFALL SUMMARY FOR $year</h1>");
    print("<table border=\"1\" >");
    print ("<tr><td>MONTH</td><td>RAINFALL</td></tr>");
    for ($count= 1; $count <= 12; $count = $count + 1)
    {
      $nextRainfall = fgets($rainDataFile);
      print ("<tr>");
      if ($count == 1)
        print("<td>January</td>");
      elseif ($count == 2)
        print("<td>February</td>");
      elseif ($count == 3)
        print("<td>March</td>");
      elseif ($count == 4)
        print("<td>April</td>");
      elseif ($count == 5)
        print("<td>May</td>");
      elseif ($count == 6)
```

```
                    print("<td>June</td>");
             elseif ($count == 7)
                    print("<td>July</td>");
             elseif ($count == 8)
                    print("<td>August</td>");
             elseif ($count == 9)
                    print("<td>September</td>");
             elseif ($count == 10)
                    print("<td>October</td>");
             elseif ($count == 11)
                    print("<td>November</td>");
             else
                    print("<td>December</td>");

             print ("<td>");

             $chartLength = ceil($nextRainfall);

             for ($numInches = 1; $numInches <= $chartLength;
                               $numInches = $numInches + 1)
             {
                print("<img src=\"InchOfRain.jpg\" />");
             }
             print("</td></tr>");
      }
      fclose($rainDataFile);
      print("</table>");
   ?>
</body>
</html>
```

Code Example: rainfall4.php

The **print()** statement inside the inner FOR loop generates an HTML **<img>** tag to display single square (the image stored in **InchOfRain.jpg**). Since this statement is inside the loop, the image will be displayed multiple times depending on the rainfall amount.

Each time the outer FOR loop repeats, the month name and the bar showing the rainfall amount will be added as a new row in an HTML table. To achieve this, we first print the **<table>** tag and the first row (containing the table headings) **before** the loop (we don't want these to be repeated!).

For each loop repetition, we print the opening **<tr>** to start a new row, then print **<td></td>** tags containing the month name so that this appears in the first column. To print the bar in the second column, we first print the opening **<td>** tag, then provide the code (including our new loop) to display the bar, and then print the closing **</td>** tag and end the row with the **</tr>** tag.

Following the outer loop, we print the closing **</table>** tag.

Selecting from a List of Data Files

Our rainfall applications have all operated on data stored in a single data file named **rainfall2007.txt**. It would be useful to apply these programs to process **any** file that contains a year followed by 12 lines of rainfall amounts.

A simple way to achieve this is to create an HTML document that allows the user to select any file that contains rainfall data. Since the user could easily mistype a filename, we can design our input form to provide a drop down list that contains the names of the available data files. The user can simply select the file that they wish to view and press Submit.

Here is the code for **rainfall5.html** which provides the user with a form:

```
<html>
<head>
  <title>RAINFALL</title>
  <link rel="stylesheet" type="text/css" href="sample.css" />
</head>
<body>
  <h1>RAINFALL SUMMARIES</h1>

  <form action="rainfall5.php" method="post">
    <p>Choose a data file (listed by year):</p>

    <p><select name="rainFile">
    <option>rainfall2003.txt</option>
    <option>rainfall2004.txt</option>
    <option>rainfall2005.txt</option>
    <option>rainfall2006.txt</option>
    <option>rainfall2007.txt</option>
    </select></p>

    <p><input type="submit" value="SUBMIT" /></p>
  </form>
</body>
</html>
```

Code Example: rainfall5.html

Now we must adapt our PHP application to receive the user's selection and open the appropriate file. This is very simple. First we add a statement to receive the file name selected by the user and store this in a variable:

```
$rainFile = $_POST['rainFile'];
```

We then refer to **$rainFile** in our fopen() statement in order to open the correct file. To accomplish this we replace:

```
$rainDataFile = fopen("rainfall2007.txt","r");
```

with:

```
$rainDataFile = fopen("$rainfFile","r");
```

Figure 9-13 shows a sample user interaction.

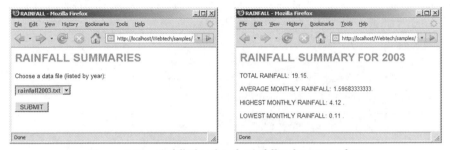

Figure 9-13: rainfall5.html and rainfall5.php screenshots

Summary

This chapter is more complicated than the previous chapters because it is more difficult to follow and apply the logic of repetition structures.

We have seen that a FOR loop is used to control a loop by counting.

A FOR loop consists of a loop **heading** that is used to control the loop, and a loop **body** that contains the statements that are to be repeatedly executed.

The FOR loop heading contains three sections, separated by semi-colons: the loop **initialization** is used to assign an initial value to the counting variable; the loop **condition** provides a Boolean expression that is tested each time the loop begins in order to determine whether or not the loop body should be processed; the loop **update** increments or decrements the value stored in the counting variable following each repetition.

The counting variable can be assigned any starting value. The counting variable can also be incremented (or decremented) by any value. These may be literal numeric values or values stored in variables.

An important application of loop structures is to process data sets in order to produce useful information. Some common processing tasks are to find the sum, average, high and low values in a set of values. Loop structures make it easy to process data sets of any size.

Loop structures can include selection structures, as well as other loops. If one loop is nested inside another loop, the inner loop will run through its entire set of repetitions every time the outer loop repeats once.

Chapter 9 Review Questions

1. Which of the following describes the purpose of a repetition structure?
    a. Choose between two or more blocks of statements based on a test condition
    b. Loop through a block of statements until a test condition changes
    c. Perform a sequence of statements in order

2. Which of the following is NOT an example of a repetition structure?
    a. for
    b. while
    c. do..while
    d. foreach
    e. if..else

3. How many times will the following loop repeat?

```
for ($count = 1; $count <= 5; $count = $count + 1)
{
   print ("<p>Hello!</p>");
}
```

    a. 1
    b. 3
    c. 4
    d. 5
    e. This is an infinite loop

4. How many times will the following loop repeat?

```
for ($count = 1; $count < 5; $count = $count + 1)
{
   print ("<p>Hello!</p>");
}
```

    a. 1
    b. 3
    c. 4
    d. 5
    e. This is an infinite loop

5. How many times will the following loop repeat?

```
for ($count = 1; $count <= 5; $count = $count + 2)
{
    print ("<p>Hello!</p>");
}
```

   a. 1
   b. 3
   c. 4
   d. 5
   e. This is an infinite loop

6. How many times will the following loop repeat?

```
for ($count = 1; $count <= 5; $count = $count + 5)
{
    print ("<p>Hello!</p>");
}
```

   a. 1
   b. 3
   c. 4
   d. 5
   e. This is an infinite loop

7. How many times will the following loop repeat?

```
for ($count = 0; $count <=6; $count = $count + 1)
{
    print ("<p>Hello!</p>");
}
```

   a. 0
   b. 4
   c. 5
   d. 6
   e. 7

8. Which of the following FOR loop headings will cause the loop to repeat the number of times stored in the variable $numTimes?
   a. for ($count = $numTimes; $count <= 5; $count = $count + 1)
   b. for ($count = 1; $count <= $numTimes; $count = $count + 1)
   c. for ($count = 1; $count <= 5; $count = $count + $numTimes)
   d. for ($numTimes = 1; $numTimes <= 5; $numTimes = $numTimes + 1)
   e. for ($numTimes = 1; $count <= $numTimes; $count = $count + 1)

9. The following code processes a file containing five positive numbers. What will the
    variable $result contain after the code is executed?

```
$result = 0;
$someFile = fopen("someFile.txt", "r");
for ($count = 1; $count <= 5; $count = $count + 1)
{
   $nextNum = fgets($someFile);
   if ($nextNum > $result)
      $result = $nextNum;
}
close ($someFile);
print ("<p>The result is $result</p>");
```

   a. The sum of the five numbers in the file
   b. The highest of the five numbers in the file
   c. The lowest of the five numbers in the file
   d. The value of the first number in the file
   e. The value of the last number in the file

10. The following code processes a file containing five positive numbers. What will the
    variable $result contain after the code is executed?

```
$result = 0;
$someFile = fopen("someFile.txt", "r");
for ($count = 1; $count <= 5; $count = $count + 1)
{
   $nextNum = fgets($someFile);
   $result = $result + $nextNum;
}
close ($someFile);
print ("<p>The result is $result</p>");
```

   a. The sum of the five numbers in the file
   b. The highest of the five numbers in the file
   c. The lowest of the five numbers in the file
   d. The value of the first number in the file
   e. The value of the last number in the file

11. The following code processes a file containing five positive numbers. What will the variable $result contain after the code is executed?

```
$result = 0;
$someFile = fopen("someFile.txt", "r");
for ($count = 1; $count <= 5; $count = $count + 1)
{
   $nextNum = fgets($someFile);
   $result = $nextNum;
}
close ($someFile);
print ("<p>The result is $result</p>");
```

    a. The sum of the five numbers in the file
    b. The highest of the five numbers in the file
    c. The lowest of the five numbers in the file
    d. The value of the first number in the file
    e. The value of the last number in the file

12. What is displayed after the following code is executed?

```
print ("<p>");
for ($count = 1; $count <= 3; $count = $count + 1)
{
   print("*****");
}
print ("</p>");
```

    a. A single line containing 5 asterisks
    b. A single line containing 15 asterisks
    c. Three lines containing 5 asterisks in each line
    d. Three lines containing 15 asterisks in each line
    e. Fifteen lines containing 1 asterisk in each line

13. If a loop is used to generate an HTML table which table tags and data should be generated each time that the loop repeats?
    a. The tags and data for the **next** table row and the columns within this row
    b. The tags and data for **all** of the table rows and columns
    c. **All** of the table tags and data including the <table> and </table> tags
    d. The tags and data for the **next** column
    e. The tags and data for **all** the table columns

14. What output does the following code generate?

```
for ($count = 1; $count <= 3; $count = $count + 1)
{
    print ("$count and..");
}
```

    a. One and..Two and..Three and..
    b. One and..Two and..Three
    c. 1 and..2 and..3 and..
    d. 1 and..2 and..3
    e. 1, 2, 3, and..

15. The following code displays the values between 1 and 25. What would you change to only display the **odd** numbers between 1 and 25?

```
for ($count = 1; $count <= 25; $count = $count + 1)
{
    print ("<p>$count</p>");
}
```

    a. Change $count = 1; to $count = 0;
    b. Change $count = 1; to $count = 2;
    c. Change $count <= 25; to $count < 25;
    d. Change $count = $count + 1; to $count = $count + 2;
    e. Change $count = $count + 1; to $count = $count + 3;

16. What is wrong with the following code which is designed to read and output five numbers stored in a file?

```
for ($count = 1; $count <= 5; $count = $count + 1)
{
    $someFile = fopen("someFile.txt", "r");
    $nextNum = fgets($someFile);
    print("$nextNum<br />");
}
close ($someFile);
```

    a. A semi-colon is missing at the end of the first line
    b. The file should be opened before the FOR loop begins
    c. The file should be closed inside the FOR loop
    d. The print statement should appear after the FOR loop ends
    e. There is nothing wrong with the code

17. What does "number crunching" mean?
    a. Breaking a number down into individual digits
    b. Processing a set of data values to obtain useful results
    c. Parsing a string of characters to see if it contains a number
    d. Creating a conversion table of some kind
    e. Reading a file of numeric values

18. Which statement is false?
    a. In PHP, the heading of a FOR loop must end with a semi-colon
    b. Loop structures can include selection structures
    c. Loop structures can include other loop structures
    d. In PHP, the counting variable that controls a for loop does not have to be named $count
    e. In PHP, multiple statements inside a loop structure must be enclosed in curly braces

19. How many columns will be displayed in this table?

```
print ("<table border=\"1\">");
for ($count = 5; $count <=25; $count = $count + 5)
{
    $result = $ccount * $count * pi();
    print("<tr><td>$count</td><td>$result</td></tr>");
}
print ("</table");
```

    a. 1
    b. 2
    c. 3
    d. 5
    e. 20

20. How many rows will be displayed in this table?

```
print ("<table border=\"1\">");
for ($count = 5; $count <= 25; $count = $count + 5)
{
    $result = $count * $count * pi();
    print("<tr><td>$count</td><td>$result</td></tr>");
}
print ("</table");
```

    a. 1
    b. 2
    c. 3
    d. 5
    e. 20

Chapter 9 Code Exercises

Your Chapter 9 code exercises can be found in your Chapter09 folder. This folder is included in your customized XAMPP installation at the following location:

   xampplite\htdocs\WebTech\coursework\Chapter09

Type your name and the date in the **Author** and **Date** sections of each file as you work on each exercise.

Debugging Exercises

Your **Chapter09** folder should contain a number of "FixIt" files. Each of these files contains PHP code that has an error of some kind. You will need to run each program in order to see the errors, and to debug and test the code to see if it works correctly. For example to run **fixIt1.php**, first run the Web server, then use the URL:

   http://localhost/WebTech/coursework/Chapter09/fixIt1.php

Code Modification Exercises

Your **Chapter09** folder contains a number of "Modify" files. Each pair of files contains HTML and PHP code that needs to be modified to meet a requirement. The requirements are included in each file. Modify the algorithms as specified, being careful to make changes to the .html and .php files as directed.

Code Completion Exercises

1. Read this exercise carefully and take your time to work out the logic. Your **Chapter09** folder contains versions of **squares1.html** and **squares1.php**. The code in **squares1.html** does not need to be changed—it just provides a form with a Submit button to run **squares1.php**. Provide a loop in **square1.php** to display the numbers 1 through 10, along with their squares. The **<hr />** tags already included in **squares1.php** simply displays a line (hard rule) across the page. Figure 9-14 shows how the output should appear.

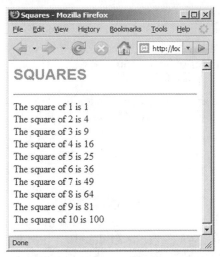

Figure 9-14: squares1.php screenshot

2. Read this exercise carefully and take your time to work out the logic. Your **Chapter09** folder contains versions of **squares2.html** and **squares2.php**. The code in **squares2.html** does not need to be changed—it provides a form with inputs for a starting number, ending number and an increment. Provide a loop in **squares2.php** to display a list of numbers and their squares from the starting number to the ending number in increments according to the increment provided by the user. Review the **TempConverter4** example if you need help. Figure 9-15 shows some sample output.

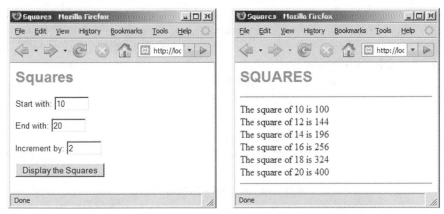

Figure 9-15: squares2.html and squares2.php screenshots

3. Read this exercise carefully and take your time to work out the logic. Your **Chapter09** folder contains versions of **weeklyReport1.html**, **weeklyReport1.php** and **weeklyData.txt**. The code in **weeklyReport1.html** does not need to be changed—it just provides a form with a Submit button to run **weeklyReport1.php**. The file **weeklyData.txt** contains a list of daily income from completed paint jobs over a one week (7 day) period. Each line contains the total income amount for a single day. Use a FOR loop to read the 7 lines from the file and include the necessary pro-

cessing to calculate the total income, the average income, and the number of days with no income. The output code is already provided — note the variable names. If your loop statements are correct the total will be $906.00, the average will be $129.43, and the number of "no income" days will be 2.

4. This program is similar to the previous exercise. Your **Chapter09** folder contains versions of **weeklyReport2.html**, **weeklyReport2.php** and **weeklyData.txt**. The code in **weeklyReport2.html** does not need to be changed — it just provides a form with a Submit button to run **weeklyReport2.php**. The file **weeklyData.txt** contains a list of daily income from completed paint jobs over a one week (7 day) period. Each line contains the total income amount for a single day. Use a FOR loop to read the 7 lines from the file. Assume that the first number represents the income for Monday, the second day for Tuesday, and so on, with the last number in the file representing the income for Sunday. For each line that the program reads from the file, display the day of the week, followed by the income for that day.

5. Read this exercise carefully and take your time to work out the logic. Your **Chapter09** folder contains versions of **currency.html** and **currency.php**. The code in currency.html does not need to be changed — it provides a form with a drop down asking the user to select a country. The PHP program already includes a selection structure that assigns the name of the currency for the selected country, along with a value to convert from US dollars to that currency (current at the time of writing — you may want to update this!).

   You need to add a table, using a loop to generate 10 rows with two columns in each row. The heading for the first column is "DOLLARS" and the heading for the second column is the currency of the country that the user selected. The first column in each table row is a dollar amount, starting with 100 and ending with 1000 in 100 increments. The second column in each row should be the equivalent in the currency that the user selected. Multiply the conversion factor by the current number of dollars to perform the conversion calculation for each row.

6. Your Chapter09 folder contains **tickerPrinter.html**, **tickerPrinter.php**, and **ticketCount.txt**. The code in tickerPrinter.html does not need to be changed. The ticketCount.txt file contains the count of tickets that have been sold. Your tickerPrinter.php file already contains code to read the number from ticketCount.txt into a program variable.

   Your job is to add a FOR loop to tickerPrinter.php that will "print" all the tickets. Instead of actually printing, you will use a print statement so that each ticket will display on the Web page as "ADMIT 1: " followed by the name of the performance (any name you want), followed by "TICKET #" followed by the ticket number. The first ticket will be numbered 1 and so on, up to the number that was read from ticketCount.txt. For example, if the performance was "Rolling Stones", and if ticketCount.txt contained the number 50, the first ticket would display as "ADMIT 1: Rolling Stones TICKET #1", and the last ticket would display as "ADMIT 1:

Rolling Stones TICKET #50". In your loop, print each ticket between <p> and </p> tags and then include a second paragraph that just prints a line of dashes. This will ensure that a line of dashes will appear between each ticket. Be sure that your FOR loop will work for any number that is stored in ticketCount.txt.

7. For this exercise you will create a program that helps the user understand his or her fuel costs. Your Chapter09 folder contains **fuelCosts.html** and **fuelCosts.php**. The code in fuelCosts.html includes a form that allows the user to enter the make and model of their car, the average fuel consumption (mpg), and the average fuel cost per gallon. Your fuelCosts.php file receives this input.

Your job is to provide a FOR loop in fuelCosts.php that displays the fuel costs for 10,000 to 100,000 miles of travel, in 10,000 increments. The fuel costs will be the miles traveled divided by the mpg multiplied by the cost per gallon. Use a table with a column for the miles traveled and a column for the fuel cost for that number of miles. Think carefully about the opening and closing <table>, <tr> and <td> tags. Which tags should appear **before** the loop, **inside** the loop and **after** the loop?

Chapter 10

"While NOT End-Of-File" — Introducing Event-Controlled Loops

Intended Learning Outcomes

After completing this chapter, you should be able to:

- Summarize the characteristics of event-controlled loops.
- Trace the processing of a simple WHILE loop.
- Design and code a WHILE loop.
- Identify and apply the standard algorithm to process a file of unknown length.
- Use a WHILE loop to process a simple data file.
- Include selection structures within a WHILE loop.
- Use a WHILE loop to process a file of records.
- Use a WHILE loop to process selected records in a file of records.
- Use a WHILE loop to process selected fields in a file of records.

Introduction

We have learned how to develop loop structures where the number of repetitions is controlled by a counting variable. However we often have to design solutions where the number of repetitions cannot be determined in advance. Under these circumstances a counter-controlled loop will not work for us. Instead of repeatedly incrementing and testing a counting variable we must design a loop that uses some other test to decide when the loop should stop repeating.

Event-controlled loops are loops that will repeat 0 or more times until a specific event occurs. In this chapter we will learn how to design and develop applications that include event-controlled loops using the WHILE loop structure. Specifically, we will learn how to use WHILE loops to process text files of unknown length containing data of some kind. We also will learn how to include selection structures in these loops to extract useful information for many different purposes. Although we will work with text files, many of the concepts and processes covered here will also apply when you move on to work with database tables and records.

Characteristics of WHILE Loops

Loops that are not controlled by counters are controlled by **events**. Consider the following instructions to inflate a tire to the recommended air pressure:

```
TireInflation:


   remove the valve cap
   check the air pressure in the tire
   WHILE airPressure < recommendedAirPressure
     add a small amount of air
     check the air pressure in the tire
   ENDWHILE
   replace the valve cap
END
```

The first two instructions direct you to remove the valve cap and check the air pressure of the tire. The next instruction is the heading of a WHILE loop which contains a condition that may be **true** or **false**. In this example the loop condition is **airPressure < recommendedAirPressure.** If this test is **true**, the instructions inside the loop are executed, then we return to the loop heading and test the loop condition again to decide whether or not to repeat the instructions in the loop. If the test is **false** that means that the tire is at the recommended pressure so we skip the instructions inside the loop and move on to the next instruction following the loop structure (in this case the next instruction is to replace the valve cap).

Figure 10-1 shows a flow chart of the same algorithm. Read the last paragraph again, this time referring to the flow chart.

Take time to study the pseudocode and flow chart versions of this algorithm carefully. Pay attention to the logical structure of the loop. Don't just look at the algorithm briefly and decide "Oh I understand—we're adding air to the tire until it's correctly inflated". That is quite correct but it's important to understand exactly how the algorithm is accomplishing this step by step so that you can apply this structure to other problems. Beginning programmers often have a lot of trouble understanding how to apply WHILE loops correctly in their own algorithms.

It helps to walk through the algorithm using some test values and following the instructions exactly. As a first example, let's assume that the recommended air pressure for a tire is 32 pounds per square inch (32 psi). You remove the valve cap and test the tire pressure, which turns out to be 28 psi. You then come to the WHILE loop heading

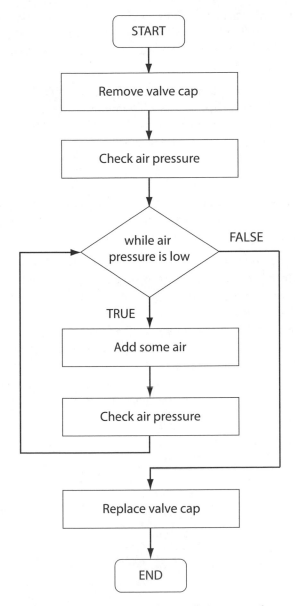

Figure 10-1: Flow chart of tire inflation example

and test the loop condition. Since the actual air pressure is less than the recommended air pressure, the loop condition it **true** so you perform the instructions inside the loop, adding some air and then checking the air pressure again. Let's say that the air pressure is now 30 psi. You return to the start of the loop and test the loop condition again. The test is once again **true** so you repeat the instructions in the loop, adding some air and testing the air pressure again. Let's say that the air pressure is now 32 psi. You return to the start of the loop and test the loop condition again. The test is now **false** since the actual pressure is no longer less than the recommended air pressure, so you skip the loop instructions and move on to the next instruction, which is to replace the valve cap.

Suppose the first time that you test the pressure, the actual pressure is 32 psi. That means that the first time that you test the loop condition the test is **false**, so you immediately skip past the loop and replace the valve cap. In this case, the loop instructions are **never** executed.

There are three important things to notice about this WHILE loop example. First, it is not possible to determine in advance how many times the loop will repeat. The loop is not controlled by a counting variable — instead the loop is controlled by an **event**. The event in this case is the air pressure in the tire reaching the recommended air pressure.

The second thing to notice is that the loop might execute 0 times. The algorithm includes an instruction to check the air pressure **before** the loop structure. If the air pressure is already at the recommended pressure the loop condition will be immediately **false** and the loop instructions will never be executed.

The third thing to notice is that the instruction to check the tire's air pressure appears **twice**. This instruction must appear **before** the WHILE loop in order to test the loop condition the first time, and this instruction must **also** be included **inside** the loop, **after** the instruction to add more air so that the air pressure will be tested again each time the loop repeats. If this instruction was not included **inside** the loop then the loop would execute forever since it would continue to refer to the results of the initial air pressure check even after more air was added. Also, if the instruction appeared **before** the instruction to add more air, the next test would be inaccurate since more air would be added **after** re-testing the air pressure. These are important logical considerations when designing an event-controlled loop.

You may be wondering "But what if there is too **much** air in the tire?" A more accurate algorithm would be:

```
TireInflation:

    remove the valve cap
    check the air pressure in the tire
    WHILE airPressure is not equal to the recommendedAirPressure
      if airPressure is less than the recommendedAirPressure
        add a small amount of air
      else
        release a small amount of air
      check the air pressure in the tire
    ENDWHILE
    replace the valve cap
END
```

If you review this carefully you will see that it handles tires that are under-inflated, over-inflated or correctly inflated. Can you draw a flow chart for this revised tire inflation algorithm?

The Structure of WHILE Loops

A WHILE loop will execute a number of statements 0 or more times, until the loop condition generates a false result. The general structure of a while loop written in pseudocode is as follows:

```
WHILE ( loop test )
   loop instructions
ENDWHILE
```

where (**loop test**) is any Boolean expression that will generate a **true** or **false** result, for example:

```
Prompt for password
Get userInput
WHILE ( userInput != correctPassword )
   Display "That is not the correct password - please try again"
   Prompt for password
   Get userInput
ENDWHILE
```

In this case the Boolean expression is **userInput != correctPassword**, which tests whether the value stored in the **userInput** variable is not equal to the value stored in **correctPassword**. The Boolean expression in a WHILE loop heading can use any relational operators (==, <=, <, >, >=, !=) and can combine expressions using any logical operators (**AND, OR,** or **NOT**).

An Algorithm to Process Files of Unknown Length

An important use of WHILE loops is to read data from a file when it is not certain at the time the program is written how much data the file will actually contain. A data file may contain a few lines of data or thousands of lines. The file may even be empty.

Consider a program that must process a file which contains the weekly timesheets of hourly employees (one timesheet on each line in the file). The program will need a loop to repeatedly read each line in the file in order to calculate each employee's pay, but how many times should this loop repeat? The length of the file may vary from week to week as employees leave or start work.

As another example, recall our **smokingSurvey.html** and **smokingSurvey.php** application that appended a new line of data to a file (**smokingSurvey.txt**) every time a new smoking survey was submitted by a user. What if we are required to write a program that will process all the submitted surveys in **smokingSurvey.txt** and produce a report? Since we may not know how many surveys were submitted, this program must be written in a manner that can handle any number of surveys in the file.

In order to process files of unknown length, we use a loop that repeatedly reads and processes lines from the file until the **end-of-file (EOF) marker** is found. The EOF marker is a special character that follows the last data value stored in a file. We can use a WHILE loop for this purpose by controlling the loop with the heading WHILE NOT EOF.

Programmers use a very standard, general-purpose algorithm to process files of unknown length. This is one of the more important and widely used algorithms for data processing so it is well worth taking the time to understand how it works:

```
STANDARD ALGORITHM TO PROCESS A FILE OF RECORDS:

   Open the file for reading

   Read nextLine from file
   While NOT EOF
      Process the data stored in nextLine
      Read nextLine from file
   ENDWHILE

   Close the file
```

Figure 10-2 shows a flow chart for the standard file processing algorithm.

This algorithm can be customized for your specific requirements by replacing the statement **Process the data stored in nextLine** with the specific instructions that your program needs to process each line in the file. Can you see how similar this algorithm is to the algorithm to achieve the correct air pressure in a car tire?

The key to understanding this file-processing algorithm is to pay careful attention to which instructions occur **before** the loop structure, which instructions are located **inside** the loop structure and which instructions **follow** the loop structure.

There are two instructions **before** the loop structure. The first instruction opens the file for reading. The second instruction reads the first line of data from the file and stores this data in a variable (here the variable is named **nextLine** but this could be any variable name). If the file is empty, this first **Read** instruction will find the EOF marker.

The loop structure appears next. The loop is controlled by the loop condition WHILE NOT EOF. Since this condition cannot be tested unless the program has already attempted to read a line from the file, the first **Read** instruction must appear **before** the WHILE loop, as shown here. The first **Read** instruction is often referred to as the **priming read**.

If the loop test is **true** (the end of the file has **not** been found), the program enters the loop structure and executes the statements inside the loop. These statements should include the instructions required to process the line of data currently stored in the **nextLine** variable, followed by an instruction to read the **next** line from the file into the **nextLine** variable. The program then returns to the start of the loop to test whether

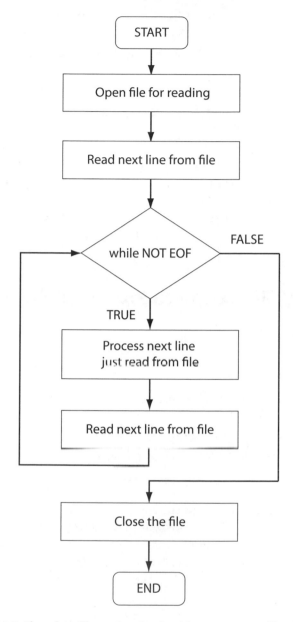

Figure 10-2: Flow chart illustrating the algorithm to process a file of records

or not the **EOF** marker was found during this last Read operation. If the EOF marker was **not** found , the loop repeats, processing the data stored in the **nextLine** variable and then reading the next line from the file. If the EOF marker **was** found, the loop is skipped and the program moves on to close the file.

Note that the last instruction inside the loop structure reads the next line from the file into the **nextLine** variable, replacing the previous value stored in that variable. For this reason it is important that the program performs all necessary processing to the line of data currently stored in the variable **before** the next line is read from the file.

The actual processing will vary according to the needs of your application and we will consider a number of examples in this chapter.

Once the EOF marker has been found, and the file has been closed, the program may need to perform additional steps to meet the application requirements. For example the program may need to display a total or average or other summary statistics.

The purpose of the priming read should now be clear: this allows the program to correctly handle an empty file. If the EOF marker is found when reading the first line, the loop structure is skipped entirely and the file is closed. The instruction to **Read nextLine from file** must therefore appear **twice** in this algorithm. It is written **once before** the loop to perform the priming read, and it must be written **again** as the **last** statement **inside** the loop to read the next record from the file after the previously read line has been processed. If you forget to include this statement inside the loop the program will repeatedly process the content of the first line in the file.

Using a WHILE Loop to Process a File of Scores

Consider the following requirement:

ProcessScores1 requirement:

Create an application that opens a file of scores selected by the user, reads each score from the file, and displays the scores.

For testing purposes, allow the user to choose between four different files: scores1.txt, scores2.txt, scores3.txt, and scores4.txt. Each of these files contains a different number of scores.

This requirement allows the user to choose between a number of different data files (all located in the **samples** folder). This will allow us to test our programs on a number of files of different lengths and containing various combinations of valid and invalid data. The **scores1.txt** file contains **five** scores, as follows:

```
89
77
92
69
87
```

The **scores2.txt** file is **empty**.

The **scores3.txt** file contains **ten scores, two of which are invalid** (these scores are out of the range 0 and 100):

```
89
77
92
69
87
101
-2
80
100
50
```

The **scores4.txt** file contains four scores, all invalid (these scores are out of the range 0 and 100):

```
-2
101
-1
102
```

Here is the algorithm for the HTML form that allows the user to select any scores file:

```
processScores1.html algorithm:
   Prompt the user for a file name
   Get fileName
   Submit fileName to processScores.php
END
```

Here is the HTML document (**processScores1.html**) that uses a drop-down list to implement this algorithm:

```
<html>
<head>
   <title>STUDENT SCORES</title>
   <link rel="stylesheet" type="text/css" href="sample.css" />
</head>
<body>
   <h1> STUDENT SCORES </h1>

   <form action="processScores1.php" method="post">

     <p>Choose the scores file to process:</p>

     <p><select name="fileName">
       <option>scores1.txt</option>
       <option>scores2.txt</option>
       <option>scores3.txt</option>
```

```
        <option>scores4.txt</option>
      </select></p>
      <input type="submit" value="Display the scores" />
    </form>
  </body>
</html>
```

Code Example: processScores1.html

Here is the algorithm for the PHP code that will open, process, and close the selected data file:

```
processScores1.php algorithm:

  Receive fileName from processScores1.html
  Open fileName as scoreFile for reading

  Read nextScore from scoreFile
  WHILE NOT EOF (scoreFile)
    Display nextScore
    Read nextScore from scoreFile
  ENDWHILE

  Close scoreFile
END
```

Note that this algorithm is based on the general-purpose algorithm that was shown previously. This requirement is simply to display each score so the instruction to process each line from the file is simply: **Display nextScore.**

Here is the PHP code for this algorithm (**processScores1.php**):

```
<html>
<head>
  <title>STUDENT SCORES</title>
  <link rel="stylesheet" type="text/css" href="sample.css" />
</head>
<body>
  <h1> STUDENT SCORES </h1>
<?php
  $fileName = $_POST['fileName'];

  $scoreFile = fopen("$fileName","r");
  $score = fgets($scoreFile);

  while (!feof($scoreFile))
  {
    print ("$score <br />");
    $score = fgets($scoreFile);
  }
```

```
    fclose($scoreFile);

    print("<p>END OF FILE REACHED</p>");
?>
</body>
</html>
```

Code Example: processScores1.php

This program receives the file name selected by the user and assigns this value to the variable **$fileName**. The file is opened for reading using the value stored in this variable:

```
    $scoreFile = fopen("$fileName","r");
```

Now the program reads the first line from the file (the priming read) and stores the content of the line in the variable **$score**:

```
    $score = fgets($scoreFile);
```

If the file contains data the first line of data is now stored in **$score**. If the file is empty, then this read operation finds the EOF marker.

Next the program encounters the heading of the while loop and tests the loop condition the first time:

```
    while ( !feof ($scoreFile) )
```

The WHILE NOT EOF test is written in PHP using a PHP function named **feof()**. This functions tests whether the EOF marker has been found. Notice the use of the NOT operator which is expressed in PHP using an exclamation mark (!). By associating this operator with **feof()** we are testing for NOT EOF. In other words, if the EOF marker has **not** been found yet, the test will be **true**, whereas if the EOF marker **has** been found, the test will be **false**.

Each time that the loop repeats, the program executes two instructions:

```
    {
       print ("$score <br />");
       $score = fgets($scoreFile);
    }
```

First the score that was previously read from the file and stored in the **$score** variable is displayed, followed by a line break. Second, the score from the next line in the file is retrieved and stored in the **$score** variable (replacing the previous score).

Note that curly braces are required to indicate which statements are included in the loop structure.

Each time the program reaches the end of the loop statements it returns to the start of the loop to test again if the line that was just read contains the EOF marker. This cycle repeats until the EOF marker has been read from the file. The loop test then generates a **false** result and the program moves on to the instructions that follow the loop structure:

```
fclose($scoreFile);
print("<p>END OF FILE REACHED</p>");
```

Figure 10-3 shows an example of input/output if the user selects **scores1.txt** from the form.

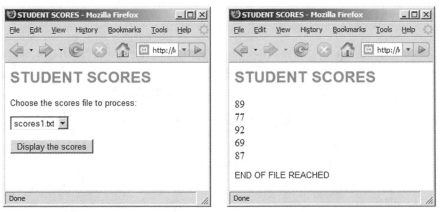

Figure 10-3: processScores1.html and processScores1.php screenshots

Figure 10-4 shows output from two other executions of **processScores1.php**. The first screen shows the output generated if the user selects **scores2.txt** which contains 0 scores (recall that this file is empty). The second screen shows the output generated if the user selects **scores3.txt** which contains 10 scores.

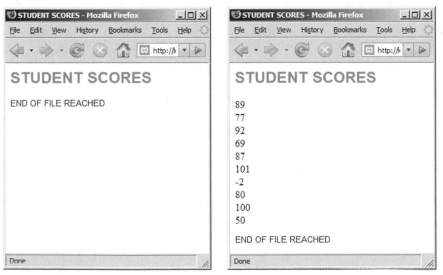

Figure 10-4: processScores1.html and processScores1.php screenshots

Including Selection Structures Inside a WHILE Loop

As you can see, the **scores3.txt** file contains two incorrect scores (scores that are either below 0 or above 100). Here is a revised requirement to handle this problem:

ProcessScores2 requirement:

Create an application that opens a file of scores selected by the user, reads each score from the file, and displays only the scores that are within the range 0..100. Out of range scores should be ignored.

For testing purposes, allow the user to choose between four different files: scores1.txt, scores2.txt, scores3.txt, and scores4.txt. Each of these files contains a different number of scores.

Let's modify our algorithm to ignore any invalid scores as follows:

```
processScores2.php algorithm:
   Receive fileName from processScores2.html
   Open fileName as scoreFile for reading
   Read nextScore from scoreFile
   WHILE NOT EOF (scoreFile)
      IF nextScore >= 0 AND nextScore <= 100 THEN
         Display nextScore
      Read nextScore from scoreFile
   ENDWHILE
   Close scoreFile
END
```

Just as in the previous example, this algorithm uses a WHILE loop to read and process each line from the file until the EOF marker is found. However in this case an **IF** structure is included inside the loop to test if the score that was just read from the file contains a value that is at least 0 and not more than 100. The score is only displayed if it is within range.

Note that the instruction to read the next score from the file is part of the WHILE loop structure but is **not** part of the **IF** structure. That's because we need to read the next score in the file **whether or not** the previous score was in range. The code for **processScores2.html** and **processScores2.php** can be found in the **samples** folder. Here is the code for **processScores2.php**:

```
<html>
<head>
   <title>STUDENT SCORES</title>
   <link rel="stylesheet" type="text/css" href="sample.css" />
</head>
```

```
<body>
  <h1> STUDENT SCORES </h1>
  <?php
    $fileName = $_POST['fileName'];
    $scoreFile = fopen("$fileName","r");
    $score = fgets($scoreFile);

    while (!feof($scoreFile))
    {
      if ($score >= 0 and $score <= 100)
      {
        print("$score <br />");
      }
      $score = fgets($scoreFile);
    }

    fclose($scoreFile);
    print("<p>END OF FILE REACHED</p>");
  ?>
</body>
</html>
```

Code Example: processScores2.php

The braces are not necessary for the IF structure since this structure contains only a single statement, but you can see these braces make it easier to follow the logic. Note once again that the instruction **$score = fgets($scoreFile);** is a part of the loop body but is **not** part of the IF structure.

Figure 10-5 shows the output that is generated if scores3.txt is selected by the user for processing. Note that the data in this file includes two out of range scores which are not displayed.

Try running the program on the other three text files to see the results.

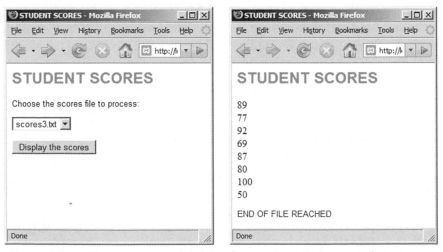

Figure 10-5: processScores2.html and processScores2.php screenshots

Using a WHILE Loop to Count, Sum and Average Data

Now let's look at a requirement to read a file of scores and perform some statistics:

ProcessScores3 requirement:

Create an application that opens a file of scores selected by the user, reads each score from the file, and calculates and displays the number of valid scores in the file (within the range 0..100), the number of invalid scores in the file, and the average of the valid scores.

For testing purposes, allow the user to choose between four different files: scores1.txt, scores2.txt, scores3.txt, and scores4.txt. Each of these files contains a different number of scores.

This requires us to process the data in these files quite differently. In order to calculate the **average** score in the file we need to **count** the number of valid scores and accumulate the **sum** of the valid scores as we read each score from the file. We must also **count** the number of invalid scores. Also, before our program attempts to divide the sum by the count to obtain the average we must ensure that the count of valid scores is greater than 0! There is always a possibility that the file contains no valid scores and an attempt to divide by 0 will crash our program. Here is the solution algorithm:

```
ProcessScores3.php algorithm:
   Receive fileName from processScores3.html

   sum = 0
   validCount = 0
   invalidCount = 0

   Open fileName as scoreFile for reading

   Read nextScore from scoreFile
   WHILE NOT EOF (scoreFile)
     IF nextScore >= 0 AND nextScore <= 100 THEN
       sum = sum + nextScore
       validCount = validCount + 1
     ELSE
       invalidCount = invalidCount + 1
     ENDIF
     Read nextScore from scoreFile
   ENDWHILE

   Close scoreFile

   Display validCount, invalidCount
```

```
   IF validCount > 0 THEN
      average = sum / validCount
      Display average
   ENDIF
END
```

The algorithm uses a variable to sum the valid scores, a variable to count the number of valid scores, and a variable to count the number of invalid scores. All three variables must be initialized to 0 **before** any of the scores are processed. The program opens the file, reads the first score from the file, then tests the WHILE loop condition. If the EOF marker was found during the first read operation, the loop test is **false** and the program will skip past the loop structure with the **sum**, **validCount** and **invalidCount** variables all still containing 0. If the EOF marker was **not** found, the loop test is **true** so the program enters the loop. If the current score is within range, the value of the score is added to the **sum** variable and 1 is added to the **validCount** variable. If the score is out of range, 1 is added to the **invalidCount** variable and the **sum** is left unchanged. The program then reads the next score and returns to the start of the loop to test whether the **EOF** marker was found during the last read operation.

This cycle repeats until the program finds the EOF marker and drops out of the loop. The sum variable will have accumulated the total of all of the valid scores, and the two counting variables will contain the number of valid and invalid scores in the file.

Following the WHILE loop structure, the program closes the file, then displays the valid and invalid score counts. If there is at least one valid score, the average of the valid scores is also calculated and displayed. The use of a selection structure here avoids a division-by-zero error if there are no valid scores in the file.

Walk through this algorithm carefully until you understand how it works. Here is the PHP code (**processScores3.php**):

```
<html>
<head>
   <title>STUDENT SCORES</title>
   <link rel="stylesheet" type="text/css" href="sample.css" />
</head>
<body>
   <h1> STUDENT SCORES </h1>
   <?php
      $fileName = $_POST['fileName'];

      $sum = 0;
      $validCount = 0;
      $invalidCount = 0;

      $scoreFile = fopen("$fileName","r");

      $score = fgets($scoreFile);
```

```
     while ( !feof($scoreFile) )
     {
       if ($score >= 0 AND $score <= 100)
       {
         $sum = $sum + $score;
         $validCount = $validCount + 1;
       }
       else
         $invalidCount = $invalidCount + 1;

       $score = fgets($scoreFile);
     }

     fclose($scoreFile);

     print("<p>Number of valid scores: $validCount<br />");
     print("<p>Number of invalid scores: $invalidCount<br />");
     if ($validCount > 0)
     {
       $average = $sum / $validCount;
       print("<p>Average of valid Score $average</p>");
     }
   ?>
</body>
</html>
```

Code Example: processScores3.php

Take some time to study this code—it incorporates most of the programming logic that we have covered so far. Run the program on each of the four scores files (**scores1.txt**, **scores2.txt**, **scores3.txt** and **scores4.txt**). The **scores4.txt** file contains only invalid scores so this will test the IF statement at the end of the program, which is designed to avoid a division by zero. Figure 10-6 shows the output when the program processes **scores3.txt** and **scores4.txt**.

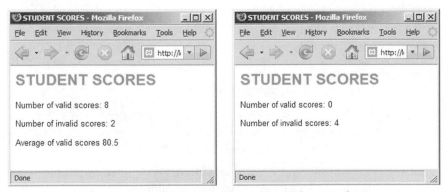

Figure 10-6: processScores3.php—two sample screenshots

Using a WHILE Loop to Process a File of Records

The previous examples in this chapter have processed files that contain a single data **value** (a score) on each line in the file. Now we will consider a requirement to process a file that contains a complete data **record** on each line:

ProcessWages1 requirement:

Create an application that opens a file that contains a list of employee timesheets, each timesheet record on a separate line. Each timesheet record contains an employee's first name, last name, hours worked and hourly wage, with each data item separated by a colon. For example:

Mike:Smith:20:12.55

The application should read all of the records from the selected file and display them as an HTML document. For testing purposes, allow the user to choose between three different files: timesheets1.txt, timesheets2.txt and timesheets3.txt. Each of these files contains a different number of timesheets.

The three timesheet files are included in the **samples** folder. The **timesheets1**.txt file contains **three records**, as follows:

```
Mike:Smith:20:12.55
Mary:King:40:17.50
Chris:Jones:35:9.50
```

The **timesheets2.txt** file is **empty.**

The **timesheets3.txt** file contains **ten records**:

```
Mike:Smith:20:10.55
Mary:King:40:17.50
Chris:Jones:35:10.55
John:Anderson:50:10.55
Anne:Frame:10:10.55
Catherine:Olson:35:10.55
Steve:Jones:35:17.50
Joseph:Canton:50:8.50
Beth:Jones:35:25.25
Peter:Anderson:16:17.50
```

The code for **processWages1.html** allows the user to select any of the three files for processing. Since this is similar to **processScores1.html**, the algorithm and code is not shown here (the file is included in the **samples** folder).

Earlier, we learned how to parse a line containing a record with multiple data items (you will recall that we achieve this in PHP using a combination of the **explode()** and list() functions). We can now apply these tools to process a file of records of unknown length. Here is the algorithm to meet the requirement for ProcessWages1:

```
processWages1.php algorithm:
   Receive fileName from ProcessWages1.html
   Open fileName as timesheetFile for reading

   Read empRecord from timesheetFile
   WHILE NOT EOF (timesheetFile)
      Get firstName, lastName, hrsWorked, hrlyWage from empRecord
      Display firstName, lastName, hrsWorked, hourlyWage
      Read empRecord from timesheetFile
   ENDWHILE

   Close timesheetFile
END
```

Here is the PHP code (**processWages1.php**) which uses the **explode()** and **list()** functions to obtain the first name, last name, hours worked and hourly wage from each line that is read from the file, and displays this information using an HTML table:

```
<html>
<head>
   <title>WEEKLY WAGE REPORT</title>
   <link rel="stylesheet" type="text/css" href="sample.css" />
</head>
<body>
   <h1> WEEKLY WAGE REPORT </h1>
   <?php
      $fileName = $_POST['fileName'];

      print ("<table border=\"5\">");
      print ("<tr><td>NAME</td><td>HOURS</td><td>HRLY
                  WAGE</td></tr>");

      $timesheetFile = fopen("$fileName","r");
      $empRecord = fgets($timesheetFile);

      while ( !feof($timesheetFile) )
      {
         list($firstName, $lastName, $hours, $payRate) =
            explode(":", $empRecord);

         print ("<tr><td> $firstName $lastName </td>");
         print ("<td> $hours </td>");
         print ("<td> $payRate </td></tr>");
```

```
        $empRecord = fgets($timesheetFile);
    }
    fclose($timesheetFile);

    print("</table>");
    print("<p>END OF FILE REACHED</p>");
  ?>
</body>
</html>
```

Code Example: processWages1.php

Note that the **<table>** tag and the first table row containing the headings are printed **before** the file is processed. Each time the loop structure repeats, a table row is created that displays the information that is parsed from the current line using the **explode()** and **list()** functions. Once the loop has completed, the ending **</table>** tag is printed. Figure 10-7 shows the output that is displayed if the program reads **timesheets1.txt**.

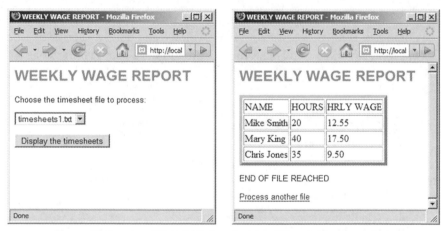

Figure 10-7: processWages1.html and processWages1.php screenshots

Processing Weekly Wages from a File of Timesheet Records

Here is a requirement to process the timesheet files and calculate and display the weekly wages of each employee:

ProcessWages2 requirement:

Create an application that opens a file that contains a list of employee timesheets, one timesheet record on a separate line. Each timesheet record contains an employee's first name, last name, hours worked and hourly wage, with each data item separated by a colon. For example:

Mike:Smith:20:12.55

The application should read all of the records from the selected file and calculate and display the employee's first name, last name and weekly wage in a check format.

For testing purposes, allow the user to choose between three different files: timesheets1.txt, timesheets2.txt and timesheets3.txt. Each of these files contains a different number of timesheets.

There is little difference between this and the previous algorithm except that here we are adding a calculation and displaying the employee's first and last name and weekly wage in the form of a pay check. We do not display the hours worked or hourly wage.

Here is an algorithm that meets this requirement:

```
ProcessWages2.php algorithm:

   Receive fileName from ProcessWages2.html
   Open fileName as timesheetFile for reading
   Read empRecord from timesheetFile
   WHILE NOT EOF (timesheetFile)
      Get firstName,lastName,hrsWorked,hrlyWage from empRecord
      weeklyWage - hrsWorked * hrlyWage

      Display"PAY TO firstName lastName
           THE SUM OF $ weeklyWage"
      Read the next empRecord from timesheetFile
   ENDWHILE

   Close timesheetFile
END
```

Here is the code for this algorithm (**processWages2.php**) which uses the PHP **number_format**() function to display the wages to two decimal places:

```
<html>
<head>
  <title>WEEKLY WAGE REPORT</title>
  <link rel="stylesheet" type="text/css" href="sample.css" />
</head>
<body>
  <h1> WEEKLY WAGE REPORT </h1>
  <?php
    $fileName = $_POST['fileName'];

    $timesheetFile = fopen("$fileName","r");

    $empRecord = fgets($timesheetFile);
```

```php
      while ( !feof($timesheetFile) )
      {
        list($firstName, $lastName, $hours, $payRate) = explode(":",
          $empRecord);
        $weeklyWage = $hours * $payRate;

        print ("PAY TO $firstName $lastName SUM
          OF $".number_format($weeklyWage, 2)."<br />");

        $empRecord = fgets($timesheetFile);
      }
      fclose($timesheetFile);
      print("<p>END OF FILE REACHED</p>");
    ?>
  </body>
</html>
```

Code Example: processWages2.php

Figure 10-8 shows the output if the program reads **timesheets1.txt**.

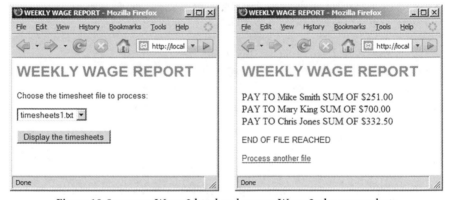

Figure 10-8: processWages2.html and processWages2.php screenshots

Processing Selected Records from a File of Timesheet Records

Often when we process a file of records, we are only interested in processing specific records. Consider the following requirement:

ProcessWages3 requirement:

Create an application that allows the user to input an employee's first name and last name, and the name of a timesheet file. The application should read all of the records from the selected file and display the first name, last name and hours worked of any employees whose first and last names match the user input.

For testing purposes, allow the user to choose between three different files: timesheets1.txt, timesheets2.txt and timesheets3.txt. Each of these files contains a different number of timesheets.

In order to meet this requirement we must develop an algorithm for an HTML form that will obtain the required user input, and an algorithm for the PHP program that will read the records in the file, test each record to see if the first and last names match those entered by the user, and display the hours worked of an employee if a match is found. There may be 0 or more records that match. Here is the algorithm for the HTML form (**processWages3.html**):

```
processWages3.html algorithm:

    Prompt for file name
    Get fileName
    Prompt for first name to search for
    Get searchFName
    Prompt for last name to search for
    Get searchLName
    Submit filename, searchFName, searchLName to processWages3.php
END
```

Here is the code for the form (**processWages3.html**):

```html
<html>
<head>
   <title>WEEKLY WAGE REPORT</title>
   <link rel="stylesheet" type="text/css" href="sample.css" />
</head>
<body>
   <h1> WEEKLY WAGE REPORT </h1>
   <form action="processWages3.php" method="post">
     <p>Choose the timesheet file to process:</p>

     <p><select name="fileName">
       <option>timesheets1.txt</option>
       <option>timesheets2.txt</option>
       <option>timesheets3.txt</option>
     </select></p>

     <p>First Name of employee:
     <input type="text" size="15" name="searchFName" />
     </p>

     <p>Last Name of employee:
```

```
    <input type="text" size="15" name="searchLName" />
    </p>

    <input type="submit" value="Display the Hours Worked" />
  </form>
</body>
</html>
```

Code Example: processWages3.html

Here is the algorithm for **processWages3.php**:

```
processWages3.php algorithm:

  Receive filename, searchFName, searchLName from
ProcessWages3.html
  Open fileName as timesheetFile for reading

  Read empRecord from timesheetFile
  WHILE NOT EOF (timesheetFile)
    Get firstName,lastName,hrsWorked,hrlyWage from empRecord

    IF firstName == searchFName AND lastName == searchLName THEN
      Display "firstName lastName HOURS WORKED: hrsWorked"
    ENDIF

    Read the next empRecord from timesheetFile
  ENDWHILE

  Close timesheetFile
END
```

And here is the PHP code for **processWages3.php**:

```php
<?php
  $fileName = $_POST['fileName'];
  $searchFName = $_POST['searchFName'];
  $searchLName = $_POST['searchLName'];

  $timesheetFile = fopen("$fileName","r");

  $empRecord = fgets($timesheetFile);

  while ( !feof($timesheetFile) )
  {
    list($firstName, $lastName, $hours, $payRate) =
      explode(":", $empRecord);
```

```
        if ($firstName == $searchFName AND
            $lastName == $searchLName)
        {
          print ("$firstName $lastName HOURS WORKED:
             $hours<br />");
        }

        $empRecord = fgets($timesheetFile);
    }

    fclose($timesheetFile);

    print("<p>END OF FILE REACHED</p>");

?>
```

Code Example: processWages3.php

Note the use of the AND operator to combine the tests for first name AND last name. Figure 10-9 shows sample input and output.

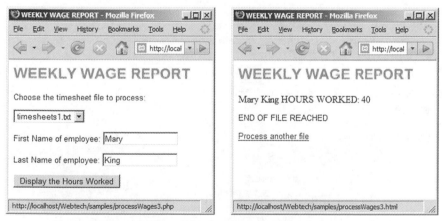

Figure 10-9: processWages3.html and processWages3.php screenshots

Processing Selected Fields from a File of Records

The last example demonstrated how to work with selected **records** in a file. Now let's see an example where we work with selected **fields** from each record.

ProcessWages4 requirement:

Create an application that reads all of the records from a file of timesheets and calculates and displays the average hours worked by the employees.

*For testing purposes, allow the user to choose between three different files:
timesheets1.txt, timesheets2.txt and timesheets3.txt. Each of these files contains a
different number of timesheets.*

In order to fulfill this requirement, our program is only concerned with the hours
worked by each employee. We need to sum and count these values to calculate the average hours worked by all employees. However in order to obtain this data, the program must still read all of the data from each line in the file, and parse the data from
each line to obtain the hours worked. We can then accumulate the total of the hours
worked and count the number of lines in the file (since this will tell us the number of
employees). Before calculating the average we must also test the count in case the file
contains 0 records. Once again we must be careful to consider which statements occur
before the loop structure, which statements should be located **inside** the loop structure and which statements **follow** the loop structure. Here is the algorithm:

```
processWages4.php algorithm:
   Receive fileName from ProcessWages4.html
   Set sum = 0
   Set count = 0

   Open fileName as timesheetFile for reading

   Read empRecord from timesheetFile
   WHILE NOT EOF (timesheetFile)
      Get firstName, lastName, hrsWorked, hrlyWage from empRecord
      sum = sum + hrsWorked
      count = count + 1
      Read the next empRecord from timesheetFile
   ENDWHILE

   Close timesheetFile

   IF count > 0 THEN
      averageHours = sum /count
      Display averageHours
   ELSE
      Display "FILE IS EMPTY"
   ENDIF
END
```

Here is the PHP code (**processWages4.php**):

```
<html>
<head>
   <title>WEEKLY WAGE REPORT</title>
   <link rel="stylesheet" type="text/css" href="sample.css" />
</head>
```

```
<body>
  <h1> WEEKLY WAGE REPORT </h1>
  <?php
    $fileName = $_POST['fileName'];

    $sum = 0;
    $count = 0;

    $timesheetFile = fopen("$fileName","r");
    $empRecord = fgets($timesheetFile);

    while ( !feof($timesheetFile) )
    {
      list($firstName, $lastName, $hours, $payRate) =
        explode(":", $empRecord);
      $sum = $sum + $hours;
      $count = $count + 1;
      $empRecord = fgets($timesheetFile);
    }

    fclose($timesheetFile);

    if ($count > 0)
    {
      $averageHours = $sum / $count;
      print("<p>AVERAGE HOURS WORKED: $averageHours</p>");
    }
    else
      print("<p>NO RECORDS FOUND</p>");
  ?>
</body>
</html>
```

Code Example: processWages4.php

Figure 10-10 shows the output if this program processes **timesheets3.txt**.

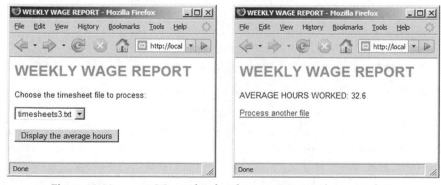

Figure 10-10: processWages4.html and processWages4.php screenshots

Processing a File of Survey Data

Let's consider one more file-processing example to demonstrate how much information can be extracted from a relatively simple data set. Earlier, we developed an application to receive smoking surveys submitted via an HTML form and append each survey to a file named **smokingSurvey.txt**. Here is a requirement to process this file and generate a report:

SurveyReport requirement:

Create an application that reads all of the records from a file that contains records of smoking surveys (each survey on a separate line in the file). Each record consists of a first name, last name, years smoked, and number of cigarettes smoked daily. The four data items in each record are separated by colons, for example:

John:Smith:2:20

The program should display: The number of surveys collected, the number and percentage of survey takers who have never smoked, the number and percentage of survey takers who have smoked, the number of survey takers who are heavy smokers (smoke 20 or more cigarettes a day for at least 5 years), the average number of cigarettes smoked daily by survey takers who smoke, and the average number of years that survey takers who smoke have smoked.

This requires us to plan carefully! We will need a number of variables to count and accumulate as we process each record from the data file. We will need variables to keep track of the number of smokers and non-smokers. We will need a variable to count the number of heavy smokers. And we will need variables to accumulate the total number of years that the smokers have smoked, and the total number of cigarettes that the smokers have smoked—we will use these to calculate the required averages. All of these counting and accumulating variables will need to be initialized to 0 before our program begins to process the file.

Each time the program processes a line from the file, we will need to test whether the survey taker entered 0 for the number smoked daily. If this is the case, we will count the survey taker as a non-smoker, otherwise we will count the survey taker as a smoker. If the survey taker is a smoker, we must add the years he or she has smoked and number of cigarettes smoked daily to our two totals. And we must test if the years smoked is at least 5 and the number of cigarettes smoked is at least 20 to determine whether or not to count this person as a heavy smoker.

We must also remember to read the next line from the file after we process each record.

Once the program reaches the end of the file it must calculate the various statistics that are required. We can calculate the total number of survey takers by adding the count of smokers to the count of non-smokers. We can calculate the percentage of smokers and non-smokers by dividing each of the counts of smokers and non-smokers by the total number of survey takers. We can calculate the average number of years that smokers have smoked and average number of cigarettes that smokers have smoked daily by dividing the appropriate totals by the count of smokers.

Here is the algorithm that meets these requirements:

```
processSurvey.php algorithm:

  Receive fileName from ProcessSurvey.html

  countHeavySmokers = 0;
  countSmokers = 0;
  countNonSmokers = 0;
  totalSmokedDaily = 0;
  totalYearsSmoked = 0;

  Open fileName as surveyFile for reading
  Read nextSurvey from surveyFile
  WHILE NOT EOF (surveyFile)
    Get firstName, lastName, yearsSmoked, smokedDaily from
      nextSurvey
    IF (smokedDaily == 0)
      countNonSmokers = countNonSmokers + 1
    ELSE
      countSmokers = countSmokers + 1
      totalSmokedDaily = totalSmokedDaily + smokedDaily
      totalYearsSmoked = totalYearsSmoked + yearsSmoked
      IF (smokedDaily >= 20 AND yearsSmoked >= 5)
        countHeavySmokers = countHeavySmokers + 1
      ENDIF
    ENDIF
    Read nextSurvey from surveyFile
  ENDWHILE

  Close surveyFile

  totalSurveys = countSmokers + countNonSmokers
  percentNonSmokers = 100 * countNonSmokers / totalSurveys
  percentSmokers = 100 * countSmokers / totalSurveys
  avgSmokedDaily = totalSmokedDaily / countSmokers
  avgYearsSmoked = totalYearsSmoked / countSmokers

  Display Survey heading
  Display totalSurveys, countSmokers, countNonSmokers,
    percentSmokers, percentNonSmokers, countHeavySmokers,
    avgSmokedDaily, avgYearsSmoked.
END
```

This algorithm includes selection structures within the loop structure. The first selection structure is used to determine whether to count the survey taker as a smoker or non-smoker. Non-smokers are simply counted but smokers require a number of processing steps; these include a second selection structure that is nested inside the ELSE section of the outer selection structure and used to count heavy smokers.

The PHP code (**processSurvey.php**) uses a table with no border to display the survey results. The table is not visible to the viewer but lines up the output nicely. An <**hr /**> (**hard rule**) tag is used to draw some separating lines across the screen:

```php
<html>
<head>
   <title>SMOKING SURVEY REPORT</title>
   <link rel="stylesheet" type="text/css" href="sample.css" />
</head>
<body>
   <?php
      $fileName = $_POST['fileName'];

      $countHeavySmokers = 0;
      $countSmokers = 0;
      $countNonSmokers = 0;
      $totalSmokedDaily = 0;
      $totalYearsSmoked = 0;

      $surveyFile = fopen("$fileName","r");
      $nextSurvey = fgets($surveyFile);

      while ( !feof($surveyFile) )
      {
         list($firstName, $lastName, $yearsSmoked, $smokedDaily) =
             explode(":", $nextSurvey);

         if ($smokedDaily == 0)
         {
            $countNonSmokers = $countNonSmokers + 1;
         }
         else
         {
            $countSmokers = $countSmokers + 1;
            $totalSmokedDaily =
               $totalSmokedDaily +  $smokedDaily;
            $totalYearsSmoked =
               $totalYearsSmoked + $yearsSmoked;

            if ($smokedDaily >= 20 AND $yearsSmoked >= 5)
```

```php
        {
          $countHeavySmokers =
          $countHeavySmokers + 1;
        }
    }

    $nextSurvey = fgets($surveyFile);
  }

  fclose($surveyFile);

  $totalSurveys = $countSmokers + $countNonSmokers;
  $percentNonSmokers = 100 * $countNonSmokers / $totalSurveys;
  $percentSmokers = 100 * $countSmokers / $totalSurveys;
  $avgSmokedDaily = $totalSmokedDaily / $countSmokers;
  $avgYearsSmoked = $totalYearsSmoked / $countSmokers;

  print ("<h1>SMOKING SURVEY REPORT</h1>");
  print ("<hr />");
  print("<p>(Report generated from data file:
     <strong>$fileName </strong>)</p>");
  print ("<table>");
  print ("<tr><td>Total number of people
     surveyed:</td><td>$totalSurveys</td></tr>");
  print ("<tr><td>Number of
     smokers:</td><td>$countSmokers</td></tr>");
  print ("<tr><td>Number of non-smokers:</td>
     <td>$countNonSmokers </td></tr>");
  print ("<tr><td>Percentage of smokers:</td>
     <td>$percentSmokers %</td></tr>");
  print ("<tr><td>Percentage of non-smokers:</td>
     <td>$percentNonSmokers %</td></tr>");
  print ("<tr><td>Heavy smokers (20+ a day for at least 5
     years):</td><td>$countHeavySmokers</td></tr>");
  print ("<tr><td>Average cigarettes smoked daily by
     smokers:</td><td>$avgSmokedDaily</td></tr>");
  print ("<tr><td>Average years that smokers have
     smoked:</td><td>$avgYearsSmoked</td></tr>");
  print ("</table>");
  print ("<hr />");

?>
</body>
</html>
```

Code Example: processSurvey.php

This is a more complex piece of code and it is worth taking some time to read through it until you understand all of the components. Figure 10-11 shows the results of processing a file of survey data named **sampleSurvey.txt** (in the **samples** folder).

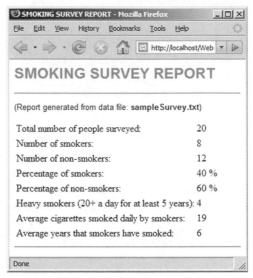

Figure 10-11: processSurvey screenshot

Using DO..WHILE or REPEAT..UNTIL Loops

Almost all programming languages provide another type of event-controlled loop, where the loop test appears at the **end** of the loop structure rather than the beginning. This structure is implemented as either a DO..WHILE loop or REPEAT..UNTIL loop, depending on the programming language. The characteristics of these loops are described in Appendix G.

Summary

Event-controlled loops allow us to repeat a series of instructions without the need to know in advance how many times the loop is to repeat. We achieve this by using a loop condition that allows the loop to repeat until some event occurs.

One example of an event-controlled loop is a loop that repeatedly reads and processes lines from a file until the **end-of-file** (**EOF**) **marker** is read. In this case the event is reading the end of file marker.

Just as a **FOR** loop is the usual choice for count-controlled loops, the most commonly used structure for event-controlled loops is a WHILE loop. The general syntax of a WHILE loop is:

```
while ( loop test )
  loop instructions
ENDWHILE
```

A WHILE loop can be used to process a file of unknown length. The standard algorithm to achieve this is as follows:

```
Open the file for reading
Read nextLine from file
While NOT EOF
   Process data stored in nextLine
   Read nextLine from file
ENDWHILE
Close the file
```

The statement **process nextLine** may include any number of instructions, including selection structures and even other loop structures. Processing may include counting, accumulating, testing, performing calculations or displaying information as required. Since the algorithm uses a loop to process one record at a time, it is important that any processing applied to each record must be performed inside the loop **before** the next record is read from the file.

When designing event-controlled loops, it is important to determine what instructions must be performed **before** the loop structure, which statements should be repeated **inside** the loop structure, and which statements should be performed **following** the loop structure.

Another type of event-controlled loop is a DO..WHILE or REPEAT..UNTIL loop, where the loop test occurs at the **end** of the loop structure.

Chapter 10 Review Questions

1. Consider a loop that repeatedly reads lines from a file of unknown length until the end of the file is reached. What term is commonly used to describe this kind of loop?
   a. A selection loop
   b. A sequential loop
   c. A count-controlled loop
   d. An event-controlled loop
   e. A for loop

2. Study the following algorithm. How many times will the user be allowed to attempt to enter a password until a correct password is submitted?

```
Prompt for password
Get userInput
WHILE (userInput != correctPassword )
   Display "That is not the correct password - try again"
   Prompt for password
   Get userInput
ENDWHILE
Display "Welcome!" message
```

   a. Once
   b. Twice
   c. Three times
   d. Four times
   e. Any number of times

3. What is the LEAST number of times this loop might repeat?

```
Prompt for password
Get userInput
WHILE (userInput != correctPassword )
   Display "That is not the correct password - try again"
   Prompt for password
   Get userInput
ENDWHILE
Display "Welcome!" message
```

   a. 0
   b. 1
   c. 2
   d. This cannot be determined in advance.
   e. This is an infinite loop.

4. Consider the following instructions for a bank teller. What event controls this loop?

```
WHILE there are more customers waiting in line
   Call the next customer
   IF the customer needs a loan
      Refer them to the Loan Officer
   ELSE
      Handle the customer's transaction
   ENDIF
ENDWHILE
```

  a. There are more customers waiting in line
  b. Call the next customer
  c. The customer needs a loan
  d. Refer them to the Loan Officer
  e. Handle the customer's transaction

5. How do we usually process a file of unknown length?
  a. Read the first line from the file, then use a loop to process the line that has just been read and read the next line, until the EOF marker is read
  b. Use a loop to read the next line from the file and process it, until the EOF marker is read

6. Which PHP function is used to test whether the End Of File marker has been read from a file?
  a. The eof() function
  b. The EOF function
  c. The feof() function
  d. The fclose() function
  e. The endOfFile() function

7. Which statement is **false**?
  a. WHILE loop structures can include selection structures.
  b. WHILE loop structures can include other loop structures.
  c. A WHILE loop can repeat 0 or more times.
  d. WHILE loops can be used to process files of unknown length.
  e. In PHP, the heading of a WHILE loop must end with a semi-colon.

8. How many scores will the following loop process?

```
$scoreFile = fopen("scores.txt","r");
$score = fgets($scoreFile);
while (!feof($scoreFile))
{
   print ("$score <br />");
   $score = fgets($scoreFile);
}
fclose($scoreFile);
```

  a. 0 scores
  b. 0 or more scores, depending on the content of scores.txt
  c. 1 or more scores, depending on the content of scores.txt
  d. 2 scores
  e. 2 or more scores, depending on the content of scores.txt

9. What does this loop actually do?

```
$number = 0;
$scoreFile = fopen("scores.txt","r");
$score = fgets($scoreFile);
while (!feof($scoreFile))
{
   $number = $number + 1;
   $score = fgets($scoreFile);
}
fclose($scoreFile);
print ("<p>$number </p>");
```

a. Displays the scores in scores.txt
b. Counts the scores in scores.txt
c. Sums the scores in scores.txt
d. Averages the scores in scores.txt
e. Adds 1 to each score in scores.txt

10. What does this loop actually do?

```
$number = 0;
$scoreFile = fopen("scores.txt","r");
$score = fgets($scoreFile);
while (!feof($scoreFile))
{
   $number = $number + $score;
   $score = fgets($scoreFile);
}
fclose($scoreFile);
print ("<p>$number </p>");
```

a. Displays the scores in scores.txt
b. Counts the scores in scores.txt
c. Sums the scores in scores.txt
d. Averages the scores in scores.txt
e. Sets each score to 0 in scores.txt

11. What does this loop actually do?

```
$number = 0;
$ageFile = fopen("ages.txt","r");
$age = fgets($ageFile);
while (!feof($ageFile))
{
   if ($age > 65)
      $number = $number + 1;
   $age = fgets($ageFile);
}
fclose($ageFile);
```

   a. Displays all the ages
   b. Counts all the ages
   c. Counts all the ages above 65
   d. Sums all the ages
   e. Sums all the ages above 65

12. What is wrong with this code?

```
$ageFile = fopen("ages.txt","r");
$age = fgets($ageFile);
while (!feof($ageFile));
{
   print("$age <br />");
   $age = fgets($ageFile);
}
fclose($ageFile);
```

   a. The first age in the file will not be displayed because two statement are in the wrong order
   b. The last age in the file will not be displayed because two statement are in the wrong order
   c. A semi-colon needs to be removed, otherwise the loop will not perform correctly
   d. The file should be opened inside the loop
   e. The file should be closed inside the loop

13. What is wrong with this code?

```
$ageFile = fopen("ages.txt","r");
$age = fgets($ageFile);
while (!feof($ageFile))
{
   $age = fgets($ageFile);
   print("$age <br />");
}
fclose($ageFile);
```

   a. The first age in the file will not be displayed because two statement are in the wrong order

   b. The last age in the file will not be displayed because two statement are in the wrong order

   c. A semi-colon needs to be removed, otherwise the loop will not perform correctly

   d. The file should be opened inside the loop

   e. The file should be closed inside the loop

14. The following code is designed to process one of the following files. Which one?

```
$value = 0;
$someFile = fopen("someData.txt","r");
$nextItem = fgets($someFile);
while (!feof($someFile))
{
   $value = $value + $nextItem;
   $nextItem = fgets($someFile);
}
fclose($someFile);
print ("<p>$value </p>");
```

   a. A file containing exactly two lines of data

   b. A file containing a list of numbers, one number on each line

   c. A file containing a list of numbers, all on the same line, separated by colons

   d. A file containing a name, colon, and number on each line

   e. A file containing a name on the first line, a colon on the second line, and a number on the third line

15. The following code designed to process one of the following files. Which one?

```
$someFile = fopen("someData.txt","r");
$nextItem = fgets($someFile);
```

```
while (!feof($someFile))
{
   list($value1, $value2) = explode(":", $nextItem);
   print ("<p>($value1 $value2</p>");
   $nextItem = fgets($someFile);
}
fclose($someFile);
print ("<p>$value </p>");
```

a. A file containing exactly one line of data
b. A file containing exactly two lines of data
c. A file containing a list of numbers, one number on each line
d. A file containing a name, colon, and number on each line
e. A file containing a name on the first line, a colon on the second line, and a number on the third line

16. What length of file can be processed using a WHILE loop
    a. Only files that contain no data (empty file)
    b. Files that contain exactly one line of data
    c. Files that contain exactly two lines of data
    d. Files that contain 0 or more lines of data
    e. Files that contain 1 or more lines of data

17. What does this code actually do?

```
$value = 0;
$someFile = fopen("someData.txt","r");
$nextItem = fgets($someFile);
while (!feof($someFile))
{
   list($item1, $item2) = explode(":", $nextItem);
   $value = $value + $item2;
   $nextItem = fgets($someFile);
}
fclose($someFile);
print ("<p>$value </p>");
```

a. Reads a file containing a list of values, one on each line, and sums them
b. Reads a file containing two values on each line and sums all of the values in the file
c. Reads a file containing two values on each line and sums the first values on each line
d. Reads a file containing two values on each line and sums the second values on each line
e. Reads a file containing two lines and sums the values on these lines

18. What does this code actually do?

```
$value = 0;
$someFile = fopen("someData.txt","r");
$nextItem = fgets($someFile);
while (!feof($someFile))
{
    list($item1, $item2) = explode(":", $nextItem);
    if ($item1 == "Smith")
        $value = $value + $item2;
    $nextItem = fgets($someFile);
}
fclose($someFile);
print ("<p>$value</p>");
```

    a. Reads a file containing two values on each line and counts the lines where the first value is "Smith"

    b. Reads a file containing two values on each line and sums the second values of the lines where the first value is "Smith"

    c. Reads a file containing two values on each line and sums the first values of the lines where the second value is "Smith"

    d. Reads a file containing two values on each line and sets the second value to 0 if the first value is "Smith"

    e. Reads a file containing two lines and doubles the value of the second line if the value of the first line is "Smith"

19. The textbook provides a SmokingSurvey example. How are the total number of surveys calculated in the algorithm for this program?

    a. By using a counter to count each survey that is read from the survey file

    b. By using counters to count the number of smokers and non-smokers in the survey file, then adding these after the file has been processed

    c. By adding the total smoked daily by all survey takers and dividing this by the number of smokers

    d. By using a form that asks the user for the number of surveys in the file

    e. The total number of surveys is not calculated in this program

20. When using a WHILE loop to read records from a file of unknown length, why is it important to read the first record BEFORE the loop test?

    a. In order to determine how many records are in the file

    b. In order to determine what type of records are in the file

    c. In case the file contains duplicate records

    d. In case the EOF marker is on the first line (the loop will then be skipped)

    e. The program should NOT read the first record BEFORE the loop test!

Chapter 10 Code Exercises

Your Chapter 10 code exercises can be found in your **Chapter10** folder. This folder is included in your customized XAMPP installation at the following location:

xampplite\htdocs\WebTech\coursework\Chapter10

Type your name and the date in the **Author** and **Date** sections of each file as you work on each exercise.

Debugging Exercises

Your **Chapter10** folder should contain a number of "FixIt" files. Each of these files contains PHP code that has an error of some kind. You will need to run each program in order to see the errors, and to debug and test the code to see if it works correctly. For example to run **fixIt1.php**, first run the Web server, then use the URL:

http://localhost/WebTech/coursework/Chapter10/fixIt1.php

Code Modification Exercises

Your **Chapter10** folder contains a number of "Modify" files. Each pair of files contains HTML and PHP code that needs to be modified to meet a requirement. The requirements are included in each file. Modify the algorithms as specified, being careful to make changes to the .html and .php files as directed.

Code Completion Exercises

1. Read this exercise carefully and take your time to work out the logic. Your **Chapter10** folder contains versions of **software1.html** and **software1.php** as well as a text file named **orders.txt** which contains a list of software orders. Each line in the file contains the name of an operating system (**Linux**, **Windows**, or **Macintosh**) followed by a colon, followed by the number of copies ordered, for example:

    Macintosh:2

    Add the necessary code to **software1.php** to process the data in **orders.txt** using a WHILE loop to calculate the total number of copies that have been ordered and to count the number of separate orders. For testing purposes, the correct total is **52** and the correct number of orders is **20** (but your code should still work correctly if you change the data in the file). Be sure to use a priming read and remember that you will need to parse each line to obtain the operating systems and number of copies for each order. The output and some other statements have been provided to save time.

2. Read this exercise carefully and take your time to work out the logic. Your **Chapter10** folder contains versions of **software2.html** and **software2.php** as well as a text file named **orders.txt** which contains a list of software orders. Each line in the file contains the name of an operating system (**Linux, Windows,** or **Macintosh**) followed by a colon, followed by the number of copies ordered, for example:

   Macintosh:2

   This exercise also processes **orders.txt** but this time you are asked to develop a WHILE loop that contains selection structures. Add the necessary code to **software2.php** to process the data in **orders.txt** and count the number of orders that request more than one copy, the number of copies of **Linux** software ordered, the number of copies of **Macintosh** software ordered, and the number of copies of **Windows** software ordered. The correct counts are **8** orders with multiple copies, **13** copies of Linux, **23** copies of Macintosh, and **16** copies of Windows (but your code should still work correctly if you change the data in the file). The output and some other statements have been provided to save time.

3. Read this exercise carefully and take your time to work out the logic. Your **Chapter10** folder contains versions of **romeReport.html** and **romeReport.php** as well as a text file named **travel.dat** which contains a list of travel reservations. Each line in the **travel.dat** file contains a single reservation: the name of a destination, number of people traveling, and number of nights staying, for example:

   Rome:2:12
   Tokyo:3:15

   The program should read the file and report the number of reservations in the file for **Rome**, and the total number of people traveling to **Rome**. For testing purposes, the correct number of reservations for Rome is **7** and the correct number of people traveling to Rome is **18** (but your code should still work correctly if you change the data in the file).

4. Read this exercise carefully and take your time to work out the logic. Your **Chapter10** folder contains versions of **findCharacter.html** and **findCharacter.php** as well as a text file named **characters.txt** which contains a list of records with character information. Each line in the **characters.txt** file contains the name of a character, the character type, the number of health tokens, number of experience tokens, and number of supply tokens. Note that these are separated by **commas** (not colons) for example:

   Mozart,Elf,10,2,25

   The form in **findCharacter.html** asks the user for a character name to search for (this file does not need to be changed). The **findCharacter.php** program receives this name and must use a WHILE loop to read the file and display the information for the character if the name is found.

Note that the program includes a variable **$notFound** which is assigned an initial value of **true**. If this variable still contains a value of **true** after the loop has been process, a message is displayed indicating that the character was not found, so be sure that your file-processing code includes a statement to set this variable to **false** if the character is found in the file. All required output statements are already provided, along with some other statements to save you some time.

Be sure to test your program with a character name that is in the file and a name that is not in the file. For testing purposes, the following names can be found in the file: Mozart, Leamus, Pete, Tara, Petal, Drake, Sert, Brian, Siren, and May.

5. Your Chapter10 folder contains **events.html**, **events.php**, and **events.txt**. The code in events.html does not need to be changed. The events.txt file contains a list of dates and performers, separated by colons, for example 1/15/2011:**Rolling Stones**. Each event appears on a separate line. Open this file in your text editor and add 5 more lines with dates and performers (feel free to also change the events already listed).

Add the necessary code to events.php to display a list of dates and performers, where each date appears as an <h2> heading and each performer appears below the date as an <h1> heading. You will need a WHILE loop to read the entries from the file and each time you read a line you will need to extract the date and performer and then print this information. Be sure to test your work.

6. Your Chapter10 folder already contains **busTravel.html**, **busTravel.php**, and **bus-Travel.txt**. You do not need to change busTravel.html or busTravel.txt. Your busTravel.txt file is a trip log that contains information about business trips, each on a separate line. Each line contains a date and miles traveled, followed by four YES/NO entries to indicate whether or not the travel for that date included breakfast, lunch, dinner or hotel. Here are examples of the first two lines in the file:

```
3/15/2011:120:NO:YES:YES:YES:
3/16/2011:100:YES:YES:NO:NO:
```

Your job is to provide the code in busTravel.php to process this file and calculate the reimbursement for these business trips. Open the file for reading, then use a WHILE loop to read each line from the file until the end of the file is reached. Each time a line is read from the file the six values must be extracted from the line and the reimbursement must be calculated as follows: The basic reimbursement will be the miles traveled x 0.35. If breakfast was included add 6.00 to the reimbursement. If lunch was included, add 8.50 to the reimbursement. If dinner was included, add 17.50 to the reimbursement. If a hotel was included, add 110.00 to the reimbursement. So for example the cost of the first line will be 120*0.35 + 8.50 + 17.50 + 110.00, which is $178.00.

(Note that these are the same calculations that you used in the corresponding Chapter 8 exercise. The only difference is that now the program should add the total reimbursement for each trip to a running total so that after the loop has completed, the total reimbursement can also be displayed.)

After the loop, the program should close the file and display the total reimbursement. If your code is correct this should amount to $884.60.

NOTE: For a more challenging and professional exercise, instead of just displaying the total reimbursement, display a table with rows for each trip, with columns that display the trip and reimbursement amounts for car use, breakfast, lunch, dinner, and hotel.

Chapter 11

Structured Data — Working with Arrays

Intended Learning Outcomes

After completing this chapter, you should be able to:

- Summarize key characteristics of arrays.
- Create an array using index value.
- Create an array using the array() function.
- Assign values to array elements.
- Access array elements in expressions.
- Create and work with arrays of strings.
- Use the sizeof() function to control a FOR loop
- Use a WHILE loop to read data from a file into an array.
- Use a FOR loop to process an array.

Introduction

Computer programs use variables to store data temporarily while the application is executing. Until now, we have created a separate variable for each value that our program needs to store. Each of these variables may only contain a single value at any time.

The use of separate variables to store various data values works well for many purposes, but there are limitations. Consider a program that uses variables to store three scores—we can create three separate variables named $score1, $score2 and $score3. To sum these values we would write $score1 + $score2 + $score3. This a little tedious with just three variables but what if we needed to write a program to sum and display 20 scores, or 100 scores, or 1,000 scores? Using separate variables for each score is now not only tedious but unfeasible. And just imagine if you wrote this code and are then told to modify your code to work with a different number of scores!

Fortunately programming languages provide more complex data structures that allow us to work with large or small groups of data values much more efficiently. One of the most widely used data structures is an **array**, which can be used store any number of data values and refer to these using a single variable name. In this chapter we will learn how to create array variables, how to store values in arrays, and how to access and process these values.

What Is an Array?

An array is a data structure that contains multiple data values, where each individual value is referenced using an **index** of some kind. The simplest type of array is indexed using integer values, beginning with an index value of **0**. Let's start with an example. Suppose that we have to write a program that needs to work with 5 scores. We could create 5 separate variables, and store our scores in each variable:

```
$score1 = 90;
$score2 = 87;
$score3 = 74;
$score4 = 80;
$score5 = 94;
```

But a better solution is to create a single **$scores** variable that will reference an array to store all 5 scores. Each of the five scores will be stored in an indexed location in the **$scores** array (we often refer to each indexed location as an array **element**). Here is one way to create an array of five scores in PHP:

```
$scores[0] = 90;
$scores[1] = 87;
$scores[2] = 74;
$scores[3] = 80;
$scores[4] = 94;
```

We now have a single array variable, **$scores**, which contains 5 values (90, 87, 74, 80, and 94). We can reference any of these values using the appropriate index position within the array, for example **$scores** [2] refers to the **third** element which contains the value **74**. Note that the five elements are indexed from 0 to 4 and not from 1 to 5 as you might expect. The reason for this is explained later in the chapter. Also note that the index value is indicated inside **square brackets** []. Be sure to use square brackets when working with array index values—do not use curly braces or parentheses.

You can also create an array of values in PHP by calling the **array**() function and sending all of the values to be assigned to the array as a list of arguments:

```
$scores = array (90, 87, 74, 80, 94);
```

This statement achieves the same result as the previous five statements combined. Instead of assigning values to each array element separately, we use the **array**() function to create the entire array in a single statement. In this example, the **array**() function creates an array with five index values ($scores[0], $scores[1], $scores[2], $scores[3], and $scores[4]), and assigns the values 90, 87, 74, 80 and 94 to these indexed locations. The function returns the complete array which is then assigned to the $scores variable.

The **array**() function can be used most effectively when the values that are to be assigned to the array are known at the time the array is created. As we shall see, that is not always the case.

Working with Array Elements

You can store, change, and access values in any element of an array variable just as with any other variable, the only difference is that you need to include the index position to identify which element is to be referenced.

You can **assign** a value to any position in an array. Just as with any variable, if an array element already contains a value, the previous value is replaced.

Here are three examples:

```
$scores[2] = 85;
$scores[3] = $exam1 * 0.85;
$scores[4] = $scores[2] + 5;
```

You can use an array element as part of an **expression**. Here are three examples:

```
$revisedScore = $scores[0] + 10;

$averageScore = ($scores[0] + $scores[1] + $scores[2] +
          $scores[3] + $scores[4]) / 5;

if ($scores[1] >= 60)
   print("PASS!");
else
   print("FAIL!");
```

(NOTE: if the array variable is referenced on the right side of an assignment, be sure that it has already received a value. For example the first example above adds 10 to the value already stored in **$scores[0]**, so **$scores[0]** should have been assigned a value before this statement is executed.)

You can **update** a value that was previously assigned to an array element. The following two examples both add a number to the value currently stored in an array element, and store the result back into the same element (replacing the previous value):

```
$scores[4] = $scores[4] + 5;
$scores[2] = $scores[2] + 1;
```

Extending an Array

Unlike most programming languages, PHP allows you to add a new element to an array at any time. For example, you can add a sixth and seventh element to the **$scores** array simply by creating these elements:

```
$scores[5] = 75;
$scores[6] = 65;
```

PHP also allows you to add new elements to the end of an array without specifying the index position:

```
$scores[] = 80;
$scores[] = 55;
```

In this case, assuming that our **$scores** array already has seven elements (indexed from 0 to 6), two new elements are created. The new elements, **$scores**[7] and **$scores**[8], contain the values 80 and 55 respectively. This feature can be very useful where new elements are added to an existing array since your application does not have to determine the next index value.

PHP provides a number of useful functions for working with arrays. See Chapter 13 and Appendix F for additional information concerning these functions.

Displaying Array Values

You can display array values in PHP **print**() statements just as any other variables. For example to display a value from the **$scores** array:

```
print("<p> SCORE 1: $scores[0]</p>");
```

When referring to an array variable directly in a print statement, be sure that there are no spaces between the array name and the square brackets containing the index.

The following example shows how you might print a **$scores** array containing five scores in an HTML table:

```
print("<h1>SCORES</h1>
   <table>
   <tr><td>SCORE 1</td><td>$scores[0]</td></tr>
   <tr><td>SCORE 2</td><td>$scores[1]</td></tr>
   <tr><td>SCORE 3</td><td>$scores[2]</td></tr>
   <tr><td>SCORE 4</td><td>$scores[3]</td></tr>
```

```
<tr><td>SCORE 5</td><td>$scores[4]</td></tr>
</table>");
```

If you're wondering how you would achieve this with an array containing many more values, we will explain that shortly.

Receiving Scores into an Array from an HTML Form

The following requirement will demonstrate various ways of working with array elements:

Arrays1 requirement:

*Create an application that provides a form for the user to submit five scores. The first three scores are **exam** scores, the fourth score is an **essay** score and the fifth score is a **project** score.*

*The applications should receive the five scores and calculate the average of the three **exam** scores. If this average is 90 or above, a 5 point **bonus** should be added to the **project** score, but the project score should not exceed 100.*

*The application should display the five scores, the **total** of the five scores, the **average** of the three exam scores, and an **explanatory message** concerning the project score.*

Here is the HTML code for **arrays1.html**:

```
<html>
<head>
   <title>Scores Entry Form </title>
   <link rel="stylesheet" type="text/css" href="sample.css" />
</head>
<body>
   <h1>Score Entry Form</h1>
   <form action="arrays1.php" method="post">
   <table>
   <tr> <td>Please enter the score for Exam 1:</td>
        <td><input type="text" size="5" name="exam1" /></td></tr>
   <tr> <td>Please enter the score for Exam 2:</td>
        <td><input type="text" size="5" name="exam2" /></td></tr>
   <tr> <td>Please enter the score for Exam 3:</td>
        <td><input type="text" size="5" name="exam3" /></td></tr>
   <tr> <td>Please enter the essay score:</td>
        <td><input type="text" size="5" name="essay" /></td></tr>
   <tr> <td>Please enter the project score:</td>
```

```
        <td><input type="text" size="5" name="project" /></td></tr>
   <tr> <td><input type="submit" value="Submit the Scores" /></td>
        <td><input type="reset" value="Clear" /></td></tr>
   </table>
   </form>
</body>
</html>
```

Code Example: arrays1.html

Our PHP program (**arrays1.php**) will receive the five values from the form, assign each of these value to an element of the **$scores** array, and then process the array as indicated by the application requirements. Here is the code for **arrays1.php**:

```
<html>
<head>
  <title> Scores Report</title>
  <link rel="stylesheet" type="text/css" href="sample.css" />
</head>
<body>
  <h1>Scores report </h1>

  <?php
    $scores[0] = $_POST['exam1'];
    $scores[1] = $_POST['exam2'];
    $scores[2] = $_POST['exam3'];
    $scores[3] = $_POST['essay'];
    $scores[4] = $_POST['project'];

    $averageExamScore = ($scores[0]+$scores[1]+$scores[2]) / 3;

    If ($averageExamScore >= 90)
    {
      if ($scores[4] > 95)
        $scores[4] = 100;
      else
        $scores[4] = $scores[4] + 5 ;
    }

    $totalScore = $scores[0] + $scores[1] + $scores[2] +
            $scores[3] + $scores[4];

    print ("Exam 1: $scores[0]<br />");
    print ("Exam 2: $scores[1]<br />");
    print ("Exam 3: $scores[2]<br />");
    print ("Essay : $scores[3]<br />");
    print ("Project: $scores[4]<br />");
```

```
        print ("<p>Your total score is: <strong>$totalScore </strong>
            out of a possible 500 points.</p>");

        print ("<p>Your average for the three exams is: <strong>
            $averageExamScore</strong>. If this average is 90 or
            above, 5 points has been added to your project score
            (up to a maximum project score of 100 points).</p>");
    ?>
</body>
</html>
```

Code Example: arrays1.php

When receiving values from a form, most of our examples so far have used PHP variables with the same name as the **name** attribute in the form. This is not required and here we simple assign the five values received from the form to indexed elements of the **$scores** array:

```
$scores[0] = $_POST['exam1'];
$scores[1] = $_POST['exam2'];
$scores[2] = $_POST['exam3'];
$scores[3] = $_POST['essay'];
$scores[4] = $_POST['project'];
```

These statements could have been written as follows:

```
$scores[] = $_POST['exam1'];
$scores[] = $_POST['exam2'];
$scores[] = $_POST['exam3'];
$scores[] = $_POST['essay'];
$scores[] = $_POST['project'];
```

since PHP will automatically create another array element each time a value is assigned to **$scores**[].

The **$scores** array could also have been created using the **array()** function:

```
$scores = array ($_POST['exam1'], $_POST['exam2'],
    $_POST['exam3'], $_POST['essay'], $_POST['project']);
```

In this case, we are using the **array()** function to create the array and assign all five values as a list enclosed in parentheses. However, as you can see, this makes the code harder to read.

The remainder of the code in **arrays1.php** contains nothing new except that array elements are being used to store the scores instead of standard variables. Trace through the nested selection structures to see that this code correctly adds a bonus to the project score if the average exam score is 90 or above, but does not allow the project score to exceed 100. Figure 11-1 shows a sample interaction.

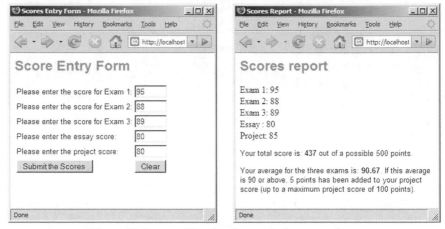

Figure 11-1: arrays1.html and arrays1.php screenshots

Arrays of Strings

Arrays can be used to store any type of data, and it is often useful to create arrays that contain character strings. For example, applications must often include statements to display various error messages. Instead of including these messages directly in your **print**() statements, it can be useful to store all the error messages in an array and then refer to them as needed. Here is how we might construct an array of standard error messages:

```
$errorMessage[0] = "ERROR: You submitted a form with empty
   fields";
$errorMessage[1] = "ERROR: You submitted non-numeric data";
$errorMessage[2] = "ERROR: The value is out of range";
$errorMessage[3] = "ERROR: Incorrect User ID";
$errorMessage[4] = "ERROR: Incorrect Password";
```

Now your program can print any error message by referencing the appropriate array element. Here are three examples:

```
if (empty ($hoursWorked) OR empty ($hourlyWage))
   print ("<p>$errorMessage[0] </p>");

if ($score[0] < 0 OR $score[0] > 100)
   print ("<p>$errorMessage[2] </p>");
if ($password != $correctPassword)
   print ("<p>$errorMessage[4] </p>");
```

This may not seem very useful, after all why not simply include the appropriate error message directly in your **print**() statements? However there are a number of advantages to this approach. First it simply helps us organize our messages and makes them easy find if we wish to change them. Second, if we need to use the same message in more than one location in our application we can avoid duplicating the message. And third, we can share this entire array of standard error messages among multiple Web applications! That means that we can use the same array in different applications without having to duplicate all that code. This approach also promotes a common look and feel between our programs which is especially important when we are developing a number of applications for the same company or Web site. In the next chapter we will learn how to store useful code such as arrays in separate files and then include this code in multiple applications without the need to copy the code.

How Large Is the Array?

As we will see, it is often useful to determine the number of elements that an array contains (often termed the **length** of an array). You can always obtain the length of an array using the **sizeof**() function, for example **sizeof**(**$scores**) would return 5 if there are 5 elements in the **$scores** array. Note that the **sizeof**() function returns the **total** number of elements in the array and not the **index position** of the last element (in the case of 5 elements the last index position would be 4 since the first element is in index position 0).

The sizeof() function is especially useful when using a FOR loop to process an array This topic will be covered later in the chapter.

Why Do Array Indices Begin with 0 and Not 1?

You may be wondering why array index positions begin with 0 and not 1. Recall that all variables are names for memory locations. Since an array uses a single name to refer to an area of memory that will be used to store multiple values, it must be able to keep track of the location of each value. The index position indicates the number of elements that each element is **offset** from the **first** memory location of the array. **So $scores[2]** is stored in a location that begins 2 elements from the array's starting memory location. The reason that the first index position is 0 is that the first element in the array is stored in a location that is 0 elements from the array's starting memory location (in other words, at the start of the memory location of the array).

Using FOR Loops with Arrays

Often we need to write instructions that process all of the values stored in an array. For example here is the **print**() statement that we used earlier to display the five values in the **$scores** array as a table:

```
print("<h1>SCORES</h1>
<table>
<tr><td>SCORE 1</td><td>$scores[0]</td></tr>
<tr><td>SCORE 2</td><td>$scores[1]</td></tr>
<tr><td>SCORE 3</td><td>$scores[2]</td></tr>
<tr><td>SCORE 4</td><td>$scores[3]</td></tr>
<tr><td>SCORE 5</td><td>$scores[4]</td></tr>
</table>");
```

The following statement finds the sum of the five values in the **$scores** array:

```
$totalScore = $scores[0] + $scores[1] + $scores[2] +
              $scores[3] + $scores[4];
```

It is tedious to write out statements that must reference every element in an array! Consider what these two examples would look like if the array contained 100 elements or 1,000 elements! In fact statements like this are often unfeasible since it is not always known in advance how many elements might be stored in an array.

FOR loops provide us with a very efficient way to process all the elements of an array for any purpose. Remember that we use a counting variable to control the number of times that a FOR loop repeats. What if we create a FOR loop with a counting variable that increments from 0 to the last index position in an array? Now we can use the counting variable inside the loop to refer to a different array index position each time that the loop repeats.

Here is a simple FOR loop that uses the loop counting variable to display the values in the **$scores** array:

```
print("<h1>SCORES</h1>");
for ($i = 0; $i < 5; $i = $i + 1)
{
    print("<p>$scores[$i]</p>");
}
```

The FOR loop is designed with a counting variable named **$i**, and the loop will repeat five times. The variable **$i** is also used **inside** the loop as the array **index**. The first time the loop executes, **$i** will have the value 0, and so **$scores[0]** will be printed. The second time the loop executes, **$i** will have the value 1, and so **$scores[1]** will be printed, and so on. It is important that the initial value of **$i** is 0, and that the loop condition is **$i** < 5 and not **$i** <= 5 since the array indices are 0, 1, 2, 3, 4.

The decision to name the counting variable $i may surprise you since we have talked about the importance of meaningful variables names. It is traditional (but not required) to use the names $i, $j, and $k to represent array indexing variables in loop structures.

If the **$scores** array contained 100 elements, we would simply change **$i < 5** in the loop heading to **$i < 100**.

Using the sizeof() Function to Control a FOR Loop

This loop becomes even more useful if we use the **sizeof()** function to control the number of times that the loop repeats:

```
print("<h1>SCORES</h1>");
for ($i = 0; $i < sizeof($scores); $i = $i + 1)
{
    print("<p>$scores[$i]</p>");
}
```

Now instead of **$i < 5**, we use **$i < sizeof($scores)** to control the number of repetitions. This ensures that the loop will process the entire array no matter how many elements are in the array! If we change the number of scores that are stored in the array we no longer have to change the loop since the **sizeof()** function will always provide the correct length. Do you see how efficient this is? Not only does this loop process a **$scores** array containing 5 scores, but the same loop would work with no change if the **$scores** array contained 100 scores, or 1,000 scores!

Again, note that the loop test must be **$i < sizeof($scores)** and not **$i <= sizeof($scores)**. That's because the last index position is one **less** than the size of the array (remember that the array index positions begin with 0).

Summing and Averaging the Values in an Array

Let's see how we can use a FOR loop to find the **sum** and **average** of the values stored in our **$scores** array:

```
$sum = 0;
  for ($i = 0; $i < sizeof($scores); $i = $i + 1)
  {
    $sum = $sum + $scores[$i];
  }
$average = $sum / sizeof($scores);
```

Before we begin the FOR loop we create a **$sum** variable and initialize this to 0. Once again the loop is controlled by a counting variable (**$i**) which will be used inside the loop to refer to each index position in the array. Each time the loop repeats, the value of the next array element is added to the value stored in the **$sum** variable. The result is assigned to **$sum**, replacing the previous value. By the time the loop has completed, the **$sum** variable contains the sum of all the values in the array.

Once the loop has completed, we also use the **sizeof**() function to calculate the average by dividing the value stored in the **$sum** variable by the length of array. Since we use the **sizeof**() function to control the loop **and** to calculate the average, this code will work no matter how many values are stored in the **$scores** array.

NOTE: as always, when you are working with loops like this, think carefully about the statements that should appear **before** the loop, the statements that are **part of** the loop, and the statements that should **follow** the loop. For example you would not want to include the statement **$sum = 0;** inside the loop structure since that would reset the **$sum** variable to 0 each time the loop repeated!

Counting Selected Values in an Array

Our array-handling loops can include any statements necessary to perform the required processing. Here is a FOR loop that includes an IF structure to count the number of **passing** scores in our **$scores** array (assuming that a passing score is 60 or above):

```
$numPassingScores = 0;

for ($i = 0; $i < sizeof($scores); $i = $i + 1)
{
   if ($scores[$i] >= 60)
      $numPassingScores = $numPassingScores + 1;
}
```

In this example, each time through the loop, the program tests whether the score at the current index position is at least 60. If it is, then 1 is added the count of passing scores.

Multiple Operations on an Array

Let's put together the previous examples, and write a program that: creates an array of 10 scores; displays the scores in a table; calculates the sum and average; counts the number of passing and failing scores; and displays the results. The program uses a single FOR loop to perform all of the necessary operations on the array. Here is the code for **arrays2.php:**

```
<html>
<head>
   <title>SCORES REPORT</title>
   <link rel="stylesheet" type="text/css" href="sample.css" />
</head>
<body>
   <?php
      $scores = array(80, 55, 75, 97, 88, 82, 59, 60, 96, 78);
      $sum = 0;
      $numPassingScores = 0;

      print("<h1>SCORES REPORT</h1>");
      print("<table border=\"1\">");

      for($i = 0; $i < sizeof($scores); $i = $i + 1)
      {
         $scoreNum = $i + 1;
         print("<tr><td>SCORE $scoreNum</td>
                  <td>$scores[$i]</td></tr>");

         $sum = $sum + $scores[$i];

         if ($scores[$i] >= 60)
            $numPassingScores = $numPassingScores + 1;
      }
      print("</table>");

      $numFailingScores = sizeof($scores) - $numPassingScores;
      $average = $sum / sizeof($scores);

      print("<p>AVERAGE SCORE: $average <br />");
      print("NUMBER OF PASSING SCORES: $numPassingScores <br />");
      print("NUMBER OF FAILING SCORES: $numFailingScores </p>");
   ?>
</body>
</html>
```

Code Example: arrays2.php

In this example, the **array**() function is used to assign 10 scores to the **$scores** array.

The FOR loop counting variable is used to reference a new array element each time the loop repeats. The loop includes statements to: display the value of the current element in a table row; add this score to the sum of the scores; add 1 to the number of passing scores if the score is 60 or above.

Following the FOR loop, the number of failing scores is calculated by subtracting the number of passing scores from the total number of scores in the array. The average of the ten scores is also calculated. The **sizeof**() function is used in both calculations in order to determine the total number of scores in the array. If you look through this code carefully you will see that you can change the number of scores initially assigned to the scores array with no other changes to the code required. This code will work correctly with any number of scores.

Figure 11-2 shows the output from **arrays2.php**. Note that the scores are numbered from 1 to 10, even though the array is indexed from 0 to 9. In order to accomplish this, the code includes a variable named **$scoreNum** which is assigned a value 1 greater than the current index position each time that the loop repeats.

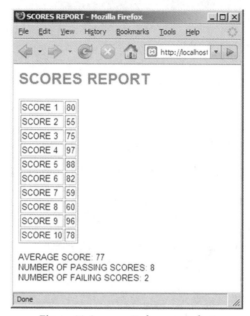

Figure 11-2: arrays2.php screenshot

Reading Data from a File into an Array

We can also read data from a file (or database) into an array. We can open the file, use a loop to read each line from the file into an array and then close the file. After closing the file, we can process the data stored in the array instead of processing this data while the file remains open.

This is actually quite an important design decision: whether to (a) **process** the lines of a file in the same loop that reads these lines **from** the file, or (b) first read **all** the lines from the file into an array, close the file, and then process the array.

The advantage of processing the lines in the file directly is that your program does not need to set aside additional memory to copy the entire contents of the file into an array. Instead each line is read and processed without being stored for further reference. This is often a good approach when processing very large files where memory usage is a significant issue.

However the disadvantage of this approach is that the file must be left open for a longer period while all the lines are processed. The advantage of first reading the contents of the file into an array and then processing the array is that the file can be opened and closed much more quickly, making it available for other applications that may need to access the file.

Another advantage of first reading the data into an array is that this separates the code that **obtains** the data from the code that **processes** the data. As long as the code that reads the file stores the data in an array, the processing code will still work. This is useful, for example, if the data source changes, or if you want to use the same data-processing code for different applications.

Let's look at an example. The following requirements may seem familiar:

Arrays3 requirement:

Write a program that processes a file named rainfall2007.txt. The file contains the year followed by 12 monthly rainfall amounts, each on a separate line. The program should display the year, total rainfall for the year, the average monthly rainfall, highest monthly rainfall amount and lowest monthly rainfall amount.

We worked with the same requirements to develop **rainfall2.php** in Chapter 9. Here we will meet these requirements by first using an array to read the 12 rainfall values from the file, then processing the array to obtain the required results.

```
arrays3.php algorithm:

  Open rainfall2007.txt as rainfallData for reading

  Read year from rainData
  FOR count = 0 TO 11
    read rainfall[count] from rainData
  ENDFOR

  Close rainData

  totalRainfall = 0
  FOR count = 0 TO 11
    totalRainfall = totalRainfall + rainfall[count]
    IF count == 0 OR rainfall[count] > highestRainfall
      highestRainfall = rainfall[count]
    ENDIF
    IF count == 0 OR rainfall[count] < lowestRainfall
      lowestRainfall = rainfall[count]
    ENDIF
  ENDFOR

  avgRainfall = totalRainfall / 12

  Display year, totalRainfall, avgRainfall, highestRainfall,
    lowestRainfall
END
```

We open the data file, read the year, then use a FOR loop to read the 12 rainfall amounts into an array (named **rainfall**), then close the file. With this approach we have opened the file only long enough to obtain the year and rainfall amounts, and then closed it. The rainfall values are now stored in an array and we use a second FOR loop to process these values by accessing each element of the array in turn.

Here is the PHP code for arrays3.php:

```
<html>
<head>
  <title>RAINFALL</title>
  <link rel="stylesheet" type="text/css" href="sample.css" />
</head>
<body>
  <?php
    $rainDataFile = fopen("rainfall2007.txt","r");
    $year = fgets($rainDataFile);

    for ($i = 0; $i < 12; $i = $i + 1)
    {
      $rainfall[$i] = fgets($rainDataFile);
    }
    fclose($rainDataFile);

    $totalRainfall = 0;
    for ($i = 0; $i < sizeof($rainfall); $i = $i + 1)
    {
      $totalRainfall = $totalRainfall + $rainfall[$i];

      if ($i == 0 OR $rainfall[$i] > $highestRainfall)
        $highestRainfall = $rainfall[$i] ;

      if ($i == 0 OR $rainfall[$i] < $lowestRainfall)
        $lowestRainfall = $rainfall[$i];
    }

    $avgRainfall = $totalRainfall / sizeof($rainfall);

    print("<h1>RAINFALL SUMMARY FOR $year</h1>");
    print("<p>TOTAL RAINFALL: $totalRainfall.</p>");
    print("<p>AVERAGE MONTHLY RAINFALL: $avgRainfall.</p>");
    print("<p>HIGHEST MONTHLY RAINFALL:
          $highestRainfall.</p>");
    print("<p>LOWEST MONTHLY RAINFALL: $lowestRainfall.</p>");
  ?>
</body>
</html>
```

Code Example: arrays3.php

As you can see, we now use two FOR loops, one to read the contents of the file into the array, and the second to process the array. Our new version requires the use of additional memory to store the array, however the file is opened and closed much faster.

By using an array, we have also separated two operations: **obtaining** the data and **processing** the data. This turns out to be very useful. If we need to obtain our rainfall data from some other source, we can replace the first loop with new code. As long as the new code stores the rainfall data in the **$rainfall** array, the second FOR loop will process the data correctly with no changes required.

Note that the first FOR loop cannot be controlled by the **sizeof**() function but must be explicitly directed to run **12** times. That's because the array size will not become 12 until **after** this loop has completed since the loop is adding a new element to the array with each repetition.

Reading Data into an Array from a File of Unknown Length

We were able to use a FOR loop in the last example because we were told that the file contained exactly 12 rainfall amounts. Often however we want to read values into an array from a file that of unknown length. In these cases we can use a WHILE loop and test for the end of file marker to decide when to stop reading more lines from the file.

In **arrays2.php** we assigned 10 scores to an array of scores and then processed the scores. Let's modify that program to read scores from a file named **scores1.txt**.

The replacement code will need to open the file, use a WHILE loop to read scores from the file until the EOF marker is found, and close the file, as follows:

```
$scoreFile = fopen("scores1.txt", "r");
$i = 0;
$score = fgets($scoreFile);

while (!feof($scoreFile))
{
   $scores[$i] = $score;
   $score = fgets($scoreFile);
   $i = $i + 1;
}
fclose($scoreFile);
```

Since a WHILE loop does not normally use a counting variable, we have created a variable **$i** to reference the next index position in the **$scores** array as the loop repeats. Before the loop begins, $i is assigned the value 0. The first line of the file is read. If this line does not contain the end of file marker, the line is processed inside the loop. The score is assigned to the next element of **$scores**, the next line is then read from the file, and the value of **$i** is incremented by 1 so that the next value read from the file will be assigned to the next index location in the array.

This sequence repeats until the end of file marker is found. If you trace through this carefully using some sample data you will see that the code correctly reads all scores from the file and assigns each score to the next element in the **$scores** array, using **$i** to indicate the appropriate index value. The code will work no matter how many scores are stored in the file (this example assumes that each score is stored on a separate line).

Take time to understand this code. Pay special attention to the need to initialize **$i** to **0** before the loop begins, and to add 1 to the value of **$i** each time the loop repeats. The complete program is provided in your samples folder as **arrays4.php**. Consider the importance of the **sizeof()** function in this code. We must use this function to determine the length of the array since we do not know the actual number of elements that will be stored in the **$scores** array until the program actually executes.

Note that this code example uses a variable named **$score** and another variable named **$scores**. Be careful not to confuse these two variables, or to use one where the other should be used. The **$score** variable is a simple variable used to store the next score that is read from the file. The **$scores** variable is an array variable, used to store all the scores. To avoid confusion you might prefer to change the name of **$score** to **$nextScore**. You could also eliminate the need for the **$score** variable entirely by reading the values directly from the file into the array, for example:

```
$scoreFile = fopen("scores1.txt", "r");
$i = 0;
$scores[$i] = fgets($scoreFile);
while (!feof($scoreFile))
{
   $scores[$i] = fgets($scoreFile);
   $i = $i + 1;
}
fclose($scoreFile);
```

Using [] with no Index Value

You may recall that PHP has a special feature that allows you to add new elements to an array without specifying the index position. We could take advantage of this feature as follows:

```
$scoreFile = fopen("scores1.txt", "r");
$score = fgets($scoreFile);
while (!feof($scoreFile))
{
   $scores[] = $score;
   $score = fgets($scoreFile);
}
fclose($scoreFile);
```

And here is the same code reading the values from the file directly into the array variable:

```
$scoreFile = fopen("scores1.txt", "r");
$scores[] = fgets($scoreFile);

while (!feof($scoreFile))
{
        $scores[] = fgets($scoreFile);
}
fclose($scoreFile);
```

Although this is a very handy feature in PHP, we have demonstrated how an index variable can be used with a WHILE loop since this can be useful for other purposes (and most programming languages require the use of an indexing variable).

Reading Selected Data from a File into an Array

In our last example, we read all the scores from the scores1.txt file into an array. What if, for our purposes, we only need an array that contains the passing scores (scores of 60 or above)? In that case we can simply test each score that we read from the file and decide whether or not to add it to the array, based on the score value:

```
$scoreFile = fopen("scores1.txt", "r");
$i = 0;
$nextScore = fgets($scoreFile);

while (!feof($scoreFile))
{
   if ($nextScore >= 60)
   {
     $passingScores[$i] = $nextScore;
     $i = $i + 1;
   }
   $nextScore = fgets($scoreFile);
}
fclose($scoreFile);

print("<p>There are ".sizeof($passingScores)." passing scores in
   the file.</p>");
```

Since the array only contains scores that are 60 or above, we can use the sizeof() function to obtain the number of passing scores that were in the file.

It is important to understand which code should be located within the braces of the IF structure, and which should not. The statements:

```
$passingScores[$i] = $nextScore;
$i = $i + 1;
```

are located inside the braces since these two statements should only execute if the next score is to be added to the array. And it is essential that the statement:

```
$nextScore = fgets($scoreFile);
```

is not inside the braces, since we want the program to read the next line from the file whether or not the current score is a passing score.

Reading Data from a File into Multiple Arrays

We might also want to read the scores from the file into two arrays, where one array will store the passing scores and one will store the failing scores. We can do this with some careful modifications:

```
$scoreFile = fopen("scores1.txt", "r");
$i = 0;
$j = 0;
$nextScore = fgets($scoreFile);
while (!feof($scoreFile))
{
  if ($nextScore >= 60)
  {
    $passingScores[$i] = $nextScore;
    $i = $i + 1;
  }
  else
  {
    $failingScores[$j] = $nextScore;
    $j = $j + 1;
  }
  $nextScore = fgets($scoreFile);
}

fclose($scoreFile);

print("<p>There are ".sizeof($passingScores)." passing scores in
    the file.</p>");
print("<p>There are ".sizeof($failingScores)." failing scores in
    the file.</p>");
```

We have added an ELSE section to our IF structure, and we are now using a $failingScores array to store any failing scores. But note also that we now need two indexing variables, one for each array. We use $i to keep track of the index of the $passingScores array, and $j to keep track of the index position of the $failingScores array. And once again, note that the fgets() statement is not included in either the IF or ELSE section, since we want to read the next score not matter whether the current score is a passing or failing score.

Reading Selected Data from a File of Records into an Array

We may sometimes need to read values from a file that contains records on each line. For example, scores5.txt contains the gender of each student as well as the score, in the following format:

m:70
f:85
f:69

In other words, each line contains a gender ("m" or "f") followed by a colon followed by a score.

If we just wanted to read all the scores from this file into an array, we can do this using the explode() and list() functions to extract the two values from each line, and then simply ignoring the gender:

```
$scoreFile = fopen("scores5.txt", "r");
$i = 0;
$nextRecord = fgets($scoreFile);

while (!feof($scoreFile))
{
   list($gender, $score) = explode(":", $nextRecord);
   $scores[$i] = $score;
   $i = $i + 1;
   $nextRecord = fgets($scoreFile);
}

fclose($scoreFile);
```

But what if we need to store the scores of male and female students in two separate arrays? We can test the gender on each line to decide which array the score belongs to:

```php
$scoreFile = fopen("scores5.txt", "r");
$i = 0;
$j = 0;
$nextRecord = fgets($scoreFile);
while (!feof($scoreFile))
{
   list($gender, $score) = explode(":", $nextRecord);
   if ($gender == "f")
   {
      $femaleScores[$i] = $score;
      $i = $i + 1;
   }
   else
   {
      $maleScores[$j] = $score;
      $j = $j + 1;
   }

   $nextRecord = fgets($scoreFile);
}
fclose($scoreFile);

print("<p>There are ".sizeof($femaleScores)." female scores in
   the file.</p>");
print("<p>There are ".sizeof($maleScores)." male scores in the
   file.</p>");
```

This example is provided in the arrays.6.php file in your samples folder. It would of course be easy to add additional code to process these two arrays and generate useful statistics regarding the performance of male and female students.

More About the explode() and list() Functions

Throughout this book we have used the explode() and list() functions to parse records that have been read from a text file. Now that we know something about arrays we can investigate the way these functions actually work, and learn how to use them for other purposes.

Let's assume that a variable named **$appointment** contains the character string **"Dentist:10:15:AM"** that has been previously read from a file. This character string contains four values separated by colons: the type of appointment ("Dentist"), the hour

("10"), the minutes ("15"), and the time of day ("AM"). As we have already seen we can extract these four values into separate variables using the explode()and list() functions as follows:

```
list($appointmentType, $hour, $minutes, $timeOfDay) =
    explode(":", $appointment);
```

After this statement has executed, $appointmentType will contain "Doctor", $hour contains "10", $minutes contains "15", and $timeOfDay contains "AM".

Let's look more closely at what is happening here.. The explode() function receives a separator value (":") and a string to be parsed ("Dentist:10:15:AM"). The function parses the string based on the separator and **returns an array that contains the extracted values**. In this case the function returns an array of four elements where the element [0] contains "Doctor", element [1] contains "10", element [2] contains "15", and element [3] contains "AM".

The list() function is a function that receives any array of values, extracts each value from the array, and assigns these values to the variables that are listed as arguments. So in this example the value stored in position [0] of the array ("Doctor") is assigned to the variable $appointmentType, the value stored in position [1] of the array ("10") is assigned to the variable $hour, the value stored in position [2] of the array ("15") is assigned to the variable $minutes, and the value stored in position [3] of the array ("AM") is assigned to the variable $timeOfDay.

We have been using the explode() and list() functions together, however this is not required. For example we might just want to store the values that have been extracted by the explode() function into an array:

```
$myAppointment = explode(":", $appointment);
```

The $myAppointment variable now contains an array with four values, for example $myAppointment[0] contains "Doctor", and so on. This variable can then be used just like any other array variable.

Similarly the list() function can be used with any array, not just an array that has been created by the explode() function. For example, perhaps your program includes an array named $regionalSales that has been assigned four regional sales figures:

```
$regionalSales = array(3245, 4674, 1674, 5878);
```

If you need to assign these four values into separate variables, you can achieve this using the list() function:

```
list($northRegion, $southRegion, $westRegion, $eastRegion) =
    $regionalSales;
```

In this case, the list() function assigns the elements of the $regionalSales array to each of the four variables, so that $northRegion now contains "3245", $southRegion contains "4674", and so on.

In summary, we can use the explode() function to parse any string that includes multiple values separated by a delimiter of some kind. The function returns an array of indexed elements, where each element contains one of the parsed values. Similarly, the list() function can be used to extract values from any array and store these values in separate variables.

A Special Loop for Processing Arrays — FOREACH

The use of a FOR loop to process every element in an array, one element at a time, is very common. As a result, many current programming languages provide a special simplified loop for exactly this purpose, usually known as a FOREACH loop. The syntax of a FOREACH loop varies between languages. In PHP the syntax is as follows:

```
foreach ($arrayName as $variable)
{
   loop instructions here
}
```

where **$arrayName** is the name of the array that is to be processed by the loop, and **$variable** is the name of a variable that will be used inside the loop and will contain the value of the **first** element in the array on the **first** loop iteration, the value of the **second** element on the **second** iteration, and so on. The loop will repeat for each array element.

To use a FOREACH loop to sum the values in the **$scores** array:

```
$total = 0;
foreach ($scores as $nextScore)
{
   $total = $total + $nextScore;
}
```

In this example the FOREACH loop processes the **$scores** array, one element at a time. Each time the loop repeats, the value of the next element in the array is stored in **$nextScore**, so this variable contains a different value from the array on each repetition.

As you can see, a FOREACH loop is simpler to construct than a FOR loop but can only be used when the entire array is to be processed, and when the loop code does not need to perform any complicated processing of the array elements (such as referring to multiple elements in a single repetition).

Multi-Dimensional Arrays

All of array examples in this chapter are "1-dimensional" in the sense that each array consists of a set of indexed elements that each store a single value. But each array element can be assigned **another array**, so that, instead of an array of single values, we have an **array of arrays**, in other words, a "2-dimensional" array. These arrays can also contain arrays, so that we can create "multi-dimensional" arrays of any number of dimensions. Multi-dimensional arrays are an extremely important data structure that can be used to store information such as topological data, weather data, flight trajectories and paths through 3-dimensional space, mathematical models, game environments, and so on. This topic is beyond the scope of this textbook but for your reference, Appendix G provides some simple examples and demonstrates some common procedures for accessing and processing elements in multi-dimensional arrays.

Summary

An array is a data structure that contains multiple data values. Each value in the array is known as an array **element** and is referenced using a unique **index** location.

A simple array uses integer values to index the array elements, starting with index position 0. The index position refers to the number of elements the current element is offset from the beginning of the array (the initial memory location).

Values can be assigned to individual array elements by referring to the array name and the appropriate index position, for example $someArray[0] − 100;

In PHP, values can be assigned to an entire array in a single statement using the **array()** function, for example $someArray = **array (100, 50, 25, 0);** will store 100, 50, 25 and 0, in array locations $someArray[0], $someArray[1], $someArray[2], and $someArray[3].

Also in PHP the square brackets can be used with **no** index location. In this case an element will be added to the end of the array with an appropriate index, for example if **$someArray** already contains four elements, **$someArray**[] = 75; will store 75 in $someArray[4] (the fifth element).

Each element of array can be used just as any other variable in programming statements.

An array element can be assigned any type of value, for example a character string can be stored in an array element.

In PHP, the number of elements in an array can be ascertained using the **sizeof()** function. Other languages provide a similar function.

Arrays are often processed with FOR loops since a FOR loop can be constructed with a counting variable that increments from 0 (the first array index location) to 1 less than the size of the array (the ending array index location). Each time the loop repeats, the current value of the counting variable can be used inside the loop to reference the next array element.

When using a FOR loop to process an entire array, the **sizeof**() function should be used to control the number of repetitions. That way the loop will work even if the size of the array is changed.

It is often useful to read data from a file into an array before processing the data. The advantage is that the file is open for the minimum time. The disadvantage is that additional memory is required to store the array.

When processing a file of unknown length, a WHILE loop can be used to store the lines from the file in an array. In that case, a counting variable will need to be explicitly created and initialized to 0 **before** the loop, and incremented each time the loop repeats. This variable will be used to add the next line in the file to the next index position in the array.

The **explode**() function returns an array where each element is one of the values that was parsed by the function.

The **list**() function receives an array and assigns the values for the array to each of the variables listed as the function argumnents.

The explode() and list() functions can be used independently as needed by the application requirements.

A FOREACH loop provides an efficient way of processing an entire array where the next element in the array is to be processed each time the loop repeats.

Array elements can store other arrays, allowing a programmer to create multi-dimensional arrays. In addition to general data processing, multi-dimensional arrays are important for modeling and simulation applications.

Chapter 11 Review Questions

1. What type of data structure is used to store multiple values using a single variable name, where each value is referenced by an index value?
    a. A selection structure
    b. A loop structure
    c. An array
    d. A numeric variable
    e. A session

2. What PHP function can be used to determine the number of elements in an array?
    a. The sizeof() function
    b. The numElements() function
    c. The length() function
    d. The array_size() function
    e. There is no such function

3. Which of the following would refer to the value stored in the **fourth** element of an array named $sales?
    a. $sales [0]
    b. $sales [1]
    c. $sales [2]
    d. $sales [3]
    e. $sales [4]

4. What value is stored in $sales[2] after the following statement is processed?

```
$sales = array (200, 300, 400, 500, 600);
```

    a. 200
    b. 300
    c. 400
    d. 500
    e. 600

5. What value is stored in $sales[2] after the following statements are **all** processed in order?

```
$sales [0] = 200;
$sales [1] = $sales [0] + 200;
$sales [2] = $sales [1];
$sales [2] = $sales [2] + $sales [0];
$sales [0] = 400;
```

a. 200
b. 400
c. 600
d. 800
e. 1000

6. What value is stored in $sum after the following statements are processed?

```
$sales = array(100, 200, 300, 400, 500);
$sum = 0;
for ($i = 0; $i < sizeof($sales); $i = $i + 1)
   $sum = $sum + $sales[$i];
```

a. 0
b. 500
c. 1000
d. 1400
e. 1500

7. What value is stored in $sum after the following statements are processed?

```
$sales = array(100, 200, 300, 400, 500);
$sum = 0;
for ($i = 1; $i < 3; $i = $i + 1)
   $sum = $sum + $sales[$i];
```

a. 0
b. 500
c. 1000
d. 1400
e. 1500

8. Which is the equivalent FOREACH loop to the following FOR LOOP?

```
$sum = 0;
for ($i = 0; $i < sizeof($sales); $i = $i + 1)
    $sum = $sum + $sales[$i];
```

  a. foreach ($sales as $nextSale)
       $sum = $sum + $nextSale;
  b. foreach ($sales as $nextSale)
       $sum = $sum + $sales[i];
  c. foreach ($sales[i] as $nextSale)
       $sum = $sum + $nextSale;
  d. foreach ($nextSale as $sales)
       $sum = $sum + $nextSale;
  e. foreach ($nextSale as $sales)
       $sum = $sum + $sales[i];

9. What, if anything, is wrong with this FOR loop?

```
for ($index = 0; $index <= sizeof($sales); $index = $index + 1)
    print("<p>NEXT SALE: $sales[$index]</p>");
```

  a. The loop variable should begin with the value 1 not 0
  b. The loop variable should be named $i not $index
  c. The loop test should be $index < sizeof($sales), not $index <= sizeof($sales)
  d. The array element cannot be displayed inside a character string
  e. There is nothing wrong with this FOR loop

10. What, is the last index position of $sales after these two statements are processed?

```
$sales = array(100, 200, 300, 400, 500);
$sales[] = 600;
```

  a. 4
  b. 5
  c. 6
  d. 7
  e. There is an error—the second statement is missing an index value between the brackets

11. What value is stored in $result after the following statements are processed?

```
$sales = array(100, 200, 300, 400, 500);
$result = $sales[0];

for ($i = 1; $i < sizeof($sales); $i = $i + 1)
{
   if ($sales[$i] > $result)
      $result = $sales[$i];
}
```

  a. The sum of the values stored in the $sales array
  b. The number of values in the $sales array greater than the first value
  c. The lowest number stored in the $sales array
  d. The highest number stored in the $sales array
  e. The last number stored in the $sales array

12. What value is stored in $result after the following statements are processed?

```
$sales = array(100, 200, 300, 400, 500);

for ($i = 0; $i < sizeof($sales); $i = $i + 1)
{
   $result = $sales[$i];
}
```

  a. The sum of the values stored in the $sales array
  b. The number of values in the $sales array greater than the first value
  c. The lowest number stored in the $sales array
  d. The highest number stored in the $sales array
  e. The last number stored in the $sales array

13. What value is stored in $result after the following statements are processed?

```
$sales = array(100, 200, 300, 400, 500);
$result = 0;

for ($i = 0; $i < sizeof($sales); $i = $i + 1)
{
   if ($sales[$i] > $sales[0])
      $result = $result + 1;
}
```

  a. The sum of the values stored in the $sales array
  b. The number of values in the $sales array greater than the first value
  c. The lowest number stored in the $sales array
  d. The highest number stored in the $sales array
  e. The last number stored in the $sales array

14. If an array named $scores is indexed from 0 to 7, what value would sizeof($scores) return?
   a. 0
   b. 7
   c. 8
   d. The sum of the scores in the array

15. Which approach uses less memory when working with large data files?
   a. Process the data while reading it from the file and close the file when done.
   b. Read the data from the file into an array, then close the file and process the data in the array.

16. Which statement is true?
   a. The list() and explode() functions must always be used together.
   b. The list() and explode() functions can be used together or independently.

17. What does the explode() function return?
   a. A list of variables, each containing one of the values extracted from the string that was passed to the function for parsing.
   b. An array containing the values extracted from the string that was passed to the function for parsing.
   c. A count of the values extracted from the string that was passed to the function for parsing.
   d. A string containing the values extracted from the string that was passed to the function for parsing, separated by a colon.

18. What does the list() function do?
   a. Sums the values that are listed as arguments.
   b. Converts the values that are listed as arguments into a single character string.
   c. Takes an array of values and assigns each value to one of the variables in the function's list of arguments.
   d. Takes an array of values and extracts these based on a delimiter.

19. An array containing a set of indexed elements that each store a **single** value is an example of:
   a. A 1-dimensional array
   b. A 2-dimensional array
   c. A multi-dimensional array

20. True or False? An array can contain other arrays as array elements
   a. True
   b. False

Chapter 11 Code Exercises

Your Chapter 11 code exercises can be found in yourB folder. This folder is included in your customized XAMPP installation at the following location:

> xampplite\htdocs\WebTech\coursework\Chapter11

Type your name and the date in the **Author** and **Date** sections of each file as you work on each exercise.

Debugging Exercises

Your **Chapter11** folder should contain a number of "FixIt" files. Each of these files contains PHP code that has an error of some kind. You will need to run each program in order to see the errors, and to debug and test the code to see if it works correctly. For example to run **fixIt1.php**, first run the Web server, then use the URL:

> http://localhost/WebTech/coursework/Chapter11/fixIt1.php

Code Modification Exercises

Your **Chapter11** folder contains a number of "Modify" files. Each pair of files contains HTML and PHP code that needs to be modified to meet a requirement. The requirements are included in each file. Modify the algorithms as specified, being careful to make changes to the .html and .php files as directed.

Code Exercises

1. Read this exercise carefully and take your time to work out the logic. Your **Chapter11** folder contains versions of **weeklyReport.html**, **weeklyReport.php**. The code in **weeklyReport1.html** does not need to be changed—it just provides a form with a Submit button to run **weeklyReport.php**. Open **weeklyReport.php** and create an array named **$weeklyContracts** that contains seven elements. Each element contains the daily income from completed paint jobs, as follows: 236.00, 284.00, 148.00, 128.00, 0.00, 110.00, 0.00. Use a FOR loop to process the array and calculate the total income, the average income, and the number of days with 0 income. The output code is already provided—note the variable names. If your loop statements are correct the total will be $906.00, the average will be $129.43, and the number of "0 income" days will be 2.

2. Read this exercise carefully and take your time to work out the logic. Your Chapter11 folder contains versions of **inventory.html** and **inventory.php**. This application allows the user to select a paint color from a drop down list. The inventory.php

program already includes an array named **$paintInventory** where each array element contains the number of cans of paint that are available for each color. The values are stored in the following order: **white**, cream, beige, yellow, green, red, maroon, blue, teal, gray, so for example **$paintInventory[0]** contains the number of cans of white paint, and **$paintInventory[5]** contains the number of cans of red paint.

The inventory.html file provides an HTML form that asks the user to select a color. Your job is to add code to inventory.php to test the color submitted by the user and display the number of cans available for that color. You will need a selection structure to determine which array element to display. For example, if the user selects "white", the program should indicate that 65 cans are available since that is the value stored in $paintInventory[0].

3. Read this exercise carefully and take your time to work out the logic. Your Chapter11 folder contains versions of **orders.html** and **orders.php**. This application allows the user to obtain a report concerning orders for blueberry bushes. Create an $orders array with the following 10 values: 2, 17, 4, 6, 1, 3, 1, 15, 1, 6. You can use any approach to create the array.

Now write the code to display the orders in a table with two columns. The heading for the first column is Order #, and the heading for the second column is Quantity. These are provided. Use a FOR loop to display rows containing the orders stored in the array. For each row, the order number will be 1 added to the index of the current array element (so the orders will be numbered 1, 2, 3, etc), and the quantity will be the value stored in the current element. Use the **sizeof()** function to control the loop.

Now add a second FOR loop to obtain the sum of all the bushes in these orders, and also count the number of orders that are for more than one bush. Use the sizeof() function to control the loop. If your code is correct, the sum should be **56** and the count should be **7**. The code is provided to display the sum and the count.

4. Read this exercise carefully and take your time to work out the logic. Your Chapter11 folder contains versions of **parking.html** and **parking.php**. This application allows a parking attendant to select a parking space number from a drop down list (there are 20 parking spaces numbered from 0 to 19). The parking.php program already includes an array named **$parkingPermits** where each array element contains the license number of the car that has a permit for the parking space with the same value as the array index. So for example the license that has been registered for parking space 0 is **"LYD EW25"** and this is stored in **$parkingPermits[0]**.

Add a single print statement to display the correct license plate number from the $parkingPermits array based on the user's form submission. The paragraph should display the permit number as well as the license number, for example:

"The license plate number for parking space 0 is LYD EW25."

5. Read this exercise carefully and take your time to work out the logic. Your Chapter11 folder contains versions of **citySurvey.html** and **citySurvey.php**. Your city-Survey.php application includes an array named **$citySurvey** that contains the results of a survey where 20 people indicated which city they would most like to visit ("London", "Paris", or "Rome"). Add a FOR loop to process this array and count the number of people who chose each of these cities. When your program has completed the loop, display the results in a table that prints the city names in the first column and the count for each city in the second column.

6. For this exercises you will create a Seating Maintenance Report for a small concert hall. Your Chapter11 folder contains **seating.html** and **seating.php**. The code in seating.html does not need to be changed. You will see that your seating.php file already includes an array named **$seating** that stores the condition of each of the 100 seats in the concert hall. The seats are numbered 1 to 100, so $seating[0] contains the condition of seat 1, and $seating[99] will contain the condition of seat 100. Each array element contains either the value "OK" or "REPAIR" (note that these are upper-case).

    Provide a FOR loop to process the array and print the numbers of every seat that need to be repaired. You will need an IF structure in the loop that uses the loop index variable to test the next element in the array each time the loop repeats. Remember that the array index begins with 0 and not 1 when you print the seat numbers. The loop should ALSO count the seats that need to be repaired and report the total count of seats in need of repair at the end of the list.

7. Read this exercise carefully and take your time to work out the logic. Your Chapter11 folder contains the files **sales.html** and **sales.php**, and also a data file named **salesData.txt**. The salesData.txt file contains the value of each sale made by two sales people named **Smith** and **Jones**. Each line in the file contains a sale person's name followed by a colon, followed by the value of a single sale. For example the first line contains **Smith:345.50** which means that Smith made a sale worth 345.50.

    Add code to sales.php to: open the file; read each line and extract the name of the sales person and value of the sale; and add the value as a new element in either the **$smithSales** or **$jonesSales** array. Remember to close the file when you are done. When the loop has completed the $smithSales array should contain the values of all of Smith's sales, and the $jonesSales array should contain the values of all of Jones's sales.

    Now use a FOR loop to calculate the total value of all the sales in the $smithSales array, and another FOR loop to calculate the total value of all the sales in the $jonesSales array. Calculate the average value for each salesperson using the totals that you just calculated, and the **sizeof()** function to obtain the size of each array.

Display the total sales value for each sales person, the number of sales by each sales person, and the average sale of each sales person, as follows:

```
Smith achieved 6 sales with a total value of $2,469.15, and
an average sale value of $411.53.
Jones achieved 4 sales with a total value of $2,411.15, and
an average sale value of $602.79.
```

Chapter 12

Associative Arrays

Intended Learning Outcomes

After completing this chapter, you should be able to:

- Summarize key characteristics of associative arrays.
- Create an associative array.
- Identify useful applications for associative arrays.
- Use a literal key value to access a value in an associative array.
- Use a variable that contains a key value to access a value in an associative array.
- Describe the structure of the PHP $_POST array.
- Summarize the basic characteristics of a Web session
- Create and destroy a Web session.
- Use the $_SESSION array to share variables between pages in a Web session

Introduction

Chapter 11 demonstrated the structure and use of arrays that are indexed with numerical values. Many languages, including PHP, also permit the use of **associative arrays**. An associative array is indexed with **character strings** that are used to describe the content of each element much better than a number. For example here is an associative array that contains scores for three exams, an essay and a project:

```
$scores['Exam 1'] = 90;
$scores['Exam 2'] = 93;
$scores['Exam 3'] = 87;
$scores['Essay'] = 78;
$scores['Project'] = 80;
```

Notice that the elements are now indexed with the character strings "Exam 1", "Exam 2", "Exam 3", "Essay", and "Project", instead of 0, 1, 2, 3, and 4. The character strings used to name each array index are known as **keys**, so for example 'Exam 1' is the key for the first element in the $scores array. Any array element can now be accessed by referring to the key used as an index, for example $scores['Essay'] uses the key 'Essay' to indicate the location of the value of the essay score. This score is stored as the fourth array element but $scores['Essay'] is obviously more meaningful than $scores[3].

Associative arrays are very useful where an array contains a relatively small number of values, and where meaningful key names can be provided for each array element.

In this chapter we will learn how and when to use associative arrays. We will also learn that the $_POST array is an example of a standard associative array, and we will learn how to start and stop and make use of Web sessions using another standard associative array, the $_SESSION array.

Using a Variable to Reference the Key of an Associative Array

Here is an associative array that contains user ID's as the keys, and user passwords as the values:

```
$userList['mike75'] = "abc123";
$userList['mary2'] = "xyz999";
$userList['chris17'] = "abc999";
$userList['chris84'] = "xyz123";
```

In this example, 'mike75' and 'mary2' are different user ID's and "abc123" and "xyz999" are their respective passwords. We can obtain the password for the person with user ID "chris17" by using this ID as the index to look up the password for this user. For example we might use this in a print statement:

```
print("<p>Your user ID is chris17 and your password is
    $userList['chris17']</p>");
```

But note that we don't have to use the **literal** key as the index value. Instead we can use a **variable** that **contains** the literal key. So for example if the variable $id already stores the value "chris17" we can obtain the password for that ID using $userList[$id].

This is very useful since it allows us to write code that looks up an item in an associative array dynamically, for example, based on user input. What if our program is designed to process a form that asks the user for an ID and password and then to check the submitted ID and password against an array of ID's and passwords to see if the password is correct? Our program would first obtain the ID and password from the $_POST array, for example:

```
$id = $_POST['id'];
$password = $_POST['password'];
```

Assuming our program has already defined the $userList array (see above), the password that the user submitted can now be tested against the ID as follows:

```
if ($userList[$id] == $password)
   print("<p>WELCOME $id! You are now logged in!</p>");
else
   print("<p>LOGIN FAILED</p>");
```

Do you see how this works? The program is using the **$id** variable that contains the ID entered by the user as the key to look up a password in the **$userList** array. If the password stored in the array at the location indicated by **$id** contains the same password that the user entered then the login is valid. For example if **$id** contains "mary2" and **$password** contains "xyz999" then the test would be:

```
if ($userList['mary2'] == "xyz999")
```

which would generate a **true** result since the value "xyz999" is stored in that location.

However if **$id** contains "mary2" and **$password** contains "xyz123" then the test would be:

```
if ($userList['mary2'] == "xyz123")
```

which would generate a **false** result.

Using Associative Arrays as Lookups

In the previous example the $userList array contained a list of user passwords that are referenced by the user ID. Associative arrays are extremely useful to store all kinds of useful lookups for any number of purposes. For example we could use an associative array to store useful information about our company:

```
$companyInfo['name'] = "Most Excellent Web Design, Inc.";
$companyInfo['street'] = "123 Main Street";
$companyInfo['city'] = "Sometown";
$companyInfo['state'] = "SomeState";
$companyInfo['zip'] = "12345";
$companyInfo['email'] = "excellent@mewd.com";
$companyInfo['phone'] = "(123) 456-7890";
$companyInfo['fax'] = "(098) 765-4321";
```

This array can now be used by any application that needs to refer to information about this company. For example, a program could display the company's e-mail address using $**CompanyInfo** ['email'].

Here is an associative array that lists capital cities, indexed by country names:

```
$capitals['FRANCE'] = "PARIS";
$capitals['ENGLAND'] = "LONDON";
$capitals['AFGHANISTAN'] = "KABUL";
$capitals['ANGOLA'] = "LUANDA";
$capitals['OLIVIA'] = "SUCRE";
```

A program could find the capital of, for example, Angola, by referring to $**capitals**['ANGOLA'].

Even better, we can look up a capital using a variable that stores the key. For Consider a program that allows the user to choose a country from a drop down list in an HTML form, using the name 'country'. The receiving program can receive the selected country and store this in a variable, for example:

```
$country = $_POST['country'];
```

The program can now use this variable as the key for the $capitals array to display the capital for whichever country the user requested:

```
print("<p>The capital of $country is $capitals[$country]</p>");
```

Consider how efficient it can be to develop associative arrays that contain useful lookups that can then be shared by different applications and programmers. Consider for example an array of state names using the state abbreviations as keys, or an array that stores explanations of different payroll codes using the payroll codes as the keys. Or an array that stores course descriptions that are indexed by the course ID's, or that stores scene descriptions for a game with the scene titles as the keys? And what if another programmer provide you with a useful associative array of this kind that saves you many hours of work? In the next chapter we will learn how to store associative arrays in separate files so that we can use them as lookups in multiple applications.

Using the array() Function to Create Associative Arrays

The PHP **array**() function can also be used to create associative arrays using the => operator to associate keys and values. For example here's how we would use the **array**() function to create our $**capitals** array:

```
$capitals = array ('FRANCE' => "PARIS", 'ENGLAND' => "LONDON",
  'AFGHANISTAN' => "KABUL", 'ANGOLA' => "LUANDA",
  'BOLIVIA' => "SUCRE");
```

This is equivalent to the method that we discussed earlier:

```
$capitals['FRANCE'] = "PARIS";
$capitals['ENGLAND'] = "LONDON";
$capitals['AFGHANISTAN'] = "KABUL";
$capitals['ANGOLA'] = "LUANDA";
$capitals['BOLIVIA'] = "SUCRE";
```

Associative Arrays and the FOREACH Loop

Sometimes we need to process every element in an associative array, for example we might need to need to sum all the elements of our $scores array to get the total score. But how can we use a FOR loop to count through the array index if the array is indexed with character strings instead of numbers? A FOR loop won't work with our $scores array now that it is not indexed numerically:

```
$scores['Exam 1'] = 90;
$scores['Exam 2'] = 93;
$scores['Exam 3'] = 87;
$scores['Essay'] = 78;
$scores['Project'] = 80;
```

Earlier we learned how to use a FOREACH loop to process a numerically indexed array, but a **FOREACH** loop is especially useful for processing an associative array. The heading of the FOREACH variable defines a variable that store the value of a single element of the array, and each time the loop repeats, the next value of the array is automatically assigned to this variable. We can include statements in the loop to work with this variable knowing that it will contain the value of consecutive array elements each time the loop repeats.

The same FOREACH loop that we reviewed earlier will work just as well with an associative array:

```
$total = 0;
foreach ($scores as $nextScore)
{
  $total = $total + $nextScore;
}
```

Just as before, the FOREACH loop processes the **$scores** array, one element at a time. Each time the loop repeats, the value of the next element in the array is stored in **$nextScore**, so this variable contains a different value from the array on each repetition.

Let's explore how we can use a FOREACH loop with our array of capital cities. We can use the same syntax to print a list of all the capital stored in the $capitals array:

```
foreach ($capitals as $nextCapital)
{
   print("The capital is $nextCapital");
}
```

But you may be thinking, that's great but what if I wanted to print the **name** of the country as well as the capital? In other words what if we want to use the key of each element as well as (or even instead of) the value of each element? This is a common requirement and the FOREACH loop allows us to access the key as well as the value using a special syntax:

```
foreach ($capitals as $nextCountry => $nextCapital)
{
   print("The capital of $nextCountry is $nextCapital");
}
```

The use of **$nextCountry => $nextCapital** in the FOREACH loop heading means that, each time the loop repeats, the **key** of the next element in the **$capital** array will be stored in the variable **$nextCountry**, and the **value** of the same element will be stored in **$nextCapital**. This is a terrific tool and you will find it useful in many applications. Note that, when using a FOREACH loop, the first variable in the heading must be the name of the array you wish to process. You can use any variable names for the key and value variables. The operator => is required between the two variables if you include a variable for the key.

More about the $_POST Array

You have learned how to create your own associative arrays but PHP also defines a number of **standard** associative arrays that you can use in any of your applications. These standard arrays provide very useful services and are readily identified by the $_ that begins the array name (this naming convention helps to ensure that you don't create an array with the same name as a standard array).

In fact you have been using a standard associative array throughout this book: the **$_POST** array. When a user submits a form that uses the **method = "post"** attribute, the PHP processor automatically creates a **$_POST** array for the program that will process the form. The **keys** of the **$_POST** array are the **names** associated with each input field in the form, and the **values** in the $_POST array are the **values** submitted by the user in these fields.

Here again is the code for **wage2.html** (our very first HTML form example):

```html
<html>
<head>
  <title>Wage Report</title>
  <link rel="stylesheet" type="text/css" href="sample.css" />
</head>
<body>
  <h1>Wage Report</h1>
  <form action="wage2.php" method="post">
    <p>Please enter your hourly wage:
    <input type="text" size="20" name="hourlyWage" />
    </p>

    <p>And the hours you have worked:
    <input type="text" size="20" name="hoursWorked" />
    </p>

    <input type="submit" value="Get Your Wage Report Now" />
    <input type="reset" value="Clear and start again" />
  </form>
</body>
</html>
```

Code Example: wage2.html

When this form is submitted, the Web server will run **wage2.php** since this program is indicated in the **action** attribute of the <**form**> tag. The **method** attribute indicates "**post**" so the wage2.php program is provided with a $_POST array that contains the values that the user submitted on the form. The $_POST array is an associative array and each element is indexed using the values specified in the name attributes of each of the input components of the form. In this case, the first input field is named "**hourlyWage**" and the second input field is named "**hoursWorked**" so the $_POST array contains two elements:

$_POST ['**hourlyWage**'] contains the value submitted by the user
in the field named "hourlyWage".
$_POST ['**hoursWorked**'] contains the value submitted by the user
in the field named "hoursWorked".

We have been writing statements in our program examples to retrieve these values from the $_POST array and store them in program variables, for example:

```php
$hourlyWage = $_POST['hourlyWage'];
$hoursWorked = $_POST['hoursWorked'];
```

In this textbook we have always copied the values from the **$_POST** array into separate variables and then used these variables in subsequent instructions. Actually it is perfectly acceptable to use the elements of the **$_POST** array directly without any need for additional variables. Values stored in the **$_POST** array can be used and modified throughout your code just as any other variables. The practice of copying **$_POST** array values into separate variables is quite common since it makes the code more readable. We have taken that approach here to help us to keep the focus on basic concepts.

PHP provides two other associative arrays to receive values from an HTML form. The **$_GET** array is used when the **method** attribute of the <form> tag is assigned the value **"get"** instead of **"post"**. The **"get"** method is less secure since the values are submitted as part of the URL, and therefore visible. The **"get"** method also limits the number of characters that can be submitted, so **"post"** is more commonly used, and this is the method we have used here.

The **$_REQUEST** array can be used to receive values from forms whether the <form> attribute has the value **"get"** or **"post"**. We could use **$_REQUEST** in all our form-processing code instead of **$_POST**. The **$_REQUEST** array is a good choice, for example, when a single program may need to handle from input from multiple sources, and where it may not be known whether the input is submitted using the **"get"** or **"post"** method.

Using the isset() Function to Combine a Web Form with the Form Processing Code in a Single Page

The PHP isset() function receives a variable name and tests whether or not the variable has already been created by the application. This is useful for many purposes, one of which is to test whether or not an element of your $_POST array was actually created before the PHP code was executed. For example if your HTML form contains a text input with the name 'age', you can test whether or not this element was added to your $_POST array as follows:

```
if(isset($_POST['age']))
```

Note that this is not the same as the **empty**() function. The test

```
if (empty($_POST['age']))
```

will tell you whether or not $_POST['age'] **contains** a value, in other words whether or not the user actually entered a value in the input box named 'age', but the test

```
if (isset($_POST['age']))
```

will tell you whether the element $_POST['age'] actually **exists**.

This is a very useful test. If the $_POST array element was created, it indicates that the application is being executed because a form that contains the application's name in the <form> tag was submitted. If this $_POST array element was **not** created, it indicates that the application is being executed as a result of a direct URL, and not because a form has been submitted.

If we can test whether or not a PHP page is executing as a result of a Web form submission, we can develop a single PHP page that contain both the Web form AND the code that processes this form. Here's how it works:

```php
if (isset($_POST['age']))
{
   // statements to process this form
}
else
{
   // print the form
}
```

In other words, if $_POST['age'] is set, that indicates that this page is executing up because a Web form was submitted, so go ahead and process the form. But if $_POST['age'] is **not** set, that indicates that the PHP page was called directly, so in that case display the Web form for the user to submit.

Confused? Let's look at a complete example. Your **samples** folder contains a file named **addTwoNumbers.html** which contains a form that asks the user for two numbers and submits these for processing by a program named **addTwoNumbers.php**. The addTwoNumbers.php application receives the two numbers from the $_POST array, adds the, and displays the results. This is the approach we've been using throughout this textbook.

But the code in these two files can be combined into a single file, using the isset() function to decide when to display the form and when to process the form. Your samples folder also contains a file named **addTwoNumbersImproved.php**. Examine the IF structure used in this code:

```php
<?php
if (isset($_POST['number1']))
{
   $number1 = $_POST['number1'];
   $number2 = $_POST['number2'];
   $result = $number1 + $number2;
   print("<h1>RESULTS</h1>");
   print("<p>$number1 + $number2 = $result.</p>");
   print("<p><a href=\"addTwoNumbers.php\">Return to the
      Input Form</a></p>");
}
```

```
else
{
print ("<h1>ADD TWO NUMBERS</h1>
    <form action=\"addTwoImproved.php\" method=\"post\" >
    <p>1st number: <input type=\"text\" size=\"20\"
    name=\"number1\" /></p>
    <p>2nd number: <input type=\"text\" size=\"20\"
    name=\"number2\" /></p>
    <p><input type=\"submit\" value=\"Tell me the sum\"
    name=\"submit\" /></p>
    </form>
}
?>
```

You can see that the IF structure is used to determine whether to **process** the form or **display** the form, depending on whether or not the application received a $_POST array element named 'number1'. If this was created, that indicates that the application is being executed because a form was submitted so the form data can be processed. If this was not received, then a form has not been submitted, so the application displays the form for the user.

Since the Web form also contains an input element named 'number2', the application would work equally well using the test:

```
if (isset($_POST['number2'))
```

The combination of a Web form with the code to process the form into a single file is a widely used design approach since it allows for more compact and modular application development.

Web Sessions and the $_SESSION Array

We use program variables to store and modify values while a PHP page is being processed but the contents of these variables are lost when the processing is completed. That has not been a problem so far since our applications have all consisted of a single PHP page. But a Web application might include multiple PHP pages that need to share information. Consider an online store, where the customer browses through many pages, adding items to his or her shopping cart. How does the application keep track of the customer's name and the items that the customer has selected so as the customer moves from one page to the next, each new page has access to these data values? What if a game application contains multiple PHP pages, each handling a different game scene? How can a page that handles one game scene pass on the information such as the player's name and current score to the page that handles the next game scene? To put it another way, if your application consists of multiple PHP pages (as most real-world applications do), how can you create variables that are **available** for use **throughout** the application, that can be used by **any** of the pages that comprise the application?

To understand this better, let's consider a simple application that handles prizes for a door raffle. The application contains three files. The first file is named **raffle.html** and presents a form to the user that allows them to enter their first name, their city, and their raffle ticket number. This form runs a PHP program named **raffle.php** which receives the first name, city and raffle ticket number, and checks to see if the raffle number is the winning number (in this case the winning number is 45768). If it **IS** the winning number, the program presents **another** form to the user, allowing them to choose from a list of prizes. This form runs a second PHP program named **choosePrize.php** which receives the user's selection and tells them how to pick up their prize. Figures 12-3 and 12-4 provide screen shots of this application.

That all seems straightforward—we know how to create and process Web forms like this. The problem is that **choosePrize.php** needs to display a message that includes the user's name and city. These two values were received by **raffle.php** from the form provided in **raffle.html** but how does **raffle.php** share these values with

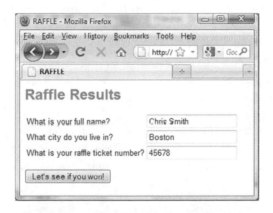

Figure 12-3: raffle.html provides the first form

Figure 12-4: raffle.php (with the second form) and choosePrize.php

choosePrize.php? It's true that **choosePrize.php** also contains a form but this form is used only to submit the user's choice of a prize. It would make no sense to use this form to ask the user for their name and city again! So how can **raffle.php** share the user's name and city with **choosePrize.php**?

There are in fact a number of solutions, but here we will use this problem to explain the use of Web **sessions**. A Web session allows us to track a user's activity from the time the session is initiated to the time the session is ended (closing the Web browser will also end the Web session). Data values that need to be used throughout the session are stored in **session variables**, which are stored independently of each page that participates in the session. These values are stored in a **$_SESSION** array, which is another standard associative array, similar to the $_POST array. All pages that participate in the session can work with the $_SESSION array, checking or changing the values of variables that are already stored in the array, or adding new variables to the array. Session variables are available to any pages that use the session from the time the session variable is added to the $_SESSION array until the session ends. Before we learn how to write code that uses the $_SESSION array, let's get a better understanding of how a session actually works.

When a user opens a Web page that initiates a session, a unique identification (UID) number is created on the Web server for that user (the user never actually sees this UID and you and your application do not need to know what it is either). Note that many users may be accessing the same Web application at the same time (for example on a shopping site or in a Web-based interactive game), and each user is assigned their own unique UID. The Web server associates a $_SESSION array with each UID, and this allows you to use the $_SESSION array to store and modify values that can be shared by any pages that participate in the session. You don't have to worry about the fact that multiple users are using your pages — the data for each user is automatically maintained in a separate $_SESSION array associated with the user's UID. This is important — you would not want your online purchases to be confused with those of **another** user!

Adding Code to Manage a Web Session

In PHP, a session is started using the **session_start**() function, and the session can be ended using the **session_destroy**() function. A session also ends if the user closes his or her browser (note that all windows for the browser must be closed before the session will end).

Every page that is intended to participate in a Web session **must** include a call to the **session_start**() function, and not just the page that you intend to be starting page. This function call **must** appear in a PHP section **before** any HTML tags that appear in the file, for example:

```
<php
  session_start();
?>

<html>
. . . HTML and additional PHP code here..
</html>
```

Each page that includes the call to the **session_start**() function can use the $_SESSION array to store, access or modify values that are to be shared with other pages that are also participating in the session.

Any page that executes the **session_destroy**() function will end the session. Once a session is ended, no pages will have access to the $_SESSION array that was created for the session and values stored in this array will be lost.

Creating, Initializing and Modifying Session Variables

Once you have included a **session_start**() call in a page that will be a part of your session, you can include code on that page to add elements to the $_SESSION array. To add a new element, simply define a new $_SESSION array key, just as with any associative array. You can then assign a value to this new element.

For example in our raffle.php program we will receive the user's first name and city from the form in raffle.html:

```
$firstName = $_POST['firstName'];
$city = $_POST['city'];
```

In order to share these values with other pages (here we want to share them with choosePrize.php), we can create two elements with key names 'firstName' and 'city' in our $_SESSION array and copy the values that were received from the form into these elements:

```
$_SESSION['firstName'] = $firstName;
$_SESSION['city'] = $city;
```

Actually you can copy these values directly from the $_POST array to the $_SESSION array:

```
$_SESSION['firstName'] = $_POST['firstName'];
$_SESSION['city'] = $_POST['city'];
```

Now the user's first name and city are stored in elements of the $_SESSION array and these can be accessed by any PHP program that is participating in the session (remember that these programs must include the call to the session_start() function). For example here's how a participating page might display the user's first name:

```
print ("<p>Hi, ".$_SESSION['firstName']."!</p>");
```

In our examples we are using the same key names for variables in our $_POST array and our $_SESSION array. This is not required—your $_SESSION variables can be given any key names.

Here is the code for the three pages in our raffle application. This code is provided in your **samples/sessions** folder. Note the use of the **session_start**() function in **raffle.php** and **choosePrize.php**, the use of the **$_SESSION** array in these programs, and the use of the **session_destroy**() function in **choosePrize.php**. Note also that the ticket number in raffle.php and the selected prize in choosePrize.php are stored in ordinary variables. That's because these variables are only needed in a single page so there is no need to share them with other pages in the $_SESSION array.

```
<html>
<head>
  <title>RAFFLE</title>
  <link rel="stylesheet" type="text/css" href="sample.css" />
</head>
<body>
  <h1>Raffle Results</h1>

  <form action="raffle.php" method="post">
  <table>
  <tr><td>What is your full name?</td>
  <td><input type="text" size="20" name="fullName" /></td></tr>

  <tr><td>What city do you live in?</td>
  <td><input type="text" size="20" name="city" /></td></tr>

  <tr><td>What is your raffle ticket number?</td>
  <td><input type="text" size="20" name="ticketNum" /></td></tr>

  </table>
  <p><input type="submit" value="Let's see if you won!" /></p>
  </form>
</body>
</html>
```

Code Example: raffle.html

```php
<?php
  session_start();
?>
<html>
<head>
  <title>RAFFLE</title>
  <link rel="stylesheet" type="text/css" href="sample.css" />
</head>
<body>
<?php
  $_SESSION['fullName'] = $_POST['fullName'];
  $_SESSION['city'] = $_POST['city'];

  $ticketNum = $_POST['ticketNum'];

  if ($ticketNum == "45678")
  {
    print("<h1>".$_SESSION['fullName'].", you won !!!</h1>");

    print("<form action=\"choosePrize.php\" method=\"post\">
        <p>Now choose a prize:
        <select name=\"prize\">
        <option>A New TV</option>
        <option>A New Laptop</option>
        <option>A New Refrigerator</option>
        </select></p>
      <p><input type=\"submit\" value=\"Click Here to Learn
        How to Obtain Your Prize\" /></p></form>");
  }
  else
    print("<h1>Sorry ".$_SESSION['fullName'].", you didn't win
      anything - better luck next time..</h1>");
?>
</body>
</html>
```

Code Example: raffle.php

```php
<?php
  session_start();
?>
<html>
<head>
  <title>RAFFLE</title>
  <link rel="stylesheet" type="text/css" href="sample.css" />
</head>
<body>
<?php
  if (isset($_POST['prize']) and isset($_SESSION['fullName']))
  {
    $prize = $_POST['prize'];

    print("<h1>".$_SESSION['fullName'].", you chose
      $prize!</h1>");

    print("<p>Bring your ticket to our <strong>"
      .$_SESSION['city']."</strong> store and we will have your
      prize ready for you!</p>");
  }

  session_destroy();
?>
</body>
</html>
```

Code Example: choosePrize.php

Validating $_SESSION and $_POST Arrays

You have to take some care to manage any page that make use of $_SESSION variables. One question you must ask is: what happens if a user links to a page "out of sequence." For example in our raffle application, what would happen if a user directly typed the URL for choosePrize.php without submitting the forms in raffle.html and raffle.php? In that case the message displayed by choosePrize.php would be missing the user's first name and city since these $_SESSION elements were not created by raffle.php. The page would also be missing the prize selection since this was not submitted by the form in raffle.php to the $_POST array.

In this case, the problem is caused by the user typing the wrong URL. This may be very unlikely since most users will have been directed to use raffle.html and will not know that choosePrize.php exists. But it is often important to handle this situation by including code to test the page and display an error message if the $_SESSION variables or $_POST variables do not contain values.

The PHP **isset**() function receives a variable name and tests whether or not the variable has already been created. This function can be used with any variable including variables that are elements of associative arrays. For example, **isset($_SESSION['fullName']')** will return **true** if **$_SESSION['fullName']** already exists, **false** otherwise.

So we can use an IF..ELSE structure to decide what actions should be performed when a player visits a page that uses a session, for example:

```
if (isset($_SESSION['fullName']) )
{
   // Statements to execute if the element exists
}
else
{
   // Error message or nothing at all if you simply wish to
   // present a blank page
}
```

Now the page will only process normally if $_SESSION ['fullName'] has already received a value from another page.

The isset() function can also be used with the $_POST array, for example:

```
if (isset($_POST['prize']) )
```

This ensures that the user came to this page by submitting a form containing an input field named 'prize'. And of course these tests can be combined to ensure that the user submitted a form to arrive at this page, and also that the required $_SESSION variables have already been created:

```
if (isset($_POST['prize']) and isset($_SESSION['fullName']) )
```

Another useful function when working with $_SESSION and $_POST array variables is the **empty**() function. In this case we can test not whether the element was created, but if it contains a value, for example we could use this in raffle.php to ensure that the user submitted a name:

```
if (empty($_POST['fullName']) )
{
   print("<p>ERROR, a name is required!</p>");
   print("<p><a href=\"raffle.html\">Return to the form</a></p>");
}
else
{
   // process the form
}
```

This section is only intended as an introduction to the general procedure for managing and validating Web sessions. You will want to study further and advance your skills before producing Web sessions that are fully secure and robust. The next section shows to manage a page that a user might visit multiple times during a single session.

Revisiting the Same Page in a Web Session

Well-designed Web applications often require the user to return to the same page multiple times. For example a game player might need to return to the same scene page, and an online shopper might return to the same product page. Your programs must be able to handle this type of activity. For example, perhaps your first game scene sets a variable named $_SESSION['score'] to 0. If the player is allowed to return to this game scene more than once while playing, it's important that his or her score is not reset to 0 each time the player visits the page. We can use our isset() and empty() functions to handle these situations.

Let's consider a simple, one page online quiz that tests a child's addition skills. The page (**mathQuiz.php** in the **samples/sessions** folder) displays either a welcome message (the first time) or the result of the previous addition (if the child has already played), followed by the current score, followed by a form that displays two random numbers between 1 and 20 and asks the player to submit the sum. This form calls the **same page** (mathQuiz.php) to receive the sum submitted by the player, check whether or not the answer is correct, display the result, update the count and score, and display the form again with two new numbers. The player can continue to play for as long as they wish. To quit the player clicks the **"Ready to Quit"** link which links to mathQuit.php. Figures 12-5 and 12-6 provides sample screenshots.

Play the game yourself so that you are familiar with how it behaves. Note that the application is located in the **samples/sessions** folder so the URL is:

```
http://localhost/Webtech/samples/sessions/mathQuiz.php
```

Before looking at the code for this application, it's important to understand why the form on the page must be designed to call the same page. It would be impractical to create multiple pages, one page for each time the player needs a form to submit another addition. Apart from the duplication of code, there is simply no way to predict how many pages the player might need!

But to use a single page requires some careful planning. Even though the player is returning to the same page each time the form is submitted, the page will be executed again for each visit. So the page will need to use $_SESSION variables to keep track of the player's score and the count of the player's attempts. The first time the player comes to the page (the start of the session) these two variables should be set to 0. These variables should not reset to 0 each time the player returns to the page. Instead, each time the player tries another addition, the count should increment by 1, while the score should increment by 1 only if the player submitted the correct answer.

The next consideration is that the page should not try to process the $_POST array the first time the page is displayed since the player has not submitted anything yet so there is nothing to process.

And last, the application requires a link to a second page that will execute if the player chooses to quit. This page will display the score and count and destroy the ses-

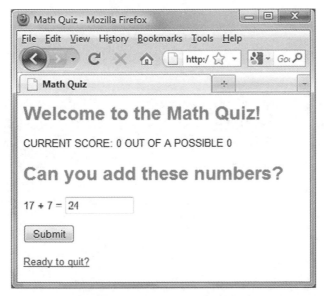

Figure 12-5: mathQuiz screenshot (initial visit to page)

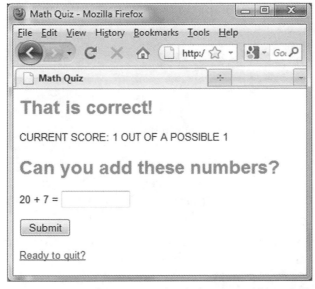

Figure 12-6: mathQuiz screenshot (subsequent visit to page)

sion so that the next time the player returns to the first page (mathQuiz.php), the game
will reset to a score and count of 0 and will display the initial Welcome message again.

Look over the code for **mathQuiz.php** and **mathQuit.php** (this is your
samples/sessions folder). Consider how this code works to allow the player to begin
playing and then playing as many times as he or she chooses to quit. Note that, if the
player quits, the mathQuit.php program destroys the session, so if the players tries
again, the score and count will reset to 0. Why? Because when the session is destroyed,
the $_SESSION['score'] variable will be lost so the test to see if $_SESSION['score'] is
not set will be true.

```php
<?php
   session_start();
?>
<html>
<head>
   <title>Math Quiz</title>
   <link rel="stylesheet" type="text/css" href="sample.css" />
</head>
<body>
<?php
   if (!isset($_SESSION['score']))
   {
      $_SESSION['score'] = 0;
      $_SESSION['count'] = 0;
      print ("<h1>Welcome to the Math Quiz!</h1>");
   }

   if (isset($_POST['userAnswer']))
   {
      $_SESSION['count'] = $_SESSION['count'] + 1;
      $userAnswer = $_POST['userAnswer'];
      $correctAnswer = $_SESSION['num1'] + $_SESSION['num2'];
      if ($correctAnswer == $userAnswer)
      {
         $_SESSION['score'] = $_SESSION['score'] + 1;
         print ("<h1>That is correct!</h1>");
      }
      else
         print ("<h1>Sorry! The correct sum of ".$_SESSION['num1'].
            " and ".$_SESSION['num2']." is $correctAnswer</h1>");
   }

   print("<p>CURRENT SCORE: ".$_SESSION['score']." OUT OF A
      POSSIBLE ".$_SESSION['count']."</p>");
   print("<h1>Can you add these numbers?</h1>");
   print("<form action=\"mathQuiz.php\" method=\"post\">");
```

```
    $_SESSION['num1'] = rand(1, 20);
    $_SESSION['num2'] = rand(1, 20);

    print("<p>".$_SESSION['num1']." + ".$_SESSION['num2']." = ");
    print("<input type=\"text\" size=\"10\" name=\"userAnswer\"
      /></p>");
    print("<p><input type = \"submit\" value = \"Submit\"
      /></p></form>");
    print("<p><a href=\"mathQuit.php\">Ready to quit?</a></p>");
?>
</body>
</html>
```

Code Example: mathQuiz.php

```
<?php
    session_start();
?>
<html>
<head>
    <title>Math Quiz - RESULT</title>
    <link rel="stylesheet" type="text/css" href="sample.css" />
</head>
<body>
<?php
      print("<h1>Thanks for Playing! </h1>");
      print("<h2>YOU SCORED ".$_SESSION['score'].
            " OUT OF ".$_SESSION['count']."</h2>");
      session_destroy();
      print("<p><a href = \"mathQuiz.php\">Try Again?</a></p>");
?>
</body>
</html>
```

Code Example: mathQuit.php

This is an important example for anyone wishing to develop Web applications. The code has been kept simple to focus on the general design—a real world application would include additional validation and features. For example, additional information about the player could be requested, and upon quitting the player's information and score could be maintained in a file or database so that the application could keep track of progress.

The **goldHunter** application in the **samples/sessions** folder provides one more example of a page that calls itself, this time to provide a simple game.

Summary

An **associative** array uses character strings to index each element. Each index of an associative array is known as a **key**. The value of each element in an associative array is referenced using the appropriate key.

A common use of an associative array is to provide **lookups.**

The standard PHP **$_POST** array is an associative array. A $_POST array is automatically created for any PHP program that receives values from an HTML form that specifies the "**post**" method. Each value submitted from the form is assigned to an element of the **$_POST** array. Each element is identified by a key using the same character string that was assigned to the corresponding **name** attribute in the HTML form.

Similarly the standard PHP **$_GET** array is created for a program that receives values from an HTML form that specifies the "**get**" method. The standard PHP **$_REQUEST** array is created for a program that receives values from an HTML form that specifies either the "**get**" or "**post**" method. The **$_REQUEST** array can therefore be used instead of the **$_POST** or **$_GET** arrays.

The **isset**() function can be used to test whether or not a $_POST array element has been created. This allows us to combine the code to display a Web form with the code to process the form in a single file.

A Web session allows multiple pages to share data. The data values are maintained in the standard PHP **$_SESSION** associative array. Each value is created using a descriptive key, and these values can be accessed or modified by any page that participates in the session. To participate in a session, each page must include a PHP section that includes a call to the **sesson_start**() function. This call must appear **before** any HTML code in the file.

A user's session can be explicitly destroyed by calling the **session_destroy**() function. When this function is called the contents of the **$_SESSION** array for that user are lost.

Since a user can enter a session from any page, and can return to any page (including a page that contains code to initialize the session variables), care must be taken to ensure that session data is handled correctly each time a specific page is visited. The **isset**() function is used to test whether or not a variable has already been created and this can be used to determine whether or not **$_SESSSION** or **$_POST** array elements have been created in order to construct various responses for a user. The **empty**() function is also useful to ensure that input was actually received into a **$_SESSSION** or **$_POST** array.

Chapter 12 Review Questions

1. What type of array uses character strings as the index of each array element?
    a. Associative array
    b. Named Array
    c. Character Array
    d. String Array

2. What type of data structure is this?

```
$menu['coffee'] = 1.75;
$menu['tea'] = 1.25;
$menu['cake'] = 2.25;
```

    a. An array indexed by numbers
    b. An associative array
    c. A single variable containing a character string
    d. A single variable containing a number
    e. A data file

3. Which assertion is true concerning the following statement?

```
$menu['tea'] = 1.25;
```

    a. 'tea' is a key and 1.25 is a value
    b. 'tea' is a value and 1.25 is a key
    c. $ menu is a key and 'tea' is a value
    d. $ menu is a key and 9.75 is a value
    e. $ menu is a value and 'tea' is a key

4. What will be displayed?

```
$menu['tea'] = 1.25;
print("<p>Tea is ".$menu['tea']."</p>");
```

    a. Tea is tea
    b. Tea is 1.25
    c. Tea is $menu['tea']
    d. Tea is $menu
    e. Tea is menu

5. A $_POST array receives values from an HTML form. Which statement is correct?
   a. The $_POST array is also called a $_GET array
   b. The values stored in a $_POST array must be assigned to variables with the same name as the keys of the $_POST array.
   c. The $_POST array must be created by the programmer.
   d. The $_POST array is used to maintain session data
   e. The keys of a $_POST array are the same as the names given to the input elements submitted from the form.

6. When should the session _start() function be used?
   a. Only in page that the user opens to start the session
   b. On every page that is part of the session

7. When should you create a session?
   a. Whenever the user will access multiple pages on your Web site
   b. Only if the user must login to your Web site
   c. Whenever data must be shared across multiple pages on your Web site
   d. Whenever data must be shared between multiple users of your Web site
   e. Whenever associative arrays are used on your Web site

8. What is the general purpose of the isset() function?
   a. Tests whether the $_POST array has been created
   b. Tests whether the $_SESSION array has been created
   c. Tests whether a particular value was submitted from a form
   d. Tests whether any variable has been created
   e. Tests whether the session has been started

9. True or False? A single PHP file can contain the code to display a Web form and the code to process the form.
   a. True
   b. False

10. Which of the following is **not** an example of a standard associative array?
    a. $_POST
    b. $_SESSION
    c. $_GET
    d. isset()

Chapter 12 Code Exercises

Your Chapter 12 code exercises can be found in your Chapter 12 folder. This folder is included in your customized XAMPP installation at the following location:

xampplite\htdocs\WebTech\coursework\Chapter12

Type your name and the date in the **Author** and **Date** sections of each file as you work on each exercise.

Debugging Exercises

Your **Chapter12** folder should contain a number of "FixIt" files. Each of these files contains PHP code that has an error of some kind. You will need to run each program in order to see the errors, and to debug and test the code to see if it works correctly. For example to run **fixIt1.php**, first run the Web server, then use the URL:

http://localhost/WebTech/coursework/Chapter12/fixIt1.php

Code Modification Exercises

Your **Chapter12** folder contains a number of "Modify" files. Each pair of files contains HTML and PHP code that needs to be modified to meet a requirement. The requirements are included in each file. Modify the algorithms as specified, being careful to make changes to the .html and .php files as directed.

Code Exercises

1. Your chapter folder contains two files named **myInfo.html** and **myInfo.php**. The myInfo.html file does not need to be changed. Open myInfo.php and add an associative array named **$myInfo**. The array should contain 8 elements that store your first name, last name, street address, city, state, zip (or postal code), email address, and phone number. Use descriptive names for each element, for example $myInfo['first name']. You can add more elements if your address requires them. Now add code that obtains the necessary values from the $myInfo array to display your name and address as it might appear on an envelope, for example:

```
Chris Jones,
100 King Street,
Chicago, Illinois 60604
```

2. Read this exercise carefully and take your time to work out the logic. Your Chapter12 folder contains versions of **inventory.html** and **inventory.php.** This application allows the user to select a paint color from a drop down list. The **inventory.php** program already includes an associative array that indicates the number of cans of paint that are available for each color. Your job is simply to complete a single line of code that will look up the color selected by the user in order to find the number of cans available in that color. The result is stored in a variable which is then displayed (the necessary print statements are provided). For example, if the user selects white, the program will indicate that **65** cans are available, and if the user selects maroon, the program will indicate that **0** cans are available.

3. Your chapter folder contains two files named **employees.html** and **employees.php.** The employees.html file contains an HTML form that asks the user for an employee ID, using a drop down list. The employees.php file receives the ID and also defines two arrays. The $salaries array contains salaries, indexed by employee ID. The **$employees** array contains employee names. also indexed by ID. Add code to display the employee's name and salary by using the ID submitted by the user to look up these values in the two arrays. For example if the employee's ID is 12345 your page should display the following:

```
Employee 12345 is Mary Smith, with a salary of $54,555.00
```

4. Read this exercise carefully and take your time to work out the logic. Your Chapter12 folder contains versions of **travelCosts.html** and **travelCosts.php.** This application allows the user to select a destination in order to find out the air fare and nightly hotel cost. Create **two** associative arrays named **$airFare** and **$hotel.** The **$airFare** array should contain the five destinations as **keys** (Barcelona, Cairo, Rome, Santiago, and Tokyo), and the fares for these destinations as **values** (875.00, 950.00, 875.00, 820.00, 1575.00). The **$hotel** array should contain the same five destinations as **keys,** and the nightly rates for these destinations as **values** (85.00, 98.00, 110.00, 85.00, 240.00).

    Use the variable that contains the destination submitted by the user to look up the appropriate air fare and the hotel rate from these two arrays, so that these will be displayed. The print statements have been provided.

5. Read this exercise carefully and take your time to work out the logic. Your Chapter12 folder contains versions of **scenes.html** and **scenes.php.** This application allows the user to select a direction in order to find out what happens.

    You do not need to change scenes.html. The scenes.php program already includes an associative array that describes different scenes using directions as keys. Your job is simply to add a single print statement to the end of the code in order to display the correct scene from the array, based on the destination selected by the user.

6. Your chapter folder contains two files named **dateConverter.html** and **dateConverter.php**. The dateConverter.html file contains an HTML form that asks the user for a day, month name, and year. The dateConverter.php file receives these three values and also defines an array named **$months** that contains the month numbers using the month names as indices, for example **$months**['**January**'] contains 1, and **$months**['**February**'] contains 2. Add code that uses the month name provided by the user to look up the month number and displays the date as three numbers separated by /'s. For example if the user submitted 2, June and 2013, the program would display:

```
The date is 2/6/2013.
```

---

7. Your Chapter12 folder contains **cityTrips.html** and **cityTrips.php**. The code in cityTrips.html does not need to be changed—it contains a form that allows the user to choose any of five cities from a drop down list in order to obtain the mileage and fuel costs to the city from NYC. Add an associative array to your cityTrips.php file that uses city names as keys to store distances to the following five cities from NYC:

```
Atlanta 880
Boston 225
Chicago 788
Detroit 614
Miami 1275
```

Now add code that: receives the city, fuel cost (per gallon), and car mileage (mpg) submitted by the user; looks up the distance to that city; calculates the fuel cost (distance / mpg * fuel cost per gallon); and then displays the city, distance and fuel cost.

8. Review the chapter material that explains the purpose and construction of applications that use Web sessions. Study the code examples carefully. Now develop a small application of your own that uses a Web session to track one or more data values between multiple Web pages (for example the user's name and a score, or a selection that the user has made on a previous page). Keep it simple and don't use more than three or four pages. As you become more comfortable using Web sessions you will be able to develop more complex applications, such as small Web-based games.

Chapter 13

Program Modularity — Working with Functions and Objects

Intended Learning Outcomes

After completing this chapter, you should be able to:

- Summarize the importance of modular approaches to software design.
- Describe key characteristics of functions.
- Explain the purpose of arguments and parameter lists.
- Write code that calls a function based on the function name and required arguments.
- Write code that receives a value returned by a function call.
- Find and use common pre-defined PHP functions.
- Use the PHP die() or exit() function to end an application's execution.
- Create a new function and use this in a PHP application.
- Create and save a library of useful functions for use with multiple applications.
- Create and use include files to avoid duplication of HTML and PHP code.
- Incorporate include files containing functions into an application.
- Explain the significance of Object-Oriented Programming (OOP)
- Summarize the general structure and purpose of an object.
- Interpret a class definition for a simple object.
- Create and use instances of a simple object using the object's Application Programming Interface (API).
- Explain common OOP terminology.

Introduction

Since the first computers appeared in the 1940s, computer technology has evolved rapidly. The first desktop computer appeared in 1982. The World Wide Web emerged in 1994. Throughout this period we have seen dramatic advances in operating systems, microprocessors, network systems, and also in programming languages. New languages are constantly being developed, not only to take advantage of new hardware and network capabilities, but also to reflect our increasing understanding of effective **software design**.

Perhaps more than anything else, modern software design is concerned with **code modularity**: development of code in separate, functional components in order to maximize **reusability** and minimize **duplication**. With the development of computer networks, the application of code modularity has extended beyond the design of individual applications to facilitate access to common code and inter-communications between applications world-wide (**interoperability**). This in turn has led to greater cooperation between software companies and developers to achieve **common standards**.

The development and delivery of common modules remains a work in progress, and many programmers continue to develop new code that simply duplicates code already written and tested. To take some simple examples, consider how many times code might have been written to perform standard tax computations on employee wages, convert temperatures, sort a list of names alphabetically, or sum a list of numbers.

Good programmers quickly learn to first research the availability of pre-existing code modules that can be used in their applications. When existing code is not available, good software design calls for new code to be developed in many small modules that each perform well-defined tasks. These modules can then be "glued" together as needed into working applications to meet specific requirements.

For example, consider the advantage of developing distinct code modules that carry out tax-related calculations, perform standard temperature conversions, or process various banking transactions? If you think about it, it makes sense to always try to develop code in small reusable modules. You can liken this approach to the way that we design and build houses. The contractor constructs a house to meet the specific requirements of the home-owner but, instead of building the entire structure from scratch, he or she makes use of pre-assembled components (doors, windows, plumbing fixtures, drywall panels, etc.). These components are designed to meet common standards so that they can be used interchangeably. Old components can be easily replaced with new and improved versions.

Just as there are entire companies whose business is to design and develop standard housing components such as windows and plumbing fixtures, so many software companies design and develop standard software components that are then sold to other developers for inclusion in working applications.

Individual code modules are called **functions, methods, sub-programs , sub-routines , or procedures , depending on the programming language.** We will use the term **function** here since this is the term used in PHP. Each function is identified by a **function name** and contains the necessary code to perform a specific, well-defined task. Functions are easy to identify in most languages — the function name is always followed by a pair of parentheses.

You have been using many pre-definied PHP functions already. For example you have used the **pow()**, **pi()**, **round()**, **ceil()**, **floor()**, and **random()** functions to perform various mathematical operations, the **fopen()**, **fclose()**, **feof()**, **fputs()** and **fgets()** functions to process text files, and the **list()**, **explode()**, **trim()**, **strtoupper()**, **strtolower()**, and **number_format()** functions to work with character strings.

In this chapter you will learn more about pre-defined functions, and also how to create and use your own functions, and how to store these in **include** files for use by any number of applications.

You will also be introduced to **Object-Oriented Programming (OOP)**. OOP is a relatively recent and very significant development in the history of software design, that dramatically improves upon earlier approaches to code modularity. An **object** essentially integrates a set of related data items (such as wage information or weather data) with a group of pre-written functions (called **methods** in the jargon of OOP) that perform useful tasks associated with the data. Programmers use the object's methods as an **Application Programming Interface (API)** to access and modify the object's data.

The OOP approach allows a degree of standardization that greatly simplifies and speeds up application development, and also encourages standard data processing solutions so that applications can share data more easily to perform electronic transactions across the world.

The entire OOP section is optional reading. The purpose of this book is not to teach OOP in any detail. However this chapter introduces the general concepts and application of OOP to prepare you for further study of this important topic.

Using Functions

As a general rule, programmers avoid writing duplicate code, whether within a single application or in different applications. Duplicate code is usually an indicator that it is time to step back and reconsider your application design. The more you program, the more you will hesitate whenever you find yourself rewriting the same (or similar) code.

One important way to minimize code duplication is to break your code down into distinct modules (known as **functions** in PHP and many other languages). Once developed, a function can be "called" as many times as needed by your application. If you design your functions carefully, it is quite likely that they can be used by many different applications. The secret to **reusability** is to develop each function to perform a single, very precise task. For example, don't design a single function to both calculate **and** print the tax on a sale. That function could not be used by an application that needed to only calculate the tax without printing it! Instead design one function to **calculate** the tax, and another function to **print** the tax. That way your applications can call either function as needed, and if an application needs to calculate **and** print the tax, it can simply call **both** functions.

As mentioned earlier, you have been using functions all along. Functions are easily recognized in PHP and most languages, because each call to a function requires you to specify the function **name** followed by a pair of parentheses. Like most programming languages, PHP supplies many useful pre-defined functions that you can use in your programs as needed.

When you think about it, a function works in your program the way an employee or contractor performs in the workplace: you call up the function whenever you need a specific task performed, and give it the information it needs, and trust that it will take care of the task for you, just as you (hopefully!) trust an employee or contractor to have the skills needed to perform their job. In either case, you do not need to know how the work is actually done.

In order to use a function you only need to know **four** things:

1. What is the name of the function?
2. What **task** does the function perform?
3. What input does the function need in order to perform its task (in other words, what **arguments**, if any, must you send to the function)?
4. What **output** does the function generate (in other words, what type of value, if any, does the function **return** to your program when it completes its task)?

Consider the **pow**() function. You know that the function name is pow, that the function's purpose is to multiply a value by itself the number of times indicated by an exponent, that the required arguments are the base value and the exponent, and that the return value is the result of this operation. This is all you need to know in order to use the pow() function in your programs.

Understanding Function Arguments

Once you know these four things about any function, you can write code to call the function, send it any values that it needs, and receive the result (if any) that the function returns. Let's look more closely at how we do this.

Many functions need to receive some values in order to perform their task. The values that we send to a function are called **arguments**. Arguments must be listed between the parentheses that follow the function name. For example, the **pow**() function needs us to supply a base number and an exponent in order to perform a calculation, so this function needs **two** arguments. If we need to obtain the value of 7 cubed, we can use **pow (7,3)**, where the base number 7 is the first argument and the exponent 3 is the second argument. We can also send values stored in variables as arguments to a function. For example if we need to raise the value stored in the variable $someNumber to the power of **5**, we can use **pow($someNumber, 5)**.

Arguments **must** be listed in the correct order! When we use the **pow**() function, the first argument must be the base number and the second argument must be the exponent. If we supplied these values in the wrong order, the **pow**() function would still work, but would generate an unintended result.

Different functions require different numbers of arguments. The **pi**() function does not require **any** arguments since it simply returns the value of PI (but notice that, since this is a function, you must still supply the parentheses). The **strtoupper**() function requires a single argument, for example **strtoupper("London")**. Here the argument is the **character string** "London" and the function will return "LONDON".

The **feof**() function also takes a single argument, for example **feof($someFile)**. In this case the argument is the **file handle** that the function will refer to in order to determine whether or not the EOF marker for the file has been read. The **fopen**() function uses **two** arguments: the **name** of the file to be opened and the **mode** (indicating whether the file is to be opened for read, write or append operations, or some combination of these), for example **fopen("textfile.txt", "r")**.

Some functions are designed so that they can be used with **different** numbers of arguments. In actuality a different version of the function is executed depending on the number of arguments that are sent. An example of this is the **round**() function. Sometimes we want round off to whole numbers and we call the function using just one argument, for example **round (14.626)** will return **15**. But other times we may want to round a value to a specific number of decimal places. In that case we can call a version of the **round**() function that accepts two arguments, for example **round (14.626, 2)**. In this case the **round**() function returns the value rounded off to the number of places specified in the second argument. In the case of **round (14.626, 2)**, the function would return **14.63**.

By the way, the **fgets**() function is another example of a function that can be used with one or two arguments. We have used the single argument version but a two-argument version allows you to specify the number of bytes that are to be returned by the read operation.

Receiving Values from a Function

As we have seen, many functions are designed to **return** a value once they have completed their task. If a function returns a value, the program that calls the function will usually want to use this value in some way.

A program may assign the value that is returned from a function to a variable for use in subsequent statements. For example in the statement **$result = pow(7, 3)**; the value returned by **pow(7, 3)**; is stored in the variable $result. Similarly in the statement **$nextLine = fgets($someFile)**; the value returned by **fgets($someFile)** is stored in the variable **$nextLine**.

A program may also use the value returned by a function directly in an expression of some kind. For example in the statement **while (!feof($someFile))** the **true** or **false** value returned from the **feof**() function is not stored in a variable. Instead it is used directly to decide whether or not to repeat the statements inside the while loop.

Similarly, the value that is returned by a function can be used directly in **print**() statements. However note that a call to a function cannot be included inside a character string that is enclosed in double quotes. That's because the PHP processor will assume that a statement such as:

```
print("<p>The square of 3 is pow(3, 2)</p>");
```

is intended to generate the string exactly as written, so this statement will produce: "<p>The square of 3 is pow(3, 2)</p>". In order to call a function within a **print**() statement we need to separate the function call from any character strings and concatenate the function call to these strings using periods (the period is the PHP concatenation operator). Here is the correct version of the previous statement:

```
print("<p>The square of 3 is ".pow(3, 2)."</p>";
```

Note that the call to the **pow**() function is now separated from the character string "<p>The square of 3 is " and the character string "</p>". These three output items are concatenated with two periods.

Researching Available Functions

An increasingly important skill for a programmer is to research the availability of existing functions and other code modules in order to reduce the need to develop new code.

PHP provides more than 700 pre-defined, or standard, functions. You can view a list of these at **http://www.php.net/quickref.php**. These are functions that the PHP processor will recognize. Don't be intimidated by the length of this list! Programmers tend to learn functions on an as-needed basis. As a programmer you will become increasingly skilled at using functions most relevant to your own work, and to quickly find and make use of new functions when you need them.

An easier way to get a feel for the more common used function is to look them by general category. For example you can see lists of functions associated with dates, math operations, string processing, file handling, and arrays at http://www.w3schools.com/php/default.asp. Lists like this are widely available on the Web. You can also find a short list of some of the most generally useful functions in these categories in Appendix F at the end of this book.

Apart from the standard PHP functions, many other useful functions have been developed by other programmers. Useful functions can be found by searching the Web, looking through programming books, requesting help from other programmers, etc. A great deal of code is freely shared but be careful to ensure that any functions that you find are intended for general use and not copyrighted.

Often collections (or **libraries**) of related functions are developed for specific purposes. Some function libraries are freely available, while others are distributed as a commercial product. If you go to work as a programmer, you may be provided with function libraries that have been developed internally to support your company's specific business applications.

Reasons to Use Pre-Defined Functions

It is often far more efficient and practical to make use of existing functions than to write new code for the same purpose, for a number of reasons:

Rapid development: Use of code that already exists reduces the time needed to develop new applications.

Improved code: Code that has already been shared has usually been evaluated by many programmers and can usually (not always!) be assumed to be accurate and efficient.

Reduced testing: Code that has been previously developed has usually already been rigorously tested, whereas any new code that you create must be tested carefully for errors.

Ease of maintenance: Code can be maintained and improved separately by different programmers or development teams.

Duplication of effort: Why write code that has already been written when your efforts are better spent developing something new?

Self-documenting code: Programmers must often maintain applications that have been developed by others. It is easier to read and understand the purpose of code that makes use of standard or commonly-used functions.

Increased standardization: The greater the standardization of code between applications, the more easily applications can work together. This is increasingly important in a global, network-based software environment.

Using die() or exit() to Terminate an Application

Some functions can be critical to know, since they handle tasks that could not otherwise be easily coded. An example is the **die**() function. Sometimes applications must be designed to end immediately in the event an error occurs. For example in Chapter 6 we saw how to work with text files. The fopen() function is used to open a file and provide a handle to the connection which is usually assigned to a variable, like this:

```
$someFile = fopen("someFile.txt", "r");
```

But what happens here if a problem occurs when the application tries to open the file? For example, what if the file does not exist? In cases such as this, the fopen() function simply returns FALSE. In our sample code, therefore, FALSE would be stored in the variable $someFile. Clearly if the file cannot be opened, the application should not be allowed to go ahead and use fgets() or the fclose() functions to process the file. Doing so would cause the application to abruptly terminate with a PHP error message. We can avoid this by testing $someFile and, if the variable contains FALSE, we can simply force the program to end with a suitable error message of our own design. The die() function will do this for us. Here is a general template for closing a program if an attempt to open a file fails:

```
$someFile = fopen("someFile.txt", "r");

if (!$someFile)
    die("<h1>File I/O Error</h1><p>Sorry, this file could not be
    opened. The application is now closing.</p>");
```

The die() function takes any message that you want to provide as an argument, and this message will be displayed before the application closes.

You may be wondering why the IF structure does not include an ELSE section to contain the code that will process the file if the fopen() operation is successful. The ELSE section is not needed here because the die() function will immediately end the application so no following code will be executed if this function is called.

PHP also provides an **exit**() function which is functionally the same as the die() function. These two functions can therefore be used interchangeably.

The die() and exit() functions can be used in any situation where you wish the application to exit immediately under some circumstance without "crashing" with a system error message. In the next chapter we will see how we can use these functions when trying and failing to connect to a database.

Creating Your Own Functions

Despite the availability of a wide range of functions designed to handle many different operations, you will still often need to develop functions of your own. When you do, you may then want to share these with other programmers.

You can create your own functions quite easily. It is useful to develop functions in groups that are related by some general purpose. We will begin by developing some functions for use with our temperature conversion applications. Many weather-related applications might need to convert temperatures between Celsius and Fahrenheit, so it makes sense to provide a library of functions for this purpose that can then be called up by any applications as needed.

Let's start with a function to convert Celsius to Fahrenheit. This function must receive a single argument (a Celsius temperature), and must return a Fahrenheit temperature. We'll call the function **toFahrenheit**() Here's how we construct the function in PHP:

```php
function toFahrenheit($celsius)
{
   $fahrenheit = (9 / 5) * $celsius + 32;
   return $fahrenheit;
}
```

The function definition begins with a **heading**: function **toFahrenheit** (**$celsius**). This heading includes the word **function** followed by the name that we wish to give the function (**toFahrenheit**), followed by a pair of parentheses that must contain a list of variables that the function will use to receive the actual arguments that are sent to it each time the function is called by a program. These "receiving variables" are known as the function's **parameters**. Each parameter must receive a value when the function is called and can be used as needed within the function to process the arguments that have been received.

In this case the **toFahrenheit**() function has one parameter, a variable named **$celsius**. Whenever we call this function, we must supply a single argument. The function will receive any value sent as an argument in the **$celsius** parameter. The **$celsius** variable can then be used within the function as needed.

For example, if we want to use this function in a program that needs to convert 20° Celsius to Fahrenheit and store the result in a variable named $fTemp, we could include the following statement:

```php
$fTemp = toFahrenheit(20);
```

The **toFahrenheit**() function will be executed and the argument **20** would be received by the function and stored in the parameter variable **$celsius**. Any reference to the **$celsius** variable inside the function would obtain the value 20, so the statement:

```php
$fahrenheit = (9 / 5) * $celsius + 32;
```

would be processed as:

```php
$fahrenheit = (9 / 5) * 20 + 32;
```

which will store 68 in $fahrenheit. The second statement in this function is:

```php
return $fahrenheit;
```

and this will return the value 68 to the calling program if the value 20 was sent to the function.

We could also call the function using a variable as an argument, for example:

```
$fTemp = toFahrenheit($someTemperature);
```

Here the value stored in the argument **$someTemperature** would be passed to the parameter **$celsius**.

So a function definition consists of the function **heading** and the function **body**. The function **body** contains the code that the function needs to perform its task. The code is provided between a pair of {} braces, and can contain any programming structures (sequential, selection or loop statements, or even calls to other functions). A function can contain any number of instructions but remember that good program design calls for each function to only perform a single task—this ensures that programmers have the greatest flexibility in the ways they can use the function in their own applications.

Our **toFahrenheit()** function contains two statements. The first statement uses the value received by the parameter **$celsius** to calculate the Fahrenheit and assign the result to the variable **$fahrenheit**. The second statement in the function is a return statement. The value that follows **return** (in this case the value stored in **$fahrenheit**) is returned to the program that called the function. If you do not include a return statement, the function will not return a value.

Do you see how this works? The function is designed independently of any program that calls it. The program that calls the function can send any numeric value, either a literal value such as **34.25**, or the value stored in a variable, such as a variable named **$someTemperature** or even a value stored in a variable that happens to be named **$celsius** (the same name as the function's parameter). The programmer who is **writing** the function simply provides a variable in the parameter list to receive the value that is sent as an argument. The programmer who is developing the program that **calls** this function does not need to know that the parameter is named **$celsius**, only that the function must be sent a number as an argument.

Here is the code for a second function, **toCelsius()** that receives a Fahrenheit temperature, converts this to Celsius, and returns the result:

```
function toCelsius($fahrenheit)
{
   $celsius = ($fahrenheit - 32) / (9 / 5);
   return $celsius;
}
```

Now we have **two** useful functions that could be used in any applications that need to convert temperatures. The mark of a good programmer is to think beyond any specific application and develop libraries of related functions that can then be used as needed to minimize duplication of code. What else might we add to our group of temperature-related functions?

Perhaps it would be useful to include functions that return the actual **conversion formulas** that are used to perform these conversions. An application can call these functions if it simply needs to display the formulas themselves. Here is the code for two functions named **strFahrenheitFormula**() and **strCelsiusFormula**() that return character strings containing the actual formulas:

```
function strFahrenheitFormula()
{
   return "Fahrenheit = (9 / 5) * Celsius + 32";
}

function strCelsiusFormula()
{
   return "Celsius = (Fahrenheit - 32) / (9 / 5)";
}
```

These two functions do not include any parameters. That's because these functions do not require any arguments. They each simply return the character string that describes the appropriate formula. Note that a function with no parameters **must** still include the parentheses in the function heading even though there is nothing between them.

Now let's add a function name **getWindChill**() to calculate the wind chill temperature. This function uses the wind chill formula developed by the US National Weather Service in 2001:

```
function getWindchill($fahrenheit, $windSpeedMPH)
{
   $windchill = 35.74 + (0.6215 * $fahrenheit) -
      (35.75 * pow($windSpeedMPH, 0.16)) +
      (0.4275 * $fahrenheit * pow($windSpeedMPH, 0.16));
   return $windchill;
}
```

Now here's a great example of why it is so useful to create a function to perform a common task! How many times would you want to see that code repeated in different programs? What would be the likelihood of errors? In fact this is a good example of a function that should be written once and then made available to programmers everywhere!

Also notice that this function requires **two** parameters. The first parameter receives the temperature in Fahrenheit and the second parameter receives the wind speed in miles per hour. In PHP multiple parameters are separated by **commas**. If you call a function with more than one parameter, be sure that the arguments that you send to the function are in the same order as the parameters in the function heading! For example if you wanted the wind chill for a temperature of 30 and a wind speed of 15, you must call the function using getWindchill(30, 15) since that is the order of the parameters. If you called the function with getWindchill(15, 30), the function would receive 15 into the $fahrenheit parameter and 30 into the $windSpeedMPH parameter so the result would be incorrect. This would result in a significant error that might be very difficult to discover. It's the kind of error that can have very serious real-world consequences: sometimes an error like this may not be caught until some time after the application has been in production. This is why careful testing is such an important part of all software development.

Where Do I Put My Functions?

Functions can be included directly in a program simply by typing the function definition in your code **before** the function is actually called. Look at the code for **tempConverter5.php** which shows how our **toFahrenheit**() function can be included directly in an application. This is a revised version of **TempConverter3.php** which used a FOR loop to display the Celsius and Fahrenheit temperatures from 0 to 100 in increments of 10. The new version defines the **toFahrenheit**() function and then calls this function each time the loop repeats in order to obtain the next conversion value.

```html
<html>
<head>
   <title>Temperature Conversions</title>
   <link rel="stylesheet" type="text/css" href="sample.css" />
</head>
<body>
   <?php
     function toFahrenheit($celsius)
     {
       $fahrenheit = (9 / 5) * $celsius + 32;
       return $fahrenheit;
     }

     print("<h1>Temperature Conversions</h1>");

     print ("<table border = \"1\"> ");
     print ("<tr><td><strong>Degrees Celsius</strong></td>
         <td><strong>Degrees Fahrenheit</strong></td></tr>");

     for($celsius = 0; $celsius <= 100; $celsius = $celsius + 10)
     {
       $fahrenheit = toFahrenheit($celsius);
       print("<tr><td class=\"center\">$celsius</td>
         <td class\"center\">$fahrenheit</td></tr>");
     }
     print ("</table>");
   ?>
</body>
</html>
```

Code Example: tempConverter5.php

You can include any number of functions in your code in any locations, as long as each function is listed before it is called. However this approach means that the function will only be available to the program where the function is actually located. If you wanted to use the toFahrenheit() function in other programs you would need to copy the function definition to each file.

In order to share functions between programs it is far more useful to store your functions in a separate file so that any programs can obtain the functions from this file and use them. A good approach is to create a number of function files so that each file contains a group of functions that are related in their purpose. This helps to keep functions organized and easier to locate. Files of related functions are often known as function **libraries**.

Creating a Library of Functions

We have created five functions. Since they are all related to temperatures, we will create a library of temperature functions by storing them in a file named **incTempFunctions.php** as follows:

```php
<?php
  function toFahrenheit($celsius)
  {
    $fahrenheit = (9 / 5) * $celsius + 32;
    return $fahrenheit;
  }
  function toCelsius($fahrenheit)
  {
    $celsius = ($fahrenheit - 32) / (9 / 5);
    return $celsius;
  }
  function strFahrenheitFormula()
  {
    return "Fahrenheit = (9 / 5) * Celsius + 32";
  }
  function strCelsiusFormula()
  {
    return "Celsius = (Fahrenheit - 32) / (9 / 5)";
  }
  function getWindchill($fahrenheit, $windSpeedMPH)
  {
    $windchill = 35.74 + (0.6215 * $fahrenheit) -
      (35.75 * pow($windSpeedMPH, 0.16)) +
      (0.4275 * $fahrenheit * pow($windSpeedMPH, 0.16));
    return $windchill;
  }
?>
```

Code Example: incTempFunctions.php

Note that this file simply contains a group of PHP functions. The file is not intended to generate a Web page and contains no HTML code and no PHP other than the code used to create the functions. It is simply a "utility" file for use by other applications. Note also that beginning and ending PHP tags are required to surround this code.

So now we have a file that contains a group of useful temperature-related functions. How do we make **use** of these functions in our programs?

Including Functions from External Files

In PHP, we can tell the processor to include code from external files before processing the PHP instructions in our applications. One way to do this is by issuing an **include**() statement. For example if we wish to include the code in the **incTempFunctions.php** file an application, we can use the statement:

```
include("incTempFunctions.php");
```

This statement **must** appear **before** any code that references the code contained in the included file. When a file is included in another file, the content of the included file is added to the existing code at the location of the **include**() statement. The code in the included files can therefore be referenced by any statements that follow this location.

Notice that we named our file of functions **incTempFunctions.php**. We can use any name for files that are to be included in other files. But using "**inc**" as the first part of the file name helps us to recognize the purpose of these files: they are not in themselves working applications but instead contain code that can be included in our applications.

Look at the code for **tempConverter6.php**. This is a revised version of **tempConverter5.php**. The new version uses the **toFahrenheit**() function from the **incTempFunctions.php** file to convert the temperature, and also calls the **strFahrenheitFormula**() function from the same file to display the formula.

```
<html>
<head>
  <title>Temperature Conversions</title>
  <link rel="stylesheet" type="text/css" href="sample.css" />
</head>
<body>
  <?php
    include("incTempFunctions.php");

    print("<h1>Temperature Conversions</h1>");
    print("<p>NOTE: These conversions use the formula:
```

```
       <br />".strFahrenheitFormula()."</p>");
   print("<table border=\"1\"> ");
   print("<tr><td><strong>Degrees Celsius</strong></td>
       <td><strong>Degrees Fahrenheit</strong></td></tr>");

   for ($celsius = 0;$celsius <= 100; $celsius = $celsius + 10)
   {
      $fahrenheit = toFahrenheit($celsius);
      print("<tr><td class=\"center\">$celsius</td>
          <td class=\"center\">$fahrenheit</td></tr>");
   }

   print("</table>");
   ?>
</body>
</html>
```

Code Example: tempConverter6.php

The first PHP statement is an **include** statement which includes the code in the file **incTempFunctions.php**.

The second **print()** statement calls the **strFahrenheitFormula()** function which returns the formula so that this can be displayed. The processor recognizes this function because it is listed in the **incTempFunctions.php**, which has previously been included. The character string returned by **strFahrenheitFormula()** is added to the output of the **print()** statement (note the use of the periods to concatenate the function call with the two character strings).

The FOR loop repeats 11 times to produce the required table rows. Each row contains a temperature conversion from Celsius to Fahrenheit. The counting variable is named **$celsius** and this variable is incremented by 10 for each repetition, with values from 0 to 100. The two statements in the loop body perform the following operations:

- The current value of **$celsius** is sent as an argument to the toFahrenheit() function. The function calculates and returns the equivalent Fahrenheit temperature which is stored in the $fahrenheit variable.
- The print statement uses the values stored in the $celsius and $fahrenheit variables to generate a new table row containing the Celsius and Fahrenheit temperatures.

Using the Same Functions in Different Programs

The value of developing a group of related functions and then storing them in a separate file is that we can use these functions for different purposes in different programs.

Consider the following requirement for another temperature-related application:

calcWindChill requirements:

Write an application that asks the user for the current temperature (in degrees Celsius) and the wind speed (mile per hour). The program should then display the wind chill for these conditions (also in degrees Celsius).

To meet these requirements, we need a form to receive the required input from the user. Here is the pseudocode for **calcWindchill.html**:

```
calcWindchill.html algorithm:

    Prompt the user for the temperature in Celsius
    Get celsius
    Prompt the user for the windspeed
    Get windspeed
    Submit celsius, windspeed to calcWindchill.php
END
```

Here is the code for calcWindchill.html:

```
<html>
<head>
   <title>WIND CHILL CALCULATOR</title>
   <link rel="stylesheet" type="text/css" href="sample.css" />
</head>
<body>
   <h1>WIND CHILL CALCULATOR</h1>

      <form action="calcWindchill.php" method="post">
      <table>
      <tr>
      <td>Enter a temperature in degrees Celsius:</td>
      <td><input type="text" size="10" name="celsius" /></td>
      </tr>

      <tr>
      <td>Enter a wind speed in mile per hour:</td>
      <td><input type="text" size="10" name="windspeed" /></td>
      </tr>
      </table>
      <input type="submit" value="Display the Windchill
         temperature" />
   </form>
</body>
</html>
```

Code Example: calcWindchill.html

Next we need to design a program to process the user input. We can use our previously developed **getWindchill**() function, but the requirements tell us to obtain the temperature in degrees Celsius, and also display the results in Celsius. Since our **getWindchill**() function is designed to receive the temperature in degrees Fahrenheit and return the wind chill in degrees Fahrenheit we will need to use the **toFahrenheit**() function to convert the Celsius input to Fahrenheit before calling the **getWindchill**() function, then use the **toCelsius**() function to convert the windchill temperature from Fahrenheit back to Celsius **after** calling the **toCelsius**() function.

Here is the pseudocode for calcWindchill.php:

```
calcWindChill.php:

    receive celsius, windspeed from calcWindchill.html
    fahrenheit = toFahrenheit(celsius)
    windchillF = getWindchill(fahrenheit, windspeed )
    windchillC = toCelsius(windchillF)
    Display celsius, windspeed, windchillC
END
```

Here is the code for calcWindchill.php:

```php
<html>
<head>
   <title>WIND CHILL CALCULATOR</title>
   <link rel="stylesheet" type="text/css" href="sample.css" />
</head>
<body>
   <h1>WIND CHILL CALCULATOR</h1>

<?php
    include("incTempFunctions.php");

    $celsius = $_POST['celsius'];
    $windspeed = $_POST['windspeed'];
    $fahrenheit = toFahrenheit($celsius);
    $windchillF = getWindchill($fahrenheit, $windspeed);
    $windchillC = toCelsius($windchillF);

    print("Temperature (Celsius): $celsius<\<>br />");
    print("WindSpeed (miles per hour): $windspeed<\<>br />");
    print("Windchill (Celsius): ".number_format($windchillC, 2)
       ."<br />");
?>
</body>
</html>
```

Code Example: calcWindchill.php

Figure 13-1 shows a sample interaction.

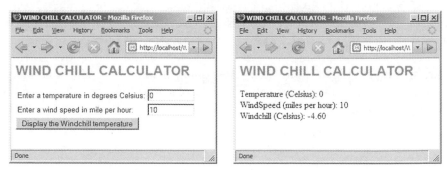

Figure 13-1: calcWindchill.html and calcWindchill.php screenshots

This example should give you a feel for the importance and value of developing libraries of useful functions. Some programmers may spend most of their time developing general purpose code libraries of this kind, while other programmers develop applications that make use of these function libraries to meet specific requirements. There is an important difference in approach. An application programmer is focused on developing a custom solution for a specific set of requirements. But a programmer who is developing general purpose code is not thinking about any specific application. Instead he or she is considering the most generally useful way to develop code functions for maximum reusability.

Learning to Think Beyond Specific Applications

As we have seen, modular programming changes the way that we think about software design. Instead of designing and developing code for a specific set of requirements, we start to think on a larger scale. Let's look at one more example of a function library.

We have already developed code to process a file of numbers containing rainfall data and then perform various operations on this data: display the numbers, calculate the total, calculate the average, find the highest rainfall, and find the lowest rainfall. These applications worked with rainfall data, but we might ask "Don't we often need to perform similar operations on all kinds of files that contain numeric values, for example files of scores, or files of payroll amounts?"

What if we simply develop a set of functions that we could use to process **any** file that contains a list of numbers? We could include a function to simply display the values in the file, and functions to obtain the total, count, average, highest and lowest values? Then we could use these functions as needed in any program required to process a file of numbers, whether the file contained rainfall, student scores, wages, ages, sales figures, or anything else. The functions would have to receive the appropriate file name as an argument in order to know which file to open, and the file would need to simply contain a list of numbers since that is what these functions will be designed to handle.

Your **samples** folder includes a file named incNumericFileFunctions.php. This file contains a number of functions that are designed to work with any file that contains a list of numbers, where each number appears on a separate line in the file. Each function uses a parameter to receive a file name, then opens the file and processes it in some way:

The **printData()** function opens the file with the filename that is sent as an argument, outputs the numbers contained in the file, then closes the file.

The **getTotal()** function opens the file with the filename that is sent as an argument, calculates the total of the numbers contained in the file, closes the file, and returns the total.

The **getCount()** function opens the file with the filename that is sent as an argument, counts the numbers contained in the file, closes the file, and returns the count.

The **getAverage()** function opens the file with the filename that is sent as an argument, calculates the average of the numbers contained in the file, closes the file, and returns the average.

The **getHighest()** function opens the file with the filename that is sent as an argument, finds the highest value of the numbers contained in the file, closes the file, and returns the highest value.

The **getLowest()** function opens the file with the filename that is sent as an argument, finds the lowest value of the numbers contained in the file, closes the file, and returns the lowest value.

Here is the code for **incNumericFileFunctions.php**:

```php
<?php

    function printData($fileName)
    {
        $dataFile = fopen("$fileName","r");
        $nextValue = fgets($dataFile);
        while (!feof($dataFile) )
        {
            print("$nextValue <br />");
            $nextValue = fgets($dataFile);
        }
        fclose($dataFile);
    }

    function getTotal($fileName)
    {
        $total = 0;
        $dataFile = fopen("$fileName","r");
        $nextValue = fgets($dataFile);
```

```
  while (!feof($dataFile) )
  {
    $total = $total + $nextValue;
    $nextValue = fgets($dataFile);
  }
  fclose($dataFile);
  return $total;
}

function getCount($fileName)
{
  $count = 0;
  $dataFile = fopen("$fileName","r");
  $nextValue = fgets($dataFile);
  while (!feof($dataFile) )
  {
    $count = $count + 1;
    $nextValue = fgets($dataFile);
  }
  fclose($dataFile);
  if ($count > 0)
    return $count;
  else
    return -1;
}

function getAverage($fileName)
{
  $count = getCount($fileName);
  $total = getTotal($fileName);
  if ($count > 0)
    return $total / $count;
  else
    return -1;
}

function getHighest($fileName)
{
  $dataFile = fopen("$fileName","r");
  $nextValue = fgets($dataFile);
  $highest = $nextValue;
  while (!feof($dataFile) )
  {
    if ($nextValue > $highest)
      $highest = $nextValue;
    $nextValue = fgets($dataFile);
  }
```

```php
    fclose($dataFile);
    return $highest;
  }


  function getLowest($fileName)
  {
    $dataFile = fopen("$fileName","r");
    $nextValue = fgets($dataFile);
    $lowest = $nextValue;
    while (!feof($dataFile) )
    {
      if ($nextValue < $lowest)
        $lowest = $nextValue;
      $nextValue = fgets($dataFile);
    }
    fclose($dataFile);
    return $lowest;
  }
?>
```

Code Example: incNumericFileFunctions.php

This library of functions can be included and used by any application that needs to process a file that contains a list of numbers, where each number is stored on a separate line in the file.

The **processScores4.php** program shows how we can use our new function library to display a list of student scores from a file named **scores1.txt**, and also display the count and average of these scores. Here is the code:

```php
<body>
  <h1> STUDENT SCORES </h1>
<?php
    include("incNumericFileFunctions.php");

    $fileName = $_POST['fileName'];

    printData($fileName);

    $avgScore = getAverage($fileName);
    $numScores = getCount($fileName);

    print("Number of Scores: $numScores <br />");
    print("Average Score: $avgScore <br />");
?>
</body>
</html>
```

Code Example: processScores4.php

As you can see by the reduced amount of code, our use of pre-written functions **greatly** simplifies the work of the application programmer!

As a professional programmer, you will probably find that your work focuses on a specific subject area. For example if you work in an educational setting you may work mostly with student records. Or you may work as an independent contractor developing Web sites for small companies. If you take care to build useful function libraries that are directly related to your work you will find that these will help you (and your programming team) create new applications quickly and easily.

More about Include Files

Do not think that PHP include files are only for use with libraries of function. Include files can be used to include **any** code in a PHP file. When you include a file, the contents of the file are simply added to the content of the current file at the location of the include statement, so you can think of this as a simple "paste" operation. Let's explore some other uses of include files.

In our chapter on arrays, we mentioned the usefulness of associative arrays to contain lookups of various kinds, for example a list of standard error messages, or a lookup of company information (address, phone, e-mail, etc.). Arrays of this kind can be developed and stored in include files (for example **incErrorMessages.php** or **incCompanyInfo.php**) that can then be included in any programs that need to reference these arrays. This promotes standards and consistency in the manner in which this information is displayed by different applications and avoids duplicating the same information in multiple applications.

As another important example, many pages on a Web site often contain the same HTML code, for example the information in the <head> section may be the same for each page, or the pages may have the same menus or footers. Instead of duplicating this material in each file, the HTML code can be saved in an include file. Note that an include file that contains only HTML code should not have opening and closing PHP tags since the file does not contain PHP code.

Your samples folder contains two examples that demonstrate more extensive use of include files. The file **includeDemo.php** uses a number of include files to: (1) add the head and foot sections to the page (**incHead.php** and **incFoot.php**); (2) make use of an associative array that contains company information (**incCompanyInfo.php**) and (3) make use of an associative array that contains a list of error messages (**incErrorMessages.php**). This program opens a file of sales data and generates a report. The file **includeDemo2.php** goes one step further and also includes **incNumericFileFunctions.php** in order to use these functions to process the data file. Look at these programs carefully to understand the value and efficiency of include files in your code.

IMPORTANT NOTE: Since the include statement is a PHP statement, **any** file that contains this statement must have a .php extension. This is true even if you only want to include HTML code in this file. And each include statement must be located in a PHP section at the location where you want the content of the include file to be pasted, even if the PHP section contains nothing more than the include statement. Actually it is quite standard for **all** files in a Web application to use .php extensions even if the file contains only HTML code. We have used files with .html extensions in this textbook only so that we can use the same file names for pairs of pages where the first .html page displays an HTML form and the second .php page contains the code to process the form.

As a Web developer, you will quickly learn to develop a library of small include files that each display individual components for your Web pages. You can then include each file as needed to assemble each page. Just as important, if you need to change a standard feature on your pages, you can make the change in the appropriate include file and all of your pages will reflect the change.

It is not the purpose of this book to provide a comprehensive description of PHP features or Web site design. You will find it useful to explore this subject further and consider other uses for include files.

OPTIONAL: Introducing Object-Oriented Programming (OOP)

The remaining sections of this chapter provide an optional introduction to OOP and may be skipped if this subject is not part of the course or study requirements. The review questions and code exercises at the end of this chapter do not refer to the OOP section.

Modular approaches to software design have led to a significant recent development in software design known as **Object-Oriented Programming** (**OOP**). Since its inception, OOP has quickly become the standard approach for most modern application development. Unfortunately it would take far too much space to examine OOP in any detail, so here we will simply introduce the concept of OOP, explain some common OOP terminology, and provide a working example that will prepare you for further study of OOP principles and practices in subsequent courses or reading.

OOP takes modular design a step further by allowing programmers to more tightly integrate groups of related data values with the functions needed to work this data to perform useful tasks. There are many examples of data values that are grouped together: employee information, student records, the grades that make up a course, weather data for a specific location, bank account information, the headers and body of an email message, etc.

The combination of a specific set of data with all of the functions needed to operate on this data constitutes an **object.** In OOP terminology, functions are usually referred to as **methods,** but since PHP uses the word function, we will use that term in our descriptions here. In object-oriented design, programmers who wish to work with the data associated with an object **must** use the functions provided for this purpose. The functions therefore provide a standard **Application Programming Interface** (**API**) to the data. The use of a standard API promotes consistency, enables rapid development, ensures compatibility, reduces duplication, increases security, and minimizes errors.

Before an object can be used, it must be first be defined. Once defined, any number of **instances** of the object can be created for use by any application. The object is often defined quite independently of its use by any specific application and, as we shall see, this independence is a significant feature of OOP design.

Before we examine important OOP terms and characteristics, let's first look at how to define a sample object and then develop a small application that uses this object. Assume that the data related to an employee's weekly wage consists of just four values: the employee's ID, number of tax exemptions, hours worked, and hourly wage. In an Object-Oriented Programming model, a programmer would not create individual variables for these values. Instead he or she would create an instance of an existing object that had already been coded. This object would have been defined to contain these four values, and would also contain a comprehensive set of functions allowing the programmer to work with this data as needed. These functions would constitute the Application Programming Interface (API) to the data. If the program required work with multiple employees, then the programmer would simply create multiple instances of the object, one for each employee, each with a unique name.

But the object must be defined before instances can be used by a program. The object's data definitions along with the functions (or methods) that allow programs to operate on this data together constitute an object **class**.

Defining an Object Class

Here is an overview of the data and functions that might constitute a **WeeklyPay** object class:

Data for the WeeklyPay class:

  empID: the employee's ID

  numExemptions: the number of Federal tax exemptions

  hoursWorked: the hours worked this week

  hourlyWage: the hourly wage

API for the WeeklyPay class. These are the names of the functions (methods) that a programmer will use to access or modify the data that is listed above:

WeeklyPay(): a special function called a constructor used only to create new instances of the object (this will be explained).

  getID(): a function used to access the employee ID

  setID(): used to modify the employee ID

  getNumExemptions(): used to access the number of exemptions

  setNumExemptions(): used to modify the number of exemptions

  getHoursWorked(): used to access the hours worked by the employee setHoursWorked (): used to modify the hours worked by the employee

getHourlyWage(): used to access the employee's hourly wage

setHourlyWage(): used to modify the employee's hourly wage

getGrossPay(): used to obtain the employee's gross weekly pay

getFedWithholding(): used to obtain the employee's federal taxes

getNetPay(): used to obtain the employee's net weekly pay

Each of the functions that make up the object's API performs a very specific and often quite simple task, so that programmers who need to work with objects of this class can easily perform any operation that is required. The idea is that a program that needs to work with the weekly pay for one or more employees can create an instance of WeeklyPay for each employee and then use the functions that make up the WeeklyPay API to work with the employee's WeeklyPay data as needed. Of course this is a simplified example. In a real world application we would include all kinds of additional data, as well as functions designed to handle tasks related to health insurance, retirement contributions and state taxes.

Coding the Object Class

Here is how a WeeklyPay object class might actually be defined in PHP (this definition is provided in the **incWeeklyPayObject.php** file in your **samples** folder). You will see that object class definitions incorporate some operators and other features that we have not seen before:

```php
<?php
class WeeklyPay
{
   var $empID;
   var $hoursWorked;
   var $hourlyWage;
   var $numExemptions;

   function WeeklyPay()
   {
     // No code. This constructor function is used only to
     // create a new instance of the object
   }

   function getID()
   {
     return $this->empID;
   }
```

```
function setID($empID)
{
  $this->empID = $empID;
}

function getHoursWorked()
{
  return $this->hoursWorked;
}

function setHoursWorked($hoursWorked)
{

  $this->hoursWorked = $hoursWorked;
}

function getHourlyWage()
{
  return $this->hourlyWage;
}
function setHourlyWage($hourlyWage)
{

  $this->hourlyWage = $hourlyWage;
}

function getNumExemptions()
{
  return $this->numExemptions;
}

function setNumExemptions($numExemptions)
{
  $this->numExemptions = $numExemptions;
}

function getFedWithholding()
{
  $fedWithholdingTaxBase = ($this->hourlyWage *
    $this->hoursWorked * 52) - (3300 * $this->numExemptions);

  if ( $fedWithholdingTaxBase >= 0 AND
      $fedWithholdingTaxBase <= 2650)
    $fedWithholding = 0;
  else if ( $fedWithholdingTaxBase > 2650    AND
           $fedWithholdingTaxBase <= 10000)
    $fedWithholding = 0.10 * ($fedWithholdingTaxBase - 2650);
  else if ( $fedWithholdingTaxBase > 10000 AND
           $fedWithholdingTaxBase <= 32240)
    $fedWithholding = 0.15 * ($fedWithholdingTaxBase - 10000);
```

```php
      else if ( $fedWithholdingTaxBase > 32240 AND
              $fedWithholdingTaxBase <= 73250)
      $fedWithholding = 0.25 * ($fedWithholdingTaxBase - 32240);
      else if ( $fedWithholdingTaxBase > 73250 AND
              $fedWithholdingTaxBase <= 156650)
      $fedWithholding = 0.28*($fedWithholdingTaxBase - 73250);
      else if ( $fedWithholdingTaxBase > 156650 AND
              $fedWithholdingTaxBase <= 338400)
      $fedWithholding = 0.33*($fedWithholdingTaxBase - 156650);
      else if ($fedWithholdingTaxBase > 338400)
      $fedWithholding = 0.35*($fedWithholdingTaxBase - 338400);
      else
      $fedWithholding = -1; // error
      return round($fedWithholding / 52, 2);
   }

   function getGrossPay()
   {
     $gross = round($this->hoursWorked * $this->hourlyWage, 2);
     return $gross;
   }
   function getNetPay()
   {
     $net = round($this->getGrossPay() -
       $this->getFedWithholding(), 2);
     return ($net);
   }
} // end of class definition
?>
```

Code Example: incWeeklyPayObject.php

The entire class definition for the WeeklyPay object is introduced with a class heading that consists of the keyword **class** followed by the name of the class. The entire content of the class definition is enclosed in {} braces. The variables that will store the data values of the object are known as **class variables** (also known as class attributes or fields). The class variables are listed separately from (usually above) the class functions. The class variables are used to store the object's data values. Note that, in PHP object class definitions, the keyword **var** is used to identify each class variable.

The class functions (or methods) are listed below the class variables. The functions will provide an interface between the class variables and any program that uses instances of this object. Most of these functions perform a simple operation of some kind that involves access to the class variables. For example the **getHoursWorked**() function simply **returns** the value stored in the **$hoursWorked** variable to the program that requests this, whereas the **setHoursWorked**() function receives a value from an application and **stores** this in the $hoursWorked variable. The words **get** and **set** are often included in object function names to indicate the purpose of the function.

You will notice that the class functions use an unfamiliar syntax to refer to the class variables. For example, rather than referring to **$hoursWorked**, the **getHoursWorked**() function refers to the variable as **$this->hoursWorked**). Remember that a function can be be considered a small independent program. Without the keyword **this**, the function would assume that **$hoursWorked** was a variable for use only within the function. The use of the **this** keyword indicates that this is the class variable **$hoursWorked** and not a local variable. This ensures that the class-level variables are not confused with any variables defined inside the functions that may have the same name.

You can see the importance of this if you look at the **setHoursWorked**() function. This function contains a parameter named **$hoursWorked**. This is a function variable that will be used to receive a value from the program that calls the function. The function is designed to assign the value received by this parameter to the class variable **$hoursWorked**. But the parameter has the same name as the class variable. The statement **$this->hoursWorked = $hoursWorked** avoids any ambiguity by using the **this** reference to specify that the value received in the **parameter** variable **$hoursWorked** is to be assigned to the **class** variable **$hoursWorked**. The use of the **this** reference ensures that these two variables are not confused although both have the same name. The reason that the reference to the class variable is named **this** is that since a new set of class variables are created for each instance of the object, the functions always work with a specific instance — "this" instance. This topic is covered next.

Creating and Using Instances of an Object Class

In order to use a class, a programmer would need to know the name of the class and also what functions are available to work with the data that the class provides. Now that the WeeklyPay class has been defined, we can write programs that create and use **instances** of this class. Our program will create **instances** of the **WeeklyPay** object as needed, one instance for each employee that our application needs to process. Each of these instances will contain its own set of class variables, in other words every new instance of a WeeklyPay object will contain its own variables to store the ID, hours worked, hourly wage, and number of exemptions, along with the set of functions (API) that the program can call as needed to work with these values.

Each new instance is created by using the **new** operator to call the **constructor** function (method) which was defined as part of the WeeklyPay class. This constructor always has exactly the same name as the class itself. The constructor method automatically creates a new **copy** (instance) of the object for use by the program. In this case the constructor method is named **WeeklyPay**() since WeeklyPay is the name of the class. The constructor method is only used to create new instances. Once the instance has been created, the other functions (methods) in the WeeklyPay class can be used to work with the class variables.

Here is how a program might create new instances for **two** employees:

```
$emp1 = new WeeklyPay();
$emp2 = new WeeklyPay();
```

The statement **$emp1 = new WeeklyPay()** is used to create a new instance of a **WeeklyPay** object and assign this to the **$emp1** variable. The statement **$emp2 = new WeeklyPay()** creates **another** instance of a **WeeklyPay** object and assigns this to the **$emp2** variable. The **new** operator is always used with the constructor method and this ensures that each instance is unique and contains its own set of data that is separate from any other instance. Here, **$emp1** and **$emp2** are two variables that each contain a unique WeeklyPay object. Each is an instance of the WeeklyPay class, and each instance contains its own set of four class variables that will store the data for a single employee.

Note that class constructor functions (methods) such as WeeklyPay() do not need to include any code — the instance will be created automatically when the constructor is called. But if your class definition **does** include code, that code will be executed at the time that the object is created.

Now that these instances have been created we can use any of the functions that make up the WeeklyPay API to operate on the data contained in each instance. For example we can set the ID, hours worked and hourly wage of the **$emp1** instance as follows:

```
$emp1->setID("111-22-3333");
$emp1->setHoursWorked(40);
$emp1->setHourlyWage(10.00);
$emp1->setNumExemptions(2);
```

In PHP we use the -> operator to associate a class function with a specific instance of the class, for example:

```
$emp1->setID("111-22-3333");
```

If we write the statement

```
$emp2->setID("222-33-4444");
```

then we use the setID() function to set the ID for the $emp2 instance. In this way we can use the functions listed in the API to work with the variables in specific instance of the object class.

Here's how we can use the **getID()** and **getGrossPay()** functions to print the first employee's ID and gross wage (wage before deductions):

```
print("<p>Employee ".$emp1->getID()." wages: $".
   $emp1->getGrossPay()."</p>");
```

We can also store the values returned from WeeklyPay functions to variables in our program. For example we might call the **getNetPay()** function in the WeeklyPay class to obtain the net wage (wage after deductions) from the **$emp1** instance and assign this to a variable named **$emp1NetPay:**

```
$emp1NetPay = $emp1->getNetPay();
```

The idea of working with objects is that, once an object class has been defined, our applications can create as many instances as needed by declaring instance variables of the class. We can then work with these by applying any of the functions defined in the API to the instance variables.

The **wage11.php** program includes the **incWeeklyPayObject.php** file that contains the WeeklyPay class definition and creates two instances of the WeeklyPay object class in order to demonstrate the use of objects in a working application. Here is the code for **wage11.php**:

```php
<?php
   include("incWeeklyPayObject.php");

   $emp1 = new WeeklyPay();
   $emp2 = new WeeklyPay();

   $emp1->setID("111-22-3333");
   $emp1->setHoursWorked(40);
   $emp1->setHourlyWage(10.00);
   $emp1->setNumExemptions(2);

   $emp2->setID("222-33-4444");
   $emp2->setHoursWorked(20);
   $emp2->setHourlyWage(15.00);
   $emp2->setNumExemptions(0);

   $emp1ID = $emp1->getID();
   $emp1GrossPay = $emp1->getGrossPay();
   $emp1Tax = $emp1->getFedWithholding();
   $emp1NetPay = $emp1->getNetPay();

   print("<p><strong>Employee: $emp1ID</strong><br />");
   print("Gross Pay = $$emp1GrossPay<br />");
   print("Federal Tax = $$emp1Tax<br />");
   print("Net Pay = $$emp1NetPay</p>");

   print("<p><strong>Employee: ".$emp2->getID()."</strong><br />");
   print("Gross Pay = ".$emp2->getGrossPay()."<br />");
   print("Federal Tax = ".$emp2->getFedWithholding()."<br />");
   print("Net Pay = ".$emp2->getNetPay()."</p>");
?>
```

Code Example: wage11.php

In this example we have simply created two WeeklyPay instances and then used the various **set** functions in the API to assign values to the four WeeklyPay data items for each of the two instances. We then obtained the ID, gross wage, federal tax and net wage from the two instances using the appropriate **get** methods. For purposes of illustration, in the case of the $emp1 instance we assigned these values to variables and then used these variables in our print statements. In the case of the $emp2 instance we included the calls to the get methods directly in our print statements.

Try writing an application that creates one or more WeeklyPage instances, and uses these to perform a task of some kind. Now consider how you might define object classes of your own. For example you might define a class to store information associated with your music collection (title, date, musical group, genre, etc), or game players in an online game (playerID, character type, game score, etc), or weather readings (temperature, wind speed, wind direction, rainfall, etc.). Once you have defined the necessary class variables, consider the actions (functions or methods) that you must provide so that applications can working with these variables, for example accessing the values stored in the variables, modifying these values, or generating useful data or services derived from these values.

The Importance of OOP

As we have seen, object-oriented programming consists of two quite distinct development stages. First an object class is defined in order to allow programmers to work with a specific type of data. The class definition identifies the data elements (class variables), and provides a set of methods to allow an application operate on the data. This work is often performed independently of any applications that will make use of the object. The designer of the object class will be thinking beyond any specific application but rather will focus on the big picture: what are all possible uses of this object? What data (class variables) should be included? What functions (methods) might programmers need to work with this data?

Once a class has been developed to define the object, programmers can create instances of this class for use within their own applications. A single application may use many different kinds of object, and the programmers who write these applications often have no involvement in the development of the object classes themselves. Often objects are developed by one group of programmers and then made available throughout an organization or even world-wide. Most object-oriented programming languages also include extensive libraries of standard objects that programmers can apply in their applications. An object-oriented programmer is comfortable combining objects to suit their purposes. A real-world wage processing application may make use of **WeeklyPay** objects for calculating wages and **Employee** objects to work with employee information. The same application might also use standard objects to create components of graphical interfaces such as **menus** and **labels** and **buttons**, and to perform transactions with databases. In a fully OOP environment, **every component of the application is an object!**

Important OOP Terms and Concepts

Here we will explore some of the terminology associated with OOP and learn more about the significance and key features of this approach to programming. The application of OOP encourages standardization and reusability of code and reduces the need for duplication and redundant testing. Another important purpose of object-oriented design is to provide greater security for critical data. The API of an object class provides a pre-programmed interface between an application and the object's data. Access to the data is limited to the functions provided in the API. This prevents unauthorized use of the data, reduces coding errors, and ensures that the data is handled correctly. We say that the data defined in an object class is **encapsulated**, in other words the data is wrapped inside the API. The API **hides** the data, protecting it from inappropriate or incorrect use.

Since the object's data is only accessible through the functions that make up the API, the key to effective object-oriented design is to develop an API that is comprehensive with regard to the data set that it encapsulates. For example, to be universally useful, our WeeklyPay class should include every function that any application might need to use when processing wages.

We have used the terms **class variables** and **class methods** to describe the components of an object class (although PHP refers to **functions**, the term **methods** is more standard when describing objects). Class variables are also called **class attributes** or **fields** or **properties.**

An object **class** defines the class variables and methods. The class variables and methods together constitute the **members** of the class. Each class is designed for a specific type of object. Collections of related classes (for example a collection of classes that define objects related to employees, or rainfall data, or graphical interface components) are often stored together in **packages.**

Another key concept of OOP is an **object hierarchy**, where the class variables and functions of one object class are **inherited** by another object class which then **extends** these with additional variables and functions for a more specific purpose. For example an **Employee** class may consist of class variables and functions common to **all** employees, while a **SalariedEmployee** class might inherit these variables and functions and provide additional variables and functions that are appropriate only for **salaried** employees. Similarly, an **HourlyEmployee** class might **also** inherit the data and functions of the **Employee** class but would add data and functions that are appropriate only for **hourly** employees.

Inheritance provides a powerful design structure for OOP and minimizes code duplication. For example by inheriting the data and functions from the **Employee** class, the **SalariedEmployee** and **HourlyEmployee** classes do not need to duplicate the same data and functions common to all employees.

Another important feature of OOP is **polymorphism**. In general usage, the term polymorphic means "many shaped". In OOP, polymorphism allows applications to determine the specific type of object within an object hierarchy that it is to be processed at the time the application is running. For example an application might not "know" until it is actually executing whether to treat an employee as a salaried or hourly employee. This type of dynamic selection provides great flexibility for software designers, and once again reduces duplication.

Fully Object-Oriented languages, such as **Java**, are designed so that **all** application development is derived from objects. OOP languages provide large numbers of standard object classes that programmers can use to develop applications quickly and easily. For example, Java provides a rich set of standard object classes for developing graphical user interfaces quickly and easily.

Don't be too concerned if this very brief introduction to OOP is a little abstract or overwhelming! The topic is introduced here only as a preview of an important subject that you will meet again if you take additional programming courses.

Summary

Code modularity is an important feature of effective software design that minimizes duplication of code, reduces testing requirements, simplifies maintenance, permits rapid development, facilitates code documentation, and promotes standardization.

Small code modules that perform single tasks may be referred to as **functions, methods, sub-programs, sub-routines**, or **procedures**, depending on the language. In PHP, code modules are referred to as **functions**.

Functions permit code to be written once and then used by multiple applications. With this in mind, functions should be designed to be as generally useful as possible. Each function should be designed to perform a single task only. Libraries of functions are files that contain a number of functions that are related in purpose.

Standard functions are provided as a standard part of a programming language. The **pow**() function is an example of a standard PHP function.

In order to use a function, a programmer must know the name of the function, the purpose of the function, the number of **arguments** that the functions requires when it is called, and the type of value (if any) that the function **returns** when it has completed its task. For example the **pow**() function requires two arguments, a base value and an exponent, and returns the value of the base raised to the power of the exponent.

Different functions require different numbers of arguments. Some may require **no** arguments. Some functions can accept different numbers of arguments. For example the PHP **round**() function can be used with one or two arguments.

If a function returns a value, the program that calls the function will usually want to use the value that is returned. This value can be assigned to a program variable for subsequent use, or used directly in an expression.

The die() or exit() functions can be used when you need the application to exit immediately, with an appropriate message for the user.

Functions can be created easily in PHP. Each function definition consists of the word function, followed by the name of the function, followed by a list of **parameters** enclosed inside a pair of parentheses. Each parameter is a variable that is used to receive a value sent as an argument by the calling program. These parameter variables can then be used inside the function. The body of the function is enclosed in braces {} and contains any code needed to perform the function's task. If the function returns a value, the code will include a **return** statement, consisting of the word **return** followed by the value that is to be returned.

In PHP, files containing useful functions can be incorporated into an application using an **include** statement, for example **include("incTempFunctions.php")**; This statement tells the processor to include the code from the file that is referenced, at the current location in the application code. The include statement must occur before any program statements that call functions from the included file.

Placing libraries of functions in separate files means that these functions can be used in multiple programs for different purposes.

A key consideration for effective software design is to think beyond any particular application requirements and ask how code might be broken down into small modules that can serve multiple applications.

Object-Oriented Programming (**OOP**) is a very important approach to code modularity. In Object-Oriented design, programmers develop a comprehensive set of **methods** (or functions) to work with a specific set of related **data**. The combination of data values and methods comprises an **object**. The methods provide an **Application Programming Interface** (**API**) that programmers can use to work with the object's data, without accessing the data directly. The data is **encapsulated** by the API, meaning that the data is hidden fro direct access. The use of a standard API promotes consistency, enables rapid development, ensures compatibility, reduces duplication, increases security, and minimizes errors.

Objects are created as **classes**. An **object class** defines a set of **class variables** (or **fields**, or **attributes**, or **properties**) and **class methods** that provide an API between the variables that contain the class data and applications that need to work with the data. Together the class variables and methods constitute the class **members** of the class).

To use an object class a programmer must create **instances** of the object, where each instance contains a unique set of data that can be accessed using the API. An instance is created using the class **constructor** method with the **new** operator. The constructor method has the same name as the class.

An important feature of OOP is **inheritance**, which allows software designers to create **hierarchies** of objects, where some objects inherit the data and API's of others, and extend these with additional data and methods.

Another feature of OOP is **polymorphism** which allows applications to dynamically determine which type of object with an object hierarchy to process at the time the application is actually running.

Chapter 13 Review Questions

1. Which term refers to small code modules that each perform a single task in PHP?
    a. functions
    b. methods
    c. sub-programs
    d. sub-routines
    e. procedures

2. Look at the following statement:

```
$result = doSomething(5);
```

How many arguments does the doSomething() function require?
    a. 0
    b. 1
    c. 2
    d. 3
    e. 4

3. Consider the following function definition:

```
function doIt($num1, $num2)
{
    $answer = $num1 + $num2;
    return $answer;
}
```

How many parameters does this function have?
    a. 0
    b. 1
    c. 2
    d. 3
    e. 4

4. Consider the following function definition:

```
function doIt($num1, $num2)
{
   $answer = $num1 + $num2;
   return $answer;
}
```

Which of the following is an acceptable way to call this function?
    a. $result = doIt(3, 4);
    b. $result = $doIt(3, 4);
    c. $result = doIt(3);
    d. $result = doIt(4);
    e. $result = doIt();

5. Consider the following function definition:

```
function doThis()
{
   return "This is a test";
}
```

How many parameters does this function have?
    a. 0
    b. 1
    c. 2
    d. 3
    e. 4

6. Consider the following function definition:

```
function doThis()
{
   return "This is a test";
}
```

Which of the following is an acceptable way to call this function?
    a. $result = doThis("Testing");
    b. $result = doThis(3, 4);
    c. $result = doThis(3);
    d. $result = doThis(4);
    e. $result = doThis();

7. What value will the following call return?

```
round(13.3478, 3)
```

    a. 13
    b. 14
    c. 13.35
    d. 13.348
    e. 13.3478

8. Which of the following is a correct definition for a function named circleArea() that receives a radius and returns an area?

    a.

```
function circleArea($pi, $pow, $radius, $area)
{
   return pi() * pow($radius, 2);
}
```

    b.

```
function circleArea($pi, $radius, $area)
{
   return pi() * pow($radius, 2);
}
```

    c.

```
function circleArea($radius, $area)
{
   return pi() * pow($radius, 2);
}
```

    d.

```
function circleArea($radius)
{
   return pi() * pow($radius, 2);
}
```

    e.

```
function circleArea()
{
   return pi() * pow($radius, 2);
}
```

9. You want to use a function named doIt() which is located in a file named incStuff.php. Which statement is needed before you can use the doIt() function in your PHP program?
    a. include("doIt()");
    b. include("doIt.php");
    c. include("incStuff()");
    d. include("incStuff.php");
    e. include("incStuff.php->doIt()");

10. How many parameters does the fopen() function have?
    a. 0
    b. 1
    c. 2
    d. 3
    e. 4

11. Which of the following is **not** an important reason to use functions in your programs?
    a. Increased standardization by using common code
    b. Increased processing power
    c. Rapid development
    d. Avoids duplication
    e. More efficient testing

12. If you use an include statement to include a file containing a group of functions, which statement is correct?
    a. You can only use a single function from the file of functions.
    b. You must use every function in the file of functions.
    c. You can use any function as needed, as often as you need.

13. How would you use the getHighest() function from the incNumericFileFunctions.php file to find the highest value in a file of numbers named numbers.txt?
    a. include("numbers.txt");
       $highNum = getHighest();
    b. include("numbers.txt");
       $highNum = getHighest("numbers.txt");
    c. include("incNumericFileFunctions.php");
       $highNum = getHighest("numbers.txt");
    d. include("incNumericFileFunctions.php");
       $highNum = getHighest();
    e. include("numbers.txt");
       $highNum = getHighest("incNumericFileFunctions.php");

14. Approximately how many pre-defined functions does PHP provide?
    a. Between 100 and 300
    b. Between 300 and 500
    c. Between 500 and 700
    d. More than 700

15. Which PHP function is used to end a program immediately, with a suitable message?
    a. terminate()
    b. end()
    c. close()
    d. die()

16. What is wrong with this function?

```
function getWeeklyWage($hourlyRate, $hoursWorked)
{
    $weeklyPay = $hourlyRate * $hoursWorked;
}
```

    a. $WeeklyPay should be a parameter
    b. The word function should not be there
    c. The heading should end with a semi-colon
    d. The return statement is missing
    e. The parameters should not have $ signs since they are not variables

17. What is wrong with this function?

```
function getBonus(wage)
{
    if ($wage > 200)
        $bonus = 75.00;
    else
        $bonus = 50.00;
    return $bonus;
}
```

    a. $bonus should be a parameter
    b. The return statement should appear before the selection structure
    c. The heading should end with a semi-colon
    d. You cannot use selection structures in a function
    e. The wage parameter should have a $ sign since it is a variable

18. When you create your own functions, how many different tasks should each function be designed to perform?
    a. 0
    b. 1
    c. 2
    d. one or more
    e. 0 or more

19. What kind of code can be included in a function?
    a. sequence statements
    b. selection structures
    c. loop structures
    d. calls to other functions
    e. any combination of these can be included

20. A function must always be designed to return a value:
    a. True
    b. False

Chapter 13 Code Exercises

Your Chapter 13 code exercises can be found in your **Chapter 13** folder. This folder is included in your customized XAMPP installation at the following location:

> **xampplite\htdocs\WebTech\coursework\Chapter13**

Type your name and the date in the **Author** and **Date** sections of each file as you work on each exercise.

Debugging Exercises

Your **Chapter 13** folder should contain a number of "FixIt" files. Each of these files contains PHP code that has an error of some kind. You will need to run each program in order to see the errors, and to debug and test the code to see if it works correctly. For example to run **fixIt1.php**, first run the Web server, then use the URL:

> **http://localhost/WebTech/coursework/Chapter13/fixIt1.php**

Code Modification Exercises

Your **Chapter 13** folder contains a number of pairs of "Modify" files. Each pair of files contains HTML and PHP code that needs to be modified to meet a requirement. The requirements are included in each file. Modify the algorithms as specified, being careful to make changes to the .html and .php files as directed.

Code Completion Exercises

1. Read this exercise carefully and take your time to work out the logic. Your **Chapter 13** folder contains versions of **paintEstimate.html** and **paintEstimate.php** as well as a file of PHP functions named **incPaintFunctions.php** which contains a list of functions.

    The **paintEstimate.php** program already includes the code to receive the inputs from **paintEstimate.html** and to display the results. Your job is to include **incPaintFunctions** in **paintEstimate.php**, and use the functions appropriately to calculate the wall area, ceiling area, total area, paint cost and labor cost. Be sure to include the file, and use the correct variables ($wallArea, $ceilingArea, $totalArea, $paintCost, and $laborCost) to send values to, and receive values returned by, each function.

2. Read this exercise carefully and take your time to work out the logic. Your **Chapter 13** folder contains versions of **softwareOrder.html** and **softwareOrder.php** as well as a file named **incSoftwareOrder.php**. The code in **softwareOrder.php** includes calls to a number of functions. Your job is to add the functions to the **incSoftwareOrder.php** file so that the program works correctly:

    The **getSubtotal()** function should receive the number of copies being ordered, multiply this by **35.75** (the cost of each copy), and return the result.

    The **getSalesTax()** function should receive a sub-total, calculate the sales tax by multiplying this by **0.07**, and return the result.

    The **getShippingHandling()** function should receive the number of copies. The function should return **3.50** if the number of copies is less than **five**, otherwise the function should multiply the number of copies by **0.75** and return the result of this calculation.

    Your functions should use the **round()** function to round off the calculations to two places before returning the results (see examples in **incWageFunctions.php** which is included with these exercises).

3. Read this exercise carefully and take your time to work out the logic. Your **Chapter 13** folder contains versions of **giveAway.html** and **giveAway.php**. Create a function named **freeTrip()** and add it to the beginning of the PHP section in giveAway.php.

    The function should include the following line to generate a random number between 1 and 5. **$trip = rand(1, 5);**

    The function should use the value stored in **$trip** to return a travel destination which will be one of the following: Aruba, Cairo, London, Rome, Tokyo.

    Add the statement in the code to call this function and display the destination to the lucky winner.

4. Read this exercise carefully and take your time to work out the logic. Your **Chapter 13** folder contains versions of **travel.html** and **travel.php** and a function library named **incTravel.php**. Look through these files carefully. The code in travel.php

must be completed so that this program will use the functions supplied in incTravel.php to obtain the air fare, nightly hotel rate, cost of the tickets, and cost of the hotel, based on the user's inputs. In other words you must complete the following statements:

```
$airFare = ;
$hotelRate = ;

$ticketCost = ;
$hotelCost = ;
```

The statements to receive the user's input and generate the output have been provided. Don't forget that you must also include the **incTravel.php** file in your **travel.php** code! Note: you can download **incTravel.php** from the Web site if it is missing from your folder.

5. Read this exercise carefully and take your time to work out the logic. Your **Chapter 13** folder contains versions of airFare.html and airFare.php and a function library named **incTravel.php**. This exercise is similar to the last one, except that here you have to first add another function named **getAirline()** to **incTravel.php** that will return an airline based on a destination, as follows:

```
Barcelona    Web Airlines
Cairo        PHP Air
Rome         Air Java
Santiago     SQL Air
Tokyo        Object-Oriented Airlines
```

Add code to airfare.php to include the incTravel.php functions, and call the appropriate functions to obtain the air fare and airlines based on the destination selected by the user. The statements to receive the user's input and generate the output have been provided (be sure to use the same variable names).

6. Your **Chapter 13** folder contains **lookup.html** and **lookup.php**. The code in lookup.html contains a form that allows the user to look up a performer. Look over this code—it does not need to be changed. The code in lookup.php includes a function named **getPerformanceDate()**. You do not need to change this function.

Modify the code in this file so that the program will use the getPerformanceDate() function to look up the date for whichever performer the user submitted.

7. Your **Chapter 13** folder contains **busTravel.html** and **busTravel.php** and also **incTravelAllowances.php**. The busTravel.html and busTravel.php files process trip information submitted by the user in order to determine reimbursement costs. This is identical to the related exercise in Chapter 8 except that now the code in busTravel.php calls functions in the incTravelAllowances.php file.

Your job is to open the incTravelAllowances.php and complete the code for these functions, then ensure that the program works correctly. Note that this is a simple exercise: these functions do not need any parameters and simply return the appropriate value. But this is a common programming task—the advantage of placing these in an include file is that they can be used by any program, and the allowances can be changed as needed in this single file.

Chapter 14

Connecting to a Database — Working with MySQL

Intended Learning Outcomes

After completing this chapter, you should be able to:

- Describe the basic structure of a relational database.
- Identify records and fields in a sample database table.
- Identify key characteristics of a Database Management System (DBMS).
- Explain the general purpose of Structured Query Language (SQL).
- Write PHP code to open and close a connection to a MySQL database.
- Identify the purpose and result of MySQL SELECT queries, that may include FROM, WHERE, and ORDER BY clauses, and relational and logical operators.
- Design, code and submit syntactically correct SELECT queries in PHP applications.
- Write PHP code to receive and process the result sets that are returned by MySQL SELECT queries.
- Identify the purpose and result of MySQL INSERT, UPDATE, and DELETE queries.
- Design, code and submit syntactically correct INSERT, UPDATE, and DELETE queries in PHP applications.
- Apply a basic error-handling template to PHP code that interacts with a MySQL database.
- Use a PHP include statement to maintain MySQL connection values more efficiently and securely.

Introduction

Chapter 6 introduced ways to work with data that must be preserved beyond the life-time of the application (persistent data). That chapter focused on the use of **text files**. We learned how to open and close text files in PHP, how to read lines from text files, and how to write and append data to text files. In subsequent chapters we learned how to process data in text files using selection and loop structures.

We are now ready to look at a more sophisticated approach to data storage and re-trieval, using relational databases. We will learn about the basic structure of **relational databases** and explore the procedures and syntax required to interact with a widely used relational database system called **MySQL**. This chapter does not provide compre-hensive coverage of MySQL but it will provide a solid introduction. You are encouraged to build on what you learn here through further reading, experimentation, and course-work.

What Is a Relational Database?

As you may recall from Chapter 6, a **relational database** allows us to store data in one or more related **tables**. Each table in a database contains **records** of some kind, and each record contains a set of specific data values, stored in **fields**. Relational database tables can be visualized, rather like a spreadsheet, as a set of rows and columns. Each row contains a record, and each column contains a field of the record. For example, Table 14-1 provides a visualization of a simple table of employee records, stored in a table named **personnel**.

As you can see, there are currently 10 records in the personnel table, presented here as 10 rows. Each record contains five fields, presented here as five columns, and each field contains a data value associated with the employee. These fields are named empID (the employee's unique ID), firstName, lastName, jobTitle, and hourlyWage.

The Relational Database Management System (RDBMS)

A single database may include any number of related tables, and a single database sys-tem may contain any number of databases. A **Relational Database Management System (RDBMS)** provides a full range of management tools for storing, managing, and using relational databases. For example, an RDBMS incorporates many useful functions that facilitate common operations such as: creating, modifying and removing databases and tables; adding, modifying, and deleting records; searching (querying) tables; generating reports; assigning user accounts. An RDBMS implements sophisticated security con-trols: each user is assigned a specific level of access to each database, table, and even to

empID	firstName	lastName	jobTitle	hourlyWage
12345	Chris	Smith	sales	12.55
12347	Mary	Peters	sales	12.55
12348	Mike	Jones	manager	24.15
12353	Anne	Humphries	accountant	25.45
12356	Ann	Jones	sales	13.75
12357	John	Jackson	reception	8.75
12358	John	King	cleaner	7.75
12360	Ken	Stewart	accountant	28.55
12361	Joan	Smith	cleaner	8.25
12363	Jesse	Andrews	sales	10.75

Table 14-1: Example of a relational database table (the personnel table in the test database on your server)

individual fields, to ensure appropriate use of the data. Communications with the RDBMS are written using the RDBMS's **Structured Query Language (SQL)**.

The effective design of an RDBMS to deliver databases and tables that are easy to maintain and search, and that do not include any unnecessary duplication of data is the responsibility of a **database administrator**. A database administrator has a range of responsibilities: the overall security, maintenance, backup and performance of the RDBMS; design, creation, and maintenance of databases and tables; creation and removal of user accounts and related access permissions that specify what each user can or cannot do; oversight of procedures and related functions that deliver useful services to programmer and end-users. Database administration is a highly skilled profession that is also in high demand. Most companies and institutions require at least one database administrator to manage their data systems.

Structured Query Language — MySQL

You have already learned how to work with text files. You have used loops to read lines from a file, one line at a time, and to extract the different values on each line based on a delimiter. You have also developed code to process these values, for example to display the contents of the file, search for specific values, perform counts and other calculations, accumulate totals, or determine highest or lowest values. All of this has required you to write your own custom code to meet the requirements of each application. This is because text files are just that, simple files of text.

Unlike text files, the databases and tables in an RDBMS are not directly accessible to your programs. Instead you must submit requests that are written in the Structured Query Language that the RDBMS provides. The RDBMS processes each request (called a **query**) and returns a result. The query language is very powerful and allows you to request a wide range of operations that relieve you from having to write so much custom code. This not only simplifies the work of the application programmer but also helps to ensure efficient data processing, simplified data management, and enhanced data security.

Each RDBMS provides its own version of SQL. We will learn to work with a freeware RDBMS, widely used for Web-based applications, called **MySQL**. We will learn to create, submit, and process MySQL queries in this chapter. A version of MySQL is installed with your Web server and has been pre-configured for your use to include the **test** database with the **personnel** table that was shown in Table 14-1.

Starting Your MySQL Server

Before you can work with the MySQL RDBMS you must start your MySQL server. **Windows** users should click the Start buttons for both **Apache** and **MySQL** in the Control Panel to start both of these servers. Windows users should also remember to stop both servers before exiting the Control Panel. **Macintosh** users running **MAMP** should check the MAMP control panel which indicates whether or not the Apache and MySQL servers are running. Start the MySQL server if is not already running (it probably started by default when you started MAMP).

Be sure your MySQL server is running before you continue. If you have any problems, check the textbook Web site for the latest instructions on configuring and starting your MySQL server.

Configuring MySQL for Use with This Textbook

In order to use MySQL with the textbook examples and exercises, you must first add the required tables and user account. You only need to follow these instructions once, but you can also repeat this step if you ever mess up and need to recreate the original tables. Start your Web server and MySQL server if you have not already done so. Now open a Web browser and type **http://localhost** to connect to the Web server, then click the **samples** folder and run the application named **mysqlSetup.html** (the complete URL is **http://localhost/samples/mysqlSetup.html**). This program will create a MySQL user named **wbip** with a password **wbip123**, and will also create two tables in the test database, named **personnel** and **timesheet** (in case you're wondering, **wbip** is just the acronym for Web-Based Introduction to Programming).

Three Ways to Work with MySQL

Once your MySQL server is running, you have three options to issue queries to the RDBMS: from the **command line**; through a **graphical interface**; or from a custom application that has been developed in a programming language such as PHP.

Since this book is focused on Web-based programming, in this chapter we will learn how to submit and process MySQL queries from custom PHP applications. The textbook Web site includes some guidelines and references that explain how to access MySQL from the command line, or from a Web-based graphical interface named **PHPMyAdmin** (PHPMyAdmin is included in your Web server installation).

Working with PHP and MySQL

You will recall from Chapter 6 that in order to interact with an external device, a PHP program must (1) open a connection; (2) perform the required operations; and (3) close the connection. We learned to interact with text files using the fopen(), fgets(), fputs(), and fclose() functions, and later we also learned to use the feof() function. Now we will learn to use some of PHP's MySQL functions that allow our programs to open a connection to a MySQL server, interact with a database, and close the connection. We will take this step by step until we have all the code needed to develop a working application.

Using PHP to Open and Close a Connection to a MySQL Server

Before we can submit queries to a MySQL database, we must first connect to the MySQL server and select the database that we wish to use. We can do this in PHP by calling the **mysqli_connect**() function, and providing four arguments: the URL of the MySQL RDBMS, a user ID that has been registered with the system, the user password, and the name of the specific database we wish to work with.

The URL for our MySQL system is **"localhost"**. A user named **"wbip"** (short for Web-based Introduction to Programming) has already been created for this system, with all privileges to create, remove, and modify databases, tables, records and fields. The "wbip" user has been assigned the password **"wbip123"**. And we will work with a database named "test".

Here is a PHP statement that uses the mysqli_connect() function to connect to the MySQL server using these arguments:

```
$connect = mysqli_connect('localhost','wbip','wbip123','test');
```

Note that there is nothing special about the variable name **$connect**, this variable can have any name. The mysqli_connect() function returns a reference to the connection which is assigned to $connect. This variable is then used in subsequent instructions when it is necessary to refer to the connection. For example, when we are finished using this database, we call the **mysqli_close**() function, using $connect as an argument:

```
mysqli_close($connect);
```

In our mysqli_connect() example, we provided literal values for the four connection values that were passed to the function as arguments. Actually, it is good practice to first assign these connection values to variables and then use the variables as arguments:

```
$server = "localhost";
$user = "wbip";
$pw = "wbip123";
$db = "test";
$connect = mysqli_connect($server, $user, $pw, $db);
```

The mysqli_connect() function will return **false** if the connection fails for any reason (for example if the user ID or password is not accepted, or if the URL is incorrect, or the database does not exist). This means that we can test our $connect variable to be sure that it doesn't contain the value **false**. Here is a general code template that ensures that we don't try to work with the database if the connection attempt fails:

```
<?php
$server = "localhost";
$user = "wbip";
$pw = "wbip123";
$db = "test";
$connect = mysqli_connect($server, $user, $pw, $db);
if(!$connect)
{
   die("ERROR: Cannot connect to database $db on server
      $server using user name $user (".mysqli_connect_errno().
      ", ".mysqli_connect_error().")");
}
// place the code here to work with the database
mysqli_close($connect); // close the connection

?>
```

The test **if(!$connect)** will be true if $connect contains **false**, and in this case the program will exit with an error message. You will recall from Chapter 13 that the **die**() or **exit**() function can be used to terminate a PHP script with an optional error message. In this case we use this function to terminate the script if a database connection cannot be achieved. The error message includes a call to the PHP **mysqli_connect_errno**() function in order to display the error number that was generated, and also calls the **mysqli_connect_error**() function which provides a description of the error that occurred (for example if the user name or password was incorrect, this function will return an "Access denied" message).

Using the MySQL SELECT Query

Now that we know how to connect to a MySQL database, we can learn how to submit and process queries. But before we can learn how to do this in PHP we must first learn the necessary MySQL syntax.

We are going to work with the **personnel** table that is included in your test database. Take a few minutes to review Table 14-1 which shows this table. The table contains ten employee records, and each record contains data stored in five fields named **empID**, **firstName**, **lastName**, **jobTitle**, and **hourlyWage**.

Remember that we cannot actually access the information in our MySQL tables directly. Instead we must issue commands (queries) using the keywords and syntax of the MySQL language. You have already learned some of the syntax of HTML, CSS, and PHP, you will now learn some MySQL. As you are discovering, a single Web-based application requires the use of a number of different languages, each with its own grammar and syntax.

First we will learn how to use the MySQL **SELECT** query to retrieve values in the fields and records of MySQL tables that match your search criteria. Here is a simple query using SELECT to search for all the fields in all the records in the personnel table:

```
SELECT * FROM personnel
```

That looks straightforward. The asterisk * between SELECT and FROM means "all fields". The word **FROM** allows a clause to be added to the SELECT query that specifies which table in the database should be searched. So this query is asking the RDBMS to send the data stored in **all** fields in all the records in the **personnel** table. The results that are returned by the query are known as the **result set**, so in this case the result set will will contain the values from the empID, firstName, lastName, jobTitle, and hoursWorked fields from each of the 10 records in this table.

What if we don't actually need the data from **all** of the fields in each record? Instead of using the asterisk to indicate **all** fields, we can specify the fields we're interested in. Here's another SELECT query:

```
SELECT lastName FROM personnel
```

This query will search the personnel table but in this case the result set will only contain the last name from each of the 10 records. We can also request data from multiple fields, separated by commas, for example:

```
SELECT firstName, lastName FROM personnel
```

This query will return the first and last names in each of the records. We can request data from any number of fields in this way, or we can use the asterisk to obtain the values from all the fields.

Selecting Specific Records

We have seen how to obtain values from specific **fields** in all of the records in the table, but how can we obtain values from just some of the records? For example, what if we're only interested in the personnel records where the job title is 'accountant'?

If we want our SELECT query to match specific records we must add another clause to our SELECT query, a **WHERE** clause. For example here's how we can find all the accountants in our table:

```
SELECT * FROM personnel WHERE jobTitle='accountant'
```

Now the result set will only contain those records that meet the criteria specified in the WHERE clause, in this case where the job title is 'accountant'. Note the use of single quotes to enclose the data value.

Note that the result set may contain 0 or more records, depending on whether or not any records in the personnel table contain this job title.

What if we wanted to look up information about a single employee? You might consider a search based on the last name field, but more than one employee might have the same last name. However each employee will always have a unique employee ID, so we can use this to search for a specific person, for example:

```
SELECT * FROM personnel WHERE empID='12347'
```

In this case note that the result set might contain 0 or 1 records, depending whether or not there is an employee record with the ID that is requested.

We can still restrict our result set to values from specific fields when we include a WHERE clause. For example, the following query will produce a result set containing the the ID, first name, and last name of all our accountants:

```
SELECT empID, firstName, lastName FROM personnel
  WHERE jobTitle='accountant'
```

Relational Operators in MySQL

Did something surprise you about the last examples? In your PHP code you have been using == to test whether or not two values are equal. But in MySQL queries we use a single = for the same purpose. Each language has its own syntax so we must be careful to apply the correct syntax depending on the language we are using.

Our WHERE clause can use other relational operators. For example to obtain the first and last names of employees who earn less than 15.00 an hour:

```
SELECT firstName, lastName FROM personnel
  WHERE hourlyWage < '15.00'
```

Similarly we can use the operators <=, >, >= and !=.

MySQL provides many other special operators that can be useful in our SELECT queries. For example:

```
SELECT firstName, lastName FROM personnel
  WHERE hourlyWage BETWEEN '10.00' AND '15.00'
```

The **BETWEEN** operator finds values **between** the two values that are provided, so this test will find all records where the hourlyWage is **greater than** 10.00 and **less than** 15.00.

We can also use the **LIKE** operator for **pattern matching**. This operator will match character strings that include **wildcard** (undefined) characters. Here's a search for all employees whose first name begins with 'Ann':

```
SELECT firstName, lastName FROM personnel
  WHERE firstName LIKE 'Ann%'
```

The LIKE operator looks for values that match the search string. If the search string contains the '%' "wildcard" character, this indicates that there may be **0 or more** unknown characters in this position, so 'Ann%' will find 'Ann', 'Anne', 'Annie', Annette', etc.

You can also use the '_' wildcard character to indicate exactly **one** unknown character in a specific location in the string. And you can combine these wildcards in any combination, for example:

```
SELECT firstName, lastName FROM personnel
```

```
WHERE lastName LIKE '%m_t%'
```

This search will find last names that include any number of unknown characters followed by 'm' followed by exactly one unknown character, followed by 't', followed by any number of unknown characters. So this search will find a match with 'Smith' or 'Lamotte' or 'Mitchell' but will not for example find 'Smart' or 'Stormont' (because the single underscore in the search string indicates that only one unknown character can occur between the 'm' and 't').

The Logical Operators AND and OR

We can also use the **AND** and **OR** operators to combine tests, similar to PHP, for example:

```
SELECT firstName, lastName FROM personnel
   WHERE jobTitle='accountant' OR jobTitle='sales'
```

Here we are searching for the first and last names of all employees who are either accountants or sales people. Now consider:

```
SELECT firstName, lastName FROM personnel
   WHERE jobTitle='accountant' AND hourlyWage < '25.00'
```

In this case we are searching for the first and last names of all accountants who earn less than 25.00 an hour.

As always be careful when to use AND and OR in your WHERE clauses. For example if you wrote a query that included:

```
WHERE jobTitle='accountant' AND jobTitle='sales'
```

then **no** records would be returned! That's because no records contain a jobTitle that contains **both** 'accountant' **and** 'sales'. So we need to use OR to find every record with a jobTitle field that contains either 'accountant' OR 'sales'.

Notice that, just as in PHP, you must provide a complete test on either side of these operators. For example, although in English you might say:

```
WHERE jobTitle='accountant' OR 'sales'
```

in MySQL this must be written as follows:

```
WHERE jobTitle='accountant' OR jobTitle='sales'
```

Ordering Your Query Results

Unless you specify otherwise, the results of your SELECT query will be returned in the order of the records in the table. Often we want to order these some other way, for example by last name. We can do this by adding an **ORDER BY** clause to our query. Consider the following:

```
SELECT * FROM personnel ORDER BY lastName
```

This query will produce a listing of all the records in the personnel table, ordered by last name. Similarly:

```
SELECT firstName, lastName FROM personnel
  WHERE jobTitle ='accountant'
  ORDER BY lastName
```

This query will produce a listing of all the accountants ordered by last name. Note that the field that you use to order the list does not need to be included in the list, so if you wanted to obtain a list of first and last names, ordered by job title, you can do that:

```
SELECT firstName, lastName FROM personnel ORDER BY jobTitle
```

And if you want to order by **two** fields, for example first by last name, and then (if a number of employees have the same last name) by first name, we can provide a list of fields in the ORDER BY clause, separated by commas:

```
SELECT firstName, lastName FROM personnel
  ORDER BY lastName, firstName
```

If you want to order by more than one field, note that the result set will be ordered, first by the first field, and then by the second field, and so on.

If you want to the results to be generated in descending order, add the **DESC** key-word after the field name(s), for example:

```
SELECT firstName, lastName FROM personnel
  ORDER BY jobTitle DESC
```

You can also specify **ASC** for ascending order, however since the default ordering is ascending this is often left out.

Viewing Your Query Results

You have just learned how to issue **SELECT** queries modified using the **FROM**, **WHERE** and **ORDER BY** clauses. But how do you submit these queries and how do you receive and view the results in PHP?

MySQL queries are submitted using the **mysqli_query**() function. This function returns the result of the query so you will want to provide a variable to receive this. Here is an example:

```
$result = mysqli_query($connect, "SELECT firstName, lastName
  FROM personnel");
```

The mysqli_query() function sends the SELECT query to the MySQL RDBMS which processes it. The result is returned and assigned to the **$result** variable ($result is a PHP variable and can have any name).

Note that you cannot use mysqli_query() to submit a query unless you have already opened a connection using mysqli_connect(). The first argument to the mysqli_query() function is the variable that references the database connection (in this case a variable named **$connect**, which we used in our previous examples).

The second argument to the mysqli_query() function is the query itself. In this example we included the query directly as the second argument but a better approach is to first store the query in a variable, and then use this variable as the second argument, for example:

```
$userQuery = "SELECT firstName, lastName FROM personnel";
$result = mysqli_query($connect, $userQuery);
```

If your query is successfully processed, the mysqli_query() function returns the result set that contains the requested fields of all the records that met the requirements of your query. Note that the query is successfully processed even if no records actually met the requirements. However if the query **cannot** be processed (for example if there was no connection to the database, or if the query contained a syntax error), then the mysqli_query() function returns **false**.

Since the variable $result contains the result that was returned by the mysqli_query() function, we should now test this variable to be sure that the query was processed successfully. If $result contains the value **false**, a simple option is to exit with an error message that includes a call to the **mysqli_error**() function to explain the error:

```
if (!$result)
{
   die("Could not successfully run query ($userQuery) from
      $db: " . mysqli_error($connect) );
}
```

The mysqli_error() function will return a MySQL error message associated with the error that occurred. Note that this function requires the $connect variable as a parameter.

What if the query was successful but no records met the requirements? We might want to print a message to report this to the user. One way to do this is by obtaining a count of the number of records that were returned by the query and testing to see if this count is 0. We can do this using the **mysqli_num_rows**() function, for example:

```
if (mysqli_num_rows($result) == 0)
{
   print("No records were found with query $userQuery");
}
else
{
   // process the result set
}
```

If our query did not generate any errors, and did not generate a result set with 0 records, we can process $result. Since the result set will usually contain one or more records, we usually use a loop that extracts each record from the result set until no more records are found. The records can be extracted in different ways. An efficient approach is to extract each record from $result into an associative array, where each of the array elements contains a value from one of the record fields, and the keys for these elements are the names of these fields. This allows us to work with these values as needed by referring to each value stored in the array using the appropriate field name.

Here's the code to process the results of our "SELECT firstName, lastName FROM personnel" query:

```
print("<h1>LIST OF EMPLOYEES</h1>");
while ($row = mysqli_fetch_assoc($result))
{
   print ("<p>".$row['firstName']." ".$row['lastName']."</p>");
}
```

The **mysqli_fetch_assoc()** function extracts the next record from $result into an associative array or returns **false** if there are no more records to extract. So each time the loop repeats, the loop heading is designed to extract the next record from the result set as an associative array into **$row**. The loop continues to do this until **the mysqli_fetch_assoc()** array returns **false**, indicating there are no more records.

Inside the loop we can provide whatever code you need to process each record according to your application requirements. In this case, we just want to display the results. Since $row contains an associative array with the values of the record indexed by the field names, we can reference, for example, the value of the firstName field using $row['firstName']. Each time the loop repeats the first and last names of the next record that was returned by the query will be processed.

Note that the query in this example is "SELECT firstName, lastName FROM personnel". That means the result set will **only** contain the firstName and lastName values from each of the records that were matched by the SELECT query. So your query must request all the fields that your program needs to work with. For example what if you need to print the empID, firstName and lastName values from the result set:

```
print ("<p>".$row['empID'].": ".
    $row['firstName']." ".$row['lastName']."</p>");
```

Now your query must request these three fields:

```
"SELECT empID, firstName, lastName FROM personnel"
```

Using an HTML Table to Display the Query Results

In this example we listed the names using HTML paragraph tags. It would of course be more elegant to display these in an HTML table:

```
print("<h1>LIST OF EMPLOYEES</h1>");
print("<table border = \"1\">");
print("<tr><th>First Name</th><th>Last Name</th></tr>");

while ($row = mysqli_fetch_assoc($result))
{
  print ("<tr><td>".$row['firstName'].
    "</td><td>".$row['lastName']."</td></tr>");
}

print("</table");
```

Putting It All Together

We have walked through the code to connect to a MySQL database, submit a query, and receive and process the query results. Figure 14.1 shows the complete code for this application.

```php
<?php
$server = "localhost";
$user = "wbip";
$pw = "wbip123";
$db = "test";
$connect = mysqli_connect($server, $user, $pw, $db);

if(!$connect)
{
  die("ERROR: Cannot connect to database $db on server
    $server using user name $user (".mysqli_connect_errno().
    ", ".mysqli_connect_error().")");
}

$userQuery = "SELECT firstName, lastName FROM personnel";
$result = mysqli_query($connect, $userQuery);

if (!$result)
{
  die("Could not successfully run query ($userQuery) from
    $db: ". mysqli_error($connect) );
}

if (mysqli_num_rows($result) == 0)
{
  print("No records found with query $userQuery");
}
else
{
  print("<h1>LIST OF EMPLOYEES</h1>");
  print("<table border = \"1\">");
  print("<tr><th>First Name</th><th>Last Name</th></tr>");
  while ($row = mysqli_fetch_assoc($result))
  {
    print ("<tr><td>".$row['firstName'].
      "</td><td>".$row['lastName']."</td></tr>");
  }
  print("</table");
}
```

```
mysqli_close($connect); // close the connection

?>
```

Figure 14.1 Code for mysql1.php

Run this program to see that it works. Now run the **mysql2.php** example which contains the "SELECT * FROM personnel" query. Note that this query returns **ALL** records and **ALL** fields from each record. If you look at the code for mysql2.php, you will see just two changes from mysql1.php. First, of course, the query itself has been changed. In addition the print statements that display the table heading and table rows have also been changed. That's because this query will return values from all five fields for each record and not just the firstName and lastName fields:

```
print("<tr><th>EMP ID</th><th>First Name</th>
    <th>Last Name</th><th>Job Title</th>
    <th>Hourly Wage</th></tr>");
while ($row = mysqli_fetch_assoc($result))
{
    print("<tr><td>".$row['empID']."</td><td>"
        .$row['firstName']."</td><td>"
        .$row['lastName']."</td><td>"
        .$row['jobTitle']."</td><td>"
        .numberformat($row['hourlyWage'], 2).
        "</td></tr>");
}
```

Now take some time to try some of the other SELECT queries that were described in this chapter. To do this, open **mysql3.php** in your text editor. This file contains the same code as mysql2.php. Modify mysql3.php as needed to try different queries and remember to modify your table each time so that only the fields included in the query are displayed. This will help you become comfortable with the process of coding MySQL queries.

Using Input from an HTML Form to Construct a Query

Instead of writing values directly into our query we can construct the query with data that has been previously assigned to variables, for example data that has been submitted from an HTML form. The form in **mysql4.html** asks the user for a last name to search for, and **mysql4.php** is coded to receive the user input into a variable named **$searchName** which is then used in the MySQL SELECT query:

```
$searchName = $_POST['searchName'];
$userQuery = "SELECT * FROM personnel
```

```
  WHERE lastName='$searchName'";
```

This query will return all fields of all records where the lastName field in the record contains the same name as the search name that the user requested.

Processing Queries with a Single Result

As we have seen, some queries will produce just one result. For example since each employee has a unique employee ID, we could look up the job title and hourly wage of a particular employee by his or her ID. This example assumes that the user has submitted an ID from an HTML form:

```
$searchID = $_POST['searchID'];
$userQuery = "SELECT jobTitle, hourlyWage FROM personnel
  WHERE empId='$searchID'";
```

Since we know that the query will not return more than one record, we can extract this from the result set without using a WHILE loop:

```
$row = mysqli_fetch_assoc($result);
print("<p>ID: ".$searchID."<br />
    Job title: ".$row['jobTitle']."<br />
    HourlyWage: $".number_format($row['hourlyWage'], 2).
    "</p>");
```

This example is demonstrated in **mysql5.html** and **mysql5.php**.

Performing Calculations with the Result Set

Note that, once we have extracted our values from the result set into an associative array, we can use the array values in calculations just like values stored in any other variable. For example if the wages of all cleaners are based on a 35 hour work week, we can construct a query to obtain the first, names, last names, and hourly wage of all cleaners:

```
$userQuery = "SELECT firstName, lastName, hourlyWage
  FROM personnel
  WHERE jobTitle='cleaner'";
```

Then our WHILE loop can loop through the result set to calculate and display the weekly pay for each cleaner:

```
print("<h1>PAY CHECKS</h1>");
while ($row = mysqli_fetch_assoc($result))
{
    $weeklyPay = $row['hourlyWage'] * 35;
    print ("<p>PAY TO: ".$row['firstName'].
      " ".$row['lastName']." THE SUM OF $".
      number_format($weeklyPay,2)."</p>");
}
```

The complete code for this example is provided in **mysql6.php**.

Performing Aggregate Operations on MySQL Queries

We have mentioned that an RDBMS provides many useful functions that reduce the need for custom programming. As an example, MySQL provides a number of **aggregation functions**, for example to find the **count**, **sum**, **average**, **minimum**, or **maximum** of the values in a specified field based on the records that meet the query criteria. No need for you to write your own code to process the records and calculate these values!

These MySQL functions are named COUNT(), SUM(), AVG(), MIN(), and MAX() and should not be confused with PHP functions. MySQL functions are used in your SELECT queries. For example, here is a query to find the average hourly wage of all employees in the personnel table:

```
$userQuery = "SELECT AVG(hourlyWage) FROM personnel";
```

If we use the mysqli_fetch_assoc() function to obtain the result set, we can obtain the result returned by the AVG function in this example by referring to **$row['AVG(hourlyWage)']**, for example:

```
$row = mysqli_fetch_assoc($result);
print("<p>Average hourly wage:
  $".number_format($row['AVG(hourlyWage)'], 2)."</p>");
```

This example is provided in **mysql7.php**.

What if we wanted to know the average hourly wage of our sales staff? We simply restrict our query as follows:

```
$userQuery = "SELECT AVG(hourlyWage) FROM personnel
  WHERE jobTitle='sales'";
```

Similarly we can find the **highest** wage paid to accountants:

```
$userQuery = "SELECT MAX(hourlyWage) FROM personnel
   WHERE jobTitle='accountant'";
```

Note that we must now refer to MAX(hourlyWage) in our print statement:

```
print("<p>Highest wage for accountants:
   $".number_format($row[MAX(hourlyWage)'], 2)."</p>");
```

Or we can count the number of cleaners:

```
$userQuery = "COUNT(empID) FROM personnel
   WHERE jobTitle='cleaner'";
```

In this case the print statement becomes:

```
print("<p>Number of cleaners: ".$row['COUNT(empID)']."</p>");
```

You are invited to play around with mysql7.php to try these and other queries that perform aggregate operations on the result set.

The aggregation functions are much more powerful than the examples shown here and can also be used to generate results by sub-groups of the result set. This is beyond the scope of this textbook, but you can research these functions to learn more of their capabilities.

Performing JOIN Operations on Multiple Tables

So far our SELECT queries have all been performed on a **single** table, the **personnel** table. An important characteristic of an RDBMS is the ability to relate records in **multiple tables**, based on some kind of relationship between the tables. This allows us to submit queries that will produce a result set that includes values from fields taken from more than one table. To demonstrate, your **test** database includes a second table named **timesheet**. Table 14-2 provides a visualization of the timesheet table, which provides a sample weekly employee **timesheet**:

Like personnel, the timesheet table currently contains 10 records, one for each employee. Each record consists of just two fields: the employee's unique ID, and the hours that the employee worked this week.

Notice that the personnel and timesheet table both include an **empID** field. This allows us to **relate** the two tables based on the employee's ID. For example we can associate the hours worked by an employee record in the timesheet table with the same em-

empID	hoursWorked
12345	30
12347	35
12348	40
12353	35
12356	20
12357	40
12358	32
12360	20
12361	32
12363	35

Table 14-2: Example of a relational database table (the timesheet table in the test database)

ployee's firstName, lastName, and hourlyWage in the personnel table by looking for records with the same empID in each table. Here is an example of this query:

```
$userQuery = "SELECT personnel.firstName, personnel.lastName,
    personnel.hourlyWage, timesheet.hoursWorked
    FROM personnel, timesheet
    WHERE personnel.empID = timesheet.empID";
```

Each field name that is used in the **SELECT** statement is now preceded by the appropriate table name, to indicate which table contains the required field. A period is used to separate the table name and the field name, for example **personnel.firstName**. The **FROM** clause lists **both** tables, separated by commas. The **WHERE** clause indicates that the results set should only include the firstName, lastName, hourlyWage and hoursWorked of an employee where a record in the timesheet table matches the empID of a record in the personnel table.

Since the result set of this query contains each employee's first name, last name and hourly wage from the personnel table and the hours worked from the timesheet table, we can use this to calculate the weekly pay checks:

```
print("<h1>PAY CHECKS</h1>");
while ($row = mysqli_fetch_assoc($result))
{
   $weeklyPay = $row['hourlyWage'] * $row['hoursWorked'];
   print ("<p>PAY TO: ".$row['firstName']." ".
   $row['lastName']." THE SUM OF $".
   number_format($weeklyPay,2)."</p>");
}
```

The complete code for this example is provided in **mysql8.php**.

This is intended as an introductory example of a MySQL **JOIN** operation, where values from multiple tables are obtained by relating the tables in some way. JOIN operations can become very complex and you will want to conduct additional research or take a database course if you are planning to apply these operations in a production application.

Using INSERT to Add Records to a Table

So far we have looked at the use of the MySQL SELECT query to search and retrieve records from an existing MySQL table. What if we want to **add** a record to our table?

To add records to a table we must use the MySQL **INSERT** query. Here's a query that will add a new record to our personnel table:

```
$userQuery = "INSERT INTO personnel
   (empID, firstName, lastName, jobTitle, hourlyWage)
   VALUES ('23456', 'James', 'Joyce', 'sales', '10.75') ";
```

The INSERT command allows you to specify a list of the fields in the new record that are to receive values, followed by a VALUES clause which lists the values themselves. The values are stored in the fields in the order that the fields are listed. You can omit the list of fields, for example:

```
$userQuery = "INSERT INTO personnel VALUES
   ('23456', 'James', 'Joyce','sales', '10.75')";
```

In this case the values are always added in the same order that the fields are listed in the table.

Here's another example where an HTML form has been used to receive the values for the new record. In this case the variables that contain these values are used to construct the INSERT query:

```
$empID = $_POST['empID'];
$firstName = $_POST['firstName'];
$lastName = $_POST['lastName'];
$jobTitle = $_POST['jobTitle'];
$hourlyWage = $_POST['hourlyWage'];
$userQuery = "INSERT INTO personnel (empID, firstName,
   lastName, jobTitle, hourlyWage) VALUES ($empID, $firstName,
   $lastName, $jobTitle $hourlyWage)";
```

The **mysql9.html** and **mysql9.php** files in your samples folder include the complete code for this example. Note that this code does not need statements to process the result set since this is not a SELECT query.

Using UPDATE to Modify a Record

We can also modify existing records using the MySQL **UPDATE** query. For example, here's a query to modify Chris Smith's job title from 'sales' to 'manager':

```
$userQuery = "UPDATE personnel SET jobTitle='manager'
   WHERE empID='12345'";
```

Here we use a **WHERE** clause to specify which record is to be updated. Note that we use the employee's empID rather than first and last names in the WHERE clause. That's because the empID uniquely identifies each employee, whereas it's possible that two or more employees might have the same first and last names. We want to make sure that the right Chris Smith is promoted to manager!

The **SET** clause is used to update the **jobTitle** field of this record to 'manager'. We can update multiple fields in this record by including a **list** of updates in the SET clause, separated by commas. For example to change Chris Smith's job title to 'manager' and **also** update his or her hourly wage to '20.00':

```
$userQuery = "UPDATE personnel SET jobTitle='manager',
   hourlyWage='20.00' WHERE empID='12345'";
```

We can also code our WHERE clause to update **multiple** records. For example here's a query that updates the hourly wage of **all** employees who earn less than 8.00:

```
$userQuery = "UPDATE personnel SET hourlyWage='8.00'
   WHERE hourlyWage < '8.00'";
```

We can add an AND operator to this query if we only want to increase the hourly wage of **cleaners** who earn less than 8.00:

```
$userQuery = "UPDATE personnel SET hourlyWage='8.00'
   WHERE jobTitle='cleaner' AND hourlyWage < '8.00'";
```

This example is provided in **mysql10.php**. Once again, note that this code does not need statements to process the result set since this is not a SELECT query.

Removing a Record

We can **delete** records from a table using the MySQL **DELETE** query. Here's a query to delete the record of employee with the ID '12345':

```
$userQuery = "DELETE FROM personnel WHERE empID='12345'";
```

And here's a DELETE query that uses the WHERE clause to delete **all** employees with the job title of 'cleaner':

```
$userQuery = "DELETE FROM personnel
   WHERE jobTitle='cleaner'";
```

Be very careful when using the DELETE query! After all, you do not want to delete records that you may need at a later date. For example we might need to look up a former employee for some reason. It is often preferable to make records 'inactive' rather than deleting them entirely. We can achieve this by adding some kind of 'status' field to the table structure. This field can store a value that indicates whether or not each record is currently active. We can then include an additional test in the WHERE clause of all our SELECT queries if we only want to search for active records. Here are two examples that assume that the personnel records contain a field named **status**, and that this field contains the value 'active' or 'inactive':

```
SELECT * FROM personnel WHERE status='active'
SELECT empID, firstName, lastName FROM personnel
   WHERE status='inactive' AND jobTitle='accountant'
```

Of course these queries could only be used if the personnel table includes the status field.

Storing MySQL Connection Data in an Include File

So far our examples have included the MySQL connection data (hostname, user ID, user password, and database name) directly in our PHP application code. This means that we would have to update **every** application whenever the connection data changes, for example if the password is changed, or the database is moved to a different host. It also means that this very sensitive data is visible to anyone viewing the application code, for example on a printed copy.

A simple solution is to move the statements that assign the four connection values to variables to a separate file. Your samples folder contains a file named **incConnect-MySQL.php** that contains the following lines:

```php
<?php
$server = "localhost";
$user = "wbip";
$pw = "wbip123";
$db = "test";
?>
```

The **mysql11.php** file in your samples folder contains the same code as mysql1.php except that these four statements have been removed and replaced by a PHP **include** statement:

```php
include("incConnectMySQL.php");
```

This ensures that the four statements will be added to the code when the file is actually processed. This is much better practice: if any of the connection data changes we only have to update the incConnectMySQL.php file and all the applications that include this file will use the new connection values. This also improves security since the values are maintained in a separate file.

Creating, Dropping, and Altering Databases and Tables

In a real-world database environment, the accounts and privileges provided to programmers usually restrict them to work with specific databases and tables, and to only use queries such as SELECT, UPDATE and INSERT. Usually only the database administrator has full privileges, that will include the ability to **CREATE**, **DROP** (remove), or **ALTER** the structure of databases and tables, or to add , remove, or modify user accounts and privileges. Programmers may sometimes function as their own database administrators, for example when working on small scale applications or Web sites.

The design and management of database systems is an extremely serious business, and great care must always be taken to prevent inappropriate use, security breaches, inefficient processing, or data corruption. This topic is beyond the scope of this textbook, but the textbook Web site includes some material to introduce the MySQL commands to create, drop, and alter databases and tables.

Summary

A **relational database** is composed of 1 or more related tables of data. Each table is composed of columns (fields) and rows (records).

A **Relational Database Management System (RDBMS)** provides a full range of management tools for storing, managing, and using relational databases.

Communications with the RDBMS are written using the RDBMS's **Structured Query Language (SQL)**. MySQL is a widely used, SQL-based RDBMS.

The effective design and management of an RDBMS is the responsibility of a **database administrator**.

There are three ways to interact with the MYSQL RDBMS: from the **command line**; through a **graphical interface** such as **PHPMyAdmin**; or from a **custom application** that has been developed in a programming language such as PHP.

The PHP **mysqli_connect()** and **mysqli_close()** functions are used to open and close connections to a MySQL server and database.

The MySQL **SELECT** query is used to retrieve values in the fields and records of MySQL tables that match specified search criteria. The values that are returned by a SELECT query are referred to as the **result** set.

A SELECT query can be defined to just return values from specific fields from each of the records that match the query.

A SELECT query can include a **WHERE** clause to match specific records.

A WHERE clause can include the use of relational operators, as well as logical operators such as **AND** and **OR**. MySQL provides a number of other operators such as **BETWEEN .. AND**, and **LIKE** (used for pattern-matching).

The LIKE operator can include the **wildcard** characters % (to indicate 0 or more characters in this position) and _ (exactly one character in this position).

A SELECT query can include an **ORDER BY** clause to define the ordering of the result set. The records returned by the result set are ordered by a specific field. If you want to order by more than one field, the result set will be ordered, first by the first field, and then by the second field, and so on.

The ORDER BY clause can include the **ASC** or **DESC** keyword after the field name(s) to indicate the result set should be ordered in ascending or descending order (the default as ascending).

PHP variables can be used in MySQL queries so, for example, input from a HTML form can be included in the construction of a query.

The PHP **mysqli_query**() function is used to submit MySQL queries. If the query cannot be submitted successfully this function returns **false**, otherwise it returns the query result.

The PHP **mysqli_error**() function will return a MySQL error message associated with a query error. This function is often used to inform the user of a problem when a call to the mysqli_query() function returns **false**.

The PHP **mysqli_num_rows**() function returns the number of records in the result set of a MySQL SELECT query.

The PHP **mysqli_fetch_assoc**() function is used to extract the next record from the result set of a MySQL SELECT query into an associative array or returns false if there are no more records to extract. This function is often used to control a WHILE loop when the results might contain 0 or more records. In that case the next record is extracted from the result set into an associative array each time the loop repeats until all the records in the result set have been processed.

The values that are returned in the result set of a MySQL SELECT query can be used in calculations. MySQL also provides a large number of functions to perform calculations that are returned as part of the result set. This removes the need for special coding by the applications. Examples of MySQL functions are **SUM**(), **AVG**(), **COUNT**(), **MAX**(), and **MIN**().

MySQL **JOIN** operations are used to relate data between multiple tables.

The MySQL **INSERT** query is used to add records to a MySQL table. The INSERT command allows you to specify a list of the fields in the new record that are to receive values, followed by a VALUES clause which lists the values themselves.

The MySQL **UPDATE** query is used to modify existing records in a MySQL table. The WHERE clause is used to match the record(s) that are to updated. The SET clause specifies the fields that are to be modified and the new values that are to be assigned.

The MySQL **DELETE** query is used to remove existing records in a MySQL table. The WHERE clause is used to match the record(s) that are to deleted.

It is a best practice to maintain your MySQL connection values in a separate file, and then **include** this file in your application code. This reduces duplication and improves security.

Usually only the database administrator has full privileges to manage an RDBMS. These privileges include the ability to **CREATE**, **DROP** (remove), or **ALTER** the structure of databases and tables, or to add , remove, or modify user accounts. Programmers may sometimes function as their own database administrators, for example when working on small scale applications or Web sites.

Chapter 14 Review Questions

1. Which is correct?
    a. A database contains tables and a table contains records and fields
    b. A table contains databases and a database contains records and fields
    c. A record contains tables and a table contains databases and fields
    d. A database contains records and a record contains tables and fields

2. In a visual representation of a table, a record is shown as a
    a. Field
    b. Column
    c. Row
    d. Database

3. Which of the following best describes a RDBMS?
    a. A test database that is included with MySQL
    b. A database used to store personnel data
    c. A language used to submit queries
    d. A system to store, manage and use relational databases

4. Which of the following best describes SQL?
    a. A test database that is included with MySQL
    b. A database used to store personnel data
    c. A language used to submit queries to an RDBMS
    d. A system to store, manage and use relational databases

5. Which of the following is true?
    a. MySQL is a version of SQL
    b. SQL is a version of MySQL

6. What value will $connect have after the following statement is executed if the connection fails?

```
$connect=mysqli($host, 'wbip', 'wbip123', 'test');
```

    a. false
    b. true
    c. no value
    d. "Connection could not be completed"

7. Look at the following statement. What is the user password?

```
$connect=mysqli('localhost', 'this', 'that', 'other');
```

    a. localhost
    b. this
    c. that
    d. other

8. Which MySQL command is used to search a table for specific fields and records?
    a. SEARCH
    b. QUERY
    c. SELECT
    d. UPDATE

9. Which fields will have values included in the result set of this query?

```
SELECT empID, jobTitle FROM personnel
  WHERE hourlyWage < 10.00 ORDER BY lastName
```

    a. empID and jobTitle
    b. hourlyWage only
    c. astName only
    d. empID, jobTitle, hourlyWage, and lastName

10. What is wrong with this query?

```
SELECT title, hourlyWage FROM personnel
  WHERE lastName=='Jones'
```

    a. You must always include an ORDER BY clause in a SELECT statement
    b. WHERE lastName=='Jones' should be IF(lastName=='Jones')
    c. WHERE lastName=='Jones' should be WHILE(lastName=='Jones')
    d. WHERE lastName=='Jones' should be WHERE lastName='Jones'

11. Which query will return the title and hourly wage of all employees whose hourly wage is at least 10.00 but not more than 20.00?
    a. SELECT title, hourlyWage FROM personnel
        WHERE hourlyWage >= 10.00 AND <= 20.00
    b. SELECT title, hourlyWage FROM personnel
        WHERE hourlyWage >= 10.00 AND hourlyWage <= 20.00
    c. SELECT title, hourlyWage FROM personnel
        WHERE hourlyWage BETWEEN 10.00 AND 20.00
    d. SELECT title, hourlyWage FROM personnel
        WHERE hourlyWage BETWEEN 10.00 AND <= 20.00

12. Which query will return the title and hourly wage of all employees whose hourly wage is greater than 10.00 and less than 20.00?
    a. SELECT title, hourlyWage FROM personnel
        WHERE hourlyWage > 10.00 AND < 20.00
    b. SELECT title, hourlyWage FROM personnel
        WHERE hourlyWage >= 10.00 AND hourlyWage <= 20.00
    c. SELECT title, hourlyWage FROM personnel
        WHERE hourlyWage BETWEEN 10.00 AND 20.00
    d. SELECT title, hourlyWage FROM personnel
        WHERE hourlyWage BETWEEN 10.00 AND < 20.00

13. Which of the last names will be matched by the WHERE clause in the following query?

```
SELECT empID from personnel WHERE lastName LIKE 'Jo%s'
```

    a. Jons will be matched but Johns and Johnson will not be matched
    b. Jons and Johns will be matched but Johnson will not be matched
    c. Jons, Johns and Johnson will all be matched
    d. None of these three last names will be matched

14. Which of the last names will be matched by the WHERE clause in the following query?

```
SELECT empID from personnel WHERE lastName LIKE 'Jo_s'
```

    a. 'Jons' will be matched but 'Johns' and 'Johnson' will not be matched
    b. 'Jons' and 'Johns' will be matched but 'Johnson' will not be matched
    c. 'Jons', 'Johns' and 'Johnson' will all be matched
    d. None of these three last names will be matched

15. Assume that the personnel table contains three records of employees with these first and last names:

```
Peter Jones
Mary Jones
Robert Johnson
```

How would these three records be ordered in the result set of the following query?

```
SELECT firstName, lastName from personnel
  ORDER BY lastName, firstName
```

    a. Mary Jones, then Peter Jones, then Robert Johnson
    b. Mary Jones, then Robert Johnson, then Peter Jones
    c. Peter Jones, then Mary Jones, then Robert Johnson
    d. Robert Johnson, then Mary Jones, then Peter Jones

16. What is the correct MySQL command to add a new record to a table?
     a. ALTER
     b. UPDATE
     c. ADD
     d. INSERT

17. What is the correct MySQL command to modify the values stored in a record?
     a. ALTER
     b. UPDATE
     c. ADD
     d. INSERT

18. Assume an application uses the following query:

```
$userQuery = "SELECT jobTitle FROM personnel
              WHERE hourlyWage > 15.00";
$result = mysqli_query($connect, $userQuery);
```

and then uses the following heading for the loop that will process the result set:

```
while($row = mysqli_fetch_assoc($result))
```

Which statement below should appear inside the loop to process the values in the result set?
     a. print ("<p>$jobTitle</p>");
     b. print ("<p>$row['jobTitle']</p>");
     c. print ("<p>$result['jobTitle']</p>");
     d. print ("<p>$userQuery['jobTitle']</p>");

19. Which statement will generate the lowest hourly wage in the personnel table?
     a. SELECT MIN(hourlyWage) FROM personnel
     b. SELECT * FROM personnel WHERE MIN(hourlyWage)
     c. SELECT hourlyWage FROM personnel WHERE hourlyWage < lowest
     d. SELECT hourlyWage FROM personnel ORDER BY hourlyWage DESC

20. What value will be stored in the lastName field of this record after this query is executed? (be careful)

```
INSERT INTO personnel (empID, lastName, firstName, jobTitle,
hourlyWage) VALUES (67890, 'Michael', 'Peter', 'cleaner',
12.50)
```

     a. 67890
     b. Michael
     c. Peter
     d. cleaner
     e. 12.50

Chapter 14 Code Exercises

Your Chapter 14 code exercises can be found in your Chapter14 folder. This folder is included in your customized XAMPP installation at the following location:

xampplite\htdocs\WebTech\coursework\Chapter14

Type your name and the date in the **Author** and **Date** sections of each file as you work on each exercise.

Debugging Exercises

Your Chapter14 folder should contain a number of "FixIt" files. Each of these files contains PHP code that has an error of some kind. Open the file in a text editor and read the comment section in the file to see what to do to fix them. You will need to run each program in order to see the errors, and to test that your fixes have worked correctly. For example to run **fixIt1.php**, first run the Web server, then use the URL:

http://localhost/WebTech/coursework/Chapter14/fixIt1.php

Code Modification Exercises

Your Chapter14 folder contains a number of "Modify" files. These contain HTML and PHP code that needs to be modified to meet a requirement. The requirements are included in the comment section of each file. Modify the algorithms as specified, being careful to make changes to the .html and .php files as directed.

Code Completion Exercises

1. Complete the code in **staffReport1.php** so that the program provides a table that shows the empID and job title of all employees.

2. Complete the code in **staffReport2.php** so that the program provides a table that shows the empID, first name, last name, job title and hourly wage of all managers and accountants. Use the * to indicate all fields in your SELECT statement.

3. Complete the code in **staffReport3.php** so that the program provides a table that shows the first names, last names and job titles of managers and sales people ordered by job title then last name.

4. Complete the code in **cleaners.php** so that the program displays the lowest hourly wage of the cleaners. HINT: use a MySQL function to accomplish this.

5. The **jobTitles1.html** file includes a form that asks the user for an employee ID. Complete the code in **jobTitles1.php** so that this program displays the employee's ID, job title and hourly wage.

6. The **jobTitles2.html** file includes a form that asks the user for a job title. Complete the code in **jobTitles2.php** so that this program displays the first and last names of all employees with this job title.

7. Complete the code in **raises.php** so that the program finds the empID for all employees who earn less than 10.00, and displays the message "Employee XXX needs a raise!", for each of these employees, where XXX is the empID of the employee.

8. Anne Humphries needs to change her last name and she has also received a promotion! Complete the code in **nameChange.php** so that the last name of the employee with ID 12353 is changed to 'Jackson' and the job title is changed to 'manager'. You can run **nameChangeTest.php** to check that the record was changed correctly.

9. The **wageReport.html** file includes a form that asks the user for an hourly wage and a job title. Complete the code in **wageReport.php** to find the empID of all employees with this job title who earn this hourly wage or higher. Note that in some cases this will return 0 records.

10. The **addSalesPerson.html** file includes a form for entering a record for a new sales person. The form asks the user for the new sales person's empID, first name, and last name. Complete the code in **addSalesPerson.php** so that this program adds this employee to the personnel table with the job title 'sales' and an hourly wage of 8.25. You can run the **employees.php** program (provided) to confirm that the new employee was added to the table. NOTE: If you make a mistake and need to delete a record, you can use the **deleteEmployee.php** file (if you do this, you will first need to modify the value assigned to the $empID variable in deleteEmployee.php in order to delete the correct record).

Chapter 15

Where to Go from Here . . .

Intended Learning Outcomes

After completing this chapter, you should be able to:

- Distinguish between customized approaches taken in this book and required PHP syntax and procedures.
- Recognize importance differences between PHP and other languages regarding variable names, variable declarations, and data types.
- Summarize the importance and role of XML.
- Describe the role of IDE's and modeling languages
- Explain the difference between client/server and server/server applications.
- List some characteristics of GUI programmers and interface designers.
- Describe the relationship between SQL and relational database systems.

Introduction

Congratulations! By now you should have a good grasp of basic program logic and design. This last chapter is designed to prepare you for next steps, whether you plan to develop your HTML and PHP skills, move on to other programming languages, or explore related technologies and career options.

Moving Forward with PHP and HTML

The primary challenge of this book has been to keep the focus on the fundamentals of program logic and design, while at the same time providing the valuable practical experience that comes with hands-on coding. In order to balance these goals in a manner suitable for beginning programmers, a number of decisions were made concerning both the approach and content of the textbook. The sample applications were all designed more or less the same way, using combinations of .html files containing simple HTML forms and .php files containing form-processing PHP code, along with small .txt files containing data. In some cases, more efficient procedures were neglected to avoid introducing too much syntactical detail or too many procedures that might distract from key learning goals and fundamental concepts.

The danger of this approach is that the reader might confuse the author's strategic design decisions with actual requirements of the HTML and PHP languages. With this in mind, here are some specific practices that were followed in this textbook for the sake of simplicity and consistency, but that are **not** required procedures and do **not** necessarily represent best practices when developing PHP applications.

Use PHP print or echo?

The textbook uses the PHP **print** statement throughout to generate HTML output. The PHP echo statement can be used just as well for this purpose. The two are almost identical in operation, and most programmers simply choose one over the other. For example:

```
print("Hello, $firstName, how are you today?");
```

could be written:

```
echo "Hello, $firstName, how are you today?";
```

Users of the **echo** statement usually leave out the opening and closing parentheses since parentheses do not work when concatenation is included in an echo statement. It should be noted that parentheses are also not required when using the print statement—we have followed this convention so that our examples are closer to the syntax of output statements in other languages.

Multiple PHP Sections

The book examples almost all follow a format where an initial HTML section is followed by a PHP section which is in turn followed by a final HTML section. In fact, a PHP file can include any combination of HTML and PHP sections in any order. A PHP file may consist **entirely** of PHP code, and may even consist **entirely** of HTML code (no PHP code at all).

Usually a working program contains many small sections of PHP code interspersed with HTML code. This minimizes the need for the escape characters needed to display quotes and other special characters in HTML code that is produced by PHP print or echo statements. The only HTML code that **must** be generated inside PHP sections is code that contains values derived from PHP variables, functions, or expressions.

HTML and PHP File Names

Most of the sample Web applications in the textbook consists of two files, an .html file that contains a submission form, and a .php file of the same name that processes the form form (for example, **wage1.html** and **wage1.php**). The chapter exercises take the same approach. This convention was used to maintain a simple "input/processing/output" model and to more easily identify the names of related files.

It is important to recognize that this pairing of .html and .php files with same name was a design decision and is not in any way a normal requirement for PHP application development. Most real world PHP applications will consist of any number of files with significant sections of code provided by include files (for more about include files, see Chapter 12). There is no requirement that .html and .php files should share the same file name, in fact all of the code files that make up a Web application are usually given .php extensions, each with a unique file name, including files that contain only HTML code.

To go further, the use of two separate files to display and process a form is **not** a best practice for PHP coding. A better approach is to combine the code to display the form and the code to process the form in a single .php file. The program uses an IF..ELSE structure to decide whether to (a) display the form to the user or (b) receive the input that the use has just submitted from the form. The action attribute of the form calls the same file that contains the file. Your **samples** folder includes **addTwoNumbers.html** and **addTwoNumbers.php**. These follow the standard approach taken in this book: providing an HTML form in an HTML file and the code to process the form in a PHP document. You will also find a file named **addTwoImproved.php**, which takes the approach described above. Study the code in this file to see how the form and the form-processing code are combined. This design can be applied to many different purposes.

Program Variables and the $_POST Array

The textbook also followed a convention of creating variables of the same name as the names assigned to HTML form components, whenever the variable was used to receive values from a form, for example: $**hourlyWage** = $_POST['**hourlyWage**'];

There is no requirement that the variable should have the same name as the name used in the form. For example, $**wage** = $_POST['**hourlyWage**']; would be equally acceptable.

Furthermore it is not necessary to assign the value from the $_POST array to a new variable. For example the program could simply use $_POST['**hourlyWage**'] throughout the code rather than assign this value to $**hourlyWage** and then use that variable in subsequent code. Many programmers follow the practice outlined in this book since it often makes the code more readable.

Camelback Notation

The book uses **camelback** notation to name variables (for example $hourly_wage). This is the convention followed by programmers working in most current languages. PHP programmers often use underscores instead of camelback notation when naming variables (for example $hourly_wage). The book also uses camelback notation when naming files. There are no conventions for naming files except that file names should never include spaces.

More about PHP

Once you are comfortable with the basics of PHP, you will want a detailed reference to PHP syntax and functions. There are many good books and online resources available. For a complete PHP reference consult the PHP home page:

> http://www.php.net/

For a very good online PHP tutorial and easy-to-use reference, try:

> http://www.w3schools.com/php/default.asp

PHP provides a very large set of useful standard functions, for many different purposes. For a list of ALL standard PHP functions, see:

> http://www.php.net/quickref.php

The list of PHP functions can be quite overwhelming. **Appendix F** provides a short list of commonly used functions that build on those introduced in this book.

Some useful and important control structures and data structures were omitted from the chapter content to ensure a "one concept at a time" learning process, and avoid the confusion that occurs when beginning programmers are provided with too many alternatives to perform the same function. The most significant omissions are the SWITCH statement, DO..WHILE loop, and multi-dimensional arrays. Appendix G provides an overview of each of these topics.

Additional material may be added after publication. Visit the book Website for the latest version of the appendices, for corrections, and for additional learning materials.

PHP and Other Languages

Much of the syntax of PHP is quite similar to that of other current programming languages, so what you have learned here can be readily applied to languages such as Java or C++. However PHP also contains quite different syntax and approaches. Here are two significant differences that might otherwise surprise you when you learn another language.

Variable Naming Rules

Each language has its own rules for naming variables. PHP uses the $ symbol as the first character of each variable name. This is unusual and, in some situations, permits practices that will not work in most languages. For example, a PHP programmer can include direct references to variables inside character strings, using statements such as: "Your pay is $$pay this week.".

The reference to $pay within the character string is feasible only because the $ symbol indicates that $pay is a variable and not simply the word "pay" that should be displayed as written. Other languages do not use the $ symbol as the first character of variable names and so these languages **require** concatenation when the values stored in variables are to be added to character strings. This is optional in PHP where it is achieved using the period as the concatenation operator, for example **"Your pay is $".$pay." this week.".**

Although concatenation is a standard feature of most languages, the period is not always used as the concatenation operator. Some languages use the + character as the concatenation operator, so the same string in, for example, a Java statement would be written as **"Your pay is " + pay + " this week.".** Note that variables do not begin with a $ character in Java.

Variable Declarations and Data Types

Unlike PHP, most languages require that: (a) variables must be declared before they can be used, and (b) the variable declaration must indicate not only the variable name but also the type of data that the variable will contain.

This requirement has many advantages. Since the variable **name** must be declared **before** use, the compiler or interpreter can catch errors caused by misspelled variables, which is not possible in PHP. The requirement to declare the data **type** for each variable determines: (a) the amount of memory that is to be set aside for the variable; (b) the range and type of values that can be assigned to the variable; and (c) the type of operations that can be performed with the variable. This provides much greater control and programming efficiency, and avoids many errors related to inappropriate use. Languages that exert significant control over variable declarations and data types are referred to as **strongly typed** languages. Java is an example of a strongly typed language.

Basic data types usually fall into four basic categories. **Integer** data types allow storage of whole numbers and permit integer operations (arithmetic operations involving whole numbers that generate an integer result). Integers are also used to store the memory locations of arrays, objects, and other data structures. **Floating point** data types allow storage of numbers with decimal places and permit floating point operations (arithmetic operations involving decimal values that generate a decimal result). The **character** data type allows storage of single characters. The **boolean** data type permits only two values: false and true (sometimes stored as 0 and 1, respectively), and permits boolean operations (comparisons that generate a true or false result).

Different languages will provide additional granularity in the choice of data types. For example the Java language provides eight basic data types (known as **primitive** data types). Four of these data types permit storage of different sizes of integer values and are termed **byte, short, int**, and **long**. Two data types permit storage of different sizes of floating point values (**float** and **double**). The other two primitive types are **char** (to store single characters) and **boolean**.

In addition to these basic types, programming languages support the construction of **complex** data types. Complex data types allow storage of multiple values that can be referenced and processed using a single variable name. Examples of complex data types are character strings (which contain multiple characters), arrays, records, and objects. In a fully object-oriented language such as Java, all complex data types (including character strings and arrays) are treated as objects.

XHTML and XML

This textbook introduces HTML and the use of Cascading Style Sheets (CSS). If you are interested in Web design and development, you will want to develop your expertise in these languages, as well as **Javascript and the Document Object Model (DOM)**, discussed in the next section.

As the Web has developed there has been an increasing awareness of the limitations of HTML. This language evolved to describe the **appearance** of information on a Web page, rather than to describe the **content** of the Web page. As a result, information on the Web is difficult to organize and search. For example, if you wanted to look for an author named "Gold," a Web search would yield many thousands of references to "gold", most of which have no bearing on authors!

With the increased use of style sheets to define the rendering of information, attention has turned to the use of markup tags to **describe**, rather than format, information. For example, what if, instead of using tags such as Gold to format an author's name on a Web page, we used tags such as <authorLastName> Gold </authorLastName> to indicate that the enclosed text is the name of an author? Now we can search the Web for an author named "Gold" by searching for occurrences of this name inside <authorLastName> tags, and that means we will find only authors with that name. We can still apply formatting to this name by simply providing the required styles for this tag in a style sheet specification.

Furthermore, HTML does not allow us to group related data such as author information into a common structure (similar to the records and fields that are intrinsic to database design). For example, what if we could develop code that could process data by referring to the tags that identify each data value? In the case of textbook information, this data might might be identified by tags such <authorFirstName>, <author-LastName>, <bookTitle>, <publisher>, < publicationDate>, etc. Now we are looking at markup tags to **describe** the data and not to **render** the data. The rendering and processing can now be handled by the stylesheet and the program code.

HTML does not permit us to create our own tags, but XML does. In fact XML (eXtensible Markup Language) allows programmers to create define groups of related tags (and attributes) to describe entire groups of related information, such as authors, books, CD's, homes for sale, bank transactions, medical information, e-mail messages, RSS feeds, even IRS forms! These definitions can be standardized as **schemas**, so that similar information can be organized consistently within an organization, or worldwide. For example a standard schema for describing the results of a specific medical test allows doctors and hospitals across the world to more easily share information about a patient or diagnostic approach.

Schemas define unique **XML languages**. When an XML language is accepted as standard, programs and people all over the world are able to exchange information and engage in transactions much more effectively and seamlessly. XHTML is a recent example of an XML language, designed to create an improved standards-based description for HTML documents. XHTML is now being replaced by HTML 5, the latest version of HTML.

Anyone interested in a career in information architecture, Web design, and information retrieval will want to become familiar not only with HTML and CSS, but also with XML and its associated technologies.

Client Side Processing with Javascript and Ajax

This textbook has focused on the use of PHP to handle all of the processing functions required by a Web application. That means that all input validation and other processing tasks must be performed on the server following submissions by the user.

This is not always very efficient. For example a great deal of input validation (for example checking that required fields are completed or checking that form entries that are supposed to numeric actually contain numbers that are in range) could be performed before a form is submitted to the server for processing. This requires the use of a client side application and in most cases that means **Javascript**.

Javascript should not be confused with Java which is a quite separate language. Support for Javascript is already provided by your Web browser and so you can include Javascript code in your HTML code (using the <script> tag). Javascript is used with the Document Object Model (DOM) interface to modify and process elements of a HTML page. In addition to providing significant form validation, Javascript provides a range of functions that allow you to build a more interactive Web interface. Most Web sites make extensive use of Javascript to achieve visually exciting, dynamic, and user-friendly interfaces. Web programmers readily share useful Javascript code snippets, and you can often find existing code that meet your own needs.

Note that Javascript is not an **alternative** to PHP. The two languages are often used together. Javascript is used to minimize the use of server-side processing, and provide a higher quality interface, while PHP manages processes that must be handled on the server, for example access to files and databases and other applications.

Also note that, although the Javascript code **executes** on the client computer, the code is still **delivered** from the server, just like HTML code). So Javascript code is still maintained on the server, which the same benefits of maintenance and ease of modification.

An important new tool for **client-side** components of client/server applications is **Ajax** (Asynchronous JavaScript And XML). Ajax makes it possible to incorporate much greater functionality on the client side, so that more processing can be shared between client and server applications without loss of security. This can result in greater efficiency, faster processing times, and less page-reloading than has been possible with more traditional client/server interactions.

The Importance of OOP

An optional section in Chapter 12 briefly introduced Object Oriented Programming (OOP). Object Oriented Programming is fundamental to a great deal of current application development. Strong relationships exist between OOP, XML, server/server application development, and database programming. If you plan a career as a professional applications programmer you will want to develop the skills that you have developed here by learning a fully object oriented languages such as Java.

IDE's, Modeling Languages and Frameworks

Programmers have access to powerful design tools to develop their applications quickly and easily. Integrated Development Environments (IDE's) are available that simplify and standardize the process of designing interfaces, objects, and application modules quickly and easily. IDE's often include **code generators** that actually produce standard code for modules from design specifications. As a programmer, you will very likely need to learn to use an IDE and other development tools that are provided in your workplace. Familiarity with a specific IDE can be just as much as a requirement for employment as familiarity with a programming language.

Modeling languages are another language-independent design tool that are often used in conjunction with (or as a component of) IDE's. Modeling languages allow programmers to design and develop software specifications and objects in a standard manner that can then be quickly implemented in code. The most widely used modeling language is **Unified Modeling Language** (UML) and you will find it useful to become familiar with UML constructs if you are planning to design applications or reviews the design specifications of other programmers.

Frameworks provide another important tool for application developers. A framework delivers previously developed and tested units of code that can be assembled and modified as needed for a specific application. Frameworks are based on common and well-defined design patterns such as the **Model View Controller** (MVC) pattern that separates the user interface of an application from its processing logic.

Client/Server and Server/Server Programming

Increasingly our software environment is network-based, and this is having a tremendous impact on software design. We have talked quite extensively about **client/server** programming in this book. Programmers must also develop and maintain **server/server** applications. Server/server applications are entirely server-based and focus on automated transactions that never interact with people. These transactions are often referred to as Business-To-Business (B2B) transactions, since they often serve to conduct transactions between businesses or business units.

Consider a program running on one company's server that must order parts from a program running on the server of another company that delivers these parts. These two programs must be able to follow an agreed upon protocol to open a connection and identify one another (**handshake**), exchange information, confirm a successful (or unsuccessful) transaction, and close the connection. Both programs must also communicate with other programs or databases to check and update inventories, initiate billing processes, etc. Millions of B2B transactions occur every day.

Clearly information standards are a vital aspect of server/server transactions. In order to exchange, for example a request for a parts order, two programs must be able to agree on the organization and structure of the request. That means that a standard data description is required, and you would be quite correct to be thinking "that sounds like a job for XML". Server/server transactions often share data derived from predefined XML languages, and **validated** against the schema for that language to ensure correctness. This common language permits a standard interface between programs that may be communicating with one another from different organizations across the world.

Server-side **scripting languages** such as PHP are used to develop server-based applications. Other important languages that are used extensively for server/server transactions are Java (in the form of Java Server Pages and Java servlets) and Microsoft's .NET technologies.

Mobile Applications

Mobile applications are developed for use on handheld devices. These applications access **the cloud** for updates and to obtain the data need to deliver useful on-demand services to the user. The term "the cloud" simply refers to resources delivered by a networked service, usually over the Internet. Mobile applications are developed for specific platforms, for example Android, iOS, BlackBerry, and Windows Mobile, using the programming language appropriate for each platform.

GUI Programming, Content Management, and Interface Design

The design and development of effective graphical user interfaces is a field of its own within software design. Interface designers and developers often combine an interest in programming with art, design, writing, multimedia/graphic arts, technical communications, or psychology. As you learn more about programming you may find that your interest tends more towards the interface, or content management. To learn more, research the more widely used graphics, animation, and drawing software, and talk to graphical designers and animators about their work. Learn to use a content management system. Look for courses, programs, and literature related to interface design, Web design, digital media, technical communications, and usability.

Database Programming and SQL

Increasingly, most applications are database-driven. The language most commonly used to communicate with relational databases is Structured Query Language (SQL). SQL comes in various flavors, customized for use with specific database vendors. PHP is commonly used with **MySql** and most PHP distributions include MySql, including your xammplite installation.

If you are planning to work as a programmer or Web developer, you will want to familiarize yourself with at least one version of SQL in order to develop applications that interact with databases. In the process, you may find yourself more deeply interested in this subject. In that case, be sure to research the fields of database programming and database administration.

Also note that XML is becoming an important feature of database-related application development. XML often serves as a standard interface that allows different database systems to more easily exchange data in standard formats.

Another important development, associated with mobile applications and cloud computing, is the increasing use of **non-relational databases**, often termed **NoSQL** databases. NoSQL databases are not always based on relational tables: they sacrifice some of the security and integrity of relational database design for the sake of faster processing, especially with regard to very large data sets.

In Summary: Follow Your Heart!

Hopefully this short overview is useful as you consider where to go next. There are many opportunities in this vast field, and it is well worth taking the time to think about your own personality, your own way of working, and your personal interests. Do you like to work with other people or do you prefer to work alone? Do you prefer **coding** applications or **designing** applications? Are you happiest when you are writing queries and reports that obtain data from databases? Are you interested in the way that different applications combine to manage the flow of information and business processes throughout an organization? Do you like testing software and resolving errors? Do you enjoy writing manuals and training people to use software? Or are you most interested in creating animations, graphics, or effective user interfaces?

Often when we begin to program, we may be surprised to find that our interests evolve as we learn more about our own aptitudes and interests. As you take next steps to develop your programming skills, keep an open mind to what is possible, work hard, have fun, keep exploring, and remember to **follow your own heart!**

Appendix A

Data Representation and Formats

This Appendix provides an introduction to data representation, explaining how bits and bytes can be used to represent any kind of data once a data representation scheme has been defined.

Introduction

Moment by moment, each one of us is constantly processing **data** in order to obtain and use **information**. We may sniff an appetizing aroma and identify the smell of apple pie, look at a tall shape above us and recognize a tree, listen to a sequence of sounds and hear music, read a series of symbols and translate these into words and sentences, or see a small red circle ahead of us and brake for a traffic light. Our **information environment** includes the natural world, other people, traffic signals, clocks and calendars, books and magazines, TV and movies, e-mail and the Web.

An increasing amount of our information environment is **digital**. Digital information is stored and transmitted in some physical form that we treat as a sequence of 0s and 1s using electronics, optics or other technologies. Data that is represented in patterns of 0s and 1s is known as **binary data.**

We can represent all kinds of information as binary data. It is just a matter of agreeing on **standard data representation schemes**, usually referred to as **data formats**. For example we use a wide range of standard data formats to represent plain text, formatted text, numbers, images, audio, videos, even program instructions. Let's get a feel for how some of these formats work.

Storing Data in Bits and Bytes

All binary data formats are based on patterns of 0s and 1s. The smallest unit of binary data is known as a **bit**, which can store a single 0 or 1 value. How many possible patterns can be stored in one bit? The answer is two, either a 0 or a 1. If one bit can store one of two possible values, how many possible patterns can **two** bits store? The answer is **four**. The first bit can store either a 0 or a 1, and the second bit can also store a 0 or 1, so two bits together could store any of the following patterns: 00, 01, 10, or 11.

Similarly **three** bits can be used to store any of **eight** patterns of 0s and 1s (000, 001, 010, 011, 100, 101, 110, or 111). **Four** bits can be used to store any of **sixteen** possible patterns (0000, 0001, 0010, 0011, 0100, 0101, 0110, 0111, 1000, 1001, 1010, 1011, 1100, 1101, 1110, or 1111), and **five bits can be used to store any of thirty two** different patterns of 0s and 1s (00000, 00001, 00010, 00011, 00100, 00101, 00110, 00111, 01000, 01001, 01010, 01011, 01100, 01101, 01110, 01111, 10000, 10001, 10010, 10011, 10100, 10101, 10110, 10111, 11000, 11001, 11010, 11011, 11100, 11101, 11110, or 11111). Do you get the general idea?

A **byte** is simply a sequence of **eight** bits, so how many different patterns of 0s and 1s can be stored in a byte? Or in two bytes (sixteen bits)? Or in **n** bytes, where **n** is any number of bytes you can think of? If you consider the examples above you will notice that the number of possible patterns doubles each time another bit is added. The number of possible combinations that **n** bits can store is 2^n. So a single bit can contain 2^1 or 2 different patterns of 0s and 1s, two bits can store 2^2 or 4 different patterns of 0s and 1s, a byte (eight bits) can store any of 2^8 or 256 different patterns of 0s and 1s. And two bytes (sixteen bits) can store 2^{16} or **65,536** different patterns of 0s and 1s.

How Multimedia Data Is Represented in Binary

It may be interesting to learn how many possible patterns of 0s and 1s can be stored in a specific number of bits or bytes but what does all this have to with data representation? Let's start with how we might use sequences of binary data to represent multimedia. Figure A-1 shows a black and white drawing of an arrow.

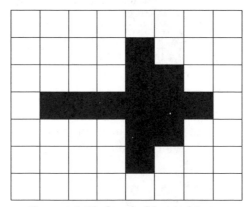

Figure A-1: Black and white pixel image

Each square in this image is a **picture element**, or **pixel**, so the drawing contains 56 pixels, some rendered in white, others in black. Since a single bit can store either a 0 or 1, we can use a single bit to store the value for each pixel. A bit that contains 0 will represent a white pixel and a bit that contains 1 will represent a black pixel. Using this scheme, here is a sequence of bits that represents the drawing:

00000000 00001000 00001100 01111110 00001100 00001000 00000000

The sequence is shown in groups of eight bits to make the pattern easier to read. Each group of eight bits represents one line of the drawing. The entire drawing can be represented and stored in 56 bits. Since there are eights bits in a byte, that means the drawing can be stored in seven bytes. Do you see how this works?

Each pixel in the black and white image could be represented by a single bit since there are only two possible values (black or white). But what if we wish to store a color image? The amount of bits needed to represent each pixel depends on how many possible colors that the pixel might contain. Let's say we want to represent an image of the same size as the one shown above, but this time each pixel can be any of 256 different colors? It takes eight bits (or one byte) to store 256 different patterns of 0'1 and 1s. If each of these 256 patterns is used to represent a different color, we will need a byte to store the color for each pixel. Fifty six bytes would therefore be needed to store the colors of all of the pixels in this image since it contains 56 pixels.

The most common method to represent colors accurately on a computer is **24-bit graphics**, which requires three bytes to represent the color of each pixel. You may recall from your physics classes that all colors are a combination of red, green and blue light. Using the 24 bit scheme, the first of the three bytes indicates the density of red light, the second byte indicates the density of green light, and the third byte indicates the density of blue light. Together the three bytes specify the overall color. This scheme allows us to specify any of 224 (16,777,216) possible colors for each pixel! A typical computer screen usually displays 1024 x 768 pixels, for a total of 786,432 pixels. If three bytes are used to represent the color of each pixel on the screen then 2,359,296 bytes are needed to represent the entire display.

In general, this method of using bit patterns to store each pixel of an image is referred to as **bitmapping**, and images stored this way are called **bitmapped** (or **.bmp**) images. As you can see bitmap images take a lot of storage space! For this reason, a number of more efficient ways have been developed to store images, using various **compression schemes** (for example **.GIF**, **.JPG**, **.PNG** and **.TIF**), or quite different schemes for representing graphical data, such as **vector graphics**. Although these methods all use different representation schemes, they all store images in patterns of 0s and 1s.

Similar binary representation schemes are used to store other multimedia formats as sequences of 0s and 1s. Examples of representation schemes for audio formats are **.AU**, **.WAV**, **.RA** and **.MP3**. Examples of schemes for video formats are **.AVI**, **.MOV** and **.MPG**.

How Numeric Values Are Represented in Binary

We have learned that multimedia can be stored in binary formats. What about numeric data? Numeric values must be stored on a computer so that we can maintain records, perform arithmetic calculations, and compare data values. In binary representation a number is represented by a pattern of 0s and 1s, just like images or other types of data. For example, since a byte can contain 256 different possible patterns of 0s and 1s we can use a byte to represent any numeric value between 0 and 255. Recall that there are eight bits in a byte. In order to store a numeric value, the rightmost bit is used to represent the decimal value 1, the next bit to the left represents 2, the next represents 4, the next represents 8, the next represents 16, the next represents 32, the next represents 64, and the leftmost bit represents 128. If the bit at any of these eight positions is set to 1, the value that the bit represents is **included** in the overall value of the number. If the bit at any position is set to 0 then the value that it represents is **not included** in the overall value of the number. Table A-1 shows how the decimal values 65, 32, 48 and 137 can be represented by a byte pattern using this scheme:

	2^7	2^6	2^5	2^4	2^3	2^2	2^1	2^0
	128	64	32	16	8	4	2	1
65 =	0	1	0	0	0	0	0	1
32 =	0	0	1	0	0	0	0	0
48 =	0	0	1	1	0	0	0	0
137 =	1	0	0	0	1	0	0	1

Table A-1: Binary representation of decimal values

The decimal value 65 is stored as 01000001. This binary sequence contains a 1 in the **64** column and a 1 in the **1** column, and 0s in all other columns. This pattern represents the value 65 since that is the sum of 64 and 1.

Similarly the decimal value 137 is stored as 10001001. This binary sequence contains a 1 in the **128** column, 1 in the **8** column, and 1 in the **1** column, and the sum of these three values is 137.

Do you see how this works? The decimal value 11 would be stored in binary as 00001011. The decimal value 0 would be stored as 00000000. How would you store the decimal value 40? The decimal value 104? What decimal value does 10101010 represent?

A single byte can only be used to store positive values in the range 0 (represented as 00000000) through 255 (represented as 11111111). We usually need to handle numbers in a much larger range than this so in fact more bytes are used to present numeric values. This scheme is also slightly modified in reality so that computer programs can handle positive or negative numbers and floating point numbers.

How Plain Text Is Represented in Binary

We also store **plain text** as binary data. Text is a collection of individual characters organized into **character strings**, for example:

"John"   "123 Main Street"   "A123-HFC"
"123-45-6789"   "Enter your password: "   "Price: $10.75"

These are examples of very small character strings. A character string could be an entire e-mail message or even an entire book! A **text file** is basically a character string stored on a disk that includes end-of line characters to mark the end of each line.

Until recently the standard representation scheme for text was **ASCII** (**American Standard Code for Information Interchange**). The ASCII system uses a single byte to store each character of a character string—each character is represented by a different pattern of 0s and 1s. Since a byte can store any of 256 different patterns, the ASCII scheme can only include 256 different characters. This works just fine to represent all of the upper-and lower-case characters of the English alphabet, as well the ten numeric digits and some other commonly used symbols that you typically find on a computer keyboard. However a single byte does not provide nearly enough different patterns to represent the character sets of all of the world's major alphabets.

For this reason the standard representation for text is now **Unicode**, which uses **two** bytes to represent a single character. Since two bytes can store any of 65,536 possible patterns of 0s and 1s, Unicode can represent any of the characters of all of the world's major alphabets (and most minor alphabets). As an example of Unicode representation, the upper-case letter 'A' is stored as 01000001 (which has the numeric value 65), the lower-case 'a' is stored as 01100001 (the numeric value 97), the space character is stored as 00100000 (which has the numeric value 32), the copyright character (c) is stored as 10101001 (which has the numeric value 169) and so on. The good news is that the ASCII values that were defined to represent the characters of the English alphabet have the same values in Unicode.

How Source Code and Markup Code Is Represented in Binary

Program source code (such as PHP code) and markup code (such as HTML code) is stored as plain text, so this code is treated just the same as any other text. Source code simply uses the syntax and key words of a programming language so that the instructions can be recognized and processed correctly buy the language interpreter or compiler. Markup code uses the < and > characters to enclose tags so that the markup instructions can be recognized and processed by the browser or other software that is processing the markup file. The < and > characters are of course text characters themselves (their Unicode/ASCII values are 60 and 62 respectively).

Since source code and markup code are written in plain text, this code can be developed and read using any text editor.

How Program Instructions Are Represented in Binary

Computer programs are basically a sequence of instructions to be performed by the computer's microprocessor. The microprocessor contains an **instruction set** which defines all of the basic instructions that the microprocessor can perform. The reason that a program written for a Macintosh computer does not run on a Pentium computer is that the computers have different microprocessors. The microprocessor's instruction set is the basis of the computer's **machine language** and the available instructions defines the tasks that the computer can actually perform. For example instruction sets include **add** instructions that allows the computer to add numbers, and **move** instructions that allow the computer to copy data between registers and other locations. These instructions are called **opcodes**. Each opcode is represented by a specific numeric value that the microprocessor uses to identify the instruction to be performed.

We have seen that numbers can be represented in binary. When the microprocessor treats a binary value as a number representing an opcode, a program instruction is executed.

How Memory Addresses Are Represented in Binary

A computer uses memory to temporarily store programs and data that are currently in use. Each byte of memory is identified by a unique **memory address**. Memory addresses are used to track where programs and data are stored while the computer is running.

Memory addresses are simply numeric values stored as a pattern of 0s and 1s. When the microprocessor treats a binary value as a number representing a memory address, data can be retrieved from, or stored in, memory.

What Else Can Be Represented in Binary?

By now you should have the general idea that binary data (patterns of 0s and 1s) can be used for any kind of data representation. It is mostly a matter of agreeing on a standard of some kind (such as Unicode for text representation, or a standard 24-bit representation for colors).

In fact you could easily invent your own representation system but, unless you can get the world to accept your new standard, your representation scheme will only work for you!

Appendix B

Files, Folders, Addressing Schemes, and Command Line Arguments

This Appendix provides a general introduction to:

- File types, disks, disk drives, files and folders
- Relative and absolute addresses, in MS Windows and on the Internet
- Command line arguments (MS DOS, Linux, Mac OS X)

File Types and File Extensions

Everything that you save on a computer disk is stored as a file of some kind. The content of each file is stored in a format appropriate for its intended use. The format is indicated by the **file type** and file names usually have a file **extension** that suggests the format that the file contains. Table B-1 shows a few examples of file types, and common file extensions.

In order to open a file you must have a program that can handle the format of the file. For example the Open Office Word Processor can handle the format of an .odt file, while any text editor can handle .txt files. Some applications can handle a number of different file types—most image processing software can open .bmp, .gif and .jpg files.

Your computer operating system can be configured to choose a default program to open files with a specific file extension. For example, in MS Windows, you might wish to specify Crimson Editor as your default editor to open files with a .php extension. In that case, if you double-clicking a file name with a .php extension, Crimson Editor will run and open the file for you. This is why .html files are opened by your Web browser when you double-click these files, and why word-processing documents are opened by your word-processor.

If no program has been associated with a specific file extension, the operating system will ask you to choose a program when you attempt to open a file of that type.

File Type	File Name Extensions	Purpose
Text	.txt	Plain text file
CSS	.css	Cascading Style Sheet (text format)
OpenDoc Text	.odt	OpenOffice word-processing document
OpenDoc Spreadsheet	.ods	OpenOffice spreadsheet
Java source code	.java	Text file containing Java source code
Java byte code	.class	Java byte code
PHP source code	.php	Text file containing PHP source code
HTML	.html, .htm	Text file containing HTML document
XML	.xml	Text file containing XML document
RTF	.rtf	Rich Text Format document
Bitmap	.bmp	Bitmap file (uncompressed image file)
JPEG	.jpeg, .jpg	JPG format compressed image file
GIF	.gif	GIF format compressed image file
SWF	.swf	Macromedia Flash file
MOV	.mov	Quick Time Movie
MP3	.mp3	MP3 Format Sound

Table B-1: Examples of file types and file extensions

Disk and Disk Drives

A computer system provides a number of disk drives so that you can store files on disks. Most personal computers include at least one non-removable "fixed" disk that has a large storage capacity and fast access times. In addition your computer will usually include drives that support portable disks such as CD's and DVD's, and portable drives such as USB drives. Portable disks and drives can be inserted and removed as needed, and used on multiple computers.

Your computer may also be connected to disk drives attached to other computers on the same network. If your computer has access to a Local Area Network (LAN), then you will probably have access to a centralized file server. The nature of your network account will determine which folders and files are accessible to you, and the type of access (for example whether you create, write or read files and folders).

If your computer has Internet access, you can access drives located on Internet-based file servers using Internet protocols. The **http** (hypertext transfer) protocol allows you to access (but not create or modify) files made available by a Web server, and the **ftp** (file transfer) protocol allows you to access files made available through an ftp server. Depending on the nature of your ftp account, you may be able to create, write or read files and folders.

Since disks are easily damaged it is important to maintain **backups** of the contents of your disks. Backups should be made on disk and drives that are distinct from your primary storage disks. Ideally your backups will be stored on disks in a separate location your computer in case of fire or some other serious accident. Network servers are a good solution for this purpose. If you don't have direct access to a network server, you can always upload copies of critical files to your e-mail service provider. You can also make up backups on CD's or DVD's and keep these at a separate location.

Files and File Folders (Directories)

Everything you save on a computer disk is saved as a file of some kind. Since there may be thousands of files on a single disk, your computer operating system provides a file management system that uses folders and sub-folders to organize your files.

Figure B-1 shows an example of file and folder organization based on the Windows operating system but the concepts are the same for any operating system. The first screen below shows the contents of a folder named **Folder Tutorial**. If you look in the address window, you can see that this folder is located on the **C:** drive, and the address of the folder is: **C:\Folder Tutorial**. The folder contains three folders named **Folder1**, **Folder2** and **Folder3**, and also three files, named **SomeFile.txt**, **SomeDocument.doc** and **SomeImage.bmp**. This example demonstrates that folders may contain sub-folders and files in any combination, depending on your organizational needs.

The second screen shows the contents of the folder named **Folder1**. This folder contains two folders (named **Folder4** and **Folder5**, as well as a file named **AnotherFile.txt**. The address of **Folder1** is **C:\Folder Tutorial\Folder1**, and the address of **AnotherFile.txt** is **C:\Folder Tutorial\Folder1\AnotherFile.txt**.

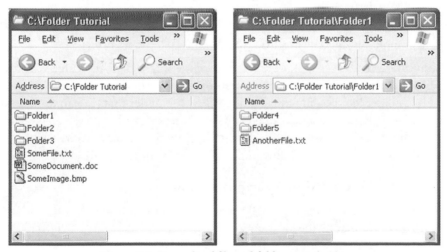

Figure B-1: Example of file and folder organization

For practical purposes there is no limit to the number of levels of folders but if you nest your folders too deeply you may find that the organization has become too complex. Plan your organization carefully so that you can find files quickly and easily. Be sure to use meaningful names for your files and folders.

Naming Files and Folders

Files and folder are identified by file names. The rules for naming files may differ depending on the operating system that the computer uses, however files and folders are often moved between operating systems (for example, you may develop .html and .php files in folders on your local Windows computer, then transfer these to a "live" Web server running on a Linux computer). With this in mind, it is a good idea to use file and folder names that will not need to be changed if they are relocated. As a general rule **avoid using spaces** in the names of your files and file folders since spaces can lead to problems when transferring files and folders between operating systems. In our Windows example, we named a folder **Folder Tutorial** which includes a space. A better name would be **FolderTutorial** (no spaces, just an uppercase letter to begin each new word in the file name) or **Folder_Tutorial** (using an underscore instead of each space).

File Addresses in Windows and on the Web

The complete address of a file is known as the file's **absolute address**. Under the Windows operating system, a file's absolute address is indicated by specifying a drive letter, followed by a folder list that indicates the exact folder location of the file, followed by the name of the file itself. For example a file named **addTwoNumbers.html** that is stored on the **C:** drive in a folder named **samples** which is in a folder named **Webtech** which is in a folder named **htdocs** which is a folder named **xampplite** will have the following absolute Windows address:

C:\xampplite\htdocs\Webtech\samples\addTwoNumbers.html

Absolute addresses of files that are accessed over the Internet are indicated with a URL (Uniform Resource Locator). A URL consists of the domain name for the Web site, followed by a folder list showing the location of the file under that domain, followed by the file name. For example a file named **addTwoNumbers.html** that is located on a Web server under the domain **www.xyz.com** in a folder named **samples** which is in a folder named **Webtech** will have the following absolute Web address (URL):

http://www.xyz.com/Webtech/samples/addTwoNumbers.html

The domain name that is used in a URL is actually pointing to an absolute address on a disk drive somewhere — the location where the Web site files and folders are located. For example, the **www.somePlace.com** domain may reference the Windows folder: **C:\xampplite\htdocs** on the Web server. In that case, the Internet URL:

http://www.xyz.com/Webtech/samples/addTwoNumbers.html

will refer to a file at the following Windows address:

C:\xampplite\htdocs\Webtech\samples\addTwoNumbers.html

Relative Addresses in Windows

Absolute addresses provide a complete path to a file. We can also reference a file location using a **relative address**. A relative address indicates the location of a file relative to our current location on the same disk. In English we might indicate relative addresses with phrases such as:

- The file **myImage.jpg** is in the current folder
- The file **myImage.jpg** is in the folder named **images**, which is inside the current folder.
- The file **myImage.jpg** is in the folder named **images**, which is in a folder named **media** which is located inside the current folder.
- The file **myImage.jpg** is in the folder that **contains** the current folder.
- The file **myImage.jpg** is in the folder named **images** which in the same folder that contains the current folder.
- The file **myImage.jpg** is in the folder named **images** which is in a folder named **media**, which is in the folder that contains the folder that contains the current folder.

We can specify relative addresses in the Windows operating system by using folder names and back slashes, along with and by using .. (two periods) when we need to indicate a "parent" folder. Here are the relative addresses of the myImages.jpg file for each of the previous examples:

- **myImage.jpg**: the file is in the current folder.
- **images\myImage.jpg**: the file is in the **images** folder under the current folder.
- **media\images\myImage.jpg**: the file is in the **images** folder, which is in the **media** folder, which is in the current folder.
- **..\myImage.jpg**: the file is in the parent folder of the current folder.
- **..\images\myImage.jpg**: the file is in the **images** folder, which is in the parent folder of the current folder.
- **..\..\media\images\myImage.jpg**: the file is in the **images** folder which is in the media folder which is in the parent folder of the parent folder of the current folder.

We can also specify a relative address starting with the root of the current drive by using a back slash at the start of our relative address, for example:

   \xampplite\htdocs\media\images\myImage.jpg

Relative Addresses on the Internet

We use the same syntax to specify relative addresses to locate files and folders on a Web server, except that Internet addresses use the forward slash (this is actually the Unix addressing scheme). For example:

 ../../media/images/myImage.jpg: the file is in the **images** folder which is in the **media** folder which is in the parent folder of the parent folder of the current folder.

Recent versions of Windows also permit the use of the forward slash to specify Windows addresses.

Using Relative Web Addresses in HTML Code

Relative Web addresses can be used when adding links to your HTML documents, for example to link to a file within the same folder or a file in another folder on the same Web site. Here are examples using relative addresses with the <**a**> **anchor** tag:

 Provide a link to contactInfo.html in the same folder as the current document:

 <a href="contactInfo.html">Contact Information</a>

 Provide a link to orderForm.html which is in a folder named **purchasing** which is located in the parent folder of the folder that contains the current document:

 <a href="../purchasing/orderForm.html">Order Form</a>

Here are examples using relative addresses with the <**form**> tag:

 Provide a link to myFirst.php in the same folder as the current document:
 <form action="myFirst.php" action="post">
Provide a link to processReport.phpl which is in a folder named **reports** which is located in a folder named **data**, which is located in the parent folder of the folder that contains the current document:
 <form action="../data/reports/processReport.php" action="post">

Here are examples using relative addresses with the <img> tag:

 Provide a link to myPic.jpg in the same folder as the current document:

 <img src="myPic.jpg" />

 Provide a link to logo.jpg which is in a folder named **images** which is located in the same folder as the current document:

 <img src="images/logo.jpg" />

Managing Files at the Command Line

Operating systems (Windows, Linux, Mac OS X, etc) manage the underlying functions of the computer. In addition to a graphical user interface (GUI), operating systems also provide a text-based **command line** interface to allow users to run programs, manage files and folders, and perform system operations. Most users do not work with (or even know about) the command line interface, preferring the user friendly GUI and a mouse to work with the operating system. For example, Windows provides the Windows Explorer interface to view and manage files and folders using your mouse.

However the command line interface can be much more efficient for certain operations, and so computer professionals often find it useful to issue operating system commands using this text-based interface.

In order to use the operating system's command line, the user must first open a **console window** which provides a **command prompt**. The user issues a command at the prompt and the pressed the Enter key. The operating system then executes the command and may display the results of the operation. The operating system then displays the command prompt, ready for the next command from the user.

The Windows command line syntax is based on Microsoft Disk Operating System (MS DOS) commands. Following are examples of MS DOS commands that allow you to work with files and folders from the command line. This list is by no means exhaustive and you will want to consult a tutorial for more information. Note that these commands are not the same for all operating systems. Linux and Mac OS X command line syntax is derived from the Unix operating system. A table comparing some common MS DOS and Unix commands is provided at the end of this section.

Note also that some commands, such as those provided here as examples, are relatively harmless. Other commands allow you to move and delete files and folders, and even reformat disk drives, destroying all data stored on them. Be very careful when issuing command line instructions!

Introduction to MS DOS Commands

To see what an MS DOS command line looks like, you first need to open a console window, also referred to as a DOS window. Click the **Start** Menu, select **Run** and type **CMD** in the text box (Figure B-2).

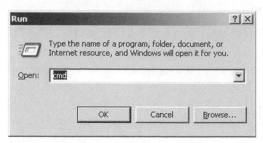

Figure B-2: Opening a console window in Windows

A console window appears with a command prompt that indicates the current disk and folder location. Figure B-3 shows an example.

Figure B-3: The DOS command prompt

A console window provides a text-based interface, so you cannot use a mouse to issue commands in this window. Instead you will type commands at the **command prompt** and press **Enter** to have the command executed by the computer. Note that the command prompt displays your current location within the file system.

In order to find out what version of the operating system is running, type **VER** at the prompt and then press Enter (Figure B-4).

Figure B-4: The DOS command prompt

The screen displays the version of Windows that is running on your machine, and then returns to the command prompt, waiting for your next command. That's the way a command line operating system works—you give a command, the command is executed, and the operating system then waits for your next command.

Your command prompt indicates the current file path, for example **C:\Documents and Settings\MOkane>**. Any commands that you give will be relative to the current file path.

Try using the following commands to become familiar with using the command line.

To clear the screen:

Sometimes it is helpful to clear the screen, for example to view a long directory all at once. Type **CLS** and then press **Enter** to clear your DOS screen.

To run a program:

You can run programs directly from the command prompt. Try typing **Notepad** and press **Enter**. If a program does not run it is because MS Windows does not know how to find it from the current file path. You can provide a complete file path (see below) or you can set an environmental variable to indicate the path (not covered in this introduction).

To view the contents of the current folder:

To view the contents of the current folder, type **DIR** and press **Enter**. A directory listing of files and folder will be displayed. Note that the list includes:

- The date and time each file or folder was created
- The word <**DIR**> if the item is a folder (DIR stands for directory)
- The size of the file in bytes
- The name of the file or folder

If the listing is too long to fit on the screen you can scroll back to view the entire list.

Or you can type **DIR/P** and press **Enter** to view a listing one screen at a time (press **Enter** for the next screen). The **P** stands for PAUSE).

You can also view a listing displayed across the screen. Type **DIR /W** and press **Enter**. The **W** stands for WIDE. This time only the names of files and folders are shown. The folders are indicated with square brackets around them.

NOTE: the /P and the /W in the last two examples are **command arguments**. These are values that the **DIR** program uses to change its behavior. Many commands provide arguments that can be used to deliver more precise direction.

To view the contents of another folder:

The DIR command can be used with relative addresses to view the content of other folder without changing your current folder location.

DIR **images** to display all files and folders in the images folder, which is located in the current folder.

DIR **media\images** to display all files and folders in the **images** folder which is located in a folder named **media** which is located in the current folder.

DIR **..** to display all files and folders in the parent folder (the folder that **contains** the current folder).

DIR **..\images** to display all files and folders in the folder named **images** which is in the same folder that **contains** the current folder.

DIR **..\..\media\images** to display all files and folders in the folder named **images**, which is in a folder named **media**, which is in the folder that **contains** the folder that **contains** the current folder.

DIR **D:\media** to obtain a listing of files and folders in the media folder on the D: drive.

You can also specify **file names** and use **wildcards** to list only files that match specific names or extensions. For example:

DIR ***.jpg** to display **all** files with a .jpg extension in the current folder

DIR **..\..\media\images*.jpg** to display all .jpg files in the folder named **images** which is in a folder named **media**, which is in the folder that contains the folder that contains the current folder.

To change drives:

To change your current location to a different disk drive, type the drive letter followed by a colon (no spaces), then press **Enter**. For example, type **D:** and press **Enter** to switch to the **D:** drive.

To change folders:

Use the CD command to change your current location to a different folder on the same drive. **CD** stands for Change Directory. In the following examples **xxx**, **yyy** and **zzz** represent the names of folders on your disk).

CD **** will change your location to the **root** folder on the current drive no matter what folder is your current location.

CD **\xxx** will change your location to a folder named **xxx** that is located in the first level of folders on the current disk

CD **\xxx\yyy** will change your location to a folder named **yyy** that is located inside a folder named **xxx** that is in the first level of folders on the current disk

CD **..** will change your location to the parent folder of the current folder (to the folder that contains the current folder).

CD **..\xxx** will change your location to a folder named **xxx** which is located in the parent folder of the current folder.

You can combine these examples to move from any folder to any other folder. Here is a more complex example:

CD **..\..\xxx\yyy\zzz** will change your location to the **zzz** folder which is located in the **yyy** folder, which is located in the **xxx** folder, which is in the parent folder of the parent folder of the current folder.

Note: before you navigate to a new folder you must first be located on the same drive as the new folder. To switch drives, see **Change Drives** above.

To copy files:

Use the **COPY** command to copy a file.

COPY ex1.java ex2.java will copy a file named **ex1.java** to a file named **ex2.java** in the same folder.

COPY **C:\xxx\yyy\ex1.java D:\zzz\ex1.java** will copy a file named ex1.java from the yyy folder, which is inside the xxx folder on the C: drive to a file with the same name in the zzz folder on a disk in the D: drive.

To rename files:

Use the **REN** command to rename a file. For example:

REN ex1.java ex2.java will rename a file named ex1.java to ex2.java

To view the contents of a text file:

Use the **TYPE** command to look at the contents of a **text** file. For example:

TYPE exam1.php will list the contents of the **exam1.php** file in the current folder.

TYPE ..\exams\exam1.php will list the contents of the **exam1.php** file in the **exams** folder which can be found in the parent folder of the current folder.

Note that the **TYPE** command just lists the contents of the file—you cannot edit a file using the **TYPE** command.

Recalling Previous Commands

You can use the **Up** and **Down** cursor keys to recall previous commands—this can save you a LOT of time when reissuing commands or using the same command multiple times with minor modifications.

Use Double Quotes when Paths Include Spaces

Use double quotes around file paths that include spaces in the folder or file names. For example the folder name **Program Files** and the folder name **Crimson Editor** both contain spaces, so in order to change to the Crimson Editor folder use:

cd "\Program Files\Crimson Editor"

Printing the Contents of the Console Window

You may sometimes want to copy your DOS screen into a document (for example in order to print the screen or include it in a report). You can do this in the same way that you can capture any window:

1. Ensure that your screen is displaying exactly what you want to capture. Click your mouse in this window to ensure it is the active window.
2. Hold down the **Alt** key and press **PrintScrn**.
3. Open a new document in your word-processor or other application that can receive an image and choose **Paste**. Your output screen will be pasted and you can then print it or use as part of the document.

Creating Batch Files

A batch file is a text file that contains one or more operating system commands. This is useful if you often have to issue the same set of commands regularly (for example to copy a set of files from one disk to another every night, or to delete temporary files). MS DOS batch files end with a **.BAT** extension and are executable. You can type a sequence of MS DOS commands into a text file, save it as a .BAT file, and then execute the file whenever you wish to simply by typing the name of the file at the MS DOS prompt, or double-clicking the file in Windows. When you do this, the commands that you typed are executed one after another.

Here is a simple example. Use a text editor to create a text file containing the following commands (each on a separate line):

DIR *.TXT
CD..
DIR/W

These commands will:

> Display all files in the current folder with a .txt extension
> Change directory to the parent folder of the current folder
> Display all files and folder in the parent folder across the screen (wide)

Note that we are not issuing these three commands at the MS DOS command prompt. We are simply typing them into a text file. The commands will not be executed until we tell Windows to process this file.

Save the file with the name "**XXX.BAT**" where **XXX** is any filename you choose, for example **TEST.BAT**. If you include the quotes when naming your file this prevents your text editor from adding a .TXT extension to your filename (some editors do this by default).

Now go to the console window, change directory to the drive/file path where your batch file was saved, type the name of the batch file at the command line, then press **ENTER**. The extension is not required (for example you can just type **TEST** if the file was named **TEST.BAT**). The instructions in the file will now be executed one line at a time. You can execute these instructions whenever you need to, just by typing the name of the batch file. You can also run the batch file by navigating to the file location in Windows Explorer and double-clicking the file.

This example contained three simple (and harmless!) instructions but could have been much longer and more complex. Real world batch programs might routinely copy files from one disk to another for nightly backup, or delete temporary files that were created each day. Programmers often use batch files to compile applications that contain many different components.

Unix Commands

Table B-2 shows some common MS DOS commands and their Unix equivalents (Linux and Mac OS X both utilize many standard Unix commands). Remember that file paths in Linux, Mac OS X or any other Unix-based operating system use the forward slash / as a separator in place of the back slash \ used in Windows file paths.

Function	MS DOS Command	Unix Command
View contents of a directory	DIR	ls
Change directory	CD	cd
Copy a file	COPY	cp
Rename a file	REN	mv
Move a file	MOV	mv
Delete a file	DEL	rm
Clear the screen	CLS	clear
Create a directory	MKDIR	mkdir
Find a string in a file	FIND	grep

Table B-2: Comparison of common MS DOS and Unix commands

Appendix C

Installing and Running Your Standalone Web Server

The Web site includes the most current instructions to install and configure your standalone Web server and MySQL server. You need to do this in order to run the sample code and develop your own applications with no need for Internet access or for an Internet Service Provider (ISP) service. Instructions are provided for Windows and Macintosh with some additional help for Linux users. The textbook Web site can be found at:

http://www.mikeokane.com/textbooks/WebTech/support.php

Using an Active Web Server

Note that you are not obliged to use a standalone Web server with this textbook. If you have an ISP service, you can use any active Web server that provides PHP versions 4.0 or 5.0 and (for Chapter 14) includes MySQL. However in these cases you will need to download the **Webtech** folder from the CD or Web site and add this to the **htdocs** folder of your Web server (or to any folder location on your Web server that can be accessed by your URL). And you will need to configure you MySQL server to include the appropriate tables and user accounts. And of course you will need to be comfortable uploading and downloading files to the server. The Web site provides details to help you use an active Web server.

Problems Using Your Web Server

The textbook Web site also provides documentation to help with most common installation problems and these can usually be resolved quickly. However note that you may experience coding when using the software that give the impression that the software has not been installed correctly. Before you assume there is an installation problem first refer to Appendix D which provides debugging help for many common coding errors.

Advanced Users

For more advanced users, the Apache Friends (http://www.apachefriends.org) Web site provides excellent documentation that explains the full functionality of the server and walks you step by step through the installation process. You may want to look this site over even if your installation went smoothly. Note that the Apache Friends site also provides the current version of the software but if you download and install this you will need to copy the textbook Webtech folder under the htdocs folder of your installation, and you will need to configure your MySQL server to include the appropriate tables and user accounts. The textbook Web site can help you with this.

By default, your Web server installation is configured for use a standalone server for learning and development and not as a functioning Web server on the Internet. However your installation is fully capable of serving as a "live" Web server. With this in mind, you may decide to configure your server to apply appropriate security settings. For more information on how to do this, read the security section on the Apache Friends site:

http://www.apachefriends.org/en/

CAUTION: Do not configure your standalone server as a live server unless you are an advanced user and have the skills to administer an active Web server!

Appendix D

Debugging Your Code

This appendix will help you find errors in your HTML and PHP code. Check the book Web site for the latest list of hints and gotchas.

Problems Viewing Your HTML or PHP Programs

This section relates to problems that occur when you attempt to open your HTML and PHP files in a Web browser. Check here if you can't seem to access your files, if you see PHP code instead of the program output, or if the browser displays previous versions of your work.

> **Problem: I start my Web server and then open a Web browser and type any URL beginning with http://localhost. When I do this, I get a message telling me that there is a problem accessing the page.**

First try just typing http://localhost and if that generates an error it means that your Web server is not actually running. Check that you started your Web server. If your server is not starting refer to the installation document for help.

If your server is running and you can access other pages on the server, refer to the next solution for help.

> **Problem: I created an HTML file or PHP program but when I try to view it in my Web browser, I get a message that the file cannot be found.**

First try typing **http://localhost/Webtech/samples/addtwoNumbers.html** in your browser address box. If this program displays and runs correctly then your Web server is running just fine so the problem is probably one of the following:

a. You typed the URL for your file incorrectly. Check the URL carefully in case you mistyped anything.
b. Perhaps you saved your file to the wrong location. Your files must be saved in an appropriate folder under the **htdocs** folder. If your file is not located somewhere under the **htdocs** folder the Web server will not be able to find it. For example if you are saving a file named **paintEstimate.html** for **Chapter05**

then this file work would be saved in the location **htdocs/webtech/course-work/chapter05**. In order to **view** the file in your Web browser you must first start your Web server and then use the URL:

http://localhost/Webtech/coursework/Chapter05/paintEstimate.html

c. Perhaps you have multiple installations of the Web server on your computer (for example one version on your hard drive and another on a portable drive). Be sure to run the version that contains the folders and files that you wish to view.

Problem: I modified an HTML file or PHP program but when I try to view it I see the previous version in my Web browser. My changes don't show up!

First check that you saved your changes!

Next, if the file is an HTML file be sure to refresh your Web browser window, otherwise the previous version of the file may be displayed.

If neither of these works, perhaps your modified file was not saved to the location that you are viewing (for example, if you have multiple installations of the server—check the previous solution for more help with this).

The last possibility is that the Web browser is in fact showing your file but your changes contain errors. To test this, try making an obvious and simple change (for example add XXX to an output heading) and see if this appears when you view the file in your browser window. If it does, you are seeing the latest version but there are bugs in your code to figure out.

Problem: I submitted my HTML form but the results appeared to come from the wrong PHP program!

Check the **action** attribute in your <form> tag. You probably pasted an incorrect PHP file name here, or else mistyped the file name.

Problem: I modified a PHP program but when I try to view it I see the code instead of the results!

That means that you are accessing your HMTL and PHP files using a Windows or Macintosh file path instead of a URL. Look in your browser's address window. The address should begin **http://localhost/** which connects to your Web server. The address should NOT begin with a Windows drive letter!

For example to open **modify1.html** located in your **Chapter05** folder, the URL would be:

http://localhost/Webtech/coursework/chapter05/modify1.html

The **modify1.html** page displays a form for user input. If you complete the form and submit it, the Web server will run the PHP program **modify1.php**. Since you are correctly using a URL the application will be processed by the Web server. The program would not run correctly if you opened the application by just clicking the file in My Computer/Windows Explorer on Windows or Finder on a Macintosh since the pages would not then be processed by your Web server.

Similarly, to run **fixit1.php** from the same folder:

http://localhost/Webtech/coursework/chapter05/fixit1.php

If your server is running and this does not work, then carefully check your file name and file path. Try the URL: **http://localhost/Webtech/**

If you see the **coursework** and **samples** folders, your server is working just fine. You can then click through the appropriate folders in your browser window until you locate the file you want (in this case, click on **chapter05**, and then click **fixit1.php**).

NOTE: If you receive PHP error messages, that means that you are accessing the server correctly but there are errors in your PHP code (see below).

In summary, here's what **not** to do when you wish to connect to your Web server in order to view files in your Web browser. Do **not** use Windows Explorer or My Computer (on Windows) or Finder (on a Macintosh) to navigate to your samples or coursework folders and then double click the files to open them. This works to view **.html** files but you are not connecting to the Web server and so any attempt to access **.php** files will simply display the source code. Always check your browser's address window—it should display a URL that begins http://localhost and not a file path that begins file://.

Problems with HTML Layout

Sometimes your HTML layout will not appear as expected. Here are some common errors:

- You mistyped a tag name.
- You accidentally typed additional < or > characters when adding tags. This may be the problem if these characters appear unexpectedly on your Web page.
- You forgot a closing tag or mistyped the name of the closing tag. If nothing appears, check that you included a closing comment tag --> at the end of your initial comment section.
- You forgot the closing </table> tag in a table. This can generate some very unexpected results so always check this if parts of your page do not display, or display in expected locations.
- You forgot to include the <form> tags around the components of your form. Remember that **all** elements of a form must be included inside the opening and closing <form> tags.
- You forgot to use double quotes around the value supplied to your attributes, for example <input type = text..> instead of <input type = "text"..>.
- You forgot to include the style sheet in your folder, or you typed the wrong style sheet file name when specifying the style sheet in your <head> section.

Locating PHP Syntax Errors

The PHP processor will generate either **parse** errors or **fatal** error messages when it cannot understand the syntax of your code. Bear in mind that the error messages are the processor's best attempt to guess the problem. The error messages indicate the line number where an error was discovered, so it helps to have line numbering switched on in your text editor if your editor provides this option.

Unfortunately, the line number that is reported is not always the line where the error actually occurs. For example, if you leave out a semi-colon at the end of a statement, and the next line begins with the name of a variable, PHP will not find a problem until it reaches the variable and you will get the message:

> UNEXPECTED T_VARIABLE on line XXX

(where **XXX** is the line number that the processor is reporting).

(**T_VARIABLE** simply refers to a program variable, just as **T_STRING** refers to a character string. The "T" stands for "Token" since all components of a PHP program are considered to be tokens.)

When you are debugging an error message, always look at the line **before** the line where the error was reported **as well as** the line **indicated** in the error message.

Keep in mind also that the error may be **many** lines previous to the line that is reported. For example you may forget to add an ending double quote to a character string. In that case the processor can only assume that all the code that follows the missing quote is still part of the character string until it either reaches the **next** double quote in your code. The processor will assume that this quote must be the closing quote that you left out, when in fact it is probably an opening quote for another character string in your code, so the error message may indicate the character that follows **this** quote. If there are not more quotes in your code, the error may be reported on the last line in the file!

Look at your error message carefully. Let's say you see an error message such as:

> Parse error: syntax error, unexpected '>' in
> /home/mikeokane/public_html/samples/addTwoNumbers.php on line 23

Look at the character that appears on this line **before** the unexpected character (in this case the unexpected character is >). If the preceding character is a quote, there is probably a quote missing somewhere in your code before this line.

Common PHP Syntax Errors

Here are some examples of common parse errors to help you debug your code. You can save some time by looking over your code for these errors before you try running the program:

Semi-colon is missing at the end of a statement.

This will generate an error message at the start of the next line.

An opening or closing quote for a character string is missing.

These are hard to track down. The error may be located many lines previous to the line that is reported.

You forgot to use \" instead of " when you wish to include a double quote within a character string.

Remember that the double quotes indicate the start and end of a string. If the string must **include** a double quote you must indicate this using \" otherwise the processor will assume the quote indicates the end of the string and will have a problem trying to process the next word in the string. A common example is when your print statement includes an HTML tag that requires an attribute. Since the attribute values are enclosed in quotes, these quotes must be escaped using \" rather than simply using ".

A function name is misspelled so the processor cannot find the function.

For example, you may have typed **ciel($number)** instead of **ceil($number)**.

An opening or closing parenthesis is missing in a function call.

For example, you may have typed **print "Hi!");** instead of **print("Hi!");**

An opening or closing parenthesis is missing in a statement that requires multiple parentheses.

These can be tough to find. For example **while (!feof($someFile)** should be **(!feof($someFile))**. It helps to count the number of opening and closing parentheses in an expression to determine if a parenthesis is missing. Be careful to add the missing parenthesis in the correct location!

An opening or closing curly brace is missing.

This problem can also be hard to find. Count your opening and closing braces to figure out what is missing. Be careful to place any missing braces in the correct location!

If you are indenting your code nicely, this will help to make a visual check. Trace through your code. Each IF section, ELSE section, and loop structure should have opening and closing braces unless they consist of a single statement.

Common Logical Errors

Logical errors will not be reported by the PHP processor. Instead the program will run but will not perform as expected. Logical errors can be caused in many ways and it is important to test your code to help locate these errors. Test with different values and try to keep these values simple so that you check the results more easily.

A useful trick when you are trying to figure out where a logical error is occurring is to add print statements to your PHP code to print out the values of each variable (along with the name of the variable) at each step. You can use some special indicator to distinguish these from your normal output, for example a sequence of asterisks. For example:

```
print("*** hoursWorked = $hoursWorked ***<br />").
```

Now you can run your program and look through your output for the *** lines and see if the variables have the values that you expect them to have. When you find incorrect values, you have a better idea where to look in your code to find the problem. When your program is running as expected you will want to remove these lines from your code (or else comment them out if you think you might need them again).

Here are some common logical errors to watch out for …

You run your program after making corrections but the corrections do not appear to have any effect.

Perhaps you forgot to save the latest version so the processor is still running the previous version. Or you may have saved your new version to the wrong location. Remember that the **localhost** domain refers to the **htdocs** folder under your **xampplite** folder, and the **coursework** files are located in this folder under **Webtech/coursework**. So if, for example, you are working on **modify1.php** for **Chapter05**, this file must be saved under your **xampplite** folder in **htdocs/Webtech/coursework/Chapter05**

If you are running the program using an HTML form, check that the form is specifying the **correct** PHP program in the form's **action** attribute. Also refresh the browser window to open the latest version of your form.

Your selection structure or loop structure is not working correctly.

There are a number of things to check in this situation:

Perhaps you added a semi-colon to the end of the heading. Remember that the headings of selection and loop structures should not be followed by semi-colons. Semi-colons are required at the end of **statements**, and the heading of a control structure is not considered a statement.

You may have used = instead of == in the test that controls your selection or loop structure. Remember that = assigns a value to a variable, whereas == compares whether or not two values are the same.

You may have forgotten to include { and } braces to surround the code in your selection or loop structure. Remember that if you do not use { and } PHP will assume that the structure only includes a single statement. In that case, any additional statements will be treated as program statements that **follow** (and are not part of) the control structure.

Be careful to **initialize** all required variables before your loop begins.

Be careful not to include statements in your selection structure or loop structures that should not be part of these structures.

Your file processing code is not working correctly.

File processing may generate many errors. If you are reading or appending to a file, be sure that the correct version of the file exists and is in the correct location (for the chapter exercises this will be the same folder as your program). Be sure that you understand the basic logic of file operations, such as the use of the priming read, how to count records, and methods of accumulating totals, determining high or low values, etc.

The best way to debug file-processing loops is to step through them carefully and be sure that each statement performs as expected. Print out the values of variables within your loop in order to satisfy yourself that these variables are performing correctly. Here are a few common file-related errors to lookout for.

When using **fopen()** be careful not to specify the wrong file name or indicate a file that is not in the current folder or has a different file path.
When using WHILE loops to read data from a file, remember that you need an **fgets()** call **before** the loop to read the first line (priming read), and you need a second **fgets()** call inside the loop, usually as the last statement. Otherwise the program will continue to read the first line each time the loop repeats.

Be careful not to test for **feof()** instead of **!feof()** in your WHILE loop heading. Remember that we are testing **while NOT EOF**.

Don't forget the **fclose()** statement and don't include this **inside** the loop!

Your output displays 0s or nothing at all where you expected your variables to display results.

There are a number of things to check in this situation:

You may have forgotten to include a $ symbol in front of a variable name.

You may have mistyped a variable name. Remember that variable names are case sensitive. Copying and pasting variable names is a good way to ensure that you are not mistyping.

You may have left out a statement that assigns a value to a variable.

If the program needs to receive data from a form, be sure to first use the form to enter the data and then press Submit. If you run the PHP program directly without using the form, the variables intended to receive values from the form will instead be assigned 0's or empty character strings.

Also check your form to be sure that your input boxes and drop down lists are listed **between** the <form> and </form> tags. If these inputs are not located within a form, the values will not be submitted.

You may have mistyped the name of a form's input field in your $_POST array reference. For example if you defined a text box with **name="hours"** in your form, the statement **$hoursWorked = $_POST['hoursWorked'];** would assign 0 to **$hoursWorked** since there is no form input with the name **"hoursWorked"**.

Appendix E

More about HTML and CSS

This book hardly begins to cover the full range of HTML tags and their attributes. This Appendix provides you with some additional references and quick answers to just a few of the questions frequently asked by students in this course. For more complete information you will want to refer to an HTML/CSS reference or google a tag or style on the Web, for example you could google "HTML hr" for more about horizontal rules, or "CSS center text" for more about setting styles to center text.

Useful HTML References

Once you are comfortable with the basics of HTML, you will want a detailed reference to HTML tags and attributes. There are many good books and online resources available. For a complete reference to current HTML standards, check the World Wide Web Consortium's (WC3's) standards page for HTML:

> http://www.w3.org/MarkUp/

For a very good HTML tutorial and easy-to-use reference, go to:

> http://www.w3schools.com/html/default.asp

Useful CSS References

Cascading Style Sheets (CSS) is a simple mechanism for adding style (e.g. fonts, colors, spacing) to Web documents. For a complete reference to current CSS standard (including tutorials), go to the World Wide Web Consortium's (WC3's) home page for CSS standards:

> http://www.w3.org/Style/CSS/

For a very good CSS tutorial and easy-to-use reference, go to:

> http://www.w3schools.com/css/default.asp

For a good reference to color names that are recognized by most browsers, go to:

> http://www.w3schools.com/html/html_colornames.asp

Inline Styles and Internal Style Sheets

In addition to, or instead of, using external style sheets, you can create **inline** styles, using the **style** attribute to apply styles to a specific occurrence of a tag in your HTML document. For example to set the color of text in a single paragraph to blue:

```
<p style="color:blue">
```

You can also include an **internal** style sheet by including a <style> tag in the <head> section of your HTML document. When you do this, the style sheet is only available to the current document. For example:

```
<style type="text/css">
   body {background-color: white;}
   p {color: blue; }
</style>
```

External style sheets, internal style sheets, and inline styles may all be used together. Inline style definitions take precedence over definitions for the same tag in either internal style sheets or external style sheets. Style definitions in internal style sheets take precedence over definitions for the same tag in external style sheets.

Deprecated HTML Tags

The specifications for HTML have evolved steadily. Many tags that were developed early on have since been **deprecated**, which means they have been replaced by more efficient solutions. At some point in the future, deprecated tags may no longer be recognized by Web browsers, so you should avoid using these tags. Examples of deprecated tags are <**b**> (bold), <**u**> (underline), <**center**> (to center text), <**font**> (to define a font).

(NOTE: Chapter 4 introduced the use of HTML **tables** for layout of Web pages. While this approach continues to be applied, the use of HTML tables for this purpose has now been deprecated in favor of page layout based on **layers**. The use of layers was not introduced here in order to keep the focus on basic programming principles.)

Frequently Asked Questions Regarding HTML Tags

How do I use a form to submit one or more values that are not provided by the user?

We have seen that forms can include fields with names that allow the user to submit values that are then passed to a PHP program's $_POST array for processing. Forms can include "hidden" fields, so that additional values not submitted by the user can also be sent to the $_POST array. This is done using an <input> tag with the type attribute set to be "hidden", and the value attribute set the required value, for example:

```
<input type="hidden" name="year" value="2010" />
```

This can be especially useful to pass a value stored in a variable from the page with the form to the page that processes the form, for example:

```
print("<input type=\"hidden\" name=\"year\" value=\"$thisYear\" />
```

However if you need to share data between multiple pages you will probably want to use $_SESSION variables. Note that a single form can combine hidden fields with fields intended for use by the user.

How do I change the background COLOR for a tag?

Use your style sheet to set the background color to blue. For example to change the entire page background:

```
body { background-color:blue }
```

To set the background color to the color indicated by #FFC088:

```
body { background-color:FFC088 }
```

How do I change the background IMAGE of my page?

Use your style sheet to set the image. For example to apply a repeating image stored in a file named test.jpg to your entire page:

```
body { background:url(test.jpg); background-repeat:repeat; }
```

To set the background with a non-repeating image:

```
body {background:url(test.jpg); background-repeat:no-repeat; }
```

How do I create a clickable image to link to another page?

Use the <**img** /> inside your <**a**></**a**> tag, for example:

```
<a href="example.html"><img src="SomeImage.jpg" /></a>
```

How do I indent a block of text?

Use the blockquote tag <**blockquote**></**blockquote**>, for example:

```
<blockquote>This text will be indented.</blockquote>
```

How do I include a citation (usually text in italics)?

Use the citation tag <**cite**></**cite**>, for example:

```
<cite>This text will be italic,</cite> but this will not.
```

How do I include lines across my Web page?

Use the Horizontal Rule tag <**hr** />

You can specify color, size and width in your style sheet.

How do I include images from other folders and Web sites?

Use the image tag <**img** /> to include images in a Web page. Here are examples where the image is in a location other than the current folder:

```
<img src="images/SomeImage.gif" /> if the image is in a folder
    named images which is in within the current folder

<img src="../SomeImage.gif" /> if the image is in the parent
    folder of the current folder

<img src="../images/SomeImage.gif" /> if the image is in a
    folder named images which is in the parent folder of the
    current folder

<img src="http://www.abtech.edu/images/tnav/HomeLogo.jpg" /> if
    the image is on another Web site
```

How do I add borders to images?

```
<img src="SomeImage.gif" border="5" /> with a border of
  thickness 5
```

How do I center paragraphs?

To center ALL paragraphs, set your p selector in your style sheet:

```
p { text-align: center; }
```

or to set an inline style for a single paragraph:

```
<p style="text-align: center;">This text is a paragraph that
  is also centered.</p>
```

How do I create numbered lists?

Use the ordered list tag <**ol**> </**ol**> with list item tags <**li**> </**li**> as follows:

```
<ol>
    <li>First item</li>      This will be displayed as item 1
    <li>Second item</li>     This will be displayed as item 2
    <li>Third item</li>      This will be displayed as item 3
</ol>
```

Use <ol type = "1"> for an ordered list that uses 1,2,3, …

Use <ol type = "a"> for an ordered list that uses a, b, c, …

Use <ol type = "A"> for an ordered list that uses A, B, C, …

Use <ol type = "i"> for an ordered list that uses Roman numerals.

Also use any starting value for your list, for example <ol start = "3">.

How do I create bulleted lists?

Use the unordered list tag <**ul**> </**ul**> with list item tags <**li**> </**li**> as follows:

```
<ul>
   <li>First item</li>
   <li>Second item</li>
   <li>Third item</li>
</ul>
```

You can specify the type of bullet, for example: <ul type = "square">

How do I create definition lists?

These lists contain terms and then indented definitions of these terms. Use the definition list tag <**dl**></**dl**> with data terms <**dt**></**dt**> and data definitions <**dd**></**dd**>, as follows:

```
<dl>
   <dt><b>Java</b></dt>
   <dd>A recent platform-independent programming language </dd>
   <dt><b>Linux</b></dt>
   <dd>An open source operating system</dd>
   <dt><b>XML</b></dt>
   <dd>eXtensible Markup Language - a data description
      language</dd>
</dl>
```

How do I set different styles for the same tag in different parts of my Web page, or set styles for different sections of my Web page (for example menus and content areas)?

This gets to more professional use of HTML and CSS for Web site development. You will want to research the use of "id" and "class" attributes and the <div> and <span> tags in relation to CSS styles in order to apply custom formats throughout your Web pages. You will also want to study current Web site design and best practices.

Appendix F

More about PHP Functions and Data Types

This Appendix provides additional PHP references, and includes a list of useful functions that will help you to expand your use of this language. The Appendix also discusses PHP's approach to data types. (NOTE: refer to Appendix D for help debugging your PHP code and Appendix G for additional PHP **operators and control structures.**)

Useful PHP References

Once you are comfortable with the basics of PHP, you will want a detailed reference to PHP syntax and functions. There are many good books and online resources available. For a complete PHP reference consult the PHP home page:

> http://www.php.net/

For a very good online PHP tutorial and easy-to-use reference, go to the excellent w3schools site:

> http://www.w3schools.com/php/default.asp

More about PHP Functions and Data Types

PHP provides many useful functions for a wide range of common programming tasks. We have used a few of these in this book. For a list of ALL standard PHP functions see:

> http://www.php.net/quickref.php

This list is quite overwhelming! It is more often more useful to see a list of functions, organized by category (for example math functions, string functions, array functions, etc). A list of this kind can be found at the w3schools site: just follow the link listed above and scroll down to the **PHP Reference** section.

To get you started, on the following pages you will find lists of the more commonly used PHP functions, by category. These include the functions that have been introduced in this book as well as many more, with short descriptions. You are encouraged to go online and research the use of any of these functions that interest you or that meet your requirements.

First, here are a few general-purpose functions that may be especially useful as you build on what you have learned in this book:

empty()	Checks whether a variable is empty, useful for validating form input. Example: if (empty($someVariable))
is_numeric()	Checks whether a variable contains a number. Example: if (is_numeric ($someVariable))
file_exists()	Checks whether a file exists before trying to open a file. Example: if (file_exists($someFileName))

```
                        {
                              ..process the file..
                        }
                  else
                              print("FILE $someFileName NOT FOUND");
```

define()	Defines a constant variable (a variable that cannot be changed). Example: define("COMPANY_NAME", "XYZ Company"); Example: define("TAX_RATE", 0.07);
phpinfo()	Displays in-depth information about your PHP installation. Try it!
isset()	Checks whether a variable contains a value. Example: if (isset($myAge)
unset()	Destroys a variable. Example: unset($myAge);

Standard PHP Array Functions

Here are some commonly used array-processing functions:

array()	creates a new array
array_fill()	fills an array with values
array_key_exists()	checks if a certain key exists in the array
array_keys()	returns the key values of an array
array_merge()	merges one or more arrays into a single array
array_pop()	removes the last element from an array
array_push()	adds one or more elements to the end of an array
array_reverse()	returns an array with the values in reverse order
array_search()	searches an array for a value and returns the key
array_shift()	removes the first element from an array, and returns the value of the removed element
array_slice()	returns specific parts of an array
array_sum()	returns the sum of the values in an array

array_unique()	removes duplicate values from an array
array_unshift()	adds one or more elements to the beginning of an array
arsort()	sorts an associative array in descending order, based on the values
asort()	sorts an associative array in ascending order, based on the values
count()	returns the number of elements in an array, same as sizeof()
krsort()	sorts an associative array in descending order, based on the key values
ksort()	sorts an associative array in ascending order, based on the key values
list()	assigns values to variables from an array
rsort()	sorts values in an indexed array in descending order
sizeof()	returns the number of elements in an array, same as count()
sort()	sorts values in an indexed array in ascending order

Standard PHP File Functions

Be careful how you use these file functions. Some have the ability to overwrite or delete files or folders!

basename()	returns the filename from a complete path name
copy()	copies a file
dirname()	returns the folder name from a complete path name
disk_free_space()	returns the available space
disk_total_space()	returns the total size
fclose()	closes a file
feof()	tests for end-of-file (EOF)
fflush()	flushes buffered output to an open file
fgets()	returns a string containing the text from the next line in a file
file_exists()	checks whether or not a file or folder exists
file_get_contents()	reads an entire file into a string
file_put_contents	writes a string to a file
fopen()	opens a file or url
fputs()	writes a string to a file, same as fwrite()
fwrite()	writes a string to a file, same as fputs()
is_executable()	checks if a file is executable
mkdir()	creates a new folder
rename()	renames a file or folder
rmdir()	removes an folder (if it is empty)
stat()	returns information about a file
umask()	changes file permissions
unlink()	deletes a file

Standard PHP Math Functions

abs()	returns the absolute value of a number
acos()	returns the arccosine of a number
asin()	returns the arcsine of a number
atan()	returns the arctangent of a number
bindec()	converts a binary number to a decimal number
ceil()	returns the value of a number rounded upwards to the nearest integer
cos()	returns the cosine of a number
decbin()	converts a decimal number to a binary number
dechex()	converts a decimal number to a hexadecimal number
decoct()	converts a decimal number to an octal number
deg2rad()	converts a degree to a radian number
floor()	returns the value of a number rounded downwards to the nearest integer
hexdec()	converts a hexadecimal number to a decimal number
hypot()	returns the length of the hypotenuse of a right-angle triangle
is_finite()	returns true if a value is a finite number
is_infinite()	returns true if a value is an infinite number
is_nan()	returns true if a value is not a number
log()	returns the natural logarithm (base e) of a number
log10()	returns the base-10 logarithm of a number
max()	returns the number with the highest value of two specified numbers
min()	returns the number with the lowest value of two specified numbers
octdec()	converts an octal number to a decimal number
pi()	returns the value of pi
pow()	returns the value of x to the power of y
rad2deg()	converts a radian number to a degree
rand()	returns a random integer
round()	rounds a number to the nearest integer
sin()	returns the sine of a number
sinh()	returns the hyperbolic sine of a number
sqrt()	returns the square root of a number
tan()	returns the tangent of an angle

Standard PHP String Functions

bin2hex()	converts a string of ascii characters to hexadecimal values
chr()	returns a character from a specified ascii value
count_chars()	counts the number of times an ascii character occurs within a string
echo()	outputs strings
explode()	parses a string into an array of substrings
fprintf()	writes a formatted string to an output stream
html_entity_decode()	converts html entities to characters
htmlentities()	converts characters to html entities
htmlspecialchars_decode()	converts specific html entities to characters
htmlspecialchars()	converts specific characters to html entities
ltrim()	removes whitespace from the left side of a string
money_format()	returns a string formatted as currency
number_format()	formats a number according to a format specification
ord()	returns the ascii value of the first character in a string
print()	outputs a string
printf()	outputs a formatted string
rtrim()	removes whitespace from the right side of a string
str_word_count()	counts the words in a string
strcasecmp()	compares two strings (case-insensitive)
strcmp()	compares two strings (case-sensitive)
strlen()	returns the length of a string
strrev()	reverses a string
substr()	returns a part of a string
substr_count()	counts the number of times a substring occurs in a string
substr_replace()	replaces part of a string with another string
trim()	removes whitespace from both sides of a string
wordwrap()	wraps a string to a specified number of characters

PHP Data Types

Variables may be used to store data of various **data types**. Each data type is stored in a different manner and allows specific operations. PHP supports the following simple data types:

> **Integer:** A whole number (**int** data type), such as -100, -1, 0, 1, 25, or 7388.
>
> **Floating point number:** A decimal number (**float** data type), such as 5.24 or 123.456789.
>
> **Character string:** A sequence of 0 or more characters (**string** data type), such as "Joe Smith", or "What is your name?" or "123 Main Street" or "<p>This is a paragraph.</p>".
>
> **Boolean:** A TRUE or FALSE value.

Unlike most languages, PHP allows you to use variables without first defining their data type. PHP evaluates each expression and determines the appropriate data types at the time a value is assigned, and when variables are used in expressions. For example:

```
$hoursWorked = 30;
$hourlyWage = 15.75;
$wage = $hoursWorked * $hourlyWage;
```

The first statement stores 30 as an integer. The next statement stores 15.75 as a float. The last statement converts $hoursWorked to a float and then performs the multiplication and stores the result as a float.

To ensure that a value is being handled as a specific data type you can **type cast** the variable, for example:

```
$hourlyWage = (float) 15;
```

This statement stores 15 as a float

```
$wage = (string) $hourlyWage;
```

This statement converts the value stored in $hourlyWage to a string and stores the string in $wage.

Note that if you cast a **float** value as an **int**, PHP truncates the value in the same way as the **floor()** function. For example **$value** = (**int**) **33.75** will store **33** in **$value**.

You can use the **gettype()** function to obtain the data of a variable. For example **gettype($hoursWorked)** would return "integer".

Appendix G

Additional PHP Operators and Control Structures

The following features are common to many programming languages, but were omitted from (or only briefly mentioned in) the chapters to reduce complexity for beginning students. These features are described here in greater detail for completeness.

Shortcut Operators

In addition to the standard arithmetic operators, most programming languages provide **shortcut operators** The operators are very efficient and commonly used when an operation is intended to change the numeric value currently stored in a variable, as follows:

Instead of:	Use the shortcut operator:
$count = $count + 1;	$count++;
$count = $count - 1;	$count—;
$value = $value + $number;	$value += $number;
$value = $value - $number;	$value -= $number;
$value = $value * $number;	$value *= $number;
$value = $value / $number;	$value /= $number;
$value = $value % $number;	$value %= $number;

Switch Structure

The SWITCH structure was not introduced in Chapter 8 in order to keep the focus on the general concept of chaining multiple IF..ELSE structures. Most languages provide a SWITCH structure that can be used as an alternative to multiple IF..ELSE structures in cases where the possible actions are all based upon the value of a single variable.

557

For example a SWITCH structure could be used instead of multiple chained IF..ELSE structures to determine which month name to display based on the numeric value stored in the variable $month:

```
switch ($month)
{   case 1: print("January"); break;
    case 2: print("February"); break;
    case 3: print("March"); break;
    case 4: print("April"); break;
    case 5: print("May"); break;
    case 6: print("June"); break;
    case 7: print("July"); break;
    case 8: print("August"); break;
    case 9: print("September"); break;
    case 10: print("October"); break;
    case 11: print("November"); break;
    case 12: print("December"); break;
    default: print("ERROR!"); break;
}
```

The variable to be tested (**$month**) appears in the switch statement heading, enclosed in parentheses. Each possible value of this variable is handled by a case statement inside the SWITCH structure. The processor tests the value in each **case** against the value stored in the variable. When a match is found, the statements following the relevant **case** are executed.

Each case may include any number of program statements and usually ends with a **break** statement. If the **break** statement is **not** included, the statements in subsequent case statements will also be processed until a **break** statement is found. This feature allows multiple cases to use the same statements, for example:

```
switch ($month)
{   case 2: print("This month has 28 or 29 days"); break;
    case 4:
    case 6:
    case 9:
    case 11: print("This month has 30 days"); break;
    case 1:
    case 3:
    case 5:
    case 7:
    case 8:
    case 10:
    case 12: print("This month has 31 days"); break;
    default: print("ERROR!"); break;
}
```

In this case, if **$month** has the value 2, the **first** case is executed. If **$month** has the value 4, 6, 9, or 11, the **fifth** case is executed. If **$month** has the value 1, 2, 5, 7, 8, 10, or 11, the **twelfth** case is executed. If **$month** has any other value the **thirteenth** case is executed.

Also by choosing where to include **break** statements, a cascade of actions can be executed:

```
switch ($movieRating)
{
   case 5: print("TOP RATING!");
   case 4:
   case 3: print("Worth seeing!"); break;
   case 2:
   case 1: print("Don't bother!"); break;
}
```

Note that the first case does **not** include a break statement. If the rating is 5, **"TOP RATING!"** will be printed, followed by **"Worth Seeing!"**. If the rating is 4 or 3, **"Worth Seeing!"** will be printed. If the rating is 2 or 1, **"Don't bother!"** will be printed.

In this example the default option is not included. This option is not needed if it is known that the variable being tested does not contain any value others than those listed.

Another Loop Structure: DO..WHILE

Most languages provide an additional loop structure that was not described here. This is the DO..WHILE or REPEAT—UNTIL loop (the specific structure depends on the programming language).

Do..WHILE and REPEAT..UNTIL loops are event-controlled loop, just like the WHILE loop. However the test that controls a WHILE loop appears at the **start** of the loop structure, and so a WHILE loop may execute 0 times. The test for DO..WHILE and REPEAT..UNTIL loops appears at the **end** of the loop structure, and so the instructions in these loops will always execute at least once.

Here is an non-programming example of a DO..WHILE loop:

```
DO
    Instruct your dog to "sit"
  WHILE the dog refuses to sit

Give the dog a treat
```

Here the test is "the dog refuses to sit" and the loop repeats as long as this test is true. Since the test is at the end of the loop, the loop instruction will always be executed at least once. In this case you want to instruct the dog to sit at least once, so this is an more appropriate loop than a WHILE loop.

Here is the same example using a REPEAT..UNTIL loop:

```
REPEAT
     Instruct your dog to "sit"
UNTIL the dog sits


Give the dog a treat
```

The REPEAT..UNTIL structure is basically as the DO..WHILE except that the logic of the test is reversed. The loop repeats **until** this test becomes true.

PHP uses the DO..WHILE structure. Here is a PHP example of a DO..WHILE loop used to display the value of 2 raised to exponents between 0 and 5:

```
$exponent = 0;
$value = 2;
do
   $result = pow($value, $exponent);
   print("$value to the power of $exponent is $result<br />");
   $exponent = $exponent + 1;
while ($exponent <= 5);
```

Note that the test of this loop structure must be followed by a semi-colon, since this is the end of the structure. Note also that braces are not required between the **do** and the **while** since these two words are sufficient to tell the processor where the loop instructions begin and end.

Multi-Dimensional Arrays

Arrays can include any number of dimensions. For example, a 2-dimensional array could store 3 scores for each of 5 students:

```
$scores[0] = array(90, 80, 92);
$scores[1] = array(82, 81, 83);
$scores[2] = array(87, 90, 84);
$scores[3] = array(78, 69, 73);
$scores[4] = array(89, 91, 92);
```

Here, the $scores array is an array that contains five elements indexed from 0 to 4. Each of these elements contains an array of three numbers, indexed from 0 to 2. To obtain the second score of the third student we can reference element 1 of the $scores[2] array as follows: **$scores[2][1]**.

If you wish to use a FOR loop to find the average score of the fifth student, you can simply refer to array $scores[4] in your loop:

```
$totalScore = 0;
for ($i = 0; $i < sizeof($scores[4]); $i = $i + 1)
{
    $totalScore = $totalScore + $scores[4][$i];
}
```

This loop will repeat for index positions 0 through 2 to add the values of each element of $scores[4].

If you wish to use a FOR loop to find the total sales for ALL FIVE students, you can use a FOR loop nested inside **another** FOR loop:

```
$totalScore = 0;

for ($i = 0; $i < sizeof($scores); $i = $i + 1)
{
    for ($j = 0; $j < sizeof($scores[$i]); $j = $j + 1)
    {
        $totalScore = $totalScore + $scores[$j][$i];
    }
}
```

This bears some review! First note that the two loop must use different counting variables so that there is no conflict when the loops are processed. Here the outer loop uses $i as a counting variable, and the inner loop uses $j.

Next note that the outer loop is controlled by **$i < sizeof($scores)**. That's because we want this loop to repeat for each of the three elements of the $scores array.

Since the inner loop is located inside the outer loop, the inner loop will be processed **entirely** each time that the outer loop repeats **once**. The inner loop is controlled by **$j < sizeof($scores[$i])**. That's because we want this loop to repeat for each of the four elements in the array stored in whichever element of the $scores array is currently referenced by $i. Make sense?

The $totalScore variable simply accumulates the values from elements of all arrays until both loops have completed.

Ragged Arrays

Each element of a multi-dimensional array such as $scores contains an array. These arrays can actually contain different numbers of elements. These are known as **ragged** arrays. For example consider a 2-dimensional array that contains donations that have been received by five different participants in a fund-raiser:

```
$donations[0] = array(25.00, 35.00, 25.00, 15.00);
$donations[1] = array(45.00, 55.00, 75.00, 25.00, 25.00, 35,00,
    50.00);
$donations[2] = array(25.00, 45.00);
$donations[3] = array(15.00);
$donations[4] = array(65.00, 35.00, 35.00, 20.00, 30.00);
```

Here is another example that demonstrates the usefulness of the sizeof() function, since this will tell us the number of elements in any array. If you needed to find the total of all donations, you can use the same pair of nested loops as in the previous example:

```
$total = 0;
for ($i = 0; $i < sizeof($donations); $i = $i + 1)
{
    for ($j = 0; $j < sizeof($donations[$i]); $j = $j + 1)
    {
       $total = $total + $donations[$j][$i];
    }
}
```

The outer loop will repeat 5 times since that is the number of elements in the $donations array. However the inner loop will repeat a different number of times for each repetition of the outer loop. That's because the inner loop is controlled by sizeof($donations[$i]), and this value will be different for each element of $donations.

Multi-Dimensional Associative Arrays

Associative arrays can also be multi-dimensional, and we can also create multi-dimensional arrays that combine associative arrays with numerically-indexed arrays. For example a 2-dimensional array could be used to store the number of cars sold by an auto sales business every quarter for 3 years:

```
$carSales["2005"] = array (121, 174, 165, 112);
$carSales["2006"] = array (134, 143, 146, 121);
$carSales["2007"] = array (101, 203, 149, 101);
```

Here, the $carSales array is an associative array that contains three elements ("2005", "2006", and "2007"). Each of these elements contains a numerically-indexed array of four numbers. To obtain the number of cars sold in the 3rd quarter of 2006 we can reference element 2 of the $carSales["2006"] array as follows: **$carSales["2006"][2]**.

If you wish to use a FOR loop to find the total sales for 2007, you can simply refer to that array in your loop:

```
$total2007 = 0;
for ($i = 0; $i < sizeof($carSales["2007"]); $i = $i + 1)
{
    $total2007 = $total2007 + $carSales["2007"][$i];
}
```

If you wish to use a FOR loop to find the total sales for ALL THREE years, you can use a FOR loop nested inside a FOREACH loop:

```
$total = 0;
foreach ($carSales as $nextYear)
{
    for ($i = 0; $i < sizeof($nextYear); $i = $i + 1)
    {
        $total = $total + $nextYear[$i];
    }
}
```

In this case, each time the FOREACH loop repeats, the next element of $carSales is assigned to $nextYear. Each of these elements is an array, so the nested FOR loop processes the array of the $carSales element that is currently stored in $nextYear, adding every value to the total. When the FOR loop completes, control returns to the FOREACH loop which assigns the next element to $nextYear, and so on.

Index